Walking *in* Grace

2026 Daily devotions to draw you closer to God

A Gift from Guideposts

Thank you for your purchase! We want to express our gratitude for your support with a special gift just for you.

Dive into **Spirit Lifters**, a complimentary e-book that will fortify your faith, offering solace during challenging moments. Its 31 carefully selected scripture verses will soothe and uplift your soul.

Please use the QR code or go to **guideposts.org/spiritlifters** to download.

Cover and monthly opener design by Nicole White. Cover photo by Raffi Maghdessian/Aurora Photos via Getty Images. Monthly page opener photos: January, Fabrice Villard/Unsplash; February, Unsplash; March, coldsnowstorm/Getty Images; April, Anna Perfilova/Getty Images; May, Oksana Schmidt/ Getty Images; June, ooyoo/Getty Images; July, gjohnstonphoto/Getty Images; August, Allec Gomez/ Unsplash; September, borchee/Getty Images; October, Wirestock/Getty Images; November, Andrei Metelev/ Getty Images; December, Marcel/Adobe Stock

Indexed by Kelly White. Typeset by Aptara, Inc.

ISBN 978-1-961441-02-6 (hardcover)
ISBN 978-1-961441-04-0 (softcover)
ISBN 978-1-961441-00-2 (large print)
ISBN 978-1-961441-01-9 (pocket edition)
ISBN 978-1-961441-03-3 (EPUB)

Printed and bound in the United States of America
10 9 8 7 6 5 4 3 2 1

Dear Reader,

Welcome to *Walking in Grace 2026*! We're so excited to bring you the newest volume of the long-running and treasured devotional volume *Walking in Grace*. Our fifty-two writers share from the heart in this volume of 365 brand-new devotions that will help you find peace and closeness with God as you spend time with Him, and in His Word, each and every day. Whether you are about to read *Walking in Grace* for the first time or you're a longtime friend and reader, welcome! We're so happy you're here.

This year, our theme is "Living a New Life," based on Romans 6:4 (ESV), "We were buried therefore with him by baptism into death, in order that, just as Christ was raised from the dead by the glory of the Father, we too might walk in newness of life." It's our hope that this scripture inspires you as you begin a new year and a new devotional journey.

In this volume, our writers reflect on all the ways that God has been active in their lives over the course of the year. Sabra Ciancanelli writes movingly about how circumstances that seem like setbacks can actually be blessings in disguise. Patricia Lorenz is inspired by some tall, resilient redwood trees to keep aging with grace and joy. Marci Alborghetti learns that she can keep walking through open doors, faithfully, and is surprised by what God shows her when she does. Gayle T. Williams connects with a stranger in an elevator and is grateful for what this encounter teaches her about prayer. Adam Ruiz is convicted of God's unconditional love when he sees a father kiss his child's head. Tia McCollors recognizes that God always leads us home, despite what detours we may encounter. Edward Grinnan reflects on how a simple verse from 1 Corinthians helped order his messy mind and desk. A quiet night as a first responder leads Erika Bentsen to reflect upon how God calls us to wait upon Him with purpose. Debbie Macomber counts her blessings and encourages us to treasure our family and traditions. Shawnelle Eliasen shares the peace and care God brought to her during a recent surgery. And those are only a few of the devotions in these pages.

Bringing you uplifting, meaningful new series is something we love to do, and this year's edition is filled with heartwarming offerings from many beloved writers. Roberta Messner shares how God has woven beauty, connection, and healing into her life—and others' lives—through the Victorian paper-punch motto samplers she describes in "Sacred Threads." Karen Valentin offers a moving account of how her family grapples with her father's passing in "Journey through Grief." J. Brent Bill meditates on God's love and care for us as he considers "The Birds of My Neighborhood." Leanne Jackson brings us a delightfully fun series of devotions about how God uses games to teach her spiritual lessons. Pam Kidd shares incredible stories of listening to the Holy Spirit and the powerful effect this practice can have in "Angel Whispers." Marilyn Turk dives into the classic book The Five Love Languages to find spiritual lessons for her marriage—and all the other relationships in her life. Jenny Lynn Keller takes us on a tour of the "Doors of Our Life" and what spiritual insights they can offer. Patty Kirk researches loneliness and provides reflections on that powerful theme, along with scriptures to help us know better how to minister to "The Lonely Among Us." Rick Hamlin ushers us through Holy Week and to the joy of Easter in "Following Jesus." Vicki Kuyper offers a short series on her breathtaking cruise through Antarctic waters. And wrapping up the year, Penney Schwab helps us connect to Jesus in the Advent series "Christmas Blessings."

We're always especially delighted to welcome back writers who had to step away from Walking in Grace. Amy Eddings is one such writer. She is back with thought-provoking and vulnerable devotions this year, and we're so happy to have her. We also want to welcome writer Norm Stolpe to the Walking in Grace fold; it's a delight to have him write for us.

Sometimes we have to say goodbye to writers for a season, and that is the case this year with Carol Kuykendall and Erin MacPherson, who aren't able to join us. We miss them and hope they can be back with us soon.

As you spend time with God this year, we pray you will be richly blessed in wisdom, encouragement, and love.

Faithfully yours,
The Editors of Guideposts

P.S. We love hearing from you! We read every letter we receive. Let us know what *Walking in Grace* means to you by emailing WIGEditors@guideposts.org or writing to Guideposts Books & Inspirational Media, 100 Reserve Road, Suite E200, Danbury, CT 06810.

January

You have taken off your old self
with its practices and have put
on the new self, which is being
renewed in knowledge in the
image of its Creator.

—Colossians 3:9–10 (NIV)

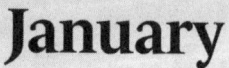

New Year's Day, Thursday, January 1

God said, Let there be light: and there was light.
—Genesis 1:3 (KJV)

The house is quiet. I sit in my dining room chair that faces the eastward-facing window, sip my coffee, and wait. My personal ritual of going to sleep at a normal hour, bypassing watching one ball drop in favor of watching the sunrise, began years ago when I was pregnant with my son, Solomon. I still have the feeling that I had discovered something sacred with my New Year's practice of intentionally waiting for the darkness to turn to light, alone, with God, reflecting on the past and imagining the future.

I love the waiting; the anticipation is truly magical. Connecting with God, I close my eyes and thank Him. I start with the coffee cup that I have used every single morning. It was mistakenly taken from my sister's house years ago, and now that she's in heaven, it makes me feel close to her.

I go over everything I am grateful for—my husband and sons, my mom next door, my scrappy little blind dog who impatiently waits to be fed, and my five cats that keep us all on our toes. I reflect on my hopes and dreams to come and go over the challenges that have healed with time and grace. The miracles I have witnessed, like the double rainbow on the anniversary of my father's passing.

Trust. I hear the word in my head. *Trust the future with the same faith that you trust the past.*

And just with that thought, the sky breaks with light like it's a response—a beautiful coincidence, to have clarity and beauty, light at exactly the moment that I surrender all fear.

Heavenly Father, thank You for shining Your glorious light on a new year.
—Sabra Ciancanelli

Digging Deeper: Proverbs 3:5–6; Isaiah 43:19

Friday, January 2

ANGEL WHISPERS: Following God's Way
He shall direct thy paths. —Proverbs 3:6 (KJV)

Another delayed flight. Here I am, stuck in a strange airport, longing for home and thinking of the $20 bill tucked in my pocket. As soon as I take a restroom break, I'm off to treat myself to some high-calorie treat in the food court.

As I pass by the lavatories, I see weariness on the face of the woman who methodically cleans the sinks one after the other, as messy hand washers hurry to meet their flights.

The voice comes: *Give the lady your $20.*

No, I respond. *I'm going to indulge myself.*

Already, I know my protestations are hopeless.

Over time, I have come to recognize these messages that float through my head, most often telling me to do things I would rather not do. I call them "angel whispers." Sometimes the whispers

incite my pride or nudge my selfishness before I give in on the second or third rerun.

The results of the whispers, if I follow their direction, are rarely obvious at first. Maybe, for me, they never are.

Now I'm washing my hands. The tired woman cleans on. I turn and pull the $20 bill from my pocket. Quickly I slip it into the woman's hand, look into her eyes, and say, "I'm supposed to give you this." I disappear, but not before I see disbelief, and possibly relief, cross her face.

Walking through the airport corridor, knowing that I've followed God's way, I smile. I imagine that in the mysterious flow of life, I've done some small thing that has worked for the good of another. All I had to do was listen and follow the path He laid before me.

Father, Your paths finally lead to inner peace. Thank You. —Pam Kidd

Digging Deeper: Psalm 32:8; Isaiah 58:11

Saturday, January 3

He is your example, and you must follow in his steps. —1 Peter 2:21 (NLT)

The road to our cabin in northern Arizona was completely blocked. Twenty inches of new snow had accumulated in the night, adding to the

record-breaking 140 inches that had already fallen that season. The snow was piled as high as the stop sign!

"We'll need to park on the main road and snowshoe in," my husband, Kevin, decided.

I nodded. We had come prepared for that possibility. I wasn't worried about the two of us getting around on the snow. We had once lived and worked in Minnesota as wilderness guides. But I wondered how our desert-dwelling dog, Mollie, would manage.

We stuffed gear into backpacks for the 1-mile trek. Kevin added a snow shovel so we could get into the front door.

"Ready, Mollie?" She met my question with eager eyes and a wagging tail. She didn't have a clue what awaited her.

Mollie bounded over the embankment—and promptly disappeared. The snow swallowed her whole. Another leap had the same result. I maneuvered her wriggling 30-pound body behind my snowshoes. "Follow me," I instructed.

We huffed and puffed our way in a winter wonderland of snow-laden pine trees. Our snowshoes created a packed trail for Mollie to walk on, but whenever she tried to go off on her own, she sank out of sight.

Later that night, as we dried out by the fireplace, I thought of Mollie's example. I knew I had some spiritual things to remember about following. And about going off on my own.

Jesus, help me follow in Your steps, so I don't find myself over my head in trouble. Amen.
—Lynne Hartke

Digging Deeper: John 10:27, 12:26

Sunday, January 4

**Write them on the tablet of your heart.
—Proverbs 7:3 (NIV)**

Every January, I set a goal to read the Bible in a year. I've done it multiple times. But is speed reading what I still need? This question needled me when our pastor assigned a simple Bible study. He asked us to study the book of John, reading five verses each day. We were to prayerfully and slowly read each assigned passage. Then we were to choose the verses that resonated with us, write down why they impacted us, and rewrite the verses in our own words.

After a week, I reread my answers. The passage in John 1 that I'd always skimmed through spoke directly to me. *Jesus was always with God from before Creation; He wasn't a late arrival on Earth* (v. 2 paraphrased). *No matter how hard the darkness tries, it can never overpower Jesus. We can trust Him to save us* (v. 5 paraphrased). *By His grace, He accepts us as His children once we recognize and accept the truth of who He is—the Creator and Savior of the world. That is all that we have to do* (v. 12 paraphrased).

How long would it take me to study and personalize the entire Bible in such depth? With

over thirty-one thousand verses, it would take 17 years! Then I saw my pastor's intent. This is exactly as Bible reading should be done. Savored daily. Pored over. Examined. Personalized. Remembered because it specifically applies directly to me now, today, tomorrow. It shouldn't be a reading race. And it definitely isn't just an old history book.

Father God, speak through the pages of Your story. I am ready to listen. —Erika Bentsen

Digging Deeper: Jeremiah 31:33; Hebrews 4:12

Monday, January 5

Do not conform to the pattern of this world, but be transformed by the renewing of your mind. —Romans 12:2 (NIV)

There's a joke among golden retriever owners: Our goldens shed twice a year, each time for 6 months. That's not far from the truth. You golden owners know what I mean.

Dark clothing? Not unless you carry a lint roller. I'd guess the average owner replaces significantly more vacuum cleaners than the rest of society. Allergies? Break out the antihistamines. Think keeping them off the furniture will help? Good luck with that.

My golden, Gracie's, most voluminous shedding happens in early winter. It always alarms me. Big clumps of fur everywhere. In the sunlight streaming through a window on a winter morning

I can see bits of her hair dancing on the air. Every year I convince myself the shedding is worse. Is it her thyroid?

This January I took her to Dr. Phillips, her vet. "I'm worried," I said, tugging a tuft of fur from Gracie's hip and holding it up. Dr. Phillips, who is regularly bemused by my overly solicitous concern for my dog's health, ran her hands through Gracie's coat. "I can take some blood," Dr. Phillips said, "but it's healthy shedding so she can grow in a new coat. Too bad we can't renew ourselves like that. It must feel good."

Back home, running the vacuum for the second time that day, I suddenly thought of Romans 12:2, about being transformed by the renewing of your mind so you can know God's will.

Isn't that a believer's version of shedding? Growing anew in our conviction of God's will? And there's no better time than at the year's dawn, refreshing our hearts and minds to be open for what God plans for the year, growing a new coat of faith.

Father, I close my eyes and renew my mind to know Yours better. —Edward Grinnan

Digging Deeper: 1 Peter 2:2–3; 2 Peter 1:1–11

Feast of the Epiphany, Tuesday, January 6

We have seen his star in the East, and have come to worship him. —Matthew 2:2 (RSV)

A few years ago I joined my son and his family in Singapore for a month at Christmastime. There, I experienced a holiday different from the way we celebrated at home. Both temperature and humidity hovered at eighty-nine, a drastic change from a New England winter. The "Christmas tree" was a potted fig tree with twinkle lights, not a fir tree. Attending a Christmas Eve service, held way downtown at midnight, proved not feasible. Of course, I savored the sights and fragrances of the Garden City with my family, but clearly something was missing—my beloved community celebration back home.

About 2 weeks later, my son's colleagues invited me to the Feast of the Epiphany service at their church. Though this was not my denomination, I knew the liturgy well and grasped at the chance to observe a familiar holiday with faith friends. And that's exactly what it was! The beloved hymns—"We Three Kings," of course—and the familiar prayers drew me into a different beloved community. Here the smiling faces in that congregation looked nothing like mine, yet I felt warmly welcomed and connected in spirit.

Millennia after Christ's birth, we no longer see that celestial star that guided the Magi. Instead, we follow Jesus to find and worship God—no matter where we are. When we seek, we will find.

Light of the world, lead us. —Gail Thorell Schilling

Digging Deeper: Matthew 2:9, 7:7

Wednesday, January 7

Every morning he makes me eager to hear what he is going to teach me. —Isaiah 50:4 (GNT)

In last year's *Walking in Grace*, I wrote how, after feeling something was missing from my morning quiet time, I heard God telling me to "listen." I then realized most of my quiet time had not included *my* being quiet. So I began listening for at least 10 minutes each day. I also wrote in a notebook what I felt I heard from God during those times of listening.

After days of checking my watch, then beginning my prayers and reading after 10 minutes had elapsed, I found myself looking at my start time but forgetting to check whether 10 minutes had passed. As the weeks went by, 10 minutes turned into 20, 20 into 30 or more. After several months, my quiet time had become a conversation time. I would listen, ask questions, then listen more.

Now I no longer check my watch. My "prayer request" time has become minimal. My listening time is nearly 100 percent of my quiet time. My "listen" notebook has grown. I often go back and reread what I've written and discuss it with God some more.

My quiet time is no longer just a time of no distractions so I can pray and read, and no longer just setting aside 10 minutes to hear. It has become a time of listening to, and talking with, God. He sets the agenda, not me. Often 2 hours or more pass before I realize it. And the insights and answers He has given me have been amazing.

Thank You, God, for our listening and conversation time together. Help me to live all You have taught me. —Kim Taylor Henry

Digging Deeper: 1 Samuel 3:9; Mark 9:7; John 10:27

Thursday, January 8

I know how to get along with little, and I also know how to live in prosperity . . . . I can do all things through Him who strengthens me.
—Philippians 4:12–13 (NASB)

When I tell people that I don't own a smartphone, they look at me as if I were an alien. Truth is, I love getting away from all my technology for several hours a day. I don't want to have an electronic pest stuffed in my pocket, pinging me when I am eating fried chicken, or during church services, or when I am flying down the freeway. I have a 60-year good driving record and I don't want to kill someone. Especially not me.

If I bought a smartphone, it would have to have a little built-in parachute, because I am an oaf, and I would drop it seventy-seven times a day. I have very large hands, so I don't do dainty little touchscreens with one pinky. I would want one with big knobs, buttons, switches, levers.

Most of all, I dislike things that pull me away from the real world around me, which is more important to me than the virtual land of Nod.

I am writing this in my doctor's waiting room. There are fourteen patients sitting here, and thirteen of them have their heads down, staring at their phones, which makes this room about as inspiring as a mortuary. The receptionist and I are the only ones having a conversation, and I'm so grateful to her just for making eye contact with me.

So, enjoy your smartphone, but don't feel sorry for me. I may be forced to buy one someday, but until then I am one of about 5 million Americans who are free from such seductive devices. God has made me happier without one.

You made us all different, Lord. Help us to appreciate those differences. —Daniel Schantz

Digging Deeper: Romans 12:6–8; Philippians 2:3

Friday, January 9

DOORS OF OUR LIFE: Front Door
Yet to all who received him, to those who believed in his name, he gave the right to become children of God. —John 1:12 (NIV)

My front door and I share a frequent difference of opinion, as one of us adapts to weather changes better than the other. Made from a solid slab of Douglas fir, the door swells during humid summers and contracts in cooler months. In contrast, my need to enter and exit the house remains the same throughout the year.

Our disagreement spiked to a boiling point last summer when the heat and humidity reached record highs and the door refused to open. In frustration I called a locksmith, and he made adjustments so that the door would function regardless of weather conditions. After I paid the bill and scolded my door for causing problems, I stood back and admired its beauty. Despite its ornery nature, the handmade creation is a work of art with beveled edges and glass pane inserts, reminding me why I selected it for the front of my house.

Ouch. I just described myself as God might see me. He created me in His image knowing I would rebel, stumble, and fall on occasion. But He also offered His Son Jesus to rescue me from each failure and guide me back to Him. By accepting God's gift, I am who He says I am—His child forever, His handmade creation, chosen by Him to be exactly where I am.

As I opened the French doors leading to the screened porch, I realized every door in my house reflected an aspect of my walk with God. A journey filled with His love and grace, even if not always gracefully walked by me.

God, thank You for opening the doors of my life to the purpose, peace, and joy You offer all Your children. —Jenny Lynn Keller

Saturday, January 10

Against all hope, Abraham in hope believed.
—Romans 4:18 (NIV)

Our congregation was one of several hosting the Kyiv Symphony Orchestra and Chorus (KSOC) during the last stop on their tour. They are part of the Music Mission Kiev, which uses sacred music to spread and share the gospel with Ukrainians. The Hope for Ukraine tour was to raise money for Ukrainians in need of humanitarian help.

There were thirty-five women in the KSOC of diverse ages; the men were not allowed to come due to the war. There were moments when the impact of the war was apparent. Every single member of the ensemble knows someone who is either fighting in the war or has been killed. Several of the women were visibly shaken by the loud noises from cars and airplanes flying overhead, sounds that often mean imminent danger back home. The ladies had a wonderful time with the church host families.

When it was time for the concert, the performers stood before the audience with confidence, energy, and joy. Their music, presence, and spirit raised the banner of faith and hope. Their voices lifted our spirits, and their courage inspired us. The next day the host families cried as the women boarded the bus to the airport to begin the trip back home to a country at war and an unknown future with faith and hope.

When I pray for people in war-zone countries who hope against hope, I remember that ensemble in prayer. When we come face to face with those who suffer and hurt, our prayers change, and we change too.

God of hope, we remember all those in war-torn countries hoping against hope and trusting You for a better tomorrow. Help us to never forget them. —Pablo Diaz

Digging Deeper: Psalm 119:49; Lamentations 3:19–24

Sunday, January 11

The God of all comfort . . . comforts us in all our troubles, so that we can comfort those in any trouble with the comfort we ourselves receive from God. —2 Corinthians 1:3–4 (NIV)

The story begins 20 years ago when a family with two small boys attended my church regularly. Then, one day they stopped coming. A divorce. We lost track of them.

A decade later, one Sunday, I read the "deceased" prayer list. Trying to discover if one name belonged to the child I remembered, I pointed to the surname and whispered to the pastor: "Is this a student?"

Yes, he answered. At Communion, I recognized the boy's mother, Lisa, nearly a stranger now. After the service, I found her. We silently embraced. She whispered, "Thank you for remembering." Lisa's college-age son had died in a skiing accident.

Now, 7 years later, Lisa sits near me most Sunday mornings. We smile and pass the peace—acquaintances, not friends.

This past Sunday, the week of my birthday, our corner of the sanctuary disintegrated into chaos. At first, I sat with my friend Sandra, suffering from dementia, lost in the liturgy, then lost among the pews. Two rambunctious boys got the best of their mother, who left early, struggling and strung out. Lisa followed her, obviously offering support. Then, before the closing hymn, I walked out. Lisa found me slumped on a staircase, sobbing. She put her arm around my shoulder. "Have you lost someone?"

Her question surprised me. "Sandra," I said, not mentioning another friend moving away this week. "And—my birthday." The sands of time—sinking through the hourglass.

"Oh, I really get the birthday thing." She didn't say much more. Didn't need to. The God of all comfort had shown His hand, sending the woman I had consoled years ago to lift me up in my own troubled times.

Lord, thank You is all I can think to say.
—Evelyn Bence

Digging Deeper: Matthew 5:4; 2 Corinthians 1:1–7

We will tell the next generation the praise-worthy deeds of the Lord. —Psalm 78:4 (NIV)

When I was a child, Dad would ramble on at the dinner table about his experience as a submariner during World War II, telling us about depth charges and the periscope. Alas, I would get too impatient to hold on to the details.

Dad died over a decade ago, but recently our son Tim did a Google search on Dad's boat—the USS *Parche*—and was stunned to read about the six war patrols it had served and the tonnage it had sunk. It was one of the most highly decorated subs in the Pacific during World War II. Tim wondered when exactly Dad was on board. Unfortunately, I didn't know. Just that he was only 19 years old when he signed up for the Navy.

Then I remembered: Dad once gave an interview to someone tracking down that information. But where was it? Enter our niece Addie, who just got her PhD in history. In a matter of minutes, she texted the link to the interview she found in the Library of Congress. All at once, I was listening to Dad.

How wonderful to get the specifics of which battles Dad was in and how he was involved. Here was a record of things he'd recounted at the dinner table.

The Bible is a book full of stories. How else would we know about Moses and Abraham and Daniel and Paul? Someone got them to tell their stories, and eventually they were written down. How grateful I was, after listening to Dad, to know that some historian had gone to the trouble of asking him about the war, recording it for posterity. Thanks, Dad, for your service and for sharing the memories when asked.

I thank You, Lord, for all the stories of faith recounted in Scripture. —Rick Hamlin

Digging Deeper: Proverbs 12:19; Joel 1:3; Philippians 4:8

Tuesday, January 13

Though your sins are like scarlet, they shall be as white as snow. —Isaiah 1:18 (ESV)

I stood there, less than thrilled, eyeing what last night had seemed a reasonable-size driveway but overnight had become roughly the size of an airport runway.

"Don't you love the snow?" my wife said.

"Why would anybody?"

"It's a picture of God's grace. Like the verse in Isaiah. It never tires of making things white and clean."

She was right, of course, but in that moment, I would have appreciated an inspirational example that wasn't so much work. Or so cold. As a kid growing up in the Arizona desert, it never crossed my mind that I might one day live where it snowed, let alone have to shovel the stuff.

We started in. Five minutes later my patience was disappearing as quickly as the feeling in my fingers and toes. Shoveling is one thing, but *re*-shoveling is a whole other ball of ice. For reasons known only to angels and meteorologists, there seems to be a rule that as soon as you finish one pass the snow starts to fall again.

"I get it, Lord. I still don't love the cold. No offense." I had to mumble this due to the fact I could no longer feel my face.

Then I heard the truck. My neighbor backed in, and with a single pass of his snowplow he cleared nearly the whole drive. I could have hugged the guy.

That's my God. Insisting on telling me He loves me even when I least deserve it.

"Thank You, Lord. I'm sorry."

Sunlight broke through the clouds.

You know what? Maybe I love the snow after all.

Heavenly Father, thank You for loving us, especially when we are unlovely. —Buck Storm

Digging Deeper: 2 Corinthians 12:9;
Ephesians 2:7–10

Wednesday, January 14

Where can I go from your Spirit? Where can I flee from your presence? —Psalm 139:7 (NIV)

I'm a cat person, but don't tell that to our little dog, Missy, a 13-year-old, 25-pound, tricolored schweenie (shih tzu/dachshund mix). We took Missy in when she was an eight-month-old puppy, after my husband's grandfather passed away. His grandmother couldn't care for a pet on her own, but she also couldn't bear to give her away. No other family members would take the dog, so she became ours by default.

Despite my preference for felines, I am Missy's person. She never lets me out of her sight. When I get up in the morning, she follows me as I go into the kitchen to start the coffee, even though she's not a coffee drinker. When I go into the bathroom and close the door, she whines to come in and join me. When I walk into my closet to get dressed, I turn around and almost trip because Missy is right behind me.

"I've never seen anything like it," says my husband, Michael. "It's like she's on an invisible leash tethered to you."

I'm not sure why Missy has chosen me, but I'm her special person. She loves being with me.

There's someone else who loves being with me. In fact, the Bible says He thinks about me constantly (Psalm 139:17–18). He chose me on purpose (John 15:16), but unlike us taking Missy in because no one else would, I am His treasured possession (Deuteronomy 7:6). There is definitely an invisible connection that tethers me to God for eternity (John 3:16). What a blessing to be God's special person!

Holy Father, I'm so grateful to be chosen and loved by You. Thank You that nothing can ever separate us. Amen. —Stephanie Thompson

---

Thursday, January 15

What does the LORD **require of you? To act justly and to love mercy and to walk humbly with your God. —Micah 6:8 (NIV)**

I turned off the nightly news, heartbroken. Again. More violence. More destruction. More greed. More people suffering greater losses than I could ever imagine having to face. How had I spent my day? Packing for a vacation. My emotions were a jumble of excitement, guilt, thankfulness, and sorrow. In a world where there's so much turmoil, is it right for me to enjoy the benefit of so many blessings? I laid my mix of guilt and gratitude at God's feet in prayer.

I didn't receive a simple answer. So many Bible verses came to mind: How wars and the poor are a constant in this present world (Mark 13:7, 14:7). How I should weep with those who weep and celebrate with those who celebrate (Romans 12:15, NASB). How I should embrace every day God has set before me (Psalm 118:24). How I should be generous with, and grateful for, all of the gifts God has given (2 Corinthians 9:11). That I should love, always love (Mark 12:30–31).

I still watch the nightly news. But I've come to view it as a catalyst. It spurs me on toward prayer. It encourages me to put myself in someone else's less comfortable shoes. It reminds me that my life is only one small story in a world of people God loves. I've come to use it as a daily challenge that helps me thoughtfully balance how to live a life that rests solely on grace.

Father, show me how to love well, with generosity and grace, in this often chaotic, confusing world.
—Vicki Kuyper

Digging Deeper: Psalm 118:24;
Mark 12:30–31, 13:7, 14:7; Romans 12:15;
2 Corinthians 9:11

Friday, January 16

"Ask, and it will be given you; search, and you will find; knock, and the door will be opened for you." —Luke 11:9 (NRSVCE)

It was the perfect storm. For a decade my husband, Charlie, and I had been in our godsons' lives. From being present at their births to weekly visits and celebrating holidays, we were a family. Then came Covid and months of awkward FaceTime calls, while we all became isolated. When the world opened up, we managed one movie before I got very sick. Over the next year, I struggled with illness and deep depression. By the time we were able to be with the boys, now both adolescents, it seemed we'd lost all intimacy. What had been easy and precious felt disconnected and broken. I was devastated.

We kept trying, though visits were fewer. Gradually, conversation flowed more smoothly as the boys realized that we hadn't deliberately abandoned them. But I thought it could never be the same, and I wondered what the new "us" would be. Would there even be a lasting us?

In struggling with this, I confronted how I'd been feeling about my relationship with God. Never once had I lost faith in Him, but my faith that He still loved me the way I'd thought He had was shaken. The desolation I felt about this overshadowed what I felt about our boys.

Recently, we took them out for dinner. Charlie and the youngest strode into the restaurant ahead of us, while the oldest lagged behind. He glanced at me quickly, and then held the door open.

I realized that God was doing the same. To discover my future—and the future of these changed relationships—I needed to walk through opened doors, faithfully.

Welcoming God, give me the courage to embrace what You will make out of my suffering.
—Marci Alborghetti

Digging Deeper: Isaiah 52:7–10

Saturday, January 17

We need not fear even if the world blows up and the mountains crumble into the sea.
—**Psalm 46:2** (TLB)

I was blessed to check off a bucket-list item by visiting Australia and New Zealand with my brother, Joe, and sister-in-law, Linda, for a month. One of my favorite places was Sydney Harbor, where the famous Opera House and the Sydney Harbor Bridge are landmarks that delight thousands of visitors daily.

One day when we took the harbor ferry to Manly Beach and sailed under the bridge, I spotted a dozen people walking up the side of the steep bridge. I learned later that at its highest point the bridge rises 440 feet (44 stories!) above the harbor, and the climb is 1,621 stairsteps.

I was shocked that people had the courage to do this amazing feat. Then a local Aussie on the ferry told me that the people climbing the bridge were tethered to a cable that would prevent them from falling over. Ah, now it all made sense.

On that trip, as we hiked steep hills and traversed sandy paths down to various beaches on rickety steps, I can't tell you how many times I reached for the hands of my brother or Linda. The relief of being tethered to someone stronger and younger than me was beyond belief.

Later when my daughter Julia was hospitalized twice in one week then had to have her spleen removed, I prayed so much that I felt tethered to Jesus. When my son Andrew set out on a trip in his 33-year-old car, all I could do was close my eyes, pray, and feel that calm sense of being tethered to our Lord.

Father, You gave me so much comfort through Your Son, a magnificent tether to help me through life's scariest moments. —Patricia Lorenz

Digging Deeper: Numbers 13:30; Acts 27:27–34

Sunday, January 18

You have given me the heritage of those who fear your name. —Psalm 61:5 (NRSVUE)

"You've grown into it," were Kate's words as I slipped on my dad's vintage brown-tweed walking hat. "Before, you were too young. You weren't ready. Now it's a style more fitting your age. Plus, I like that your head is warm," said my style-consultant, safety-officer wife as we were leaving for church.

The Dorfman Pacific, a rough-woven, wool-brimmed hat, was a gift from my dad. Over a decade ago, during the difficult time of downsizing for Dad's move into a memory-care facility, we sorted through an upper closet full of assorted caps. Baseball-style "trucker hats" with mesh back panels, low-crown "dad hats" of soft cotton... Dad's thumb to the right meant a keeper. Thumb to the left, a giveaway.

Then came the vintage walking hat. I'd admired similar headgear worn by my boss at the National Defense University. Seeing my dad's puzzled expression as he pondered the hat, I asked whether

I could take it. With his affirming glance, the classic headpiece became mine.

It took a few years till I was comfortable wearing it. Now, with my wife's approval, I was ready.

I'm honored to don the legacy symbolized by my dad's hat. His faith-filled energy and affirmation animate and encourage me. He's long been my hero.

Yet I also recognize others who sustain me in the faith. Fourth-grade Sunday school teacher Verda Minor; fifth-grade educator Rheta Bangma; Uncle Gerhard Sampson, whose Lutheran Brethren piety graces my soul.

So, come polar-vortex chill or wintry-mix slush, in wearing my dad's old-school hat, not only is my head warmed, but also my heart. I am grateful.

Gracious Father, we are thankful for spiritual mentors who've impacted our lives. May we continue to reflect their goodness, honor Your name, and be blessed. Amen. —Ken Sampson

Digging Deeper: Psalm 16:6; Proverbs 10:7; John 14:27

Martin Luther King Jr. Day, Monday, January 19

Remember the days of old; consider the years of many generations; ask your father, and he will show you, your elders, and they will tell you. —Deuteronomy 32:7 (ESV)

A single brick. It's the only tangible reminder I have left after the demolition of the childhood church that helped form my faith.

I'd confessed my faith while sitting on the wooden pews among my family, been dipped in the cool water of the baptism pool, and lent my alto voice to the youth choir. I'd recited memorized scriptures for Easter, attended vacation Bible school, and performed in plays for the Black History Month program.

Whenever I sat in the pews, I was fully aware that I was sitting among history. Sunday dinners in the church fellowship hall after service were times that I learned about how the congregation had contributed to the advancement of African American people from their own little corner of the world. They held prayer walks, used the church as a voting precinct, and took care of one another. Small, quiet moments in a large, bold movement.

When I look at my single red brick picked up from among the fallen edifice, the words of Rev. Dr. Martin Luther King Jr. come to mind: "We are not makers of history. We are made by history." Although the physical building has fallen into piles of rubble, my faith and relationship with God remain steadfast and immovable.

Father, thank You for the history of my rich heritage and how Your lovingkindness stretches across generations. You are the same today, yesterday, and forevermore. —Tia McCollors

---

Tuesday, January 20

Knowledge puffs up while love builds up.
—1 Corinthians 8:1 (NIV)

Our first snowfall in the Nashville area this year
brought an array of emotions. I was excited to
watch the glowing snowflakes falling from the
sky, while my big kids prophetically bragged about
week-long school closures. I, too, looked forward to a
slower pace—working remotely and not having to
taxi my teen girls to school, jobs, and social events.
Yet I also knew a heavy snowfall would lead to
cancellation of our community's MLK Day events.

When MLK Day arrived, I felt excitement over
a day of rest and recharge. I also looked forward
to connecting with my family, something that's
increasingly difficult due to busy schedules. My
husband and I enjoyed a movie focused on the Civil
Rights era. I checked in with my kids on a deeper level
than I had in a while. I also phoned my oldest son,
who recently moved into his own apartment, and
used the ample snowfall as an excuse for a longer
phone conversation than usual.

Later on, once it became clear that a full week
of school closures was inevitable, I realized MLK
Day had been exactly the kind of day Dr. King
would have smiled upon. He loved his family and
often spoke of his four children during his famous

speeches. Dr. King also once said, "Without love, there is no reason to know anyone, for love will, in the end, connect us to our neighbors, our children, and our hearts." While we didn't spend MLK Day listening to speeches by community leaders nor marching through the streets like Dr. King did during the civil rights movement, my family enjoyed a day of connection and love with one another. I think Dr. King would have approved.

Lord, may we remember that our most important mission is to love God and love people.
—Carla Hendricks

Digging Deeper: 1 Corinthians 13; Galatians 5:6

Wednesday, January 21

Jesus answered, "Everyone who drinks this water will be thirsty again, but whoever drinks the water I give them will never thirst. Indeed, the water I give them will become in them a spring of water welling up to eternal life."
—John 4:13–14 (NIV)

I've heard the sage advice my whole life: A healthy person should drink eight glasses of water a day to stay hydrated. Most people know water is necessary to sustain life, and a person can only live a matter of days without it.

Water intake requirements vary from person to person, but that 64-ounce amount fits for me. So every morning, I fill up my forest- green, 40-ounce, insulated Stanley tumbler. I keep it nearby and sip on the straw until mid-afternoon when I'm ready for a refill. Having water within arm's reach allows me to drink all the water I need to feel my best. Thanks to my Stanley, I'm certain to stay hydrated.

Just as I need to stay physically hydrated to be my optimal self, I need to stay spiritually hydrated to be the person God created me to be. Being spiritually filled isn't as easy as filling my Stanley cup and sipping on the straw throughout the day, but when I intentionally seek God first thing in the morning, read His Word, pray, and listen for His voice—not just once, but throughout my day—I'm more likely to be filled with His Spirit.

Thanks to His living water, I'm able to stay spiritually healthy with a fully hydrated soul and be my best.

Just as I thirst for water, I thirst for You, Lord. Fill up my soul as I take sips of Your living water throughout the day. —Stephanie Thompson

Digging Deeper: Isaiah 58:11; Jeremiah 2:13; John 4:4–15

Thursday, January 22

[The lepers] called out in a loud voice, "Jesus, Master, have pity on us!" When he saw them, he said, "Go, show yourselves to the priests." And as they went, they were cleansed. —Luke 17:13–14 (NIV)

I had been struggling with a health problem when my friend Joann, who lives in another city, called and left a message saying she just wanted to hear my voice. Knowing her to be a devoted Christian, I sensed God working through her on my behalf.

Turns out, Joann had received a vision about my health, resulting in a miraculous lifting of my spirit. But lingering concerns kept me from moving forward to spread the good news. God's promise to me via Joann was as timely as spring rain, but I decided I should share my blessing only when the symptoms were fully gone.

Six months later, I was visiting out of state when I heard a young preacher, A. J. Mosley, say, "Testify to what you already know!" The Spirit nudged me: I was not to allow myself to subconsciously doubt my healing. After all, didn't God deserve enthusiastic credit for what He had already done?

Like the lepers who were cleansed "as they *went* [emphasis mine]," it was time for me to move forward, telling others of the relief that God had provided. Why sit in silence when Jesus had clearly spoken? "Go, show yourselves," He said. He had done His part. My part was to walk in the grace and mercy He had granted.

And like the one out of the ten lepers who had the godliness to return to Jesus offering gratitude, today I humbly give thanks.

Jesus, I can never adequately thank You for the love You've already shown me, but I will always try. —Jacqueline F. Wheelock

Friday, January 23

Abraham called that place The Lord Will Provide. And to this day it is said, "On the mountain of the Lord it will be provided." —Genesis 22:14 (NIV)

"I don't understand how I got here," my daddy says. His green eyes are troubled. He runs a hand over his distinguished gray beard.

My father's in the hospital. His hip broke on a record-breaking day—12 inches of snow hid Midwest highways. Daddy waited in a small-town emergency room for 3 days. Finally, he was transferred to a larger hospital for surgery. He came through well physically. But my wise, knowledgeable father is confused.

"It's OK, Daddy," I say. "Things will come together."

Daddy nods, but I can see that he's not sure.

Things have been hard for weeks. Mama had a stroke last month. Daddy's in for a long haul, and I'm worried his mind won't return. My sister and I struggle, and the ruts in our relationship are apparent now. Anxiety makes camp in my heart.

As Daddy's eyes grow heavy, I only know to pray.

I close my eyes, and I see Abraham. He takes young Isaac up the mountain. They trek, step after step, sticks bound to the boy's back. How can Abraham prepare to offer his son as a sacrifice? He hadn't heard of resurrection. Who would think of a ram in a thicket? Yet Abraham trusted. He trusted the Lord to provide when he didn't know the way.

And the Lord was faithful.

I listen to Daddy breathe, and his ragged respiration becomes baby-sweet. Something in my chest changes too. I don't know what will happen with my parents. But my heart becomes a mountain, and it's a place of certainty.

I know God will provide.

Lord, I trust even when I don't know how You'll provide. Amen. —Shawnelle Eliasen

Digging Deeper: Psalm 28:7; Isaiah 26:3; Philippians 4:19

Saturday, January 24

As many as received him, to them gave he power to become the sons of God, even to them that believe on his name. —John 1:12 (KJV)

I read somewhere that one should take a break between workouts to allow one's muscles to rest.

I took a 3-year break, just to be sure.

I finally returned to the gym last month, and the results are astounding. In a few short weeks, I've lost zero pounds and taken—let me measure— 0.0 inches off my waist. It's unbelievable I could work out regularly and achieve no apparent effect. Meet the new paunch—same as the old paunch.

This frustration isn't new to me; it mirrors my prayer life. I go long stretches without genuine, meaningful conversations with God—then, after my sudden return, I wonder why the results aren't instantaneous, as if God were an ATM, dispensing grace at the push of a button.

I know my workouts need to be more committed and consistent; ditto with my spiritual life. I've decided to add two new (old) exercises to my routine:

Bend my knee. Bow my head. Repeat.

Give me strength to seek You regularly, Lord, and courage to hear. —Mark Collins

Digging Deeper: Matthew 17:20; Revelation 5

Sunday, January 25

"Come," [Jesus] said. Then Peter got down out of the boat, walked on the water and came toward Jesus. —Matthew 14:29 (NIV)

I watched my husband tromp into the winter woods for a walkabout with our daughter. They'd invited me to go along, but I'd elected to stay in where it was cozy and warm. "No, thanks," I'd said with a shudder. It was cold out there today!

But as I tossed another log into our woodstove, I found myself second-guessing my decision. Sure, it was cold out there. But it was also a beautiful day. The sun was out, and I had winter gear. I wouldn't freeze. Was the possibility of a little discomfort worth missing out on an opportunity to connect with my husband and daughter?

Ugh, I thought to myself with frustration. I hate it when I fall into this trap—mixing up things that actually need avoiding with things I just fear might cause me discomfort.

It's not just cold walkabouts either. It also happens sometimes when I'm faced with people or situations that feel different or difficult to understand. It's so easy to end up thinking it's the situation—or something about the person—that's at issue rather than recognizing that familiar wobble for what it is: my comfort zone resisting God's invitation to stretch myself and grow. To learn something new and connect with the people and the world around me. A world that's *so* much bigger—and, yes, sometimes colder and snowier—than my cozy, but narrow, comfort zone.

I know, God, that all too often, shying away from something because I'm afraid it'll make me uncomfortable is the very same thing as shying away from You. Please help me to be cognizant of my comfort zone's pull, so it doesn't keep me from the plans You have in store for me. —Erin Janoso

Digging Deeper: Luke 5:4;
Ephesians 1:19

Monday, January 26

Children are a heritage from the Lord, offspring a reward from him. Like arrows in the hands of a warrior are children born in one's youth. Blessed is the man whose quiver is full of them. They will not be put to shame when they contend with their opponents in court.
—Psalm 127:3–5 (NIV)

One would think that as mature adults my husband, Wayne, and I would be wise enough to make big decisions together. How I wish I could say this were true. For months, I'd been experiencing throbbing pain in my right foot. The solution was bone fusion surgery, which would leave me immobile for 8 or more weeks. About the same time, the discomfort in my husband's knee intensified to the point he was willing to undergo complete replacement surgery.

Without giving the matter a second thought, we both scheduled our surgeries a week apart. A week apart! Really—*what were we thinking*?

I came home from the hospital in a wheelchair, and Wayne followed in a walker. Neither of us could help the other. I couldn't even dress myself without difficulty, and forget about getting myself through the bathroom door.

Our daughter Adele came to our rescue. Shortly after my surgery, she moved in and spent the next 9 weeks caring for us. Honestly, I don't know what we would have done without her. She cooked our meals, made sure we each took our medications at the proper time, and generally loved on us. Her presence blessed us every single day.

Over the years I've come to appreciate and treasure the children You have given us, Lord. Our quiver—and our hearts—are full of gratitude.
—Debbie Macomber

Digging Deeper: Proverbs 17:6, 20:11

Tuesday, January 27

While we have opportunity, let's do good to all people. —Galatians 6:10 (NASB)

Our oldest child was turning 50. We had plans for a celebration that would take place after her birthday in early January, but I wanted her to have something on "the day." I wrote a card to mail and planned to tuck in a fifty-dollar bill. Our small-town bank had permanently closed, but we could withdraw cash with our grocery store purchase.

All went well—until I was handed two twenties and a ten. I needed a fifty. There were none in the till. I was told to ask at the other checkout stands. By the third of four I'd had no success. In that line stood a friend who responded, "I think I have a fifty."

She came over to me and opened her wallet. There was a nice crisp fifty! It had arrived in a

Christmas card. We traded bills. I said, "You are a blessing to me."

Startled, she answered, "I don't think I've ever been a blessing before."

Now I was the one surprised. *How could anyone go through life not knowing they have been a blessing? Has no one told her?* I thought. I promised myself we would have a future conversation.

I'd gone to the store for a fifty-dollar bill—which God had supplied in an unexpected way. With the provision—the blessing—He had shown me, this was no ordinary fifty. This one had a mission beyond a birthday gift. My friend needed to know her life has touched others with fulfillment—to understand she is a blessing to us.

How many people are missing out on their own blessing because I neglect to say, "You are a blessing to me"?

Father, the good that I say and do not only blesses others—it blesses You. —Carol Knapp

Digging Deeper: Psalm 21:3; Proverbs 11:25, 16:24

Wednesday, January 28

May the Lord direct your hearts to the love of God and to the perseverance of Christ.
—2 Thessalonians 3:5 (NASB)

I sat at my desk, my head in my hands, and sighed deeply. For weeks I'd struggled to get my computer fixed. I'd had some software incompatibility issues rolled together with hardware malfunctions. Tech support would identify a problem and fix it, but after a few hours my computer would crash. *If manufacturers weren't constantly changing technology, maybe they'd perfect something!*

Finally I threw up my hands and thought, *Enough! I'll order a new computer.* The shiny new computer had a Windows 11 operating system. I'd been on Windows 10. I hunted for the correct icons, while inwardly growling, *Windows 10 worked just fine!* But within a couple hours of loading my programs, the machine locked up five times and black-screened twice. I boxed it up and sent it back.

That evening I plopped down in my recliner and clicked on a Christian program. The host mentioned that oftentimes she asks God to show her how much He loves her. *God, I'm beyond frustrated and worn down. Will You show me how much You love me?*

While I was sorting paperwork the next day, my phone rang. It was a longtime friend and prayer partner. She greeted me with the words, "I felt God leading me to call and tell you that I love you." My heart of frustration melted. The world would constantly be changing, trying to obtain perfection. But the love of God for His children would remain—a perfect thing—throughout eternity.

It still took a couple more weeks to get my computer fixed, but I wasn't frustrated anymore. Because the One who never changes loves me.

> **Lord, when life throws challenges my way, remind me to focus on You and Your unchanging love. Amen.** —Rebecca Ondov

Digging Deeper: Deuteronomy 7:9; Psalm 139:17–18

Thursday, January 29

A joyful heart is good medicine.
—Proverbs 17:22 (ESV)

I dashed into the shoe store, intent on checking another errand off my to-do list. But I was stopped short just inside the door by their 75 percent off clearance rack. There, on its top shelf, was a pair of boots unlike any I'd seen before. Their bottoms were a normal- enough black. But there was something about their shaggy sheepskin uppers— dyed all the colors of the rainbow—that caught and delighted my eye in a way most things don't. It was like they spoke to something within that felt simple, happy, and alive.

Be reasonable, though, the rational side of my brain, surprised by this frivolity, argued. *You'd never* actually *wear them. They're way too bold*. I sighed, and—realizing it was probably true—I left the store empty-handed.

But I went back for the boots the next day. I'm so glad they were still there because, as it turns out, my rational brain was wrong: I wear the boots— often. And whenever I do, it never fails that there'll be a passerby or two who does a quick double take.

"Oooh!" they'll exclaim, as their eyes—previously focused elsewhere—flicker up to meet mine. "I just *love* your boots!" It's always said with such feeling that it's impossible not to smile back.

Every time, I walk away from those encounters with my heart full, in awe of how God is able to use a pair of boots, of all things, to orchestrate moments of such delight and connection between total strangers. Even my rational brain agrees by now that there's nothing frivolous about that!

Thank You, God, for the things that delight my heart, and for the ways You use them to bring joy into my life and the lives of others.
—Erin Janoso

Digging Deeper: Mark 10:15; Romans 15:13

Friday, January 30

Post this at all the intersections, dear friends: Lead with your ears, follow up with your tongue, and let anger straggle along in the rear.
—James 1:19 (MSG)

So many of the conversations I find myself in these days feel fraught and fragile. So quickly friendship and conviviality can turn to contention, even at my dinner table.

One night just recently in our dining room, a close friend brought up politics when the coffee was served and said something that surprised others around the table. Within a few seconds, an argument was off and running. Everyone had been enjoying one another's company up until that moment. I thought good friends were about to actually storm away into the night until someone found it in them to say, "OK, let's stop this and remember who we are."

Remember who we are. I liked that, because misunderstandings are so easily created.

It reminded me of another misunderstanding, several years ago, when my daughter remarked that we should go where her friend's family was going on vacation.

"Why there?" I asked self-consciously.

"Because they said it was a good place, and you said we're going to the Badlands," my daughter said.

When I explained the difference to her, we laughed.

Misunderstandings aren't always that easy to defuse; unlike the recent political conversation, this was a simple case of not understanding what a name meant. But in all situations, I try to remember that defusing tension is never possible unless we remember who we are: people of God who love first and listen most, leading "with our ears," as the verse in James says.

Dear God, go ahead and whack me somehow when I lead with my voice or my opinions, and instead remind me to listen with my ears tuned to the sound of Your love. —Jon M. Sweeney

Digging Deeper: Proverbs 18:13

Be joyful in hope, patient in affliction, faithful in prayer. —Romans 12:12 (NIV)

My dear friend Susann had walked through a year of her young son's leukemia. After his diagnosis, time had moved quickly, and CJ and his parents were suddenly thrust into a whole new world filled with hospital stays, chemotherapy treatments, and many days of CJ not feeling well. Yet through it all, CJ has maintained an optimistic disposition, and soon the children's hospital staff began looking forward to his stays. CJ is a force—a force of infectious joy and hope, even more so since his diagnosis.

So when Susann invited me to CJ's eleventh birthday party, I was excited to celebrate this sweet boy. Due to the time of year, and the countless viruses wreaking havoc around our town, the family planned a drive-by birthday party to protect CJ's health. I drove toward their home, my car loaded with balloons, a birthday gift, and me wearing my #TeamCJ T-shirt.

As I arrived, I expected a line of cars ahead of me and guests waving and passing gifts through car windows to the birthday boy. Instead, adults were gathered around the back lawn chatting and laughing while CJ and his friends slid down a gigantic inflatable slide. We sang happy birthday to CJ and ate an octopus-decorated birthday cake. His parents shared words of thankfulness for CJ and the friends gathered, and they explained the surprising turn of events—CJ was having a good week, and they'd decided to celebrate him with a more typical, kid-friendly party. After gathering for those few minutes, CJ begged to be excused to slide some more.

I marveled at the joy around me. But I shouldn't have been surprised. I already knew that the birthday boy lives with the "inexpressible and glorious joy" mentioned in 1 Peter 1:8 (NIV)!

Lord, grow my faith, so I can face life's challenges with infectious joy. —Carla Hendricks

Digging Deeper: Isaiah 40:30–31; 2 Corinthians 4:16–18

LIVING A NEW LIFE

1 _____

2 _____

3 _____

4 _____

5 _____

6 _____

7 _____

8 _____

9 _____

10 _____

11 _____

12 _____

13 _____

14 _____

15 _____

16 _____

17 _____

18 _____

19 _____

20 _____

21 _____

22 _____

23 _____

24 _____

25 _____

26 _____

27 _____

28 _____

29 _____

30 _____

31 _____

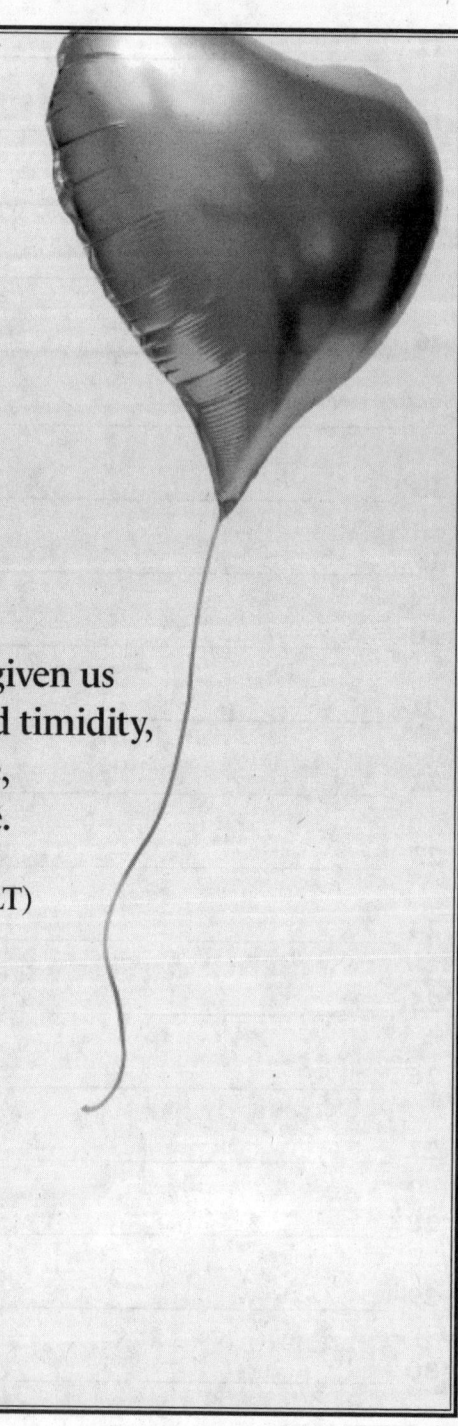

February

For God has not given us
a spirit of fear and timidity,
but of power, love,
and self-discipline.

—2 Timothy 1:7 (NLT)

If I then, your Lord and Teacher, have washed your feet, you also ought to wash one another's feet. —John 13:14 (ESV)

"The wise ones know we're in this together, and we're all just walking each other home." I found this quote on author Parker J. Palmer's social media feed. Palmer's quote simmered in my mind for weeks, especially the second part of the quote. I spent time in prayer, contemplating these words. They seemed profound, but I couldn't fully digest their meaning.

After a while, I thought less and less about the quote that had stirred my soul until one very ordinary Sunday during worship. A fellow parishioner stood to read collective prayers, and she suddenly stopped after the words, "For all those who . . ." I gazed up toward the altar. She stood paralyzed with her hand over her mouth. Her daughter, seated behind me, rushed to the altar. With her mother pointing to the paper highlighting where she left off, the daughter read out, "For all those who have died . . ." I realized this prayer must have stirred up grief for the woman, since she had lost her husband within the past year. Her daughter finished the prayers, wrapped her arm around her mother, and guided her back to her seat.

This beautiful act of love brought me to tears. While I expected to figure out Parker J. Palmer's words with my mind, the Lord spoke to my heart in the love-laden actions of a daughter. On that Sunday morning, I found "walking each other home" needed no great theological epiphany—just love, true presence, and the ultimate home of homes.

Heavenly Father, may I have a heart to truly accompany others on their way home to You.
—Jolynda Strandberg

Digging Deeper: John 13:31–35;
Romans 1:1–7, 13:8–10

Monday, February 2

Whatever is true, whatever is honorable, whatever is just, whatever is pure, whatever is lovely, whatever is commendable, if there is any excellence, if there is anything worthy of praise, think about these things. —Philippians 4:8 (ESV)

Soon after we married, my then-husband and I strove mightily to have children. He was 48 years old; I was 39. I was slightly insulted when I read the fertility doctor's official diagnosis: "advanced maternal age."

During my first round of in vitro fertilization, I became pregnant. But within a week, an ultrasound showed the tiny embryo had died. We were crestfallen but immediately turned our thoughts to another attempt.

Still smarting from the previous loss, I decided this time to approach my treatments with cool indifference and low expectations.

Fertility treatments require daily blood draws. I was already moody because of the hormones I was taking, but now I was sullen and grim. I kept a poker face through each appointment and ignored anyone who wished me luck. I thought if I anticipated failure, I would not be shocked by it.

Failure did come. We tried two more times before we stopped. To my surprise, my strategy didn't protect me from grief, anger, and resentment; it heightened them. Looking back on that joyless year, I see I had been nurturing them all along.

My fear of pain was far more debilitating than the pain itself. Fear clouded my judgment and eroded my belief in grace and divine mercy. Had I focused on those praiseworthy gifts from the God who loves me, I might have rejoiced in modern medicine, given thanks for skilled phlebotomists, and enjoyed the camaraderie of my husband as we walked that rocky road together.

God, in times of trouble, guide my attention to what is excellent and praiseworthy, and away from my fear of suffering. —Amy Eddings

Digging Deeper: Romans 12:12

Tuesday, February 3

The LORD is good to all; he has compassion on all he has made. —Psalm 145:9 (NIV)

"My mustache is touching my upper lip," Daddy says. "I never let it get like this." My father is in skilled care recovering from a broken hip. He's fiercely independent. Here he feels stripped of that freedom. Even his ability to practice self-care has been sacrificed.

"Surely there's a pair of scissors on this wing, Papa," my 22-year-old son, Samuel, says. "I'll go see what I can find." Soon he returns with a pair of small scissors. "I'll help you, Papa. I know that soon you'll do this on your own, but today I'm here to help."

I watch my gentle but strong-willed father relax. He yields to Samuel's care. Six-foot-four Sam places a towel over Papa's shoulders then bends low to begin the trim. As I watch, I remember Papa teaching Sam to hold a hammer. To disassemble delicate inner workings of clocks. To plant seedlings.

Help from the heart is rich in compassion.

One of the character traits of the Lord, firmly rooted in the Word, is compassion, and this attribute is powerful in the room today. It threads through the relationship of grandson and grandfather. It's in the tender balance of practicality and dignity. When Sam trims my father's mustache with respect, I see compassion from the Lord flow generation to generation.

Samuel eventually stands back and studies his work. "It looks good, Papa. Next time, I'll bring better tools and a mirror. Then you can shape the rest up."

This act of compassion may seem simple, but to my father it was a great blessing indeed.

Lord, let Your compassion flow through me. Amen. —Shawnelle Eliasen

Digging Deeper: Psalm 103:13; Matthew 9:36; Mark 6:34

Wednesday, February 4

Miriam the prophet, Aaron's sister, took a timbrel in her hand, and all the women followed her, with timbrels and dancing. —Exodus 15:20 (NIV)

I have a blue tambourine on the far corner of my desk. It's there to remind me to praise God and to rejoice in His salvation. It also reminds me of my friend Judy, who gave me the musical instrument in the first place. Our ladies' Bible study class had been reading through the book of Exodus in the Old Testament. One morning Judy arrived with a box of jangling tambourines—one for every woman in the class. She urged us to shake them every time we were grateful for one of God's blessings. Like Miriam on the banks of the Red Sea, Judy wanted to lead us in praising God with thanksgiving in our hearts.

That morning, as we read the Scriptures to learn more about the mighty God we serve, one woman or another would rattle her tambourine as she felt blessed by a particular Bible verse. This resulted in others lifting their own to join in. Throughout the months that followed, we brought our tambourines to class—the cheerful jangling of the instruments was a constant reminder to praise the Lord.

Judy continues to be a sister of encouragement. My blue tambourine serves as a constant reminder to be more diligent in offering prayers of thanksgiving rather than my usual petitionary prayers. When my young grandchildren lift the instrument from my desk to give it a shake, I urge them to shake it fervently, and to thank God for something specific as they do so. Like Judy, I want to be a sister of encouragement too.

Dear Lord, keep me ever mindful of all You have done for me. —Shirley Raye Redmond

Digging Deeper: 1 Chronicles 16:34; Psalm 28:7; 1 Thessalonians 5:16–18

Thursday, February 5

JOURNEY THROUGH GRIEF: My Sister's Passage

He will wipe every tear from their eyes. There will be no more death or mourning or crying or pain, for the old order of things has passed away. —Revelation 21:4 (NIV)

Angels—actors dressed to look like Victorian antiques—floated above our heads, while confetti fell like snowflakes from their elaborate wings.

My boys and I were enjoying a mesmerizing performance by Cirque du Soleil with an unusual theme for a circus: death. In the show, a clown imagined his own funeral, but the show was far from solemn. While parts were beautifully haunting, the rest was simply joyful. Life, death, and the afterworld were celebrated with dancing, laughter, jubilant music, and acrobatic acts that seemed to defy human possibility.

I was still wrapped in my post-show euphoria when I got home and opened a message from my brother-in-law.

"Your sister has passed over peacefully in her sleep," it read.

I didn't move. I simply looked at the words silently until I heard myself quietly say, "OK."

I waited for a different reaction, but nothing else came.

I had felt fear when she first told me about the cancer, and guilt for being so far away. I'd felt hopeful after a successful treatment, then crushed when the cancer progressed anyway. Helplessness, anger, desperation, and sorrow were just some of the emotions that flowed through me during my sister's illness.

Yet in the quiet of my home, as I learned her fight was over, what flowed through my body was surprisingly light. My sister was released from her frail body the same day I witnessed a stunning rendition of heaven and death, filled with beauty, celebration, and joy.

Thank You, Lord, for reminding me that death is a passage to something even more glorious than the most gifted artists can imagine or express.
—Karen Valentin

Digging Deeper: Matthew 5:4; 1 Corinthians 15:55

Friday, February 6

He has made everything beautiful in its time.
—Ecclesiastes 3:11 (NIV)

Early morning drives home after dropping my children off at school are my time to mentally prepare for the day. I think about what seems to be a never-ending to-do list and other family obligations.

But as I neared my fiftieth birthday, my morning reflections began to change. It was less about my checklist of responsibilities and more about the person I wanted to become. Was I living the life that God had intended—with all His plans and promises? I still had unrealized dreams, dreams that I had honestly intended to attain much earlier in life.

One winter day my thoughts were spurred by a particular house that I passed daily. It was an older home that sat far from the road, partially shaded by trees. The lawn was vibrant and remarkably green, a stark difference from the brown and dormant grass of every other recently constructed house I passed, including mine. Obviously, these homeowners had found a way to cultivate and grow their specific type of grass so that it reached its fullest potential.

I returned home and pulled into the garage. God's voice was clear. If I planted the seeds He had given me and tilled the soil with work and faith, my life would reach its full potential as well. It could be bountiful and prosperous, despite my age. I thanked God for reminding me that He is not slow in keeping His promises, so I should be quick in trusting His process.

God, help me to be patient until it's my season to flourish. You see from the beginning to the end, so You know what's best for me. Even though I may make many plans, I trust You to guide my steps in Your perfect timing. —Tia McCollors

Digging Deeper: Proverbs 16:9; Romans 8:28; Galatians 6:9; 2 Peter 3:8–9

Saturday, February 7

Above all, love each other deeply, because love covers over a multitude of sins. —1 Peter 4:8 (NIV)

The card had to be just right. It was for Elizabeth "Tibby" Sherrill, one of the most gifted inspirational writers of all time and a mentor to me since the 1990 *Guideposts* Writers' Workshop. My sister and I sat at my old farm table, crafting over one hundred valentines using vintage materials. Rebekkah had given herself the title of Quality Control, insisting that every Victorian postcard, scrap of ribbon, and bit of lace be glued to perfection.

A medication had affected my fine motor coordination. I was sure I'd never measure up to my sister—or to Tibby. I willed my hands to center the embossed angel on the cardstock. *Would she like the palette of pinks?* Would it mean as much as her own love-inspired missive she'd sent me, the one I'd discovered in a stack of bills that freezing, long-ago day? En route to the Cleveland Clinic for surgery, I'd stopped for fuel. A gust of wind had snatched the envelope from my hands. But not Tibby's words from my heart: *I always look for your stories, Roberta.* Me? *My* stories?

My heart swelled at the memory. With the steadiest script I could muster, I wrote, *Beloved Tibby Sherrill* on the envelope. Then mailed it to Loveland, Colorado, to receive the town's special annual Valentine's Day postmark.

A thank-you letter came quickly. Ever gracious, Tibby said she adored my little offering. I guessed love had covered my multitude of imperfections. But there was more. It was her first Valentine's Day without John, the love of her life. February 14 was also her birthday! The perfect day for a reminder of God's love in action.

Tibby is still sending love letters to the world, Lord, in the stories she taught us all to write. Thank You for Your living valentine.
—Roberta Messner

Sunday, February 8

**Let us consider one another in order to stir up
love and good works. —Hebrews 10:24 (NKJV)**

Are you among the millions who will watch the
Super Bowl? I was a kid when the first was played
between the Packers and the Chiefs in 1967 (the
Packers won handily). It was a big deal then and an
even bigger deal now.

Who could have imagined that Super Bowl
Sunday would become a virtual global holiday, with
the glitzy halftime entertainment drawing as many
viewers as the actual game? The commercials are
over the top. The game itself is gladiatorial. We're
not exactly feeding Christians to the lions, but we
are celebrating young men risking their health for
our entertainment. Billions of betting dollars change
hands.

I ought to be playing fetch with Gracie instead
of watching this decadent spectacle. Yet I wouldn't
miss it.

My wife, Julee, used to say that I would watch
anything with a score. But does the Super Bowl serve
some deeper need? Our yearning for connection
and community and tradition; to cheer for a cause,
however transitory; to be part of something bigger
than our daily toil through the power of shared

experience. A contest produces a clear winner. The outcome is definitive, unlike so much of life. It creates heroes and provides inspiration through the stories of players overcoming adversity and doing good beyond the field of play.

Today, when I inevitably tune in to the Big Game, I will consider that God allows us the gift of our mortal amusements so that we can gather with our family and friends to cheer and celebrate and bond through traditions that grow bigger than ourselves.

Lord, I love to cheer for something, especially if it has a score. I exult when my team wins. But I reserve the greatest exultation for that contest where my soul is won by You.
—Edward Grinnan

Digging Deeper: Ecclesiastes 4:9–12; Galatians 6:2

Monday, February 9

For we know that if the earthly tent we live in is destroyed, we have a building from God, an eternal house in heaven, not built by human hands. —2 Corinthians 5:1 (NIV)

My dad grew up in a beautiful home in a nearby town. In the 1990s, a decade after both my grandparents were gone, Daddy sold the house, a tough but practical decision. But he and I both still miss the old home; we drive past on days we feel particularly nostalgic.

On one such day recently, alone in my car, I felt the familiar pull to what I had always known as "Big Daddy's house." A young man was out cutting the grass in what used to be my grandfather's vegetable garden. I couldn't help but flag him down and ask about the place while sharing its history. "Don't you love that green-and-white Italian marble fireplace?" I asked.

"Oh, there's no fireplace anymore," he replied. "The owner renovated years ago."

As I drove away, tears came to my eyes. How dare anyone desecrate Big Daddy's house!

I probably shouldn't have told Daddy. He was as upset as I was. Over the years, we'd tried to think of ways to buy the house back and move it to another location. It was just talk, but a way of never really closing the book, I suppose. "I guess now we don't have to think of how to get it back," I told Daddy. "It's no longer the house we remember."

I'll always treasure the memory of that house. But instead of mourning the loss of an earthly dwelling, I'm trying to focus on anticipating my heavenly home—a home that will never change and that we'll never have to leave.

Father, I long to see the home Jesus has prepared for us! —Ginger Rue

Digging Deeper: John 14:1–31; Philippians 3:20–21

Tuesday, February 10

[King David's] servants covered him with blankets. —1 Kings 1:1 (GNT)

I remember lying in a hospital bed following a difficult childbirth and feeling tangible relief as a kind nurse surrounded me with prewarmed blankets. Ahhh, so comforting, like stepping into a steaming hot bath or drawing near a bonfire's blaze on a chilly evening.

Warmth brings life-giving comfort. That concept struck me afresh last winter when visiting my daughter, who lives in a remote part of Scotland. A mom of five children under age ten, she lives in a 100-year-old manse—a rough fixer-upper with stone walls that leak air like a sieve amid ongoing renovations. With the kitchen unfinished, meals for this family of seven were being prepared using a two-burner hotplate. I stood before the hotplate and shivered as strong winds whipped about outside and cold air seeped inside. On the counter sat a single mug containing tea brewed hours earlier, now cold.

I retrieved a saucepan and poured the tea into it, warming it on a burner and pouring the steaming liquid back into the mug. Just then my daughter entered. "Here is your tea," I ventured.

She paused and drew back slightly, saying, "It's cold."

"I heated it up for you," I said, handing her the warm cup. Tears sprang to her eyes, and I watched her hands curl around the cup as she lifted it to her lips. The comfort of warmth.

Thank You, Lord, for the sense of relief and relaxation that warmth provides. Please show us ways in which we can provide life-giving warmth both physically and spiritually to others.
—Lisa Livezey

Digging Deeper: Ecclesiastes 4:11; Job 31:20; Ezekiel 18:16; John 18:18

Wednesday, February 11

Do not conform to the pattern of this world, but be transformed by the renewing of your mind. Then you will be able to test and approve what God's will is—his good, pleasing and perfect will. —Romans 12:2 (NIV)

Recently someone said that I was born "old." Although it stung a little, he had a point. I know music from previous generations better than the songs from my own. I read the classics more than modern novels. I am happier with a horse than with a computer game. I can quote entire scenes from 1950s movies, but I draw a blank at current film-star names. I can read clocks with hands, write in cursive, and drive a stick. I prefer reading a paper book over a digital download. My friends are trending 10 or more years older than I am. Let's not even get started on my ideas of fashion, which might be considered

"John Wayne meets Annie Oakley." Isn't Gucci a type of lizard?

But my God is timeless. He is yesterday, today, and tomorrow. He is my constant. His Word is just as alive and pertinent right now as it was centuries ago. He isn't a God of the past; He is the future! He is here for all people, whether we push the cutting edge or dawdle along behind, oblivious to the whims of society.

The important thing is that God loves me just as I am, where I am, and who I am. He made me in His image. And that's the only trend that I really need to follow.

I want to fit in with You, Lord, not this earth.
Please help me to honor You in all that I do.
—Erika Bentsen

Digging Deeper: Proverbs 4:25;
Colossians 3:2; Hebrews 3:1

Thursday, February 12

Do you not know that your bodies are temples of the Holy Spirit, who is in you, whom you have received from God? You are not your own.
—1 Corinthians 6:19 (NIV)

For me, this year held a narrative that is oh-so-common but was completely foreign to me. I had a scan. They saw something. I had a follow-up. They saw more.

You all know the tale. Maybe you've had friends, parents, or children walk this path; maybe you have personally walked this path. For me, it was totally uncharted territory. One day I was on vacation. The next day, I had a breast cancer diagnosis.

I would love to say I handled it beautifully, but that would be a lie. I joked to my friends that I wanted to be described as "a light to no one." I spent many hours over the next 9 months crying in the shower. There were bright times, too, of course. Having children means life goes on, even when your life as you know it is ending and a new one begins.

In those early days, the only comfort I had was that while this was new information to me, it wasn't to everyone. While I had only just discovered this awful thing inside me, it had likely been there for years. God had known all along, and I knew He would hold me as I kicked and cried through it all. The only thing that really changed that night was my knowing.

As I write this, I am days away from my last dose of radiation. I still don't know what will come next along this not-so-fun path. But I know God already knows, and He'll be beside me no matter what it is.

Lord, hold me close. Whether my path is full of roses or loaded with thorns, be my comfort and my strength. —Ashley Kappel

Digging Deeper: Matthew 10:31; Hebrews 13:8

Friday, February 13

For whoever has despised the day of small things shall rejoice. —Zechariah 4:10 (RSV)

Lately I have had a bad case of the small-town blues. There are days when our little 3-by-4-mile town of Moberly, Missouri, puts me to sleep. Every day I go to the same places, like the library, the thrift shop, and the Christian college where I used to teach. I drive the same streets and see the same people. After 60 years here, I could do it blindfolded.

One morning I was working on a Bible lesson, poring over a map of Palestine in the time of Christ, when it struck me that Jesus lived and worked in a very small world. Bethlehem and Nazareth were both under a thousand in population. Jerusalem was just about the same size as Moberly. The entire Holy Land was small enough that Jesus walked the length and breadth of it. You could put several Holy Lands inside our state of Missouri.

For a person who was building a worldwide Kingdom, Jesus certainly started out small. But then, He was not a material man building a brick-and-mortar kingdom. Mostly He spent 3 years just visiting with people and telling stories about His new spiritual Kingdom that would endure for all time, and inviting them to join it.

So, I have revised my view of small towns. I have set a goal of visiting with at least one new person a day. All of a sudden people are coming out of the woodwork! Moberly has become a very big place. If I live to be 100, I will never meet all the interesting people in this town.

I thank God that I now have eyes to see this town and its people the way He does.

Thank You, God, for showing me just how large a small town can be when I take an interest in Your children. —Daniel Schantz

Digging Deeper: Micah 5:2; Matthew 25:23

Saturday, February 14

**Tell the Israelite people to bring Me gifts.
—Exodus 25:2 (JPS)**

"Where'd they get all that stuff?" A preteen child directly behind me in the synagogue asked that question of the adult accompanying him. I assumed it was his mother. The voice was skeptical, but also curious. The mother shushed him. It was, after all, the middle of the service, and the rabbi had just read about God's first instructions on the building of the *Mishkan,* the portable tabernacle that would contain the Ark for the Torah on the Israelites' travels through the wilderness.

When the service was over and we were in the social hall for the potluck lunch, I deliberately sat at the same table with the boy and his mother. I told them I had heard the boy's question, and I was wondering where *he* thought the "stuff" might have come from. After he got the "ancient aliens could have dropped it" out of his system, I encouraged him to think that God might have supplied whatever the Israelites needed, just like giving them the manna. I thought he might disregard that idea, but he became thoughtful and after a moment said, "So do you think if I needed something, God might give it to me?"

I waited to see if his mother would chime in, but she did not. "Well," I said, "God knew what they needed, because God had asked them for that stuff. So God can certainly provide what you need if it will help you perform your obligations to God."

He did some more thinking. "How do I know what God wants?"

I said, "Right now, ask your mom. You'll know when you can figure it out for yourself."

Sometimes I wonder if I will ever find what I need, Redeemer of my people, but I know You will show it to me in Your own time. —Rhoda Blecker

Digging Deeper: Numbers 18:6; Genesis 33:11

Sunday, February 15

The Lord will rescue me from every evil attack and will bring me safely to his heavenly kingdom. —2 Timothy 4:18 (NIV)

One Sunday I was really missing my family. My four children, their spouses, nine grandchildren, great-grandson, brother, sister, nieces, and nephews all live in eight other states far from Florida, where I live.

I forced myself to keep busy, hoping to ease my loneliness. I stayed longer in the pool. At home I framed five watercolor pencil abstracts I'd made for the upcoming Art, Books and Crafts Fair. I made curry dip for the first time and ate it with fresh pea pods and celery sticks. Painted three jars for the ABC Fair. Took a nap. Thinking it was Saturday, I walked downstairs to get the mail. No mail. Watched a Netflix movie. Texted a granddaughter but no response. Kids in their twenties are very busy.

At 4:30 I realized it was Sunday and I hadn't been to church, so I attended the 5 p.m. teen mass, thinking, *Hopefully I'll see someone I know and I'll feel less lonely.* At church I prayed with the congregation, sang a few songs, listened to the sermon, waved to strangers during the sign of peace, and received Communion.

Amazingly, I also stepped out of my lonely mood. It hit me when Father Rob said, "Every one of you has been called by God, because you're here." Whoa! I am called by God because I'm here? Yes! I worshipped, listened, sang, prayed, smiled, received, thanked God for my beautiful family, and spent time thinking how I can give more of myself to God's cause.

I needed that reminder.

Lord, sometimes I need a reminder that I am called to be Your servant. When I serve You, loneliness doesn't have a chance. —Patricia Lorenz

---

Presidents' Day, Monday, February 16

Show proper respect to everyone, love the family of believers, fear God, honor the emperor.
—1 Peter 2:17 (NIV)

While touring Andrew Jackson's Hermitage in Tennessee, I purchased a book called *Lives of the Presidents*, which includes interesting "firsts" established by early presidents.

James Polk was the one who began using "Hail to the Chief" to signal a stately entrance—a desire for ceremony that made him distinctly unlike George Washington, who was so mortified to be announced at one reception that he began arriving early at others to avoid it.

John Adams was first to occupy the White House—during a time when bathrooms were outdoors and water five blocks away. It was Andrew Jackson who arranged for running water in the White House.

Martin Van Buren was the first president born into citizenship in the United States. Previously, the office holders began life as British subjects.

James Polk held the first Thanksgiving dinner. Franklin Pierce was responsible for installing central heating in the White House and displaying the first Christmas tree there. The first telephone user in the presidential residence was Rutherford B. Hayes—his number was 1.

Andrew Johnson's wife taught him to read and write, as he had never attended school. James Garfield became the first president to campaign in both English and Spanish. Electric lights were installed in the White House by Benjamin Harrison, whose family so feared shocks they were afraid to turn them off.

Presidential image often balances on accomplishments in office. But beneath their role as leader of the United States, presidents are human beings trying to manage life and family as well as country. They need every prayer.

Heavenly Father, fulfill Your good purposes through our nation's leaders. —Carol Knapp

Digging Deeper: Proverbs 16:12–13; Matthew 28:18; 1 Timothy 2:1–4

Tuesday, February 17

Now is the acceptable time; look, now is the day of salvation! —2 Corinthians 6:2 (NRSVUE)

My daughter is apparently a budding philosopher. When she was just eight years old, she said to me one day on the walk home from school: "Tomorrow is not a thing."

I was puzzled. "What do you mean?" I said.

Very matter-of-factly, she replied, "Because tomorrow is today, if it's tomorrow."

How could I argue with that?!

It all seemed so very clear to her. And when I've returned to thinking about this conversation in the years since it took place, I keep returning to the idea that she was right. My little girl spoke wisdom that day.

There is only today, or at least there's only supposed to be today, on the way of Jesus. Whatever will happen today will come, and I will hopefully respond to it as I should, as God gives me strength to do.

So when my daughter comes home from school today, I'm not going to check my phone for texts or messages while she tells me how the day went. I will focus exclusively on her. And when we are eating dinner tonight, I won't start talking about what we should do this weekend. I will talk about today.

What comes tomorrow, I'll deal with tomorrow.

What a difference it could make in my relationships if I really lived this way.

Dear God, remind me to pay attention to You, to be fully present with the people I meet each day, to pay heed to the moment of now as I've never done before. Amen. —Jon M. Sweeney

Digging Deeper: Matthew 5:1–48, 6:1–34

Ash Wednesday, February 18

For as the heaven is high above the earth, so great is his mercy toward them that fear him. As far as the east is from the west, so far hath he removed our transgressions from us. —Psalm 103:11–12 (KJV)

Before giving away my vintage carousel projector, I flashed a hundred or so Kodak slides on the dining room wall. A few days later—on Ash Wednesday—a neighbor teen pointed to a pile of slides on the table. "What are these?" she asked.

"Cameras and pictures used to be different," I explained. "You needed a machine to show them on a screen or wall." I set up the projector. She manned the clicker, and I narrated personal scenes scattered across decades: my favorite pets, Christmas gatherings, graduations, and names of friends and family, some of whom were still nearby and some now absent.

After she left, energized by nostalgia, I perused a basketful of snapshots that supplemented the slide show: toddler days, a wild-hair stage as a young adult followed by tempered silver-tone waves. The afternoon slipped by. As I prepared dinner, I savored pleasant memories—highlights of a lifetime.

But what about the other thousands of forgettable, even regrettable, days? The mundane, sad, or solitary moments? The irksome encounters? The cranky comments? The confession-worthy things I had "left undone" and those I "ought not to have done," to quote *The Book of Common Prayer*?

On Ash Wednesday at church we read Psalm 103, placing into the hands of our merciful God *all* our days and ways—even those never captured by a camera.

Lord, on this day especially, but also every day, You draw us quietly, or dramatically, by Your mercy to Your mercy. Thank You. —Evelyn Bence

Digging Deeper: Psalm 103

Thursday, February 19

DOORS OF OUR LIFE: Garage Door

In his kindness God called you to share in his eternal glory by means of Christ Jesus. So after you have suffered a little while, he will restore, support, and strengthen you, and he will place you on a firm foundation. —1 Peter 5:10 (NLT)

Life in the mid-South offers four distinct seasons, each one with advantages and disadvantages depending on your preferences. Fall ranks the highest on my list, with its changing leaf colors and mild temperatures. Winter always places last, because of the potential for ice, sleet, and snow. Our cars share the same opinion, and all of us enjoy protection from the elements courtesy of the house and garage.

Years ago my appreciation of the garage skyrocketed when it temporarily stored the belongings of others. As their storage extended into winter, I balked at leaving our cars in the cold, and our vehicles agreed with me. None of us were happy about the situation, especially when the temperature dipped below freezing and ice pellets dropped from the sky. By morning a coating of ice welded the car doors shut and painted the windows a frosty white.

When a heavy snowfall blanketed the area weeks later, my window-scraping efforts resulted in half-frozen hands. This painful experience recalled the time I made a major decision outside of God's will and inflicted severe heartache on myself and others. On the day I realized my error and returned to His purpose for my life, I have no doubt the heavenly hosts celebrated the happy occasion. The joy of being where you belong is worthy of praise.

On the day we opened our garage doors and drove the cars into their assigned spots, I like to think they also delighted in returning home.

Heavenly Father, give me a humble spirit, a repenting heart, and a reminder when I reflect neither one. —Jenny Lynn Keller

Digging Deeper: Psalm 143:10; Isaiah 66:1–2; Luke 15:3–10

Friday, February 20

We rejoice in our sufferings, knowing that suffering produces endurance, and endurance produces character, and character produces hope, and hope does not put us to shame, because God's love has been poured into our hearts through the Holy Spirit who has been given to us. —Romans 5:3–5 (ESV)

I was in the throes of filling out financial aid forms with my son, Henry. My dining-room table was covered with old tax records, and there had been a lot of changes to the online form since we last filled it out. On top of that, the site kept crashing. The deadline was looming, so there was no option but to keep going.

I looked out the window. The leaves of the trees had fallen, and a host of sparrows were scattered on the lawn. This winter had been strange. Unseasonably warm days juxtaposed with frigid cold. I sighed and got up to get a drink.

A flash of purple out the window by our mailbox caught my eye. Lilacs. How could that be? Our neighbor's line of lilacs was blooming.

I got up and went closer to the window, and then, putting on my shoes, I walked outside to get a closer look.

My neighbor joined me, and we stood beneath her row of blooming bushes.

"Something, right?" she said. "I've never seen anything like it. Blooming in February."

"It's crazy," I said.

We both went back inside, and I searched for answers online and discovered that lilacs bloom out of season when they are under stress. I thought about nature's beautiful message, that hardship can bring beauty, that we can bloom not in spite of our challenges but because of them.

Dear Lord, thank You for the intricate lessons You place in my life that show how intimately

connected You are to everyone and everything here on earth. —Sabra Ciancanelli

Digging Deeper: Psalm 55:22; Proverbs 3:5–6; Matthew 6:34; John 14:27

Saturday, February 21

Many waters cannot quench love, nor can rivers drown it. If a man tried to buy love with all his wealth, his offer would be utterly scorned. —Song of Solomon 8:7 (NLT)

My husband and I are in midlife. Saturday night we watched the 2007 movie *The Bucket List.* It was a little corny for our tastes, but the next day, when we went to church and the Sunday sermon was about following your dreams, we both took notice at the repetition of this message. *Was God prompting us? Should we make a bucket list?*

I grabbed a pen and paper, and we sat down to talk. What do we want to accomplish before we die? What is our dream? How can we get fulfillment from life before it's too late? The rest of the day, we talked about it on and off—places we wanted to go, experiences to be had, sights to see, exotic destination vacations we wanted to take. So much to do and so little time!

Then reality set in. With a daughter in college, our funds were limited. Michael's elderly grandmother now lived with us, so while we could take short vacations, extended travel was out of the question.

Plus, shouldn't we be saving for retirement, since that was on the horizon?

Later in the evening when Michael took the dog out, he texted me a picture of the big, bright, full moon glowing in the clear ebony sky. I joined him on the back porch. It was breathtaking! We sat together, hand in hand, and stared up into the heavens.

Having a great love to share my life with didn't make my bucket list, but at that moment I realized *who* I was with was far more valuable than where I would go or what experience I could have. With the blessing of true love, my bucket list is complete.

Thank You for giving me my spouse, Lord, and that reminder of how important he is to me. May I remember there is nothing greater than love. —Stephanie Thompson

Digging Deeper: Proverbs 18:22; Song of Solomon 6:3; 1 Corinthians 13:13

Sunday, February 22

Those who cling to worthless idols turn away from God's love for them. —Jonah 2:8 (NIV)

I leaned forward as my pastor spoke about the error of always having to be heard: "I've got to get my point out!" he said, mimicking a fictional conversationalist. And then he admonished, "That's some idolatry you can do without." The idolatry of which he spoke was pride.

My thoughts scurried toward the ancient practice of worshipping images carved from wood and stone—something *I* would never do. But *pride*—as an idol? If an intangible like pride can be an idol, I reasoned, then what about envy and unforgiveness—anything we cling to more than God?

I remembered a passage from the book of Jonah: "Those who cling to worthless idols turn away from God's love for them." True, in modern times, we encounter little of the Old World wood-and-stone icons, but is it possible that unseen idolatry in our very souls is as rampant as painted images were on shelves of antiquity?

When we hold fast to intangible idols such as "You hurt me; I'll never forgive you," we—as Apostle Paul so aptly wrote in Galatians 2:21 (KJV)— "frustrate the grace of God." What true Christian wants to do that?

Perhaps we should not look at houses and cars—and even offspring—as the only modern-day candidates for idolatry. Maybe we should also consider eliminating the idols of hatred and bitterness to which we too often cling. And isn't it comforting to know that disabusing ourselves of these petty idols results in a covering of grace that was always ours?

Lord, I know You have brought me out of the miasma of unforgiveness. Yet sometimes I linger at the edge. Help me to walk in the grace You have provided for me. —Jacqueline F. Wheelock

---

Monday, February 23

I was sick, and you visited Me.
—Matthew 25:36 (NKJV)

The dire news swept through our parish: Our music minister's husband had encephalitis, which affected his speech. Prognosis uncertain. Our music minister, Heather, resigned from her ministry to care for him at home. Protecting her husband from potential infection and monitoring his impaired functioning now separated her from her church community 20 miles away. Her mother visited from the opposite coast but eventually returned home. Though Heather worked her second job remotely, she now faced a new reality: social isolation.

A few months later, when germs posed less threat but Larry still needed constant care, Heather invited me to join her for companionable knitting. As she crocheted, she voiced dismay at her isolation and frustration at her husband's prognosis: gradual improvement over several *years*.

Perhaps prompted by the Holy Spirit, I remembered a woman who had worked as a nanny for a disabled child years ago. The family had a recipe box full of cards with contact information, each one a potential helper. Perhaps we could set up a similar volunteer brigade?

Within 3 days, Heather drafted a "Friends of Larry" spreadsheet. Perhaps not surprisingly, the divinely inspired rota of eager friends included a speech pathologist, retired physical therapist, and retired occupational therapist, along with friends from choir. Some days the professionals would offer therapy. Other days we just watched Larry sleep. Every day, we gave Heather hugs and household support. Once again, Heather had her beloved community—just in a new venue.

Lord, You taught us that where two or three are gathered in Your name, You are with us—anywhere. —Gail Thorell Schilling

Digging Deeper: Job 6:14; Proverbs 17:17; Matthew 18:20

Tuesday, February 24

THE BIRDS OF MY NEIGHBORHOOD: God's Faithful Care

Now to the King eternal, immortal, invisible, the only God, be honor and glory for ever and ever. Amen. —1 Timothy 1:17 (NIV)

Drifting off to sleep the other night, I heard the distinctive hoot of a great horned owl.

One of the largest of the owls, it has long, earlike tufts and intimidating yellow eyes. It's a predator that can take down birds and mammals larger than itself. Great horned owls are active mostly during the night, especially at dusk and before dawn. For all their calling at night, they are pretty silent during the day.

As I found out one day. The few times I have encountered this awesome owl, since I'm not active at night, has been on late afternoon walks in the woods. One time I probably was walking too close to the pair's unseen-by-me nest for their comfort. The male silently swooped down. I didn't hear it or even see it coming. At first all I saw was a blur of motion, and then the big bird buzzed me. I have to admit, I jumped in fright.

As I continued my walk and thought about my owl experience, I was reminded of one of my favorite hymns. Its lyrics say about God:

Unresting, unhasting, and silent as light
Nor wanting, nor wasting, thou rulest in might.

That's how the owl seemed to me. Always alert. In day or night. Unhasting and silent, but even during the day, when I supposed it to be resting, it was watchful. In that way, I thought of our Creator God who is always surveying His creation and creatures. Not as prey or threat, like the owl, but with sustaining and loving care. The God who loves us more than we can know.

O ever-vigilant God, teach me to rest in Your faithful, loving care knowing that You are always watching over me and all of Your creation. Amen.
—J. Brent Bill

Digging Deeper: Psalm 104

Wednesday, February 25

Your basket and your kneading trough will be blessed. —Deuteronomy 28:5 (NIV)

"Do you want to get ice cream cones?" I asked.

Eighteen-year-old Gabriel's green eyes went wide as he glanced from the driver's seat. "It's the snowiest day of the winter," he said.

It was true. The snowfall had begun deep in the night and continued throughout the day. Gabe was home from college and was helping me get necessities.

"Something warmer?" I asked. "OK, hot fudge sundaes!"

Gabe smiled.

Soon we sat in our warm car outside the Dairy Queen spooning hot fudge as snow swirled outside our window. We talked about a snow fort he and his brothers built years before. About hitting the hill with their given-by-Grandpa runner sleds. About the five-brother lineup of boots by our old back door. Reminiscing brought joy for the blessings we'd had, but it also brought a pang of pain and a sense of loss that was sharp as the wind.

"We had some good times, didn't we, Gabriel?" I asked. I put my spoon on the dashboard and looked at my son straight-on. A tightness formed in my chest.

Gabriel tugged his new knit cap and then spoke with the compassion of a good, godly man. "We sure did," he said. "But I have to say, Shawn, that this here is pretty good too." The boys call me Shawn when they're teasing. But I knew that under the folly was straight, solid truth.

Gabriel reached over, squeezed my hand, then handed me that red plastic spoon. We finished our sundaes as the world went white.

Yes, this was pretty good too.

O Lord, even when I look back with longing, You still provide for me. My basket is blessed. Amen.
—Shawnelle Eliasen

Digging Deeper: Numbers 6:24–26;
Psalm 34:8

Thursday, February 26

May the Lord give you discretion and understanding. —1 Chronicles 22:12 (NIV)

Driving to a restaurant one afternoon, a truck in front of me suddenly stopped. The driver exited, walked to the other side of his truck, and began pounding at the window where a female passenger sat.

Not knowing the story, my mind filled in the blanks: *Is she safe? Should I call the police?* I waited a bit before deciding to leave. Later, at the restaurant, I wasn't feeling good about my non-response.

Soon a young family of four entered the restaurant. I watched as the youngest son took his dad's hand and kissed it. Thanking his son, the dad then kissed the top of his son's head. This act of love profoundly moved me. Before I left the restaurant, I thanked the family for the healing image they had provided for me.

Later, praying about the experience, I felt God saying, "I love you, even within your limitations." I know that God loved me wholeheartedly, without reservation! I didn't respond as I would have liked this time, but there had been many times before when I did intervene. And God's unconditional love was clear.

It took some time, but I was finally able to let go of my guilt. I discovered that being honest with myself and embracing God's unconditional love allows me to accept my own limitations. What a gift that has been.

O Lord, I thank You for Your unconditional love. Amen. —Adam Ruiz

Digging Deeper: Job 34:16; Mark 12:33; 1 Corinthians 14:15

Friday, February 27

SACRED THREADS: Remember
I will remember the deeds of the Lord; yes, I will remember your miracles of long ago. —Psalm 77:11 (NIV)

I pause at the collection of Victorian paper-punch samplers hanging on the walls of my century-old log cabin. Their words were stitched by long-ago artists, a symbol of faith-filled lives. They tell the story of my life. In many ways, they guide that life.

They are sometimes called "the poor person's stitchery," their perforated paper purchased by mail for mere pennies. Threads folks had on hand were often implemented, picked out from a favorite pillow or whatnot. Many were worked by invalids not long for this world.

One stitched in blues says *Remember Me.* My mind travels to my mother in her struggle with cancer, the final night she spent in her earthly home where I grew up. It was the first snowfall of the season; the temperature had dropped to 20 degrees. Mom struggled to coax open the heavy wooden front door, stuck her head outside, then shut it with a shiver. Turned to my daddy and said: "Jim, I've told you before, but I haven't told you enough. Thank you for this nice, warm house." No one had to tell me what she'd be telling God that last night at 607 Madison Avenue. *I've told You before, Lord, but I haven't told You enough. Thank You.* Then her long list of rememberings, of gratitude.

Hands across time nudge *me* to remember. May their stitchery speak to *your* spirit, as you, too, remember the deeds of our Lord.

I remember the folks who looked ahead in time to create beauty for me to love, Lord. Thank You.
—Roberta Messner

Digging Deeper: Deuteronomy 4:9;
Psalms 77:11–12, 103:2–5

From him the whole body, joined and held together by every supporting ligament, grows and builds itself up in love, as each part does its work. —Ephesians 4:16 (NIV)

I love African violets, particularly ones with dark purple blooms. I've tried many times to grow them successfully, but I haven't managed to do so. Either the leaves burn because of too much exposure to the sun, or the plants shrivel and stop blooming altogether.

My friend Donna, however, is the African violet queen. She raises them with great success. Even when I follow her advice, I've not been able to replicate her efforts. When I lamented my failure, Donna looked at me with a half-smile, saying, "Yes, but you write books and devotions. I can't even write an interesting Christmas letter. If the whole world grew houseplants, there'd be no books."

Her words gave me pause. It's true. We all have gifts with which to serve the Lord and His people. Not just spiritual gifts such as preaching, teaching, and making disciples, but also other gifts equally important in the Kingdom.

Donna blesses others with her houseplants. I bless others through my writing. Everything falls under the Lordship of Jesus—from car repair, healthcare, and accounting to farming and the arts. We all have a meaningful job in the Kingdom of God.

Will I give up trying to grow African violets? Probably not. But it's more important that I bloom for Jesus using the gifts He has blessed me with.

Lord, let my service to You be diligent and wholehearted. —Shirley Raye Redmond

Digging Deeper: Psalm 100:2; 1 Corinthians 10:31; Colossians 3:23

LIVING A NEW LIFE

1. _____

2. _____

3. _____

4. _____

5. _____

6. _____

7. _____

8. _____

9. _____

10. _____

11. _____

12 _____

13 _____

14 _____

15 _____

16 _____

17 _____

18 _____

19 _____

20 _____

21 _____

22 _____

23 _____

24 _____

25 _____

26 _____

27 _____

28 _____

March

Do not conform to the pattern
of this world, but be transformed
by the renewing of your mind.

—Romans 12:2 (NIV)

Be firm and be calm. —Isaiah 7:4 (JPS)

Often when my meetings and deadlines pile up, I begin moving much too fast and feeling much too stressed. Recently, on one of those occasions, I remembered a time when Father William, the priest at the monastery where I attended a retreat, was driving me to the Seattle-Tacoma airport to catch my flight home to Los Angeles.

Traffic on Interstate 5 north of Seattle slowed to a crawl, then came to a stop altogether. Since Father William was driving, I was free to think about the quiet, prayerful 2 weeks I'd just spent at the monastery. When I left the hectic work I did every day in Los Angeles and got to ease into the serenity of my nuns' Benedictine spirituality, it never failed to relax me. I'd spent the first week there with my husband, Keith, and then stayed on my own the second after he'd flown back to LA so that he wasn't neglecting his business for too long a time.

Father William had been visiting for that second week as well, and since we were leaving at the same time, he had volunteered to drive me to the airport. We had been a little late leaving—it was really hard to say goodbye, for him and for me—which meant that we had left with only a little extra time before I needed to check in for my flight.

As the gridlock barely inched forward, Father William turned to me and asked, "What would it do to your serenity if you missed your plane?"

I thought about that for a few seconds, testing out whether I wanted to shake off the remnants of the past 2 weeks in anticipation of the return to "normal" life. Then I answered, "There will be another plane."

Calm acceptance has never been easy for me, as well You know, God, and I thank You for the times I can experience it. —Rhoda Blecker

Digging Deeper: Jeremiah 46:27; Lamentations 3:25

Monday, March 2

Do not be anxious about anything, but in every situation, by prayer and petition, with thanksgiving, present your requests to God. And the peace of God, which transcends all understanding, will guard your hearts and your minds in Christ Jesus. —Philippians 4:6–7 (NIV)

I'd been wrestling in prayer over the many changes happening in our lives. Retirement hadn't quite worked out as I'd expected. My husband, Wayne, and I had purchased a winter home in Arizona, but now he was reluctant to spend 3 to 4 months away from his beloved workshop. We'd both experienced health issues. The death of a lifelong friend had left me dealing with fresh waves of grief. So many concerns crowded my heart.

After my morning prayer time, our puppy, Bullet, wanted my attention. He loved to play fetch. I'd toss him a play toy, and he'd scurry and race after it, often sliding across the tile floor in his rush to capture his prize. Then he'd bring it back to me to toss again. Only he'd refuse to release it. I'd bend over and point to the floor, letting him know he had to let go before I would continue the game. Once Bullet realized I wasn't going to toss the toy until he set it down, he reluctantly did so, only to snatch it up again before I had a chance to capture it.

I smiled at his unwillingness until I realized this was exactly the game I'd been playing with the Lord. With many of my prayers, I'd give them to Jesus, then fret and grab them back again. So many of the concerns I'd offered up had claw marks. Our silly, fun-loving puppy had taught me a valuable lesson that day. Let go and let God.

Father, help me rest in Your grace and to be willing to trust in You. —Debbie Macomber

Digging Deeper: Psalms 37:5, 56:3–4

Tuesday, March 3

"I have the right to do anything"—but I will not be mastered by anything. —1 Corinthians 6:12 (NIV)

I have to go to the emergency room."

My body had signaled something was wrong. And with both my husband and me at the age where we shy away from night driving, an unexpected trip to the hospital wasn't something we relished—neither the drive into the city nor the myriad diagnoses that could be waiting. Given my history as a cancer survivor, any unusual bodily malfunction sent my mind flying back a quarter of a century earlier to the many hours spent at the oncologist's office.

Yet I managed to sit through the long hours in the ER, the Holy Spirit providing calm I knew wasn't mine. The symptoms suddenly stopped, and shortly thereafter the doctor came in to see me. The results he stated were typical for people with the gastro-intestinal bout I'd experienced months earlier.

But I had chosen to ignore that experience and the doctor's recommendations that followed. After all, didn't I have the right to delicious food sometimes?

Paul's message from 1 Corinthians hit its mark: I had a right to eat what I loved, but it was not always the right thing to do. I could either obey the medical advice or find myself back in the ER. Or worse. Blessedly, I had received a wake-up call and not a death knell; still, I needed to revisit my lifestyle— principally my diet. Head cleared, I better understood the apostle's words. I wouldn't be mastered by my so-called rights.

To quote the lyrics of Fred Hammond in his song "Call Me Righteous," it was "a grace thing." God's grace awakened me to what my body needed (or didn't need) and, in so doing, gave me pause to see the essential wisdom before me: the Holy Spirit's unfailing guidance.

Father, help me to see that my choices,
compared to Your Spirit's, are deeply flawed.
—Jacqueline F. Wheelock

Digging Deeper: Deuteronomy 30:19;
Proverbs 3:5–6; Galatians 6:7

Wednesday, March 4

Let us run with endurance the race God has set before us. —Hebrews 12:1 (NLT)

My 11-year-old granddaughter, Lula, left the starting line at full tilt, easily pulling far ahead of the rest of her elementary- school track meet competitors. Unfortunately, the race my granddaughter was running was not the one set before her. Four months earlier, Lula had placed second in the 50-yard dash against elementary school girls from over thirty local schools. But today's event was a 1,000-meter cross-country run. In under a minute, Lula was exhausted and gasping for air. When she finally crossed the finish line, Lula was walking, accompanied by the very last of the participants in her grade.

At the next meet, Lula took the lesson she'd learned a week earlier in stride. Literally. She slowed down. She tried pacing herself with the "rabbit," a high school athlete who ran with the group, encouraging runners to keep going and stay on course.

As I watched Lula focus less on speed and more on endurance, Hebrews 12:1 came to mind. How was my own spiritual race going? That race is a one-person event, with my only competition being me. After all, no member of the human race runs an identical track. The starting line, terrain, obstacles, and length of the race are as unique as each individual's story. My race may be solo, but I'm never alone. Along with the "great cloud of witnesses" cheering me on, Jesus is always beside me, encouraging me toward the Finish Line.

Jesus, thank You for being my "rabbit," for keeping me on track, and for inspiring me to keep going when my spirit lags. —Vicki Kuyper

Digging Deeper: Isaiah 40:31; 1 Corinthians 9:24–27; 2 Timothy 4:7

Thursday, March 5

Jesus Christ is the same yesterday and today and forever. —Hebrews 13:8 (NIV)

When I finally returned to my old gym in downtown Manhattan to retrieve my gym bag and the other things I'd abandoned in my locker, it was 4 years after that day in March 2020 when the city shut down in the tightening grip of Covid-19.

Even as the trainers were rolling up mats and breaking down equipment, I had taken one last, frantic cycling class, riding as hard as I could, fearing I might not be back for some time, if at all. I'd stuffed my gym things in my locker thoughtlessly, not imagining it would be *this* long. A few hours later I was on a train headed for the hills. The city hadn't held such foreboding since 9/11. How could we have imagined what was coming and the changes it would bring?

Now, on this day, I felt like an anthropologist pawing through my old stuff. Along with socks and riding shoes and cycling pants and water bottles, there was a manuscript I'd been reading for work. A meeting agenda. A reminder for a dental appointment. One of my books that I'd signed for a fellow gym member to give him the next time I saw him. A birthday card from a friend. So much had changed in these strange few years. None of us quite the same.

How much change can one take? The world changes. Our lives change. Our bodies change. Our families change. We change. Sometimes life feels like a funhouse floor, always shifting.

But God never changes. He authored all that is, has been, and ever will be. His constancy gives us strength to face what comes next. To trust that as we move through life, we move through Him.

With You, Father, no change is too great.
—Edward Grinnan

Digging Deeper: Joshua 1:9; Philippians 4:6–7

Friday, March 6

Wake up! Strengthen what remains and is about to die, for I have found your deeds unfinished in the sight of my God. —Revelation 3:2 (NIV)

My wife, Pat, and I toured the prison where the movie *The Shawshank Redemption* was filmed. The evening before, we had watched the movie. After being there, we viewed the movie again, identifying places we'd been. My favorite line in the movie is when Andy says to Red, "It comes down to a simple choice . . . get busy living or get busy dying!"

At the time, I was recovering from a second surgery for kidney cancer. Although all went well and the outlook is good, it was my second occurrence. A troublesome reality that stayed in my mind. *Will I have more occurrences? Will one partial kidney sustain my active life? How long do I have?*

Andy's quote reminded me of a wonderful devotion from Daniel Schantz in *Daily Guideposts (Walking in Grace) 2021* that I read while I was healing from the first surgery. Daniel brought Revelation 3:2 to life for me. *Strengthen what remains*—red-letter words of Christ. Words I never noticed. Words that provide the path I need to stay focused living.

Each day I thank God for what I still have and ask His help to do what it takes to grow stronger spiritually, physically, mentally, and emotionally to better serve Him. I've learned that doing what I can to strengthen what I have left is all I can do.

The rest is in God's hands. And I am at peace and treasuring, like never before, each new day.

Dear Lord, thank You for the ways and people You use to help us find a route out of our struggles. Help us never give in to setbacks. Give us eyes, ears, and a discerning heart to sense Your guidance!
—John Dilworth

Digging Deeper: Deuteronomy 30:19; Joshua 1:9; 1 Thessalonians 5:16–18

Saturday, March 7

Your eyes saw my unformed body; all the days ordained for me were written in your book before one of them came to be. —Psalm 139:16 (NIV)

Throughout my childhood into early adulthood, I was blessed to be raised by *three* parents: my mother, my father, and my maternal grandmother. My grandmother lived with me until she passed away at the fantastic age of 94. Living with my grandmother instilled in me a love for my elders, which has continued throughout my life.

My mother lived all the days of her life with her mother, and when my parents married, my grandmother moved in with them. When I was born, my grandmother helped raise me, treating me more like a beloved daughter than as her seventeenth grandchild.

As my grandmother got older, I saw firsthand the attentive care that my mother and her four sisters showered upon her. They took turns hosting her at their homes, providing her with a variety of comforts to let her know that she was loved and respected. I suppose that God enabled me to see that perfect example to show me how to be a patient and loving caregiver to my father.

As my father entered his ninety-fifth year, the family determined that he would get the best care in a nursing care facility near his home. Certainly it was a difficult decision to make. But considering that my first paying job was as a weekend recreation supervisor at a nursing home in my hometown of the Bronx, New York, I was aware of the benefits of 24-hour care for my dad.

We certainly don't know what the Lord has in mind for us. While He knows His plans for our lives, we must live our lives with loving attention to those around us, daily trusting in Him to prepare us for what is to come.

Father, thank You for Your guidance and direction, as evidenced in Your Word. —Gayle T. Williams

Digging Deeper: 2 Chronicles 14:11; Isaiah 26:3–4

Sunday, March 8

This vision is for a future time. It describes the end, and it will be fulfilled. If it seems slow in coming, wait patiently, for it will surely take place. It will not be delayed. —Habakkuk 2:3 (NLT)

After worship and preaching a sermon titled "Waiting with Hope," I greeted attendees in the back of the sanctuary as they exited. One member of the congregation, Cindy, shook my hand and said, "God's waiting room is a difficult place to be." She waited for 36 years for an answered prayer. Although it was a long and difficult process, her faith in God increased.

The concept of "God's waiting room" resonated with me. I reflected on my longest wait for an answered prayer—26 years. I was 10 years old when I started praying and waiting for my dad to return to faith and church life. I grew into a young man, attended college, got married, and started a family without an answered prayer. Graduated from seminary, got ordained, and served a few congregations as I waited upon the Lord.

While I waited, God was at work in my own life. Helping me grow in my faith. Teaching me that waiting is part of the faith journey, and His ways are not our ways. Waiting all those years was filled with different emotions: sadness, disappointment, frustration, confusion, hope, peace, trust, and more. Some days I even forgot about the prayer request.

Twenty-six years later, when I least expected it, God answered the prayer. I was surprised and overwhelmed with joy and gratitude all at the same time.

I have been in "God's waiting room" many other times in my life. I'm still learning to persevere as

I trust God's wisdom and will for my life. It's a lifetime journey; some days are easier than others.

Lord, teach me to wait and trust Your timing, will, and wisdom for my life. —Pablo Diaz

Digging Deeper: Psalm 27:14; Isaiah 40:30–31

Monday, March 9

But He said to them, "Beware, and be on your guard against every form of greed." —Luke 12:15 (NASB)

I was lying in bed feeling sorry for myself. Medical necessity in our son's family meant I needed to stay with the grands—which I loved doing. However, the stay was scheduled to begin on a Wednesday I'd already packed with plans of my own—activities that I'd eagerly awaited.

A Latin phrase, *carpe diem*—"seize the day"— hovered in my thoughts. On its heels came a quiet caution: *Don't crave the day.* I remembered a Bible story when a complaining band of the wandering Israelites craved meat in the wilderness (Numbers 11:4–34). Finally God sent quail to satisfy their craving, but it did not end well.

One by one, I pried loose my hold on each Wednesday event I had "craved." Only after that did our son call to say I wasn't needed until Thursday.

I needed a repeat lesson a few months later when our daughter and family moved 2,000 miles to Kentucky—following God's leading. I wanted them close to me, as they had been for almost 9 years. I had "seized the day" during that time—collecting many great memories—but now I found myself hearing again, *Don't crave the day.*

Just as I had coveted a future day, I now did the same with past days. Neither put God first. They put me first. God's days to me are His gift. Craving the day is a misguided attempt to claim them for myself. Seizing the day—accepting whatever He sends—is honoring what is His.

Holy Spirit, I live my days so much wiser when I listen to You. —Carol Knapp

Digging Deeper: Numbers 11:4–34; Psalm 90:12; Hebrews 13:20–21

Tuesday, March 10

Look carefully then how you walk, not as unwise but as wise. —Ephesians 5:15 (ESV)

"Let's go chasing waterfalls," my husband, Kevin, proposed as he walked into our home office. "After all the rain, there should be water at Carney Falls."

I didn't need to be asked twice. I had been staring at my phone for 10 minutes, reluctant to begin a difficult conversation with a friend. I had been putting it off for days. One more delay couldn't hurt, could it?

After parking at the trailhead, Kevin and I hiked over several ridgelines, past prickly pear and cholla cacti. The air was full of moisture. Our terrier-mix, Mollie, romped through one mud puddle after another. Soon we reached our destination at the desert waterfall that contained water only after a rainstorm. Mollie immersed herself in the pool at the base, lapping up water with smiling eyes. On the return hike, her wet ginger fur attracted debris, prickers, and mud. She needed a bath.

But once we arrived home, I put it off. Surely Mollie's bath could wait until after I had my own shower. How much dirt could one 30-pound dog have in her fur, anyway?

Apparently, quite a bit. By delaying her bath, I had to wash not only Mollie but also two throw blankets, a comforter, a couch cushion, and the floor. She had left drying chunks of mud everywhere. My delay had caused more work, not less.

Later in my office, with a damp, but clean, Mollie next to me, I picked up my phone and left a message with my friend. "Can we get together for coffee next week? I'd like to talk."

Jesus, give me wisdom for when to tackle difficult things—whether bathing dogs or hard conversations. Delaying might mean more work later. —Lynne Hartke

Digging Deeper: Proverbs 13:4; Hebrews 6:11–12

What are mere morals that you should think about them . . . ? Yet you made them only a little lower than God and crowned them with glory and honor. —Psalm 8:4–5 (NLT)

Sometimes the shortest offhand phrase can put someone's mind at ease.

An older colleague I haven't seen in decades recently contacted me. She wanted to send me a book she treasured—a first-edition 1975 hardback copy of *Angels: God's Secret Agents* personally inscribed by author Billy Graham with a verse from Psalm 91, an assurance of angelic guardianship. "I was going to leave the book to someone in my will, but why wait?" my friend said as she made the offer.

I appreciated the thoughtful gesture, though I doubted the volume was estate-worthy in terms of its monetary value. Two weeks later—nothing in the mail—she wrote again. She couldn't find the book. Someone likely had borrowed it, she said, noting that she lives in senior housing, in close quarters with others. "I think it will turn up somewhere, sometime, and when it does, it's yours."

I responded, "I anticipate it when it's found but no worries if someone else is enjoying it."

She answered quickly, "You're so understanding, dear Evelyn. 'No worries' is just what I needed to hear."

Now, rereading these email exchanges, I identify an unintended progression: Appreciate. Anticipate.

Alleviate. (I admit that I'm a sucker for alliteration.) I'm going to remember this tack. In some small measure, it might encourage me again to be a human "secret agent" of grace.

Lord, let the words of my mouth—and keystrokes—glorify You and be a blessing to others. —Evelyn Bence

Digging Deeper: Psalm 19

Thursday, March 12

For now we see only a reflection, as in a mirror, but then we will see face to face. Now I know only in part; then I will know fully, even as I have been fully known. —1 Corinthians 13:12 (NRSVUE)

My wife and I were taking the train down to Washington, DC, traveling with our two sons, William and Tim, 7 and 4 at the time. Growing up in New York City, they'd been on subway trains multiple times but never on a big train with a long stream of cars and comfy seats to stretch out on.

We took the escalator down to the tracks at Penn Station, finding seats next to the window where they could gaze out. "All aboard," the conductor called. We slowly moved out, heading west and then south. For a long while the train traveled in a tunnel, under the Hudson River and across to New Jersey until it finally came out into the sunshine with the Newark skyline in the distance.

That's when seven-year-old William exclaimed, in amazement and wonder, "This train goes outside!"

Don't all trains go outside? But then again, he'd never been on a train like this. Some of the subways do stream aboveground, but we rarely took them. This train went outside.

Isn't it a good reminder of how limited our point of view can be, even as adults? What do I know of someone else's life and their struggles? What can I see through their eyes? What do I see through God's holy lens? How can I work to have that wisdom and perception? Sometimes I think I'm not unlike William, until I imagine being shown a heavenly vision and finally exclaiming, "This train goes outside."

Lord, help me to see clearly. —Rick Hamlin

Digging Deeper: Psalm 119:105; Matthew 6:33; John 4:24

Friday, March 13

I meditate on your precepts and consider your ways. —Psalm 119:15 (NIV)

If you haven't been touched by cancer treatment in your life, let me tell you a little about what it's like. There's often surgery, some amount of chemotherapy, and, at times, radiation. For my cancer, I needed thirty doses of radiation, which worked out to treatments on every day, Monday through Friday, for 6 weeks straight.

I'm a numbers gal, so once I knew I needed thirty doses, I made myself a calendar so I could cross out the days. Imagine my surprise when I realized the thirty treatments, after factoring in weekends, would come out to 40 days in total—my own personal Lent.

My Lenten practice has always been unique. I used to stress about finding something to give up, and then I adopted the practice of picking things up—more time in prayer, more good deeds done, more pages read.

"Well," I said, "I guess this year we're meditating." Each weekday as I applied lotions, drove to the facility, and lay still for 10 minutes on a cold surgical table, I tried my best to center myself and just be grateful—grateful for treatment, grateful for the techs, grateful for the women who had tested this technology years ago so that I could endure it.

There isn't an Easter at the end of my Lent. I'll move on to the next stage of my treatment. But there will be celebrating. If I've learned anything this year, it's that life is for living and we need to celebrate each opportunity we're given. As author Kate Bowler wisely said, "I want to live every day until I die." That is exactly my plan.

Lord, thank You for the seasons of my life that allow me to pause, breathe (hold that breath!), and reflect. —Ashley Kappel

Saturday, March 14

May he give you the desire of your heart and make all your plans succeed. —Psalm 20:4 (NIV)

"Sit here, Mom, where the sun comes in," my oldest son, Logan, says.

I take a seat on soft brown leather that's been gently warmed by the sun. Logan's dog, Old Sport, is on my feet, his blanket-body also a comfort. I'm visiting the two of them for the weekend. Logan and I will paint his writing room to change it from harsh red to new-growth green.

We drink coffee while sunshine presses through century-old windows. Logan sits across from me in a wooden Mission-style chair. He's at home in his newly purchased 1924 charmer with its lead glass, built-in cabinets, and a staircase that sings a song all its own.

"I'm proud of you, Logan," I say. "I'm proud of your hard work and that you've done this all on your own."

Logan nods, but those words seem to hang in the air. *On your own.* I know that he longs for someone to share this home with. When his belongings gave this home old-gentleman class, there was something absent. Our family prayed through this home when Logan first moved in, but when I move throughout this lovely place, I'm still praying. Without ceasing. Logan knows what he's looking for in a wife, but mostly he knows what he wants to give her.

"Well, let's get started, Mom," my son eventually says.

And as Logan paints the trim and I roll great swaths of hopeful green, I pray a silent blessing over Logan.

And I trust the Lord to provide.

Lord, You are the giver of all good things. In Your timing, please provide. Amen.
—Shawnelle Eliasen

Digging Deeper: Numbers 6:24–26; Job 38:41; Colossians 1:11

Sunday, March 15

For I the Lord do not change. —Malachi 3:6 (RSV)

A gentle buzz circulated at Sunday coffee hour. Upon seeing our new rector, a little girl had exclaimed, "Mommy! We have a new God!" We chuckled that the three-year-old could mistake a rector in his robes for the Almighty.

But the tot's perception of a "new God" gave me more to ponder than the sermon. I reflected how, in a world wracked by continuous shifts, rifts, and upheavals, God does not change. We humans enjoy benign changes like the maturing and flowering of plants and friendships. Other changes, such as watching our children grow or parents decline, tug at our hearts. But it's those shattering changes—the dreaded diagnosis, the severed relationships, the disasters, both natural and human-made—that gnaw at our hope. Without control over our lives and loved ones, we feel helpless.

Yet...

God has promised to remain constant, even as we humans struggle to adapt in an unstable world. Over and over, Scripture reminds us that God is faithful through all generations (Hebrews 10:23), that God is our refuge (Deuteronomy 33:27), that God offers everlasting love (Jeremiah 31:3), that God will never leave us (Psalm 102:12). May the observant three-year-old thrive in our beloved community, and may she grow to know that the God who loves her unconditionally will do so forever.

Eternal God, thank You for Your unchanging love and protection, which the world can never give.
—Gail Thorell Schilling

Digging Deeper: Psalm 102:27–28;
Hebrews 13:8

Monday, March 16

Being confident of this, that he who began a good work in you will carry it on to completion until the day of Christ Jesus.
—Philippians 1:6 (NIV)

"No, Erin, that's still not enough," my trumpet teacher said. "I want you to yell. Like actually *yell*. Like this..."

I covered my ears as he took a deep breath and demonstrated. The sound filled the room and then some. It also filled me with dread, because I knew I'd be expected to copy his sound with my own.

All this had started when he'd asked me, for the hundredth time, for "more sound, *more!*" My idea of what that meant hadn't even come close to his, so we'd put the trumpets down, and now here we were, yelling—like, with our voices. Or he was, anyway.

Given how impossible this entire exercise felt to me, I could hardly believe how unself-consciously he was able to make such a ridiculously huge sound. I guess I'd assumed doing that would be mortifying for anyone.

Apparently not. I'd found yet another stumbling block that was uniquely mine. *I don't need another one of those*, I thought with a sigh. But, in an oddly positive way, it also felt like I'd discovered something important about myself—a place within where God had already been working. Now that this exercise had hauled it into the light of day, I'd be able to work at it with curious intention, since being able to see an obstacle often makes it easier to overcome.

I smiled. Maybe this "yelling" business wouldn't be impossible for me forever, after all.

Thank You, God, for the opportunities You provide me to know myself better, so that I might continue to grow ever closer to the person You'd have me become. —Erin Janoso

Digging Deeper: Lamentations 3:40; Matthew 19:26

THE BIRDS OF MY NEIGHBORHOOD:
Practicing Stillness
Wait for the Lord; be strong and take heart and wait for the Lord. —Psalm 27:14 (NIV)

It was a gray day, and I wanted more light than what was available up in my office. So I set up my laptop in the great room with its two-and-a-half-story windows overlooking the woods and creek. As I sat back to write, I noticed the sweeping motion of a huge bird.

It was a great blue heron. Herons are magnificent—they're large and often silent as they glide. Unless they're startled. Then they take flight with a loud, scary squawking that reminds me of pterodactyls in old movies!

Today, the bird just sat far out on the limb and tucked his head under his wing. Motionless. Patient. Resting.

I'd seen this before. That was during the pandemic when we had worshipped via Zoom from our homes. Every Sunday for a month or more, a great blue heron would alight on the same limb just as worship started. Then, as we closed, his wings would stretch, and he'd glide away.

I thought that, in my busyness, God had led me to the great room and invited the heron to be a model for me this day. I had been rushing a lot lately. So I closed my laptop and looked out to the tree. There, against the gray sky, my companiable bird sat, a dark silhouette. My breathing slowed. My body relaxed. We both waited patiently.

After about an hour, his head came up. He stretched his giant wings and silently swooped away, gliding along the creek in benediction. And I returned to my day.

Lord, the psalmist urges us to be still and know that You are God. Lead me into a life of inner stillness, even when I am outwardly busy. Amen.
—J. Brent Bill

Digging Deeper: Psalm 33:20–22

Wednesday, March 18

Only be careful, and watch yourselves closely so that you do not forget the things your eyes have seen or let them fade from your heart as long as you live. —Deuteronomy 4:9 (NIV)

My scrub brush followed the kitchen tiles' grid lines. Back and forth. With each pass, the grout grew lighter—slowly changing from dark gray to taupe. It must have held years' worth of grime.

During my first few months of homeownership, I had focused on immediate tasks. Unboxing possessions. Repairing the roof. Building a fence for my Labrador. When I had completed those tasks, I started deep cleaning room-by-room, which was taking weeks to complete.

As I scrubbed around the kitchen island, I encountered a particularly stubborn line of grout. Even after several passes, it remained as dark as ever.

Looking closely, I noticed the adjacent tile was slightly different from the others. It was a replacement. Which explained why this grout wasn't cleaning up like the rest.

The grout used in the repair had been color-matched to the dirty grout.

I wondered if, when making the repair, the previous owner had forgotten that the grout was once light. The change in color must have happened incredibly slowly, shifting the status quo imperceptibly.

I thought of the way my life had shifted in the last few months. Since I'd purchased my home, I'd spent innumerable hours on home projects. The early projects were necessities. But I had moved to tasks of lesser importance. Were they taking up too much of my time? Was I neglecting more important aspects of my life?

I stood up.

I could add grout replacement to my to-do list. But, instead, I decided to leave the lines as they were: a stark symbol of awareness and priority.

Father, grant me awareness and align my priorities to Your Word and Your will.
—Logan Eliasen

Digging Deeper: Joshua 4:1–7; Psalm 78:9–16

Thursday, March 19

ANGEL WHISPERS: Listen and Act
For the eyes of the Lord run to and fro.
—2 Chronicles 16:9 (KJV)

On an assignment in another city, I'm on my way to an interview. My directions say "turn right," but an angel whisper says "turn left." I hesitate and go with the whisper.

Some people hear God's messages as the Holy Spirit. In my simple way of thinking, I imagine that God has untold numbers of angels, ready to whisper His suggestions to us. We, on the other hand, are free to listen or not.

I'm never completely sure, when I go with the inclination to believe the message, if I'm actually receiving a nudge from God. I check my watch. Being late for an appointment isn't wise, I chastise myself.

At that moment, on the road ahead, I watch, horrified, as a car slips over the road's shoulder and into a ravine and out of sight. No one else is around.

I stop. I rush over, look down, and see a young, terrified girl emerging from the car.

I slip down the bank and put my arm around her. She's unhurt. I help her sit on a big smooth rock near her car. "I'm going for help," I assure her. It was before cell phones were common, and there were no phones nearby. "Someone will be back soon."

Already I had noticed a church up ahead. I hurried there, found the minister, explained the situation, and saw him take immediate action.

Arriving at my meeting in the nick of time, I sat in reception and in wonder.

I don't consider myself unique or chosen. If I hadn't listened to the whisper, God would have likely offered the opportunity to comfort the frightened girl to someone else.

But I had listened, and the pleasure of remembering was mine.

Father, You give us many opportunities to reach out to those in need. All we have to do is listen and act. —Pam Kidd

Digging Deeper: Matthew 6:26; John 12:36

Friday, March 20

Fear not, for I am with you; be not dismayed, for I am your God; I will strengthen you, I will help you, I will uphold you with my righteous right hand. —Isaiah 41:10 (ESV)

The alert text reported that a telephone number I didn't recognize had left the Willy Wonka group. Willy Wonka group? I figured it was either a scam or a mistake. Willy Wonka? I searched my mind.

I was telling my husband about it when my son Henry said, "Willy Wonka, that's from the fifth-grade field trip. Remember we went to the city and saw the play? You were a chaperone. Remember?"

I thought about the field trip. We had fun on the long bus ride with the fancy seats that reclined, and the play was magical, held in a small theater where my son's class took up the first floor. That was a long time ago, 7 years, to be exact. Henry is in his senior year and is hearing back from colleges. I have had three or four phones since then and yet, somehow, I am still in the Willy Wonka group.

As I revisited the past, I faced what I have intentionally avoided. I imagined how the house will feel without Henry nestled in his spot in the corner of the sectional, head down, consumed in a sketchbook.

The other day my mom said, "It really is amazing how we age, isn't it? So much learning to let go."

Now, as I scroll through my texts, I see the alert and think about how my little boy is more than 6 feet tall and ready for the future. I am probably the last member of the Willy Wonka group, and for some reason, as I hold on to the crumbs of his school experience, that makes me smile.

Heavenly Father, I know You are with me, guiding me through life's transitions and helping me learn the grace of letting go. —Sabra Ciancanelli

Digging Deeper: Psalm 139:13–14, 23–24; Jeremiah 29:11

DOORS OF OUR LIFE: Bathroom Door

This is my command—be strong and courageous! Do not be afraid or discouraged. For the Lord your God is with you wherever you go. —Joshua 1:9 (NLT)

When you live with three indoor cats, you're never alone in any room of the house. One of them always follows us everywhere we go. The only exception is when all three race to the kitchen at mealtime, or scurry to favorite hiding places when the vacuum cleaner appears. Thank goodness they're not watchdogs, considering their priorities consist of food, sleep, and trailing us.

But what's their purpose for following me into the bathroom? Everyone deserves a little privacy now and then. Not according to these three felines, and I quickly learned closing the door caused more problems. Imagine a toddler throwing a tantrum, and you get the picture. The funniest episode occurred when my largest cat paid me a bathroom visit, left the room, and later returned to find the door closed. Bless his meowing heart, he spent significant time and energy attempting to squeeze his well-fed body under it to rejoin me.

While his silly antics made me laugh, they also reminded me of my unsuccessful attempts years ago to do the opposite—put distance between me and God. As with my cats, I soon learned there was nowhere to hide from His presence. The Lord kept His promise never to leave or forsake His children by pursuing me with tender and unfailing love. Regardless of how far I ran or how many times I closed the door in His face, my Heavenly Father invited me to return home and welcomed me with open arms when I finally did.

God, thank You for following us everywhere we go and loving us along the way.
—Jenny Lynn Keller

Digging Deeper: Psalm 139:1–10;
Jonah 1:1–3, 2:1–10

Sunday, March 22

JOURNEY THROUGH GRIEF: Holding On

My sheep listen to my voice; I know them, and they follow me. I give them eternal life, and they shall never perish; no one will snatch them out of my hand. —John 10:27–28 (NIV)

"They should have walked with him at the respite place," I seethed. "He was walking fine before he went there!"

I'd just flown to Florida from New York City, 2 weeks too late. While my mother had been resolving a health issue of her own, my father had been placed into temporary respite care for 5 days. Since then, he'd begun to decline.

"Come on, Papi," I said, dragging his legs over the side of the bed, "you can walk. You just forgot how."

My mother implored me to leave him alone, worried he'd fall, but I knew he had the strength to do it. He'd had the strength to overcome extreme poverty in his youth, which claimed his father and two younger siblings. His strength beat out cancer, a quadruple heart bypass, a stomach aneurism, and surgery that caused him to bleed internally. He was strong enough to work hard all his life, beginning as a child when he labored in sugarcane fields. His strength would get him back on his feet again.

I lifted his body and held him up, begging him to stand. Slowly I could feel the weight of his body lighten until he was standing on his own. I cheered and pecked his face with kisses. Mami cheered, too, as he humbly smiled. Soon he was walking everywhere, even venturing for walks with me outside.

Weeks later I went back to New York reassured by yet another demonstration of my father's strength. I didn't yet know it was his last, or that he had simply done it for the love of his daughter.

Father, thank You for giving us the power of Your strength, even when things seem hopeless.
—Karen Valentin

Monday, March 23

**I have my eye on salt-of-the-earth people—
they're the ones I want working with me . . . .
But no one who traffics in lies gets a job
with me; I have no patience with liars.
—Psalm 101:6, 8 (MSG)**

I've been a father of young children for 30-plus
years. My kids range in age from 32 to 14, and by the
time my youngest goes off to college, I will be 64.

I've made mistakes along the way. Some, in
fact, are not really mistakes; they are more of what
might properly be called lies.

For instance, I taught my oldest children that
Santa and the Easter Bunny were real. This was
what we called a *cute* lie, or maybe a lie for their
own good. Perhaps it was, until they wept at the
dinner table when I came clean and told them
the truth.

Even worse, I taught my youngest not long ago
that I was able to read her mind. To reinforce my
instructions to pick her toys off the floor of her room
or not to take more than two cookies from the jar,
I said: "I can see what you're thinking. I know what
you're doing, even if I'm not in the room." And
because she trusted me, she believed. This was,
I guess, my version of Santa's "He sees you when

you're sleeping; he knows when you're awake."
I eventually had to sit her down and confess too.

I regret these lies now. If I could do it all over, I wouldn't lie. I feel that God has matured me in love so that I am now able to speak truth more consistently.

First John 4:17 says: "Love has the run of the house, becomes at home and mature in us" (MSG). It's taken me a long time to get there.

I'll tell the truth today, God. —Jon M. Sweeney

Digging Deeper: John 8; Ephesians 4:25

Tuesday, March 24

The pleasantness of a friend springs from their heartfelt advice. —Proverbs 27:9 (NIV)

I've joked that my friend Linda is a "Scriptural ATM": whenever I need wise counsel, she effortlessly dispenses direct Bible quotations, with chapter and verse, on command. It's not that she has a photographic memory; it's the result of many years of hungrily devouring God's Word.

I have another friend a lot like Linda. If you've been reading this book for a few years, you know her too. Her name is Shawnelle, and she writes many of the devotions you read. Shawnelle spends so much time in God's Word that her own conversation echoes the structure and cadence of biblical language. She loves the Psalms, and her natural voice is so lyrical and gorgeous, so effortlessly filled with perfect metaphors, that I think David himself would be proud.

Over the years, I've found myself going to both Linda and Shawnelle when I need advice or encouragement. They always know exactly which verses apply to whatever my situation may be at that moment. Every single day, I pray that I will become wise like these dear friends and hide God's Word in my heart (Psalm 119:11) as they have.

Proverbs 12:26 tells us that the wise choose their friends carefully. I'm not yet a Scriptural ATM, but with friends like Linda and Shawnelle, I hope to get there one day.

Father, thank You, thank You, thank You for my wise and godly friends! Help me follow their advice and example. —Ginger Rue

Digging Deeper: Proverbs 13:20, 27:17

Wednesday, March 25

We know that in all things God works for the good of those who love him, who have been called according to his purpose.
—Romans 8:28 (NIV)

For months, my husband and I were given one blow after the other. Every area of our lives was affected. Health, finances, personal and professional relationships, work, and more. The hardest part was that every issue was brought about from an outside force that we couldn't control.

I was drained, emotionally, mentally, physically, and spiritually. Whenever one thing would resolve, another thing was thrown at us. As an author, I felt this deeply. It's hard to focus and feel creative when you are exhausted. Not only that, but I was writing a fictional story that dealt with the Salem witch trials. It was the hardest story I've ever researched or written.

While writing the story, one of my characters was struggling to understand God's purpose in allowing such suffering to occur, and I realized I was also asking God that same question in my own life, though to a lesser degree.

As the story unfolded, God began to whisper an eternal truth to my character and to me. We don't always know why God allows difficulties in our life, but we know that He sits with us during those long days, months, or even years. His love comforts us, even if we never understand His purpose. The Salem witch trials brought about the eventual end of harsh Puritanical law in Massachusetts. Those who suffered through it might not have known what God was doing, just as I'm not always sure what God is doing in my life. But there is a reason for everything He allows, and there is comfort in that truth.

Lord, even when I don't understand why You allow pain and suffering in my life, help me to trust that You have a purpose for everything.
—Gabrielle Meyer

Thursday, March 26

Therefore encourage one another and build each other up, just as in fact you are doing. —1 Thessalonians 5:11 (NIV)

"Hey, do you wanna grab a cup of coffee with me tomorrow?" an acquaintance from community band asked after rehearsal.

I was surprised by the question. I'd always enjoyed our friendly hellos each week, but we'd never conversed outside rehearsal's bounds. I hesitated, imagining the inevitable awkwardness at the coffee shop—all those mutual decisions that'd need to be made. Where would we sit? Would it be one check or two at the register? What would we talk about? Just the thought of it all made me anxious. But I decided to take the leap anyway. "Sure!" I replied.

Awkwardness did make a few appearances during our visit. Choosing a table *was* strangely difficult, but once we sat down, conversation flowed.

She explained she'd made the coffee invitation because she'd recently realized that while she had several close friends who lived out-of-state, over the past few years, her local circle had dwindled down to nobody. And even though invitations were hard for her, living with that status quo had become harder, so here we were. I'd had no idea. But I recognized the vulnerability and the courage that lived within what she'd just shared. I was so grateful I'd accepted this invitation—and not only for my new friend's sake.

As I walked back to my car post-coffee, I noticed the smile on my face and lift in my step. Everything seemed just a bit brighter than it had before. I'd needed this every bit as much as my new friend had. God had known that all along. And now I did too.

Thank You for the opportunity to know this new friend, God, and for the reminder that we can find You in the connections we discover between each other. —Erin Janoso

Digging Deeper: Ecclesiastes 4:9–12; Ephesians 2:22

Friday, March 27

SACRED THREADS: Birthday Blessing
Therefore we do not lose heart. Though outwardly we are wasting away, yet inwardly we are being renewed day by day. —2 Corinthians 4:16 (NIV)

For my 60-plus-10 birthday, I treated myself to a Victorian paper punch motto sampler listed on the Ruby Lane antiques site. It featured a charming white-roofed cottage in a pastoral setting. The nostalgic sentiment, *Home Sweet Home*, was stitched in my favorite color, red; the sampler's frame was an intricately carved walnut from the Adirondacks. I telephoned the vendor to ask about the improvised, make-do mat that appeared to be fashioned of crinkled tinfoil.

I was mentally replacing that mat when she gushed, "Don't you just love it when something lives 175 years and it's still wearing its story?" I stole a glance in a too-close-for-comfort mirror. No, not really.

I set to work prettying up my own aging packaging. I started with a pair of boots in a patchwork of embroidered fabrics and floral-painted leather, topped off with colorful suede fringe. When I entered a restaurant, a woman I'd known for years, who was normally too well-behaved to wear boots like those and too polite to comment on them, came over. "Please tell me *you* added the fringe on those shoes, Roberta," she said a little too loudly. The little girl at a nearby table couldn't take her eyes off my boots. She ambled over and stretched out a pair of her own, remarkably similar. "I guess all the kids are wearing them," the lady sniffed, eying us both.

"I *like* them!" the little girl cooed. Her delicious giggle, despite two missing front teeth, awakened something long lost to me. I might be hitting 70, but it suddenly felt like seven.

I'm all the ages I've ever been, Lord. You already knew that. It's why You sent me stitchery and a young sweetheart who knew what I needed.
—Roberta Messner

Saturday, March 28

This is love: not that we loved God, but that he loved us and sent his Son as an atoning sacrifice for our sins. —1 John 4:10 (NIV)

I arrived at my new friend's home, hesitantly, the week before Easter. She had invited me during a women's Bible study group at a new church I was attending. I was quite unsure of myself, as I was struggling with the loss of my marriage and also the rejection of some close friends and family because of my recent divorce.

I thought of reasons to cancel before going but decided that a fresh start was a good step. This new friend had also been through a recent divorce, after similar struggles in her marriage, and was finding her new normal as well. If anyone could understand what I was feeling, she could. However, I still couldn't shake the sense of shame. I felt like an unlovable outcast who had failed my children, myself, and God.

As she welcomed me into her home and took care of the final touches, she pulled out a special box filled with some very fancy glasses for us to use. When she opened the box and revealed the extravagant, beautiful details, I couldn't help but feel that God was using that moment to show me that He sees me as I was seeing the fancy glasses: I am extraordinarily important to Him, and He sees me through the blood of Jesus as a royal heir with Christ and as forgiven and loved.

Lord, I am humbled and thankful that You don't look at me and see where I have fallen short. You see me through the love and sacrifice of Your Son. Help me find joy every day in knowing I am worth that much to You. —Nicole Garcia

Digging Deeper: Jeremiah 29:11; Romans 5:8, 8:38–39; Ephesians 3:17–19

Palm Sunday, Sunday, March 29

FOLLOWING JESUS: Trusting in His Guidance

Go into the village ahead of you, and immediately as you enter it, you will find tied there a colt that has never been ridden; untie it and bring it. If anyone says to you, "Why are you doing this?" just say this: "The Lord needs it and will send it back here immediately."
—**Mark 11:2–3 (NRSVUE)**

Jesus knows. Jesus is way ahead of us. Jesus asks us to do things that don't seem possible, and yet they happen just as Jesus has said.

I love celebrating Palm Sunday. What a joy to wave those palm fronds in the air as we march around the block, outside church, singing hosannas, declaring whose we are and who is still coming.

Inside church, listening to the story of Holy Week acted out by fellow parishioners, I fold a sliver of palm into a cross to keep beside my bed until next year's Ash Wednesday when it can be burned and turned into those ashes that mark us as God's own.

It's a joyful day. Yet it's a prologue to unaccountable pain, sorrow, suffering, and abandonment. It's the lead-up to something Jesus promised and yet must have seemed inconceivable to His disciples—the Resurrection.

In that respect, Palm Sunday feels like an underpinning to every day. Celebrations are called for, mundane preparations are made, and mystical messages are received, even if we can't account for them. Then tragedies happen. What are we to do? How are we to respond?

We do as Jesus asks, trusting, believing, hoping, praying, rediscovering ourselves on the way. Did the disciples know exactly what was coming? Hardly. But what Jesus said turned out to be true. They found the colt for the Lord to ride on.

Lord, help me trust in Your guidance as I follow You. —Rick Hamlin

Digging Deeper: Psalm 118:26; Zechariah 9:9; John 12:13

Monday, March 30

Start children off on the way they should go, and even when they are old they will not turn from it. —Proverbs 22:6 (NIV)

My children, who all live 1,000 or 2,000 miles from my home in Florida, each have unique things that they do when they're visiting me.

Jeanne and I paint side-by-side when we're together. She creates fine art while I dabble with watercolor pencils or fabric paint on glass jars.

When Julia visits, she and I have tea in the mornings. One of our lunches together is always a Cuban sandwich at our favorite little beachside restaurant, Kooky Coconut.

Michael calls me from his car when he's driving to one of the cities in the Midwest for his job. Sometimes we FaceTime when he's out walking so I can enjoy his nature walks along with him while he tells me about his life, kids, and career.

Before Andrew died in 2024, he and I would talk politics, rummage through my family heirlooms, and go out for liver and onions with bacon on top whenever he visited me.

One morning when I was alone in the pool saying my morning prayers, I started thinking about my children and those special things that we enjoy one-on-one. I wondered if there was anything in my relationship with Jesus that was unique.

Maybe it's when I get to church 10 minutes before Mass starts, sit in the back pew, and spend quiet time in a place where I know God is present. Maybe it's that moment I put my feet on the floor each morning, when I say fast prayers for each of my children and grandchildren.

My goal now is to create more unique one-on-one times with Jesus. Perhaps a half-hour of prayer in the beautiful garden outside church each week? Donating weekly to the food pantry for the poor? Sending snail-mail, handwritten note cards to friends who live alone?

Jesus, I want to have a unique, one-of-a-kind relationship with You. Help me find the ways.
—Patricia Lorenz

Digging Deeper: Isaiah 49:15–17; 1 Timothy 4:11–13

Tuesday, March 31

So do not throw away your confidence; it will be richly rewarded. —Hebrews 10:35 (NIV)

Our family was fortunate enough to take a ski trip over spring break. After a few days on the slopes, my daughter Olivia, son Beau, and I were ready for a break, but my son James, age nine, was desperate for more time on skis. We had scheduled a day for my husband, Brian, to ski alone, but when James asked if he could tag along, Brian readily agreed.

While the kids and I explored local playgrounds, Brian and James rode gondolas to high heights and skied bowls down. We met up at the end of the day, and James was bursting with confidence and stories. As we ate ice cream, he told us the tale of the pink lady.

"Dad and I were skiing and this lady, she was in all pink, came screaming down the slopes," he said. "She was waving her arms and screaming, 'I'm gonna fall!' but she was skiing fine, Mom! She kept screaming over and over again, 'I'm not gonna make it!' and then she fell. And I think if you think you'll fall, you will."

James went back to licking his ice cream, and the rest of us let his words settle over us. How right he was! If you think you're going to fall, you probably will.

That ski trip is long behind us. These days we've adapted James's wisdom to be our family mantra: Whether you think you're going to have a good day or a bad one, you're right. Mindset is everything in this life, so make today a good one.

Lord, help me remember that my days are Your days. Give me confidence for my trials and grace for my failures. —Ashley Kappel

Digging Deeper: Psalm 71:5; Isaiah 32:17

LIVING A NEW LIFE

1 _____

2 _____

3 _____

4 _____

5 _____

6 _____

7 _____

8 _____

9 _____

10 _____

11 _____

12 _____

13 _____

14 _____

15 _____

16 _____

17 _____

18 _____

19 _____

20 _____

21 _____

22 _____

23 _____

24 _____

25 _____

26 _____

27 _____

28 _____

29 _____

30 _____

31 _____

April

Praise be to the God and
Father of our Lord Jesus Christ!
In his great mercy he has given us
new birth into a living hope
through the resurrection
of Jesus Christ from the dead.

—1 Peter 1:3 (NIV)

Wednesday, April 1

. . . Thy wondrous works declare.
—Psalm 75:1 (KJV)

I was sitting in a law office with my parents; Paddington, the director of our Children of Zimbabwe nonprofit; and a range of Zimbabwean lawyers. We were far removed from home and all the distractions of work and other commitments. Here, we were cast into a no-frills, "let's get to work" atmosphere.

Honestly, I liked the feeling. We were, after all, here to get things done.

Beginning in 1999, when my parents traveled to Zimbabwe for my mother to write about the many AIDS-orphaned street children, our family had been hooked. After my sister, Keri, first traveled to Zimbabwe, she returned regularly along with Dad and Mom. Finally I, and later my wife, Corinne, and our children, joined them there too.

At first we simply fed children on the streets and got them into school. When a generous donor helped us buy a rural farm, we began taking in orphans and raising them as a family, headed by Paddington and his wife, Alice. We ministered to the greater rural community, feeding them, offering empowerment projects, and finally building a school and a library.

Now, sitting in this law office watching the reactions of the lawyers as we told our story, I saw amazement that we had come so far. For the first time, I sat back and saw all this from an outsider's perspective.

God, I thought, *only You could accomplish all this through inexperienced people and caring donors. Only You could see the needs of rural schools and hungry children.*

I was sitting, I realized, in the midst of a miracle.

"Now," the lead lawyer, Byron, said, "let's move forward on this. You want to buy more property, build a clinic?"

My mind was buzzing with one word: *Miracle?* I was silently asking God.

Father, Your wonders are far above my pay grade. Thank You. —Brock Kidd

Digging Deeper: Psalm 107:8; Proverbs 30:18; Isaiah 9:6

Maundy Thursday, April 2

FOLLOWING JESUS: Filled with God's Love
Then [Jesus] took a loaf of bread, and when he had given thanks he broke it and gave it to them, saying, "This is my body, which is given for you. Do this in remembrance of me."
—Luke 22:19 (NRSVUE)

When we get together with friends, we generally look for a chance to do it over a meal—lunch, dinner, or brunch after church. We fill our bodies with good food as we fill our souls with conver-sation, shared remembrances, laughter, and a photo or two from our phones, or we'll record the event with a new photo, friends gathered around the table. We'll treasure the memories long after.

Jesus knows people well. He chose a meal, the last meal Jesus would have on earth, to give us a way to remember Him forever afterward. I love celebrating Communion, but there's something especially poignant about celebrating it on Maundy Thursday at church. That word "Maundy" comes from the Latin *mandatum*, which means "command" or "mandate," as we say in English.

I can't help recalling Jesus's command: to love our neighbors as ourselves. Here in this church where we feed our neediest neighbors at our Saturday Kitchen, where we say healing prayers, where we sing songs of joy, where we hear God's Word, where we share news at coffee hour, where we gather for Bible study, where we teach our children, we practice that love.

And once a year we remember this gift on the night when Jesus would be betrayed, His betrayer there at the table with Him. Hatred might fill our world, but there's something much bigger. God's love fills our bodies and souls.

I take from You, Lord, only so that I can give back, like You. —Rick Hamlin

Digging Deeper: Mark 14:22–24; John 6:53; 1 Corinthians 11:23–26

FOLLOWING JESUS: The Promise of Easter

When it was noon, darkness came over the whole land until three in the afternoon. At three o'clock Jesus cried out with a loud voice, "Eloi, Eloi, lema sabachthani?" which means, "My God, my God, why have you forsaken me?"
—Mark 15:33–34 (NRSVUE)

Some 30 years ago, our younger son, Tim, broke his femur on Maundy Thursday—an accident at nursery school—and had to be in traction for 26 days. I spent that night with him in the hospital as he tossed and turned in a noisy shared room. I was hoping to make it to church on Good Friday to sing in the choir, with my wife, Carol, covering for me.

Then the news came: William, his older brother, had chicken pox—a mild case, but still. I rushed to be with him, and Carol and I began a tag-team process of caregiving. One of us would be at the hospital with four-year-old Tim while the other was home with seven-year-old Will.

Is it any wonder that I dread Good Friday every year, those 3 hours that we remember Christ's suffering? "Were you there when they crucified my Lord?" we sing. *Yes, I was,* I echo the thought. Haven't we all had a dark night of the soul at some point?

It's often hard to carry the larger picture with us. Will's chicken pox turned out to have a silver lining. Why? Because Tim had been exposed, he was given a single room, and he was able to get some much-needed rest. What a relief. And I don't doubt that his period of suffering as a child served him well later on in life, when he became an ordained minister. God shows us how to use our suffering for good.

Lord, let me hold to the promise of Easter in dark times. —Rick Hamlin

Digging Deeper: Isaiah 53:5; Matthew 12:40; 1 Peter 2:24

Holy Saturday, April 4

FOLLOWING JESUS: Holding On to Faith
Nicodemus, who had at first come to Jesus by night, also came, bringing a mixture of myrrh and aloes, weighing about a hundred pounds. They took the body of Jesus and wrapped it with the spices in linen cloths, according to the burial custom of the Jews. —John 19:39–40 (NRSVUE)

Holy Saturday, that day between days when Jesus's disciples must have felt distraught and lost. Was this the way it was supposed to end? Where was the Messiah now? It wasn't any of the twelve who prepared Jesus's body for burial but two secret followers, Joseph of Arimathea and Nicodemus.

Nicodemus, a Pharisee, first came to Jesus at night probably because he didn't want to be seen listening to this controversial figure. I have a copy of the scene by the American artist Henry Ossawa Tanner hanging over my desk, a white-bearded Nicodemus on a dark rooftop with Jesus illuminated by light coming up the stairs, a reflection of his own illuminated being.

What does Jesus say to him? Nothing less than that famous verse, John 3:16 (NKJV), "For God so loved the world that He gave His only begotten Son, that whoever believes in Him should not perish but have everlasting life."

Yet here is Nicodemus now, engaging in the rituals of death. What a lonely, sad process. One wonders how he could hold on to that promise of eternal life. But he took on the job, doing what needed to be done, sparing no expense.

Don't we all have Holy Saturdays in our life, where we do our best to follow through on what we believe, even when the answers seem so unclear? No Easter yet. Just a tomb.

Lord, help me hold on to my faith when the truth seems so far away. —Rick Hamlin

Digging Deeper: Psalm 31:1–2; Matthew 27:57–59; 1 Peter 4:1

Easter Sunday, April 5

FOLLOWING JESUS: Easter Joy
If we died with Christ, we believe that we will also live with him. —Romans 6:8 (NRSVUE)

It was one of the most unusual Easters I'd ever experienced. We got up at dawn, as usual, to celebrate our risen Lord. We were at an Episcopal monastery, and the service came with familiar language. "The Lord is risen," the celebrant said. "He is risen indeed," we replied, and of course we sang, "Now the green blade riseth from the buried grain...."

The hills outside were green indeed, but not with new growth; some of the trees were losing their leaves, and the flowers were mostly evergreen shrubs. We were in South Africa, at the Holy Cross Brothers monastery where our son, Tim, was lodged for 10 months, doing volunteer work at their school. But here, it wasn't spring; it was autumn instead.

It made me rethink the springtime imagery we associate with Easter. The lily seems like a perfect symbol of the Resurrection and new life. But then aren't the seasons cyclical, the spring flowers fading into summer before the leaves fall and winter comes? On the other hand, there's nothing cyclical about Christ's Resurrection. Our ideas about death were completely rewritten that first Easter. As the Apostle Paul wrote, "For if we have been united with him in a death like his, we will certainly be united with him in a resurrection like his" (Romans 6:5, NRSVUE).

"Our Lord has written the promise of the resurrection, not in books alone but in every leaf in springtime," Martin Luther once said. It can be written in the beauty of autumn, too, as it was that South African Easter.

Thank You, Lord, for giving us life eternal, Easter celebration forever. —Rick Hamlin

Easter Monday, April 6

FOLLOWING JESUS: Resurrection Power
**Very truly, I tell you, you will weep and
mourn, but the world will rejoice; you will
have pain, but your pain will turn into joy.
—John 16:20 (NRSVUE)**

The story was titled "The Magic of Three Days,"
and I discovered it in the decades-old archives
of *Guideposts* magazine. I read it years ago, but
the message has always stuck: A woman coming
out of church on Easter Monday paused to chat
with an older woman sitting there on the steps,
who was selling corsages and boutonnieres on an
open newspaper. Despite her apparent financial
challenges, the older woman looked happy.

"Why not?" she said when asked. "Everything
is good." A surprising answer for someone who
seemed to have so little. She wore her troubles well.
On that Easter Monday she explained just how and
why, referring to Jesus's Crucifixion and all He had
suffered. Good Friday was surely the worst day in
the world, and look what happened 3 days later.
"When troubles come," she said, "I've learned to
wait 3 days."

What a helpful lesson that has been. Hardships,
medical disasters, financial worries, family

troubles—whatever it is, know that God is there with you, and then trust in the power of time to change everything. Give it the magic of 3 days.

Easter isn't over. It's just beginning, and it never stops. God's resurrection power is always with us. You don't feel it just now? Wait a few days. I recently heard some tough news from a friend, and now I'm praying for her. The answer will come, I'm sure of it. I've experienced Easter, after all, and I am still there with it.

Lord, I give thanks to You for this Easter journey. Every day has been a blessing. And the blessings never stop. —Rick Hamlin

Digging Deeper: Jeremiah 10:2; Matthew 12:40; Acts 12:4

Tuesday, April 7

Therefore we do not lose heart. Though outwardly we are wasting away, yet inwardly we are being renewed day by day. —2 Corinthians 4:16 (NIV)

The other day I caught a commercial for Olay skincare and had to smile. My mother used Olay.

Back then it was called Oil of Olay, and there was only that one product, a facial lotion that pledged to preserve one's youthful complexion. My mother was not vain. She rarely wore makeup, except possibly a little blush and lipstick if she and my dad were going out. She hated getting her hair done and refused to dye her premature gray, claiming that's how God obviously preferred her.

Her one capitulation to vanity was Oil of Olay. If ever I was at a loss for what to get her for Mother's Day or her birthday, I couldn't go wrong with Oil of Olay.

One day, well into her senior years, I found my mother regarding her complexion in a mirror. "I should sue Oil of Olay," she said.

I stifled a laugh then caught her smiling. "All the money I wasted on that stuff!" she said, shaking her head. Well, Oil of Olay was hardly Chanel.

I stood behind her and studied her reflection. In my mind I saw her face in time lapse, milky-skinned in her wedding photo, tanned from weekends at the Jersey shore, tear-streaked after losing a child, rosy-cheeked shoveling snow in Michigan. Practically overnight, the spidery creases and papery wrinkles appeared, smile lines stamped deep at the corners of her mouth and eyes. Life's signature. Nothing Oil of Olay could do about it.

She ran her fingers down her cheek, and I hugged her from behind. "I think this is the way God prefers you," I said.

Lord, life leaves its marks on us, but so do You, deep on our eternal souls. —Edward Grinnan

Digging Deeper: Psalm 92:12–15; Proverbs 16:31

Wednesday, April 8

Do not be anxious about anything, but in every situation, by prayer and petition, with thanksgiving, present your requests to God.
—Philippians 4:6 (NIV)

After comparing paint swatches for almost an hour, I had narrowed my selection to several shades of green. I was painting my writing room. Presently, the room was an angry red. Every time I sat down at my desk to write, I felt anxious. As a full-time lawyer, I experienced daily stress from my deadlines. I didn't need a paint color adding to my anxiety.

I approached the paint counter for help with my final decision. "Which of these colors do you think is the most calming?" I asked the employee. I fanned out the swatches on the counter.

The employee studied the colors. "This one," she said, pushing forward a deep green.

"Great," I said. "I'll take a gallon."

The employee started mixing the color. "What color are you painting over?" she asked.

"Bright red," I said.

"You'll need to use a primer first," she said. She pointed to a shelf of white cans. "Otherwise the red will bleed through."

I perused the cans of primer. As I did so, I thought about how my work stress was bleeding into other areas of my life. Was painting my writing room just a cover-up of a deeper issue? Was I addressing symptoms rather than the cause?

When the employee was done mixing, I paid for the paint and a primer. I was ready to replace bright red with deep, cool green. But first, I would take my worries to the Lord—the One who could exchange anxiety for peace and promises.

Lord, help me to rely on You when I am filled with worry and anxiety. —Logan Eliasen

Digging Deeper: Psalm 55:22; 1 Peter 5:6–7

Thursday, April 9

May our sons in their youth be like plants full grown, our daughters like corner pillars. —Psalm 144:12 (NRSVCE)

I often stifle laughter when working out on the treadmill in our building's gym. Our apartment is near a large engineering company and naval base, and many residents are young adults who place great importance on their physiques and strength. So there's a lot of weight lifting accompanied by groaning, grunting, and big pieces of equipment being dropped dramatically on the floor. These gym-goers are so earnest, and having several decades on all of them, I'm amused by their commitment to something I don't consider very important in the greater scheme of things.

Occasionally I hear them discussing workout plans, what foods to eat, alternative cardio exercises, how often to rest, etc. They are very serious, often advising and encouraging one another. One afternoon I was alone with one young man, who was working out intensely as usual; when he took a break, I asked why it was so important to him and his peers.

After politely trying to hide his surprise at the question, or maybe that the resident old gal had actually spoken to him, he answered, "It's about perseverance and community. That's how we build strength and get to know one another. We get stronger separately and together."

I felt a little ashamed at having dismissed their efforts as not particularly important. I realized that I put as much emphasis on my prayer time but hadn't considered how much stronger prayer could be when joined with the commitment and faith of others. Maybe it was time for the old gal to learn from the youngsters.

Father, help me to pray with—and learn from— everyone You send into my life. —Marci Alborghetti

Digging Deeper: John 15:12–17; Romans 14:10–13

Friday, April 10

Always take time to talk to God. Put your mind on what you are saying. And thank God for what he has done. —Colossians 4:2 (WE)

House-sitting for my sister is a bit like getting paid to go on a retreat. Her home, nestled in the foothills of Pikes Peak, backs up to hiking trails leading into the Rocky Mountains. From her back deck, I've enjoyed watching deer, wild turkeys, bobcats, hang gliders, and stupendous sunsets. During the summer months, the deck is also the perfect place to recline in a lounge chair and read.

I was doing exactly that when I heard what sounded like a hornet circling my head. Glancing up from my novel, I found myself eye-to-beak with an iridescent green hummingbird. It hung in the air, wings beating furiously, while its body remained motionless. After a few magical seconds, it continued on its way.

The next day, the same thing happened. My first thought was how blessed I was to have such a lovely wild creature drop by to say hi. Then I noticed my lounge chair was positioned right under the empty hook where my sister hangs the hummingbird feeder. My bird friend wasn't saying hi; he was asking, "Where's my lunch?!"

My brief avian encounter reminded me of how often I treat God the same way. My prayers are often a "fly by," where I ask for something without even stopping to say hello. Taking a lesson from the hummingbird, I put down my book and took time to really talk to the One who's always ready to listen.

Lord, I'm sorry for the times my prayers sound like a spoiled child always asking for more. Please know I'm grateful for You, not just for what You provide. —Vicki Kuyper

---

Saturday, April 11

Therefore encourage one another and build each other up, just as in fact you are doing.
—1 Thessalonians 5:11 (NIV)

My wife, Elba, got caught up in the pickleball frenzy that is going around the country. Her girlfriend Cindy invited her to play, and Elba was immediately hooked. Pickleball is a paddle sport that combines elements of tennis, badminton, and ping-pong using a paddle and a plastic ball with holes. Elba had never played sports before, so I was surprised but happy for her. She is exercising, meeting people, and having fun in a new community.

Elba would come home after playing and tell me how she served and returned the ball and met people of all ages and skill sets. Some evenings she asked me to watch a video on YouTube of people playing pickleball and explain the rules of the game to me. One morning, at her invitation, we played together for the first time . . . and we have continued playing. When I don't have a good day at the court, Elba encourages me.

I never imagined that after four decades plus of marriage we would be playing a sport together and having a great time. On the court, we are happy and stronger together. I trust and lean on her to cover her side of the court and play to her strengths. We offer tips to each other on ways to improve our skills and play better as a team.

Playing pickleball has been a gift and blessing for our relationship and friendship. We encourage each other on and off the court. Our hope is to play until our bodies tell us to stop. Hopefully not anytime soon.

Lord, may we be open to new and unexpected activities that help us build and strengthen our relationship with loved ones and friends.
—Pablo Diaz

Digging Deeper: Proverbs 27:17; Ecclesiastes 4:9–10

Sunday, April 12

Remember the long way that the Lord your God has made you travel. —Deuteronomy 8:2 (JPS)

For the second time that afternoon, I walked purposefully into a room and stopped because I couldn't remember what I'd come in for. The first time it had been the kitchen; this time it was my office, with its three filing cabinets, stacks of paper on the desk, and piles of books that didn't fit on any of the packed shelves in the spare bedroom, the library, the living room, or the downstairs family room.

I'd been aware of the possibility of memory loss since I'd gone on Medicare, and it terrified me. In order to stay sharp, I was doing a sudoku every morning and a crossword puzzle every evening. Since fifth grade, I'd never had any reason to doubt the power of my memory. My teacher had told the class that she thought I had an eidetic memory, though I didn't think so at all. My husband, Keith, said he never lied to me because I remembered every word he ever said. And my friend Dawn called my memory my "superpower."

Standing there in the office, I felt frustrated that I couldn't instantly remember what I had come in for. Then my gaze fell on the little ceramic wall plaque that Keith had given me. It said, "Be still and know that I am God" (Psalm 46:10, NIV). So while I didn't know exactly what was happening, I slowed down and reminded myself that my mind had been God-given. It wasn't so different from those filing cabinets in my office. If I stood still and waited patiently for the drawer to open, it would. And soon enough it did, giving me the information I needed.

The older I get, the harder I have to work for what used to come easily, Lord of all strength. Please, as I try harder to remember, keep remembering me.
—Rhoda Blecker

Digging Deeper: Psalms 71:9, 119:49

Monday, April 13

Walk with the wise and become wise.
—Proverbs 13:20 (NIV)

A favorite part of walking my dog each day is listening to the birds. On one recent outing, I heard so many different trills that I thought a bird convention must be going on in the branches above me! I stopped and lifted my gaze, laughing when I saw that there was no convention—all the various melodies had come from one single mockingbird.

I remember learning from a research paper I wrote in junior high how these amazing creatures imitate the sounds around them. Some mockingbirds have even been known to "mock" the sounds of chainsaws and lawnmowers. They so easily pick up and mimic what they hear.

All this made me think of how each of us becomes an amalgam of the people who have influenced us. I'm sure I'm not the only one who has heard my mother's words come out of my own mouth or passed along a saying I learned from a grandparent. Long after people have passed away, parts of them live on in us. The trick is to choose carefully whom we "mock" with our words and attitude.

Oh, how I hope to be warm and funny like my dad, hardworking like my mom, and kindhearted like my friend Honey! I hope to imitate my former headmaster's encouragement and wise counsel, to overflow with the love of Jesus like Ginny, to be a listening ear like Carolyn, ready to serve like my mother-in-law, and slow to speak like my husband. I hope my life's song borrows melodies from all the wise and wonderful people I've known.

Father, let me imitate others as they imitate Christ. —Ginger Rue

Digging Deeper: 1 Corinthians 11:1; Hebrews 13:7

Tuesday, April 14

THE BIRDS OF MY NEIGHBORHOOD:
On Still Waters

The Lord is my shepherd; I shall not want.
He maketh me to lie down in green pastures:
he leadeth me beside the still waters.
—Psalm 23:1–2 (KJV)

Still waters. That's where I find the ducks when I'm out on my walks. About 10 years ago, during a massive flood, one section of our creek rerouted itself. In the aftermath, the old creek bed went mostly dry except for about four sections, which became ponds. These ponds are fed by the many underground springs that crisscross our land. They are calm and smooth-surfaced, secluded and surrounded by trees. A perfect place for ducks.

There are about four flocks of them here. They habituate to these same locations every year. If I am quiet enough, I can walk close to the water's edge and watch them bobbing along the surface, occasionally diving for a fish or bug, and quietly calling to each other.

It took me a while to realize that they prefer these quiet waters to the rushing creek or the wind-tossed lake nearby. They are literally bobbing on the psalmist's still waters, surrounded by silent woods.

They, like the psalmist, remind me that I need still waters. I need times when there are no waves to toss me about. I need the safety of my familiar places. The places where my family is, where my fellow Quakers worship, where my spirit finds rest. I need to let the Lord lead me to those locales. Away from the white water of a life I often make far too busy for my soul's own good. I need to be, like my friends the ducks, on still waters. Safe in God's haven.

Dear Eternal Shepherd, lead me to Your green pastures and into the still waters where my soul finds rest and safety. —J. Brent Bill

Digging Deeper: Psalm 107:23–31

Wednesday, April 15

THE LONELY AMONG US: Alone in a Crowd

His purpose was for the nations to seek after God and perhaps feel their way toward him and find him—though he is not far from any one of us. —Acts 17:27 (NLT)

I'm a fix-it sort of person. Tell me a problem, I spout solutions. If I haven't had the problem myself, I question the sufferer closely, then move to the next problem-solving phase: research. Your cloud files suddenly disappeared? Your dog can't walk? I'm on it. I've watched videos on everything from lawnmower repair to endarterectomy while troubleshooting others' struggles.

Recently several friends complained of loneliness. Their problem, internet experts said, is common these days. The US surgeon general has even issued an advisory on "Our Epidemic of Loneliness and Isolation." Counterintuitively, loneliness—or "perceived social isolation," as psychologists call it—typically occurs in social contexts. First-year university students often suffer intense loneliness, though surrounded by lonely hordes just like them. Indeed, one of my lonely friends had recently embarked, after years of actually being alone, on communal living. Another was loneliest when surrounded by his wife's many friends.

The Gospels feature the powerful story of a lonely woman among the throngs. She's been menstruating for 12 years. (If I knew her today, I'd be offering endometriosis advice.) Her affliction makes her perpetually unclean in Old Testament law, perpetually cut off from others.

She sneaks up behind Jesus, desperate for help but so hesitant to ask for it she hardly dares touch the hem of His cloak. Jesus's warm response—He calls her "daughter"!—heals not only her physical ailment but no doubt her loneliness as well.

We're never actually alone, even in an epidemic of perceived isolation. God waits nearby, eager for us to reach out and discover His love.

Help me remember to seek Your company, Lord, when I'm lonely. —Patty Kirk

Digging Deeper: Matthew 9:20–22; Luke 8:40–47

Thursday, April 16

The Lord is near to all who call on him.
—Psalm 145:18 (ESV)

I've seen a lot of the world, but this particular trip came prepackaged with an added level of stress. My brother-in-law and I had been contracted to explore and video a flooded mine in the Amazon jungle with our remote operated vehicle (ROV) for an adventure TV series.

The scene entailed packing our 200 pounds of gear more than 300 yards down into a shaft to groundwater level, launching the ROV, filming, then hauling everything back out. On top of this . . . bats. Thousands of them. Along with piles and piles of droppings. We would have to cover our skin and wear goggles and face masks the entire time we were in the mine. To make things extra fun, the shaft interior would top 100 degrees.

On the trek out, I began to struggle under the heat and weight. "Lord, I'm not sure I can do this . . ."

"Of course you can't."

"I need You."

"When don't you?"

"Help."

He did.

Back out in the sunlight the jungle spun. I leaned my hands on my knees, pulling in ragged breaths. I whispered a prayer of thanks.

This life is, at best, an uncertain journey through a whole lot of unexplored jungle. We might even find ourselves in a bat-filled mine shaft or two. The great joy of the believer is that we never travel alone. Whether in valley shadow or mountaintop sun, we have a constant Friend. We are foreigners here, yes, but we have a Guide. One who speaks the language. One who knows every step and every pitfall the trail holds. One who never, ever leaves our side.

God, I need You. Not only in the tough times but in the good as well. Thank You for Your faithfulness. I am weak, but You are strong. —Buck Storm

Digging Deeper: Deuteronomy 31:8; Psalms 23:4, 46:1–3

Friday, April 17

**When I called, you answered me.
—Psalm 138:3 (NIV)**

Bundles was our first fur baby, a beautiful black Lab whose death sent me to the depths of despair. I was inconsolable after Bundles died. I spent a lot of time reliving his final days—days filled with pain for him.

One night, about a month after his death, I prayed to know that Bundles was OK and that we would be reunited in heaven.

That night, I had a dream. In the dream I was downstairs in our house when Bundles suddenly appeared! He was barking and wagging his tail. I said, "Bundles! Are you OK?" He said, "Yes, I am fine. See?" Then he ran around me over and over and jumped up and down trying to give me kisses. "See? No more pain. I can run and play all day long." Then a friend of mine named Sister Chloe appeared in the dream. There was an aura of gold all around her. She said, "Adam, Bundles only remembered being loved. Through it all, he knew he was loved."

Then the dream ended.

When I awoke, I felt indescribable joy and gratitude. I knew for certain that there is a God; that there is a heaven; and that we will all be reunited there one day. I was so grateful that God gave me this dream with Bundles.

O God, may we never cease from praising You for the way You answer our prayers. Amen.
—Adam Ruiz

Digging Deeper: Psalm 150; Isaiah 12:4; Matthew 9:8

Saturday, April 18

See the way God does things and fall into line. Don't fight the facts of nature. —Ecclesiastes 7:13 (TLB)

I am very embarrassed to admit how impatient I am, even at my age. For example, when we moved outside the city limits of Moberly, Missouri, there were no trees on our new property. So I bought the biggest trees I could afford and planted them. I fertilized and watered them often, hoping to speed up their growth, but they just stood there like statues and didn't grow. Some of them even died.

Meanwhile, some little saplings that I bought for a song and just poked into the ground were growing like teenagers and soon caught up with the expensive trees. So, I checked my tree books and discovered that I had done everything wrong. Turns out that the larger the tree you plant, the longer it takes to overcome transplant shock, several years in some cases. During that time the trees are vulnerable to stress.

By overfertilizing and overwatering my trees, I made the roots lazy. They had no incentive to reach out, so they just circled the base of the tree, enjoying the steak dinners and fine wines I lavished on them, but I was killing them with kindness.

Looking back, I can see that my impatience was born of anxiety: a fear that I would not live long enough to see these trees in maturity. It was a failure to trust God with my future.

I now realize that small trees are beautiful, too, and it's a pleasure to watch them at every stage of growth.

Father, help me not to ruin the present by dwelling too much on the future. —Daniel Schantz

---

Sunday, April 19

**O Lord, our Lord, how excellent is thy name in
all the earth! who hast set thy glory above
the heavens.** —Psalm 8:1 (KJV)

Millie, our pit bull mix, is getting old. Aging has its
symptoms, and Millie has developed a new one:
getting me up for a bathroom break at 2 a.m.—and
that is getting old real fast.

I'll admit it here: Sleep is my false idol. I crave
sleep. I worship sleep. I would even dream about
sleep if I could just get to sleep. But I rouse myself
to respond to nature's call, wandering out into the
darkness, wearing flannel jammies and a scowl.
Millie begins sniffing every corner of the yard,
looking for exactly the right spot to do her business.

This is where the grumbling begins (not that
I grumble—heaven forbid! Who would complain
after being awakened at 2 a.m. for a late-night
adventure? Except maybe everyone?). I close my
eyes and turn my head skyward in frustration.

And that's when it happens. When I open
my eyes, I am treated to the heavens—the Big
Dipper, Venus, Jupiter, and Orion in the winter.
I am reminded, again, of the vastness of space, the
planets in their courses, my place in the universe.
And somewhere in the black night, my black mood

lifts as I remember that heaven awaits those willing to open their eyes and accept, with gratitude, the gifts of this life and the promise of the next.

Lord, let me always remember that You have surrounded me with wonderful things that sing always of Your glory. —Mark Collins

Digging Deeper: Psalm 148; Hebrews 1

Monday, April 20

[Jesus] would withdraw to deserted places to pray. —Luke 5:16 (NABRE)

Some people like the mountains, some like ocean beaches, but I like deserts. The vast, rocky, cacti-riddled landscapes of the American Southwest in particular fascinate me. Deserts are often described as barren, empty wasteland, but to me, they are full of life and a quiet, mystical energy.

It made sense, then, that I decided to take a trip to a desert shortly after my divorce. I mapped out a weeklong journey from Las Vegas to the Mojave Desert and Joshua Tree National Park. I rented a car and got on the road.

On a whim, I decided to visit Death Valley. It wasn't part of my itinerary, but it was only a 2-hour drive from downtown Las Vegas. Why not give it a look?

My ears popped as I drove down to the salty, sparkling valley floor. Mountains stained pink, chocolate brown, beige, and copper green towered above me. There was no gas, no water, no food for 75 miles. I was acutely aware of being alive.

There wasn't another car in sight on the two-lane road. The speed limit was 35 mph, but I floored it to 60. I rolled all the windows down, gripped the steering wheel with my knees, and spread my arms wide, laughing and crying and screaming "Ahhh!" into the wind.

The years leading up to my divorce had been so hard. Yet here I was, my bruised heart filled with joy in the midst of an unyielding, thirsting land.

I've been to Death Valley just that once, but I wander in deserts of the spirit all the time. May I bring to them my curiosity. May I withdraw in them to pray.

God, keep me open to the gifts of deserts, within me and without. —Amy Eddings

Digging Deeper: Psalm 63:1; 1 Thessalonians 5:16–18

Tuesday, April 21

We have many parts in the one body, and all these parts have different functions.
—Romans 12:4 (GNT)

A few years ago I applied to volunteer at the local Concord Homeless Resource Center, where people who are unhoused can come for coffee, snacks, extra socks, or underwear. Here's where folks can sit indoors and chat, do a load of laundry, or take a shower.

Under the guidance of longtime volunteers, I circulated with a tray of cookies or sandwiches, poured coffee, and answered requests for personal items like toothpaste. I spoke with the clients, some of whom could not answer or make eye contact. The first month passed well, until a skirmish broke out between two older men who hurled curses at each other. I felt uneasy.

I talked to my mentors, who assured me that the volunteer position wasn't a good fit for everyone, and no one would think less of me if I decided that I wasn't cut out for it. I left and felt like a failure because I cringe around discord and harsh language. Couldn't I muscle through, turn a deaf ear—all the clichés for carrying on? I could not. My background simply hadn't prepared me for this work.

Within a few weeks, I reassessed my people skills and realized some unique ones. For example, I'm at ease with crying babies (even on planes). I can comfort weeping friends and teach people to write their stories. I can speak in front of a large audience.

I still admire the resilient folks who work with unhoused clients at the center. As for me, well, I'm needed elsewhere.

Lord of all, keep us mindful of our talents and guide us to where we can best use them.
—Gail Thorell Schilling

Digging Deeper: 1 Corinthians 12:4, 12–27

Consider the lilies how they grow: they toil not, they spin not; and yet I say unto you, that Solomon in all his glory was not arrayed like one of these. —Luke 12:27 (KJV)

The two college girls pushing a cart at Goodwill wanted to be anywhere else. "Papaw thinks I can find an outfit in this mess for 20 bucks," the one with the long brown curls was saying. "Says the landfills are overflowing with clothes and there's plenty of good stuff here." She held up a garish, seen-better-days shirt. The little blonde giggled. "He's got to be kidding."

I sized the granddaughter up. I could spend Papaw's money and have some left over. Pass on a lesson about sustainability and stewardship of our planet too. When she eyed the plaid cargo pants in my cart, I showed her the attached $148 price tag from Nordstrom's. I had neither the frame nor the frame of mind to wear them, but I'd been holding on to them for something. "These look about your size," I told her. "Slip them on over your jeans."

The pants fit like they were made to order. She loved the soft-brushed cotton fabric. What's more, the pants boasted a purple Goodwill tag, the week's half-price color. We found her a great Supima cotton T-shirt and an edgy cropped jean jacket "with just the right amount of grunge." I'd never paid for grunge myself, but it picked up the blue in the plaid. King Solomon couldn't have touched it.

With a grand total of $11.49, she could swing by McDonald's on the way to Papaw's. He'd be happy to see her embracing thriftiness. And maybe God would be happy to see her making wise use of His gifts too.

With an eye for beauty down pat, she'll learn about sustainability in due time, Lord. We got us a resale convert in the making. —Roberta Messner

Digging Deeper: Genesis 1:28, 2:15

Thursday, April 23

All their neighbors assisted them. —Ezra 1:6 (NIV)

I admire my neighbor Kim, pastor's wife and homeschooling mother of six children. She seems to keep things "all together," even with her youngest child, Ezra, having Down syndrome. Recently, at age eight, Ezra needed hip surgery, and Kim was dreading the 8-week recovery in which Ezra would be confined to a body cast. I pondered how to help a mom who seemed so organized.

Praying for Ezra on surgery day and beyond, I thought about Kim. I hesitated to offer a meal, since one of her children had food sensitivities, but the inner nudge continued. Eventually I texted Kim about bringing over some soup and she accepted immediately. Before long I was in her kitchen emptying homemade lentil soup into a large pot atop her stove.

Kim's husband walked in, carrying Ezra—full of smiles. A bright blue cast encircled Ezra's waist, extending down his right leg. I remarked how it complemented his eye color, and his blue eyes sparkled back at me joyfully. Kim showed me a photo taken days before the surgery, with Ezra in a bumblebee costume as part of his role in a student play. His older siblings were thrilled when he recited his one line perfectly!

Driving home afterward, I gave thanks for having pushed through my hesitation to help. My contribution was small, but the blessing for me was big in seeing the joy and grace evident in Kim and her family. Whether wearing a body cast or cast in a play, Ezra was surrounded with love and uplifted in every way.

Thank You, Lord, for blessing both giver and receiver. Help us not to hesitate when You nudge us to reach out to someone. —Lisa Livezey

Digging Deeper: Psalm 41:3; Proverbs 11:25; Isaiah 46:3–4; 2 Corinthians 9:7

Friday, April 24

If you falter in a time of trouble, how small is your strength! —Proverbs 24:10 (NIV)

If all goes well, my son Solomon will graduate this spring. Right now, he is furiously working on his senior project of scoring a film. Four years ago, when he enrolled, composing music was not even on his radar. He had his thoughts fixed on studying advanced calculus. But in his freshman year, he struggled with his professor's approach, and the experience jaded his love of the subject. After passing the class, he announced he was never doing calculus again.

A chance elective course on opera steered him to music, and with it came a passion and a drive I had never seen. He worked for days fine-tuning his work, and one of his pieces was selected for an orchestral concert.

On the big night, while he was on stage introducing his work, his infant mobile flashed in my mind's eye. All those years ago, I became obsessed with finding the perfect mobile. I found a state-of-the-art one that played Beethoven, Bach, and Mozart and was very expensive. We didn't have a lot of money, but I didn't hesitate to purchase it.

Fast-forward to this moment with our family in the audience, Solomon on stage, the room filled with music that came from somewhere deep inside him, and I thought of all the things that aligned to get us here—that mobile over his crib and even that difficult professor were part of the plan, laying the framework for him to discover this yearning and find his voice.

Heavenly Father, thank You for Your nudges, especially the ones that seem like setbacks but are detours to better places. —Sabra Ciancanelli

Digging Deeper: Proverbs 3:5–6;
John 16:33; 1 Peter 5:10

**Make allowance for each other's faults,
and forgive anyone who offends you.
—Colossians 3:13 (NLT)**

I stood at the sink creating a green salad when my phone dinged with the arrival of a text. It was a friend asking me to help her with an event. I jotted back that unfortunately I had plans, but I wished her the best. I wasn't prepared for the lightning bolt of criticism in her response. I took a deep breath. *Of all the rude things to say!* Jody had been working a high-stress job the last couple years, and today I felt like I was her punching bag.

The whole rest of the afternoon I banged pots, clattered dishes, and steamed about how she'd responded. I tried to think of witty ways I could defend myself the next time we had a conversation. Over the last year she'd turned into a grump. *Do I really want to be treated that way?*

As I sat down for dinner, I received another text. It was a picture of a friend's chicken with her feathers all fluffed out, two baby chick heads barely poking out. Mama had covered them with her feathers to protect them, so they'd be safe from the world.

I felt a ping of conviction. That's exactly what I should have done. Instead of drawing an emotional sword toward Jody, God wanted me to cover her with His feathers. The next day I dropped by with some treats for her and asked if I could pray with her. She grabbed both my hands and exclaimed, "Yes!"

Lord, forgive me for reacting with a sword. Thank You for reminding me that You want me to respond with the mortar of prayer—to build strong-as-brick relationships. Amen.
—Rebecca Ondov

Digging Deeper: Ephesians 1:15–23; Philippians 1:9–11

Sunday, April 26

For the LORD is good; His mercy is everlasting and His faithfulness is to all generations. —Psalm 100:5 (NASB)

Ever since my centenarian aunt told me, "You are a precious morsel in the Lord's hands," I think of this when I see that tiniest of creatures, the hummingbird. I was privileged to witness an Anna's hummer, one we do not have in north Idaho, in her flower bed in Southern California. Our regulars are the Calliope and Rufous.

Years ago my husband, Terry, and I camped with our young children at Priest Lake, at the northern end of Idaho's panhandle, and were lost in wonder when we spotted a nesting hummingbird tucked secretly among the pine boughs in the campground. Our four children are now in midlife—our son unable to work, gripped with chronic fatigue syndrome from a long-term virus. Terry and I had lived away for decades and, having moved back to Idaho's Panhandle, were camping in our same favorite campground.

I sat quietly in my beach chair on a summer morning watching the sun rise above the mountains. The lake stretched as far as I could see, water still as the ones described in Psalm 23. I caught movement and turned toward the shallows. A Calliope humming-bird hovered above the water, dipping its beak, taking sips from the lake.

I was wide-eyed in awe. All that vast water, and this "precious morsel" drinking from a seemingly infinite supply. A Spirit-led thought rose inside me. *This is how I am with God. I drink from His eternal cup. From His infinite supply.*

My heart lifted for our son. To see God's bounty from a hummingbird perspective made His endless provision spectacular. I needn't worry—He would provide. I left the beach pumped with "precious morsel" praise.

**Jehovah Jireh—Lord our Provider—
You never run out of just what I need.**
—Carol Knapp

Digging Deeper: Nehemiah 9:20–21;
Job 12:7–10; 1 Corinthians 12:13

SACRED THREADS: A Father's Enduring Influence

Whoever fears the Lord has a secure fortress, and for their children it will be a refuge.
—Proverbs 14:26 (NIV)

In all my years of antiquing, I'd never seen this sampler. *What Is Home Without a Father?* it asked. The condition of the unframed paper was pristine, save for the broken red stitches on the word *Father* and the tangle of threads on the back. The perfect companion for my *What Is Home Without a Mother?* sampler. Why was a chill running up and down my spine?

While Dad had been a great provider and teacher, he'd been much like that sampler's broken, tangled threads. Alcohol had numbed his childhood pain, but we kids paid the price. When he retired from the railroad and lost the structure of work, his drinking escalated. I was the one he called, the one who signed commitment papers to a psychiatric facility. It was there that Dad turned his life over to God. For the remaining 21 years of his life, he never drank another drop of alcohol. Lived a life of courage, humor, storytelling, and generosity.

When I found myself addicted to prescription opioids in my own retirement years, the memory of Dad's battle was a strength and refuge from beyond this world. He'd been much like me, tangled threads of contradiction. The same father who'd once drunk too much had put Mom and me on a train bound for hope in search of a cure for my condition that mystified local doctors. En route to pull a double shift to fund the best healthcare money could buy, Dad found a porter to help my mother and me with our luggage. "My baby's going to the doctor," he said, kissing the top of my head.

"Could you find her one of your *Sleep Like a Kitten* pillows?"

Yes, Lord, my story on a sampler. My home wouldn't have been complete without my father.
—Roberta Messner

Digging Deeper: Exodus 20:12; Deuteronomy 5:16

Tuesday, April 28

God brought Abram outside beneath the nighttime sky and told him, "Look up into the heavens and count the stars if you can. Your descendants will be like that—too many to count!" —Genesis 15:5 (TLB)

As an older retired woman, I started feeling that I wasn't contributing enough to society. I could no longer use my education, career, and talents to define who I am. In truth I felt lost and wistful for the old days when I was out speaking to hundreds of people or having another book published.

Then I read a fact that changed my perspective. In order to be born, I needed two parents, four grandparents, eight great-grandparents, sixteen second great-grandparents, and so on up to 4,094 ancestors just from the past 400 years. Imagine all the struggles, battles, wars, love, happiness, disease, sadness, pain, joy, disasters, medical problems, highs, lows, financial angst, fears, and

173

successes all my ancestors had to go through just for me to make it into existence.

Passing my life stories and experiences down to my children, grandchildren, and great-grandchildren seems a worthy endeavor. Thinking about the thread of life from Adam and Eve to my own existence somehow makes me proud that I even made it. With God's help I was given life and opportunities that most of my ancestors never had.

Now the older I get, the happier I am to share my past with those coming after me. And the really cool part is that my kids and grandkids seem to enjoy the stories I remember about my parents and grandparents. Instead of life passing me by I now have a purpose—to keep the thread of our lineage spiced up with all the stories I know about our ancestors.

Heavenly Father, never let me forget that I am a link in the long chain of family before me. Help me honor and respect them all. —Patricia Lorenz

Digging Deeper: Leviticus 26:45; Hebrews 11:11–13

Wednesday, April 29

Praise the Lord, my soul, and forget not all his benefits. —Psalm 103:2 (NIV)

"I didn't see one deer while you were out of town!" exclaimed my husband's 94-year-old grandmother, who lives with us. In order to give Mam Ma pleasure and something to look forward to each day, my husband, Michael, spreads corn behind our backyard fence each afternoon. So, of course, that's why Mam Ma didn't see any deer—Michael wasn't home to perform his unseen duty of buying the deer corn, hauling it home from the feed store, and walking to the back fence in all types of weather to sprinkle it on the ground to attract the woodland creatures she watches from the coziness of indoors.

"Does she think they just come to our yard on their own?" Michael asked.

I couldn't help but laugh. It was a thankless job that went unnoticed until Michael didn't do it.

That got me to thinking. Michael performed many jobs that *I* took for granted—making the bed each morning, mowing and weed-eating our 1-acre lawn, taking out the trash, cleaning cat litter boxes, gassing up our daughter's car, holding down a good job all these years to support our family. I pulled him close. "Honey, thank you so much!"

There was Someone else I'd taken for granted too. That vibrant sunrise when I walked the dog. The cool early morning temperatures that quenched the sweltering heat wave we'd had. Air I breathe and gravity that keeps my feet on the ground. The blessings of home, prosperity, health, love, and life. I whispered a prayer: *Dear God, thank You so much.*

Forgive me, Lord, when I take You and the wonderful life You've given me for granted. May I always recognize Your work in the world and thank You for my blessings. —Stephanie Thompson

---

Thursday, April 30

Return to your rest, my soul. —Psalm 116:7 (NASB)

Every cactus was blooming on a perfect spring
evening at the Desert Botanical Gardens in Phoenix.
The orange, pink, yellow, and white blooms were
arrayed around the garden in a flowering rainbow.
My daughter, Katelyn, and I arrived after work to
search for nesting birds. To be honest, I also needed
a break from my overloaded calendar. My hectic life
had left me hollow and exhausted.

We photographed a mourning dove guarding
her two chicks in a palo verde tree and another in
the bend of a thorn-covered cholla. Encouraged
by this success, we checked for birds in the empty
cavities of saguaros. Passing one tall giant, we
noticed a Western screech owl, identified by
the tufted ears. He was so well camouflaged we
thought it might be plant debris, but then he
blinked.

The saguaro cavity—called a boot—was
probably created by a Gila woodpecker looking for
a meal. To protect itself from the open wound, the
cactus produced a secretion that hardened, creating
a callous shell. Once the boot was abandoned, the
owl moved in. In the hollowed-out, empty space, the
owl found a home and a place of rest.

People gathered around us to see why we were aiming our cameras skyward. When we pointed to the owl, they were incredulous. "How did you ever see it?" they wondered.

"We found what we were looking for," we explained. I knew the words pertained not only to a nesting owl, but also to my overloaded calendar. It was time to create empty space and make a home there.

When I have room to breathe, O Giver of Rest, may I not rush to fill it. Amen. —Lynne Hartke

Digging Deeper: Job 12:7–10; Matthew 11:23–30

LIVING A NEW LIFE

1 _____

2 _____

3 _____

4 _____

5 _____

6 _____

7 _____

8 _____

9 _____

10 _____

11 _____

12 _____

13 _____

14 _____

15 _____

16 _____

17 _____

18 _____

19 _____

20 _____

21 _____

22 _____

23 _____

24 _____

25 _____

26 _____

27 _____

28 _____

29 _____

30 _____

May

In everything give thanks; for this is
the will of God for you in Christ Jesus.

—1 Thessalonians 5:18 (NASB)

Friday, May 1

Therefore keep watch, because you do not know the day or the hour. —Matthew 25:13 (NIV)

The ability to wait effectively is more challenging than I anticipated. I am a first responder with our local ambulance service. Our shifts run a minimum of 12 hours. We cover 1,500 square miles of rural area with a handful of towns with populations in the low hundreds. We average one or two calls per shift.

The running joke is that no one on shift had better say the "Q-word." A call always seems to drop within moments of commenting on how "quiet" our area has been. I try to study EMS skills or work on writing or illustration projects while I listen for our tones on the emergency scanner. Concentration on a task is sometimes difficult, since I'm not just waiting; I'm waiting expectantly for the tones to drop, ready to respond. When other agencies are toned out, I imagine what I would do for the patient if it was my call. Sometimes I'll study that condition or scenario.

Recently I'd studied the book of Revelation. Numerous verses throughout the Bible stressed the need to keep a vigilance of expectation of Jesus's return. It's not a matter of complacently dreaming about some distant day. We are commanded to actively study His Word, share His message with others, and expect Him to appear at any moment. No one but the Father knows the time of Jesus's return. We are to wait with purpose.

That reminds me. I've got a lot of work to do before God's call drops.

Lord, please keep me alert and prepared as I anticipate Your call. It sure seems quiet down here... —Erika Bentsen

Digging Deeper: Matthew 24:42–44, 25:1–13; Mark 13:32–37

Saturday, May 2

Confess your sins to each other and pray for each other so that you may be healed. The prayer of a righteous person is powerful and effective. —James 5:16 (NIV)

Riding in the elevator at my dad's nursing home, a woman sharing the car with me abruptly turned to me and asked, "Do you pray?" I was surprised by the question, but even more surprised by how quickly and easily I answered: "I do."

There was a time, not too long ago, that I would have hesitated to tell a stranger that I was a believer who prayed. But now, as a more mature Christian, I didn't feel any need to hedge my answer.

"Will you pray for my mother?" she asked, and I could see the tears in her eyes. "I want her to go to the hospital, but I have to convince the doctor to send her."

And at that moment, we arrived at her floor and she exited the elevator.

I didn't know exactly what I was to pray for, but I asked the Lord to grant guidance to the doctor and to her, so that they might come to the best solution for her mother. I kept my word and prayed fervently until I reached my floor.

In addition to praying for her mother's situation, I asked God to lead the lady toward Him, allowing her to know Him well enough that she feels able to offer prayers herself. Or perhaps she already has a relationship with Christ and simply wanted someone to pray along with her. Whatever the reason, I am grateful that I could.

Father God, thank You for using me to show Your love to others. I am grateful for the ability to connect with You in prayer for myself and for others. —Gayle T. Williams

Digging Deeper: Deuteronomy 4:7; 1 Kings 8:28

Sunday, May 3

The earth is the LORD's. —Psalm 24:1 (KJV)

The sight of a rainbow trout reflecting the sunlight in a Colorado mountain stream is beyond description. In the distance, the snowcapped Rocky Mountains provide a breathtaking backdrop to a river flanked by spring willows, silver aspen, and evergreen pine trees.

Each year my dad, our friend Bob Schwartzman, and I come here to challenge the fish and immerse ourselves in the beauty of God's handiwork. We laugh and joke, catch beautiful fish, snap photos with our phones, and then quickly release them back into their environs.

But this year, as we reach the river on our first morning, something is terribly wrong. The mountains are shrouded in gray smoke, and the smell of distant fires two states away hovers in the air. On the airport TV, we had seen faraway wildfires devouring portions of the West Coast. We hadn't realized that the repercussions of the fires had come this far.

In his sermons Dad often spoke of the earth as God's garden. He encouraged his congregation to find the peace that nature offers. He emphasized our responsibility to care for God's great creation.

Now we were seeing how the careless acts of a few individuals could lay waste to a giant slice of that creation, destroying not only the glory of God's earth but also homes, businesses, lives.

I set my eyes on the smoky landscape and breathed in the tainted air, remembering blue skies and clear water and countless trout released to swim another day. I vowed to God, in that moment, to be His messenger and a steward to His earth, to honor the great gift God has given us through His creation. Isn't this everyone's responsibility?

Father, remind me and keep me aware of my responsibility to Your creation. —Brock Kidd

Digging Deeper: 1 Chronicles 11:14; Job 12:8

183

Monday, May 4

The word of the Lord came to me [David], saying, Thou hast shed blood abundantly, and . . . shalt not build a house unto my name.
—1 Chronicles 22:8 (KJV)

I paused to admire a tree bowing to the wind. Never having written a line of verse worth its ink, I somehow knew, in the midst of the tree's dancing, there was a poem in there somewhere. Yet I also knew that, in Mississippi, that same tree could turn into the weapon of a mean tornado by day's end.

King David's character is another example of the vicissitudes of God's creation. He is revered for memorable lyrics such as "The heavens declare the glory of God" (Psalm 19:1, KJV), and "The Lord is my shepherd" (Psalm 23:1, KJV). But David was as responsible for the snuffing out of thousands of lives as he was for soothing the soul. His warring nature ultimately caused God to prohibit him from building the temple.

He seems a strange mix—his poetry standing alongside his battle weaponry—but David is not so different from us. The power of Christ helps us cool our instincts toward battle—resisting that urge to snap at our children or lash out over disagreements with our loved ones or our office mates.

Though the temple of his dream was denied him, David refused to take his eyes off God. He could have defied the Lord and leaned into that warring side of himself, attempting to build anyway. But he chose to blot out the noise of ambition, focusing on the eternal temple God has for those who love Him. And isn't it soothing to know that no matter our propensity toward conflict, if we remain focused, we can always find peace and refuge in God's love?

Lord, thank You for blessing me with the timeless poetry of Your servant David.
—Jacqueline F. Wheelock

Digging Deeper: Psalms 19, 22, 51; James 3:5–12

Tuesday, May 5

So faith comes from hearing, and hearing through the word of Christ. —Romans 10:17 (ESV)

This morning I allowed myself to half overhear a podcast on somebody's device across the coffee shop, one of those hot, crowded establishments that creates baroque coffee concoctions that make my plain little cup seem like an outcast. Maybe I should have just gone to the corner Greek diner. But if I had I would have missed the podcast. An up-and-coming Christian singer being interviewed was asked what kind of faith she grew up with. "Oh, it was just, you know, a plain vanilla faith."

I almost spit out my basic brew. Two objections immediately presented themselves. First, there is nothing plain about faith, but we'll get to that later. Second, this common calumny that vanilla is somehow ordinary, even boring, is a grievance of mine. To my taste buds the fruit of the orchid confers the most exquisite pleasure, and culinary experts consider it a complex flavor.

Credit the Spanish conquistador Hernán Cortés for having the taste to bring vanilla to Europe from the New World. Europeans used it to sweeten chocolate until the apothecary to Queen Elizabeth I started using it on its own to create sweet treats the queen went wild for. Soon the French were using it in ice cream, and the rest is history.

More recently, traces of vanilla were found in ancient wine jars in Jerusalem, enjoyed, archaeologists believe, by the Judahites before the city was destroyed.

So, for me a plain vanilla faith is just right. Plain for humility, vanilla for the sweetness of my Lord.

Lord, Your grace is sweet and pure and feeds my soul. —Edward Grinnan

Digging Deeper: Psalm 119:103; 2 Corinthians 5:7; Hebrews 11:6

Wednesday, May 6

Finally, brothers and sisters, whatever is true, whatever is noble, whatever is right, whatever is pure, whatever is lovely, whatever is admirable—if anything is excellent or praiseworthy—think about such things. —Philippians 4:8 (NIV)

I struggled with math from elementary through high school. I sought tutoring to understand and properly execute mathematical precepts. Oftentimes I felt defeated in my mind before I attempted a problem.

I had a middle-school teacher who would always tell us to put on our thinking caps. She wanted us to be confident in our abilities and to make positive thoughts our first thoughts. She also reminded us that to solve our problems, we first and foremost needed to apply the appropriate formula. That formula would never change, and it always worked.

Recently as I approached my yearly appointment to track a previous health diagnosis, worry had begun to creep into my mind. I began to second-guess certain parenting decisions and reconsider recent financial obligations. I'd made my fears bigger than my faith.

Put on your thinking cap. I recently heard those words again from the nudging of the Holy Spirit. God's Word is a formula that never changes. His formula for my anxiety was to meditate on His Word and think on the good things. I placed my mind on God's unfailing love and compassion for me. He'd never failed and He never would. I centered my thoughts on His grace, His mercy, and the things that grew my faith instead of my fear. That turned out to be *my* winning formula.

Lord, when worrisome thoughts overcrowd my mind, I will set my ears and thoughts on Your still, small voice. Your Word and presence give me peace. —Tia McCollors

---

Thursday, May 7

Commit to the LORD** whatever you do, and he will establish your plans. —Proverbs 16:3 (NIV)**

My Labrador, Old Sport, pawed at the door. Time for his afternoon walk. I grabbed his leash and a light jacket for myself.

Upon opening the door, I knew that spring had finally come to the Midwest. Nearly overnight, the scenery had changed dramatically. Green growth had pressed through gray mulch. Buds had formed on trees. Once-spindly shrubs were now heavy with flowers.

This landscaping was new to me. When I'd purchased my home in March, the yard was covered by a sheet of snow. When that had melted, I'd seen brush and branches—placeholders for warmer seasons. But now I could see beauty and detail.

Ornamental grasses were placed in the back. Low-growing flowers were in the front. Hedges sheltered delicate plants, forming a wind barrier. I recognized the assortment of species of plants— different varieties that would bloom in different months. Someone who had come before me had placed each plant with purpose.

Sport and I walked around the yard, exploring the new growth. As we did, I thought of the importance of intentionality—living a life of purpose. Beauty like this didn't come from apathy or inaction. It required dedication and deliberation.

I wondered if I was living my life intentionally. Was I using my time and attention in ways that blessed others? When I was gone, would people see the deliberate patterns of a life well lived?

I knew that, as seasons changed, I would continue to uncover intentionality in my yard. And I resolved that, during that time, I would work to become a man of dedication and purpose.

Father, give me wisdom in the choices I make. Help me to plant blessings for others to reap.
—Logan Eliasen

Digging Deeper: Matthew 5:14–16; Ephesians 5:15–16

Friday, May 8

Peter came and said to him, "Lord, if my brother or sister sins against me, how often should I forgive? As many as seven times?" Jesus said to him, "Not seven times, but, I tell you, seventy-seven times." —Matthew 18:21–22 (NRSVUE)

There are two people in my life, one close friend and the other a family member, who seem to be unable to remember the terrible things I have done or said to them in the past. Truly. I am not kidding.

"You seriously don't remember when I was 16, fresh with my driver's license, and I got three tickets in the space of 3 months, including one for deliberately driving the wrong way on a one-way street?" I said incredulously to my father recently.

"No, I don't," he said. "Sorry."

"Don't be sorry," I said.

How is this possible? I have often wondered. My dad also doesn't remember rude things I have said, actions I have done, and inactions where I should have taken action, all of which would have easily wounded less forgiving people forever.

If you, reader, have wronged me in the past, I likely remember it too well. I hold grudges. I'm not proud of it. God help me. I'm working on this, I promise.

In that pinnacle of Jesus's teachings, the Sermon on the Mount, He talks about the necessity of forgiving others who have wronged us.

But it is my father's inability to remember my sins of all kinds that reminds me more than anything else in this world of grace.

Lord, give me the gift of forgetting other people's sins. Help make my forgiveness real, but allow me also to forget. —Jon M. Sweeney

Digging Deeper: Mark 11:25

Saturday, May 9

A certain Samaritan ... when he saw him, he had compassion on him. —Luke 10:33 (KJV)

That Saturday in May when 90-degree temperatures wilted me, I bussed to Boston alone to take a harbor cruise. Indeed, the breezy voyage refreshed me.

Back at the dock, I strolled the Harborwalk, a paved pathway edging the Atlantic Ocean. I had gone about 100 yards when I tripped and plunged headfirst onto the sidewalk. My head! My hip! I lay dazed on the pavement. A young woman retrieved my hat and offered help. Before I could respond, a young steward from the party ship moored alongside the walk bounded down the gangway and knelt over me.

"Don't move! . . . Now sit up very slowly. . . . Stay here." He sprinted back to his vessel and returned with a bottle of water, an ice pack, and a bandage that he applied to my bleeding elbow.

"I must go, but I'll send someone to check on you!" He disappeared into a throng of caterers wheeling chafing dishes on board. I eased onto a park bench, sipped the water, and held the ice against my throbbing hip. Minutes passed, then a different steward asked how I felt. I never saw my Good Samaritan again.

Back home, bruised but fine, I tried to trace him through his name tag. The ship's website offered email links for reservations, but none for personal communication. I sent a thank-you note anyway. Was it forwarded? I'll never know, but I do know that when I needed help, God appeared immediately in the compassion of a stranger.

Lord of Mercy, like my Good Bostonian, may I, too, be quick to help those in distress.
—Gail Thorell Schilling

Digging Deeper: Deuteronomy 31:8; Zechariah 7:9; Matthew 5:7

Mother's Day, Sunday, May 10

Therefore encourage one another and build one another up, just as you are doing.
—1 Thessalonians 5:11 (ESV)

Ding! A brown-faced Bitmoji with curly black hair and glasses popped onto my phone screen that Sunday morning. The caricatured avatar held a cartoon card that read: "Happy Mother's Day! Love, me."

My friend Renee! We'd prayed together years ago at Moms in Prayer meetings. Every Friday morning a group of us with high school kids poured out our hearts to God and one another. My daughter, Micah, was a freshman then. Renee's daughter was a senior.

When Micah was young, I remembered thinking it odd when other mothers wished me a happy Mother's Day. After all, I wasn't their mom. I was only celebrating Mother's Day because I had a child. Motherhood didn't feel special to me. Many women held the title. I couldn't understand why anyone, other than my husband and daughter, might reach out to me on a holiday that honors moms.

Then Micah grew. Adolescence arrived with preteen drama that morphed into teenage angst.

The constant euphoria I felt when Micah was a baby, toddler, and child deflated as my husband and I parented an independent young woman who made mistakes and experienced life on her terms. The hot-air balloon ride of parenthood now felt more like being a passenger on a runaway roller coaster operating in the dark without seat belts.

Gazing at Renee's greeting, tears filled my eyes. Motherhood could sometimes be a thankless job. I treasured recognition from others—not just someone I raised, but someone who knew both the joy and heartache that came with membership in the mom club.

Lord, thank You for the fellowship of other mothers. They remind me that motherhood is a blessing as well as a divine privilege.
—Stephanie Thompson

Digging Deeper: Proverbs 31:25; Ecclesiastes 4:9–10; Matthew 18:19–20

Monday, May 11

Weeping may endure for a night, but joy comes in the morning.—Psalm 30:5 (NKJV)

It had been a year since sweet Alex had passed away after a tragic motorcycle accident. The 21-year-old college student who played high school football with my son Christian had lived with passion and vigor. I grieved with his mom when she lost her only child, and cried through his beautiful standing-room-only funeral. The day of his funeral had been an appropriately overcast, rainy day, and the tears of Alex's mourners only added to the gloom.

A year later, I attended a celebration Alex's parents hosted to celebrate what would have been his twenty-second birthday. It was a gorgeous sunny day. They live in our neighborhood, so I drove around the corner to attend what turned out to be not a solemn remembrance ceremony but a full-out, multigenerational celebration. We reminisced over his life while enjoying beef and chicken tacos and tortilla chips with guacamole and queso, followed by birthday cake. His mom spoke a few words in honor of her son, then we joined in a toast to Alex.

The parents reminded us to grab party favors on the way out, favors that included a temporary tattoo of Alex's face with that sweet smile. Not a huge fan of temporary tattoos, I placed mine on my refrigerator as a reminder of Alex and his short but impactful life. It also reminds me of what God whispered in my heart when I left the party: "Troubles don't last always," as the old Southern folks used to say. Even the darkest times of grief and pain can turn into days of gratitude, joy, and even celebration.

Father, help me cling to You on dark days, knowing that You are faithful and will usher the sun and joy back into my life. —Carla Hendricks

---

Tuesday, May 12

You did not choose me, but I chose you and appointed you so that you might go and bear fruit. —John 15:16 (NIV)

Our younger son, Tim, was being ordained a deacon in the Episcopal Church, donning a clerical collar for the first time, 6 months before his full ordination as a priest. The ceremony was held in Los Angeles, near his sponsoring parish, and his wife, Henley, had flown out there with him to be in the pew looking on. Alas, we couldn't be there to celebrate. We had another responsibility—staying home in New York to babysit their almost two-year-old son, Silas.

At least we could watch the service, live streamed from LA. What a moving event, hearing the hymns and prayers, watching our son kneel and be blessed into this life of ministry, the culmination of a long journey. I could picture him singing in choir as a boy and clutching his hands reverently in prayer at church—or folding up a program into an airplane ("Don't throw it in here, Tim"). He was so reverent that my wife, Carol, used to call him the "Pious Tot." He was a little less pious as a teenager (you should have heard his rock band).

But all that changed. He'd spent 3 years in seminary, and soon he'd be working in a church in Connecticut, nurturing others, maybe kids who are on a spiritual journey like his. I wished I could tell their parents, "You never know what your children will do when they grow up." We couldn't have ever guessed.

All that we could do was be full of wonder at how God had worked in his life. And was still working.

Dear Lord, let me trust that You are working in ways I might never imagine. May I live to see and understand, giving thanks. —Rick Hamlin

Digging Deeper: Jeremiah 1:5; Romans 7:6; 1 Peter 4:10

Wednesday, May 13

ANGEL WHISPERS: Mysteries of Hope

He answered and said unto them, Because it is given unto you to know the mysteries of the kingdom of heaven, but to them it is not given. —Matthew 13:11 (KJV)

He was my seventh-grade chorus director. He was mean. Or at least he seemed that way to me.

All through the course, he hammered us with the same song: "You'll Never Walk Alone." Forget fun. We were made to sing the song over, and over, and over. The man seemed driven to get the song right. He was fairly young. I don't remember his name.

But, believe me, I might well die with that song on my lips. Singing it again and again, it reminds me to walk through life's storms, with my head high; the song takes away all fear of the dark.

And don't we all know how this enduring song ends? By promising us that we never really walk alone.

My talent was lacking, and I promptly forgot the chorus at the end of the term. Except for this: a short time later, I heard that the young director had died. It seems that he had a terminal illness of which he was well aware.

Suddenly the song took on a different meaning, until it became a sort of permanent angel whisper in my life. Had the teacher been determined to imprint words of encouragement on his students? Or had he simply wanted to create something beautiful before he left the earth? Either way, I detected a mysterious form of an angel whisper. A gift to all who chose to hear.

Why did that director give his students that song? Did he know the repercussions of hope, that it continues to inspire? Only the great Whisperer we call God knows the answer.

Father, Your mysteries are unending, and there is hope in every whisper. —Pam Kidd

Digging Deeper: Lamentations 3:21–23; 1 Corinthians 4:1

Thursday, May 14

How long will you grieve my spirit, and crush me with words? —Job 19:2 (JPS)

After my husband, Keith, died, I was shattered, but I thought my grief would diminish steadily over time, like the half-life of a plutonium isotope. I pictured it that way—a lump of some harmful substance that shrank a bit, until one day it would be gone.

I tried to ignore the ambush of sudden hurt when a day was special: our anniversary, his birthday. I avoided the places we had been together, because the sting of spending time there alone contradicted my notion of a predictable decay rate. I refused to acknowledge that my theory had no basis in fact.

Then a "happy birthday" call to one of the wives who had been in a couples *havurah* (extended family) with Keith and me in Los Angeles had to be truncated because her husband had just been brought home from the rehab he'd been in since a stroke. As the call ended, I beat back the jealousy that rose instantly in me. Every one of the four other couples in the *havurah* was still together, and I had been alone for more than 10 years. To distract myself, I went online to read *The Washington Post*, but the first thing I encountered was an article about a couple in the Netherlands who had chosen to die together, holding hands.

I started sobbing. I knew instantly that the idea of grief disappearing was very wrong. I called a wise friend, who listened as I babbled how stupid I had been. When I had calmed enough to let him get a word in, he said quietly, "It's not that grief gets less. Your life grows around it."

I know we only borrow each other from You, God of Hosts, but I wish with all my heart that You didn't take them back when we're not ready to give them up. —Rhoda Blecker

Digging Deeper: Psalm 10:14; Jeremiah 51:8

THE LONELY AMONG US: Church Friends
Where two or three are gathered in my name, I am there among them. —Matthew 18:20 (NRSVUE)

Though I attended church weekly as a child, I've struggled to commit to regular attendance as an adult, always finding reasons to move my family from our current church to a new one. At our first church, I was nudged into leading children's church but yearned to be among more mature believers, learning. Later, my teenage daughters needed a youth group. This church's sermons clashed with my political views. That church's congregation was too old. Or too small. Too whatever.

Whenever we're between churches, I reconsider Scripture's scanty instruction concerning church attendance: "Let us consider how to provoke one another to love and good deeds, not neglecting to meet together, as is the habit of some, but encouraging one another, and all the more as you see the Day approaching" (Hebrews 10:24–25, NRSVUE). Nonattendance *can* become as habitual as attending. I know from experience. Also, I shouldn't attend just to get something myself but to provoke and encourage others.

Recently, upon hearing that an almost-forgotten woman from a church we attended long ago was terminally ill, I suddenly appreciated the obvious reason believers shouldn't neglect meeting together: church attendance connects us. Judithanne's illness provoked me to bake bread for her and her husband, Donald, and to rediscover how much I liked them both. How could I have lost contact with them?

After Judithanne died, my husband and I started meeting regularly with Donald, initially as a ministry but soon from pure enjoyment, illuminating how the special companionship of fellow believers had been missing from our lives. Church—that is, meeting with fellow believers and thereby with God Himself—can be a powerful anti-loneliness agent.

Help me keep on meeting with fellow believers, Father, as is Your will. —Patty Kirk

Digging Deeper: Deuteronomy 31:12–13; Acts 2:42–47

Saturday, May 16

A person of too many friends comes to ruin, but there is a friend who sticks closer than a brother. —Proverbs 18:24 (NASB)

When I wrote my first devotional for *Walking in Grace* (then *Daily Guideposts*), I was an energetic young man in my thirties and the father of three small children. Now I am 73 years old and my wife, Beth, and I have five grandchildren. Time moves so quickly for all of us!

A few weeks ago some cherished friends called us in Macon, Georgia, and asked us to meet them in Birmingham, Alabama, to attend a wedding together for the children of mutual friends. We knew this couple when I was their pastor in Waco, Texas, 16 years ago. We really miss them, and Beth and I jumped at the opportunity. We quickly made motel reservations and drove 4 hours to join them.

The weekend was delightful. We talked, laughed, shared memories, and realized that senior adulthood can be a unique season of great joy and celebration.

As they say in Georgia, "There ain't no friend like an old friend!" and there is much wisdom in this colloquial adage. The most important investment in our life is not financial security. Rather, it is our relational investment in friendship, family, and God. Money in the bank can pay the heating bill, but it is friendship that brings true warmth to our lives.

Dear God, help me nurture and support my old friends, my current friends, my lonely neighbor, and nameless strangers. And thank You, my Father, for Your eternal friendship. Amen.
—Scott Walker

Sunday, May 17

JOURNEY THROUGH GRIEF: Letting Go
**There is a time for everything, and a season
for every activity under the heavens.
—Ecclesiastes 3:1 (NIV)**

My instinct was to jump on the next flight to
Florida. My father had become bedridden once
before—just over a month ago—and I was able to
help him back on his feet. This time he refused to
eat as well. I panicked.

My father had already suffered from the pangs
of hunger as a child; I couldn't bear the thought
of him starving toward the end of his life too.
I need to help him now, I thought, but finances and
responsibilities at home made it a challenge to
leave immediately.

"Kevin," I implored my cousin, when he went to
visit my father. "Listen to me . . ."

I shared with him all the tricks I knew to get my
father to eat, take his pills, and communicate. In
the meantime, I worked to figure out a way to get
there as soon as I could.

A few days later Kevin called to let me know my
father wouldn't budge, and I needed to prepare
myself for the end.

"No," I said. "I know once I get there, he'll listen to me."

The moment I said this, I realized that my father had most likely been ready to die the month before, when I insisted he stand and fight. Perhaps my desperate need to keep him tugged on his need to appease the daughter he loved so much. I knew if I went there, we could do it again. But was I doing the right thing for him, or was I causing him more suffering by insisting that he keep fighting? As incredibly difficult as it was, I stayed home.

I did the most loving thing I could do for my father: as he reached for the Lord, I let him go.

Lord, give me the strength to fight when I need to, and the wisdom to let go when it's time.
—Karen Valentin

Digging Deeper: Psalm 46:10; Matthew 11:28

Monday, May 18

DOORS OF OUR LIFE: Back Door
Follow God's example, therefore, as dearly loved children and walk in the way of love, just as Christ loved us and gave himself up for us as a fragrant offering and sacrifice to God.
—Ephesians 5:1–2 (NIV)

Our house sits on a hill in the middle of woods we share with a variety of critters. Deer visit us daily, and foxes, raccoons, turkeys, hawks, and owls make regular appearances. As the seasons change, so do our views of the river below and surrounding mountains. By opening our back door, you enter the screened porch I call my exterior oasis. A fireplace offers year-round enjoyment except on the coldest days. Within the pest-free environment we eat, read, and take an occasional nap in the great outdoors, the only noise made by happy songbirds. The tranquility never fails to relax my mind and body. I'm at peace with the world and wish the serenity could last forever.

On one spectacular afternoon, I opened the back door, and the sweet scent of my nearby hydrangea blooms reminded me of the Apostle Paul's words about a heavenly fragrance. Through Jesus offering His life as a sacrifice for me, my wish for everlasting peace is granted. By opening my heart to Him, I'm filled with His love and moved by His command to love others. In sharing His love, I'm given the opportunity to witness the beauty of changed lives, a splendor far exceeding what's outside my back door.

Nowadays when my hydrangeas bloom, I think of Christ's ultimate gift to the world—opening the heavenly door for me and others. All we have to do is follow the fragrant aroma and walk inside.

God, thank You for providing Your Son as the way to eternal life with You. Help us to love others as You love us. —Jenny Lynn Keller

Digging Deeper: Psalm 36:5–10;
Matthew 22:37–39; John 13:34–35;
Romans 5:6–8

Encourage each other. —2 Corinthians 13:11 (NLT)

The morning sun streamed through my office window as I glanced at the Letters to the Editor column. Recently I noticed the letters had become combative and divisive. It felt like our community was being fractured, pulled apart by our differing opinions about politics and other current events. *God, is there something that can be done?*

My thoughts were interrupted by the bellow of a cow. Several of my neighbors and I leased our pastures to a rancher for his cows. A week ago, he moved his herd from his ranch to the leased land, dividing the cattle between several of our places. Even though the pastures were about a quarter-mile apart, the cows and calves kept watch on one another.

Soon all the cows bellowed nonstop—from all the pastures. I stepped out onto my loft deck to see what was going on. One cow had escaped by slipping through the barbed wire fence and was going on a walkabout through the neighborhood. I burst out laughing. It reminded me of the twilight bark in the movie *101 Dalmatians*. It was as if they were hollering words of encouragement to her. I imagined what they were saying: "Hey, you forgot your baby! Watch out for the road! Eat some tall grass for me!"

After the cow was put back in the correct pasture, I marveled at how even cows kept an eye out for one another, bellowing what seemed to be encouragement. That was something I could do for friends, to help build community. I pulled out a couple cards, wrote fun notes to friends, and giggled when I mailed them.

Lord, thanks for showing me an easy way to build community. Amen. —Rebecca Ondov

Digging Deeper: Romans 1:10–12; 1 Thessalonians 5:11

Wednesday, May 20

He is like a tree planted by water, that sends out its roots by the stream, and does not fear when heat comes, for its leaves remain green. —Jeremiah 17:8 (ESV)

There is a tree in my hometown that stands prominently in the middle of a farmer's cornfield. I've taken photos of it and admired its stature: proud and tall, beautiful in the morning and night, balanced and grand, graceful in the winter and hopeful in the spring. I have memories of passing by it on the bus when I was in elementary school. Years later, when I moved back home, I told my sons that it had given me comfort growing up, something to look forward to seeing just by being there.

So when I rounded the bend of Curly Corner's Road and saw it broken to pieces, my heart sank, and I welled up and cried.

I must have looked out of sorts when I unpacked groceries, because my son Solomon asked what was wrong.

"You're crying about an old tree, Mom?" he responded when I told him.

I tried to explain that it was more than an old tree. It was a symbol of . . . a symbol of . . . I struggled for what it was a symbol of. Perseverance? No. Strength? No. I don't know. Life. A symbol of life?

Later that night, when I had tea with my mom, she said, "My granddaughter Regina called. Her favorite tree fell, and she was sad."

"That was my favorite tree."

"That's everyone's favorite tree," Mom said. And so I decided the tree must have been a friend, a teacher, showing us our shared connections over the mysterious and beautiful relationship we have with nature.

Heavenly Father, thank You for the beauty and wisdom of Your creation. —Sabra Ciancanelli

Digging Deeper: Psalm 1:3; Proverbs 11:30; Matthew 7:17–18; Revelation 22:2

Thursday, May 21

When I look at your heavens, the work of your fingers, the moon and the stars that you have established; what are humans that you are mindful of them, mortals that you care for them? —Psalm 8:3–4 (NRSVUE)

Like a lot of people, I was awestruck when pictures from the 1990 Hubble Space Telescope began to be published. I was fascinated by the clarity of the details and seeing them on digital screens rather than in newspapers or even magazines. I wanted to reach through the screen and touch the texture of Saturn or feel the swirl of a galaxy that had always seemed a blur. I know technology enhanced the images, but I was entranced even more by the beauty than the science.

As I am writing this, we are starting to get not just images but profoundly puzzling insights from the 2022 James Webb Space Telescope. Hard to imagine what's coming. My mind boggles at the realization of the vast distances traveled by the light and radiation we observe in such great detail. We are watching black holes gobble up stars in real time. I keep reading of unexpected findings. "That shouldn't be there." "This changes everything we thought we knew." Good science is humbling.

I love when beauty and puzzles in the universe draw me into spiritual mystery. Much more is going on than can be seen and measured. Science will never reach a final conclusion but must keep exploring. We humans are simultaneously amazing and finite. The God of these wonders welcomes us into a relationship of exploration, intimacy, and love. Yes, this is personal. I am part of this universe that we will never fully explain, and I am embraced by God who loves all of us, not just me.

God of wonder, as I am astounded by the universe, draw me into Your steadfast love that endures forever. —Norm Stolpe

Digging Deeper: Job 38:4–7; Psalms 19:1–6, 136:5–9

Friday, May 22

Do you not know that in a race all the runners run, but only one receives the prize? So run that you may obtain it. —1 Corinthians 9:24 (ESV)

"*Go!*" the announcer shouts, causing the line of preteens to dive into the water.

"Go, Rachel!" my family yells over the crowd. I fall behind, though. I'm not a fast swimmer. "You've got this!"

As the other kids finish swimming and move to biking, the sideline quiets. The other families follow their kids; my family stays.

I'm the last one out of the pool. I drag myself out of the water, run to my bike, grab my gear, and start pedaling. I'm tired, but I'm a better biker than swimmer. Soon I pass someone, then another. I get to the end and slide off my bike. Time for the last segment, running.

I don't start too fast. I keep my pace steady. I start gaining. I pass a few more kids, until there's only one girl ahead of me.

She looks back and sees me. She starts to run faster, but I keep my pace. Ahead of me I see her starting to slow down. I pass her. We play leapfrog a few more times—she bursts past but then loses her momentum and slows down as I pass her. I'm almost to the end, and I speed up.

Dad and some of my siblings run alongside me as I go down the final stretch. I'm the first girl through the finish line.

Although this was many years ago, I still remember this race as my first big lesson in endurance: My race had its ups and downs, but I persevered. With encouragement from my family, I raced with endurance. Now when challenges arise, I know I can face them with God. He'll help me get to the finish line.

Lord, please help me to not give up during discouraging times, but rather to press on and focus on the end goal. —Rachel Thompson

Digging Deeper: Philippians 4:13; Hebrews 12:1–3

Saturday, May 23

In all things you yourself must be an example of good behavior. —Titus 2:7 (GNT)

I was browsing a tool sale in the garage of a retired mechanic. The tools were old, some of them even obsolete. *That's me*, I thought. *Obsolete.* Since I retired from teaching, everything had changed, and I felt like I no longer had anything of value to say.

The mechanic, who had been watching me closely, suddenly spoke up. "Did you used to live over on Fourth Street, way back when?"

I nodded. "That was many years ago."

"Well," he went on, "I remember you. Me and my brothers were just kids, and we lived next door to you. I used to watch you building and fixing things in your backyard. You showed me how to work with wood and how to fix things, like my bike. You're the one who got me interested in tools, which have been my whole life."

I was stunned. I had no memory of teaching those rambunctious boys anything. I was dirt-poor back then, a beginning teacher, trying to improve our old house with some homemade furniture and to keep our old car running.

On the way home I thought more about those four boys, and then about all the other children in my life, such as our neighborhood kids, my great-grandchildren, and children who see me at our church who have read my children's books.

I decided that I am not entirely obsolete after all. As long as little eyes are watching me—and they always are—I am still teaching, in the universal language of example.

Father, I thank You for all the good models You provided for me when I was growing up.
—Daniel Schantz

Digging Deeper: Matthew 5:16;
1 Peter 2:21

Sunday, May 24

**[Jesus] said to them, "Cast the net on the right-hand side of the boat and you will find the fish."
—John 21:6 (NASB)**

In Jesus's encounter with Nathanael, He tells him he has no deceit, and He has seen him under the fig tree—before Nathanael has come anywhere near Him. An astonished Nathanael asks, "How do You know me?" (John 1:48, NASB) and proclaims Jesus the Son of God.

Nathanael appears a second time when Jesus is on the beach after His Resurrection. He is fishing with several of the disciples—casting their net all night without success. Jesus calls to them to cast on the right-hand side of the boat.

When they do, the net is weighted with fish. Nathanael is working side by side with Jesus's inner group—yet he wasn't one of the chosen twelve. I wonder why. It seems he would have made a terrific disciple. He had "cast his net" toward Jesus from the moment he met Him.

Nathanael knew that God's work went far beyond His impact on any one person. I see him humbly disregarding position and loyally filling in wherever he was needed.

Ever since I bragged to my third-grade teacher, "I read on the sixth-grade level," I have struggled with grabbing the limelight in certain areas. I can dazzle in conversation. I can lead the charge in biblical insight. I'm happy to tell of my good deeds. The list is painful.

Nathanael's "no deceit" story shows that pride and boasting—hurt feelings and grudges—have no place in the water between my boat and Jesus.

Jesus, I don't have to fill my net. I cast it toward You, and You take care of the rest. —Carol Knapp

Digging Deeper: John 1:45–51, 21:1–11; Philippians 2:1–4

Memorial Day, Monday, May 25

Now therefore, our God, we thank You and praise Your glorious name. —1 Chronicles 29:13 (NKJV)

I open our front door, and the day is bold and beautiful. The promise of summer is a heartbeat. It pulses through the sunshine. The cloudless sky. The song of the birds. I stand and watch as the Boy Scouts walk down our block bearing flags.

Two young men pause and place an American flag in the holder embedded in our lawn. The breeze lifts the fabric and there's a wave of red, white, and blue. To me, it looks different than it did last year.

In the fall, I had the blessing of accompanying my daddy, a Vietnam veteran, on an Honor Flight. We flew from Iowa to Washington, DC. I stood by Daddy in solemn silence as we paid our respects at the memorials and at the Tomb of the Unknown Soldier. The veterans wore bright yellow windbreakers. I felt out of place in this sacred sea. They understood the deep meaning of sacrifice.

The inscription above the west portico at Arlington National Cemetery, translated from Latin, reads "It is sweet and proper to die for one's country." That fall day, my father and I peered from our bus window at rows after rows of white crosses, pristine in the glory of the sun. Those who gave their breath for the benefit of others.

This giving is more than I can understand.

But now, as I stand behind the glass of my storm door window, I pause as Old Glory rises and falls. Maybe I don't have to understand to be grateful. Maybe my thanksgiving can rise high as the heavens on this perfect, peaceful day that indeed came with a price.

Lord, thank You for those lives that were cut tragically short. They gave the ultimate sacrifice. I thank You for providing for our country. Amen.
—Shawnelle Eliasen

Digging Deeper: Isaiah 41:13; Philippians 4:19

Tuesday, May 26

He who forms the hearts of all, who considers everything they do. —Psalm 33:15 (NIV)

I was miserable. Days ago, a close friend and I had had a falling out. What had started as a simple difference of opinions had escalated until we were truly arguing. It'd been awful, and my brain had not stopped running and rerunning all the painful, angry details since.

Then, so abruptly it could only have been an answer to prayer, those ceaselessly looping thoughts did something unexpected—they shifted. It felt like God had dropped a different lens in front of my eyes, or removed blinders I hadn't even known I was wearing. Suddenly I was able to see the whole situation from a very different point of view—one that looked very much like my friend's. And it was so reasonable, I realized sheepishly, my anger and hurt melting away.

Our ideas had never actually been in conflict. It had only been my fear and insecurity saying otherwise. Our approaches had just been different. But I could see now that different wasn't the same thing as bad. We were separate people with different brains and life experiences. Of course we weren't going to come at everything in the same way. One of us didn't have to be wrong for the other to be right.

It turns out—to my surprise—it's entirely possible to hold, with respect and love, multiple differing yet valid points of view about something at once. It is, after all, what God's all-encompassing love does for each of us, each and every day.

Thank You, God, for this example of Your all-encompassing love at work and for granting me the opportunity to open my mind further, to include more of what's true about Your creation.
—Erin Janoso

Wednesday, May 27

The God of all grace, who called you to his eternal glory in Christ, after you have suffered a little while, will himself restore you and make you strong, firm, and steadfast. —1 Peter 5:10 (NIV)

I drove past the large lake in the neighborhood I used to live in while bringing my kids to their father's house. This was our first year co-parenting after divorcing, and so much about it was difficult.

The lake had always been a place of solitude for me. When my son had brain surgery as a baby, I had strolled around that lake with his carriage to give us both serenity. In the evenings, the dramatic sunset colors in the sky, set behind palm trees, would gloriously refresh my tired spirit. In springtime, the calls of many different baby bird breeds were peaceful music to my ears.

The beauty of the lake was a loss I hadn't even realized I was grieving. That evening, I posted on local social media groups asking for suggestions on a close alternative. I received some recommendations and drove to a new-to-me lake spot before dawn the next day. I hiked through the dark with a flashlight to find the recommended trail. I finally arrived at a majestic pier extending out onto a massive lake. A friendly group of park attendees and I stared in collective awe at the fiery colored sunrise, while ospreys and herons flew by and tiny baby alligators swam near their mothers.

I was grateful that in this time of pain and loss, God had led me to a friendly community and a magnificent lake where I could go to feel restored.

Thank You, Lord, for showing me that You see the desires of my heart. Grant me something vibrant and life-giving in every desert I walk through.
—Nicole Garcia

Digging Deeper: Psalms 51:12, 67:1, 71:20–21; Isaiah 40:31

Thursday, May 28

Pride goes before destruction, a haughty spirit before a fall. —Proverbs 16:18 (NIV)

Fifth grade has been our first foray into competitive softball. My husband, Brian, has wrangled a team of 10-year-old girls from our recreational league to play some fun weekend tournaments against traveling softball teams that practice day in and day out while our girls, well, don't.

In spite of that, our girls were holding their own with my daughter, Olivia, pitching. Batter after batter she would get two easy strikes in and then start celebrating on the mound, her little shoulders starting to shimmy just enough that she could never get that third strike over the plate.

"Don't celebrate!" her dad called out. "Just throw your pitches!" If you've pitched before, you know that routine is the name of the game—throw the same pitch the same way every time. If you start to strut, you're going to be off your rhythm.

We didn't win that game—the other team got several walks and stole around the bases—but we did learn a lot. Olivia learned there's a difference between confidence and celebration, and that one is needed during the trial on the mound and one is better suited to the dugout after the inning is over.

Her mama learned a lot too. While it's important to note milestones in each trial, it's even more important to keep the celebration for the victory. How often do I stop just short of finishing a task to treat myself, then never pick it back up? How many times do I celebrate being almost done, and then never finish?

These days, we encourage Olivia to keep a laser focus on her goal until her task is finished, until she has run her entire race. Then, of course, we celebrate like crazy.

Lord, help me keep my eyes on the prize and push until the work is done. Then give me rest.
—Ashley Kappel

Digging Deeper: Psalm 118;
Isaiah 14:29

SACRED THREADS: Where It All Began

Start children off on the way they should go, and even when they are old they will not turn from it. —Proverbs 22:6 (NIV)

My favorite sampler of all was a gift from my friend Sue. It features a little steepled building with stylized stitches in red: *Little Church Around the Corner.* I attended a church like that 8 days a week, even before I was born. There was Monday night Bible study, Tuesday visitation, Wednesday prayer gathering...

The Sunday evening hymn sing was the best of all. I couldn't have been more than 7 when Mother let me move my pigtailed self to the piano side of the sanctuary—up real close where I could watch the pretty blonde lady with the flying fingers. Her name was Sue, and she became a lifelong friend.

Much later, as an adult, a lifetime of tumor pain led to addiction to prescription meds. When I finally hit the crisis point, I threw a change of clothes in a crumpled brown grocery sack and took my shame to Sue. My body, mind, and spirit were a prison cell. I was the inmate. But instead of steel bars, Sue fixed me a bed-and-breakfast-worthy room cozied with timeworn quilts and a *Gone with the Wind* lamp. She hugged me and went downstairs.

The piano strains from the living room below awakened something that had died inside me. Withdrawing from opioids had rendered me too weak to even pick up my purse, but my soul began to sing. "God Will Take Care of You." "What a Friend We Have in Jesus." "Jesus, Jesus, Jesus, There's Something About That Name." Sue with the Flying Fingers was playing to an audience of one, reaching—and freeing—the prisoner at the top of the stairs.

The church of my childhood never, ever left me, Lord. Thank You. —Roberta Messner

Digging Deeper: Psalms 40:3, 98:1

Saturday, May 30

Grandchildren are the crown of the elderly.
—Proverbs 17:6 (CSB)

When my husband, Kevin, and I decided to take our grandson, Micah, to Washington, DC, I worried about keeping an active 11-year-old boy occupied with our planned agenda to visit the monuments and Smithsonian museums. Would Micah be bored? Would we discover common interests? Would we experience the dreaded preteen eye roll?

As a fact-loving kid, Micah enjoyed the museums. The displays provided plenty of data for his favorite game: Stump the Grown-ups.

"Who was the tenth president of the United States? What's the largest land mammal in North America? Who was the first man to walk on the moon?" His nonstop questions continued as we headed outside to see the monuments.

I could tell Micah was getting antsy, so we were happy to arrive at a kite festival near the Washington Monument.

Soon Micah had a traditional diamond-shaped kite in his hands. As an Arizona boy who lived where there was little wind, he had never flown a kite before. I did not consider myself an expert, but soon I was giving directions.

"Let out more string. Shift your weight to the left. Watch out for the person behind you!"

For more than an hour, Micah soared his kite while we snapped photos against the iconic backdrop, thankful for this bonding activity that would be a lasting memory. As we headed back to the hotel—the new kite carefully folded in Micah's backpack—our grandson flashed the biggest grin.

"Hey, Grandma. What's the capital of New Hampshire?"

Jesus, thank You for stories and experiences that connect the generations. Amen. —Lynne Hartke

Digging Deeper: Psalms 100:5, 127:3–5

Sunday, May 31

Be strong in the Lord, and in the power of His might. Put on the whole armor of God, that you may be able to stand against the wiles of the devil. —Ephesians 6:10–11 (NKJV)

Walking into church, I recognized the first distinctive chords of "I Bind Unto Myself Today," also called "St. Patrick's Breastplate." I gestured approval to the usher, who smiled back. David, our former music director, played organ renditions of the hymn the week of St. Patrick's Day. The congregation sang the beloved behemoth on Trinity Sunday, one week after Pentecost. But David retired, and the new music man didn't know this treasure, the longest and most complicated song in the hymnal. We didn't hear it for 5 years, until David's funeral last spring. And then we sang it this morning.

I can't shake loose the striking chords and affirmations. Legend attributes the text to St. Patrick, claiming that it provides divine protection from an enemy ambush. It vigorously claims the power of God, of faith, of love, and of the beauty and power of nature. Then the prayer takes an unexpected turn in tone, liltingly affirming Christ's comprehensive personal presence—with, in, behind, before, beside, and above . . . "to comfort and restore me." The finale? A return to the dynamic holy binding of oneself to "eternal Father, Spirit, Word."

The song prompts me to turn to the apostle's exhortation in Ephesians 6. Both texts expect me to put on protective gear. Both remind me of God's power and presence.

Lord, as I bind myself to You, help me remember that You are the One who saves the day.
—Evelyn Bence

Digging Deeper: Ephesians 6:10–19

LIVING A NEW LIFE

1 _____

2 _____

3 _____

4 _____

5 _____

6 _____

7 _____

8 _____

9 _____

10 _____

11 _____

12 _____

13 _____

14 _____

15 _____

16 _____

17 _____

18 _____

19 _____

20 _____

21 _____

22 _____

23 _____

24 _____

25 _____

26 _____

27 _____

28 _____

29 _____

30 _____

31 _____

June

For it is by grace you have been saved,
through faith—
and this is not from yourselves,
it is the gift of God—not by works,
so that no one can boast.

—Ephesians 2:8–9 (NIV)

Monday, June 1

ANGEL WHISPERS: Giving Freely

. . . freely give. —Matthew 10:8 (KJV)

Driving home, the angel whisper comes. And it's a doozy.

Give your blue car to Billy's family, it says.

"No," I say out loud. We have just managed to buy a station wagon with a small inheritance. If we could sell our blue car—as opposed to giving it away—it would put us a bit ahead financially for the first time in our marriage.

Give your blue car to Billy's family.

Volunteering at our elementary school, I had gotten to know Billy well. Word was that his family ran a small dairy farm for a local man who was known to hold his workers in servitude. After meeting Billy's mother and visiting with her, I discovered that this was indeed the case. The "boss" had confiscated her and her husband's driver's licenses and threatened to have them arrested if they moved from the little trailer in the mud field where they lived.

Give your blue car to Billy's family.

Back home, I walked into my husband's study. "We're supposed to give Billy's family our blue car." David's face was ashen with disappointment, but we both knew that an escape plan was the only hope for this good family. Determined, we had a lot of work ahead. Dispelling the boss's threats, paying fines for a minor traffic violation, buying insurance, and finally driving Billy's mom to the Department of Motor Vehicles to renew her license.

What a day it was, as David, our children, Brock and Keri, and I stood and watched her drive the blue car away, license in hand, to pick up her family and head north.

A few weeks later we got the letter: "Our relatives got my husband a plumber's job. We have our own place. Billy's in school. We are free. Thank you . . . "

Father God, thank YOU. —Pam Kidd

Digging Deeper: Proverbs 3:27; Hebrews 13:16

Tuesday, June 2

In your unfailing love you will lead the people you have redeemed. —Exodus 15:13 (NIV)

Even after I received degrees in theology and was working in church ministry, the thought that God loved me was more of a head experience than a heart experience.

All of that changed one day when my wife told me, "Our puppies really love you." Wow! Something instantly shifted inside of me.

Reflecting on this, I realized that doing things for other people always kept me in control of my relationships. It was actually easier for me to give than receive. Then I thought about God's love for me. To receive God's love meant I had to be vulnerable. But what if God's love was withdrawn?

What if God's love asked difficult things of me? What if I have to be beholden to God? It felt scary.

But now, with my puppies in my lap, it all felt different somehow. Their love is freely given, just as God's love is freely given. As they lay in my lap, one sleeping and one looking at me adoringly, I rested in their love, knowing that it was unconditional. They helped me see God's unconditional love for me in a whole new way—as a place of safety and rest. Something to seek out rather than to seek to control.

God had to use puppies to break through my fragile heart. As I type this, Molly and Buddy are playing by my feet. What an extraordinary gift.

O Lord, may my life be a lifelong praise to You. Amen. —Adam Ruiz

Digging Deeper: Deuteronomy 6:5; Isaiah 54:10; Matthew 12:18

Wednesday, June 3

Carry each other's burdens, and in this way you will fulfill the law of Christ. —Galatians 6:2 (NIV)

Frustrated with my friend Leanne, I headed out to work in my garden. I figured I could take out my displeasure by weeding between the rows. Leanne and I had planned to attend a Bible conference in October. I made sure she was committed, because several times in the past she had canceled at the last minute. As soon as the registration was open, I paid for the conference and booked the hotel and flights.

Now, a week before we were scheduled to leave, Leanne did it again. She called, apologized with some flimsy excuse, and canceled. Remembering our all-too-short conversation, I yanked at a stubborn weed.

All the planning, all the expense. I should have known. What kind of friend was she, anyway?

I continued grumbling under my breath as I worked my way down the row. With my energy spent, I looked down at the pile of wilting weeds and realized they were like my negative thoughts: useless. Instead of letting my disappointment get the better of me, I needed to pray and uncover the real reason Leanne had canceled, convinced it wasn't the one she'd mentioned.

With my head and my heart in a better place, I called Leanne and asked what I could do to help her. It didn't take long to learn she'd been going through a difficult time fighting depression. We discussed what was going on in her life, and afterward she agreed that the best way to deal with the darkness was to step into the light.

Leanne and I thoroughly enjoyed the conference. We were blessed by every single session—so much so that we both signed up for the same conference the following year.

Friends are precious, Father, and I thank You for Leanne. Help us continue to encourage each other.
—Debbie Macomber

Digging Deeper: Ecclesiastes 4:9–12; Proverbs 27:17

Thursday, June 4

Everything they do is done for people to see.
—Matthew 23:5 (NIV)

"Hey, Mom," Aurora piped up from the back seat, where she'd been reading a magazine on our drive home from school. "Did you know that the word *polite* comes from *polish*?"

I hadn't known that, but we both wanted to know more, so when we got home, we looked the words up in the Online Etymology Dictionary. And sure enough—it said that *polite* comes from the Latin word *politus*, which means "refined, elegant, accomplished"—literally "polished," because it is the past participle of *polire*, "to polish, to make smooth."

"So they're both about how people act and how things feel on their surfaces," I told Aurora. I thought of the Pharisees and the well-polished exteriors of their cups. Jesus made no secret about what He thought of those, yet it's still a trap I fall into all the time. Because working on polishing the inside of my cup means I first must allow it to be seen, and it's so much easier to worry about policing behavior—mine and others'—than it is to risk showing those imperfect, unpolished parts of myself to the world.

But then I think about those moments when I've felt most loved. It sure wasn't when I'd finally managed to convince someone of my refined manners or perfect rule-following. Quite the opposite. It was when all those things failed me, and, braced for rejection, I'd found real and tender acceptance instead.

In moments like that, I'm so grateful to know that God's already fully aware of what's on the inside of my cup, and that His strength is made perfect via those very weaknesses.

Your love is perfect, God. I'm not. Thank You for sharing it with me anyway. —Erin Janoso

Digging Deeper: Matthew 23:25–26;
2 Corinthians 12:9

Friday, June 5

You make known to me the path of life; you will fill me with joy in your presence, with eternal pleasures at your right hand. —Psalm 16:11 (NIV)

I'm sometimes asked how I find ideas for my devotions. I'd love to say they are divinely given, but it's not that easy and I'm not that blessed. I think the Lord wants me to work a little harder.

The first devotion I ever wrote, some 30 years ago, was a story about a minor spat between my late wife, Julee, and me concerning the exact measurement of ingredients for perfect guacamole. I had no idea what to do with the piece until my editor pointed out that buried in the disagreement was a faith lesson about marriage and love.

That was good writing advice and even better spiritual guidance. I became a kind of detective searching for clues of God's presence in my daily life. The more I searched, the more I discovered evidence of His divine touch in the otherwise most ordinary moments—bathing my dog, interviewing a prospective employee, changing a flat tire, filing my taxes. Nothing was too small for God to have a part in. It was for me to recognize those conjunctions.

Not all these clues amount to a devotion. Most don't. But they open my eyes to the tangible wonder of God's presence, reminders that moment by moment I never walk through life alone. I believe everyone can find these clues whether they write devotions or not—for the lesson is in the moment, there for us to discover.

Where did I get the idea for this devotional? One of you asked!

Lord, help my soul see what my eyes don't.
—Edward Grinnan

Digging Deeper: Psalms 23:1–6, 27:4

Saturday, June 6

Peace I leave you, My peace I give you; not as the world gives, do I give to you. Do not let your hearts be troubled, nor fearful. —John 14:27 (NASB)

My sister and I stood at the sliding glass door of our oceanfront hotel in the Bahamas watching the unexpected storm. Rain pelted the glass. The wind rattled the windows with its fury. The sea raged. Yesterday it had been a lovely, tranquil blue. Today it was gray, foamy, and fierce. Sandy enjoys watching storms. Me, not so much. Besides, the weather was keeping us confined to our hotel instead of strolling the beach to look for shells and enjoying conch stew on the restaurant's patio.

Ever cheerful, Sandy retrieved a deck of cards from her suitcase and challenged me to a gin rummy competition. As I tried to swallow my disappointment, I couldn't help but think of other unexpected squalls in life that dash one's hopes and ruin one's plans—tragic accidents, job loss, the death of a loved one. I reminded myself that Jesus, the master of the sea, calmed the storm without any difficulty at all. He understands life's storms too.

American author Willa Cather once said, "There are some things you learn best in calm, and some in storm." That's true. Through the squalls of life, I've learned patience. I've witnessed goodness and kindness. I've learned to trust God more fully, knowing He is more than able to see us through any situation in life, no matter how overwhelmed we might feel at the time.

The Lord indeed saw us through that squall too. He blessed us the next day with sunshine, which we enjoyed immensely while relishing another bowl of spicy conch stew on the restaurant patio.

Precious Jesus, thank You for being with me during life's storms.
—Shirley Raye Redmond

Sunday, June 7

**I consider that the sufferings of this present time
are not worth comparing with the glory that is to
be revealed to us. —Romans 8:18 (ESV)**

On a balmy June Sunday, I glanced down at my
phone and saw a message from Snow's caretaker.
Six months prior, our family had made a tough
decision to rehome our horse, Snow, since my
daughter's skill had outgrown her and we wanted
Snow to be able to teach other little girls to ride.
The message explained Snow had had an accident
and would be euthanized the following day.

My family was completely gutted. With tears and
a heavy heart, I and my children, Jacques and JoElla,
rushed immediately to Snow's side. Not knowing
the condition we would find her, we prayed for
Snow's comfort and prayed we would have strength
for the goodbye we never planned on having.

When we reached Snow, she was alone in a
stall and immediately whinnied when she saw us.
She remembered! She put her head down, like old
times, and I rubbed the top of her forehead. We
spent some time with Snow, then clipped part of
her tail to take home with us, thankful Snow's new
caretaker allowed us this time with her.

On the way home, Jacques asked why I took part of her tail. I explained there was a horsey-people saying, "The best horses in heaven—they have no tail." I explained our piece of Snow's tail would be a physical remembrance to keep her close to us.

We commemorated Snow's place in our lives with a bracelet and an ornament. Our little mementos of Snow still remind us that God bestowed the blessing of a lifetime on our family when He gave us Snow to love.

Dear Lord, may we continually seek Your comfort in times of hardship and open our hearts to Your blessings. Amen.
—Jolynda Strandberg

Digging Deeper: Psalm 147:2–6; Matthew 5:2–11; Revelation 21:1–4

Monday, June 8

In peace I will lie down and sleep, for you alone, Lord, make me dwell in safety.
—**Psalm 4:8 (NIV)**

"Let's go see the birds," my mom said as we entered the zoo with my three kids in tow. "They sound like they're wide awake this morning!"

When we rounded the corner to the outdoor bird area, a maze with netted sections for the various birds, we saw that they were indeed wide awake, and frantic! The zookeepers were in the netted enclosures trying to capture the small birds, who were flying desperately around the exhibits. Normally these birds sat mostly still, chirping happily. Today they looked panicked.

That's when we saw it—sitting on a branch right above the nets was a large wild hawk. We don't live far from the zoo, and we'd seen this hawk before. She sits royally, perched high in tall oak trees.

"They don't know they're safe," Olivia, my nine-year-old, said of the birds flapping wildly in their cages. "They think the hawk can get them." She was right, and that's why the zookeepers were working to capture them and place them in indoor enclosures until the hawk moved along.

How many times do I see challenges and trials, the looming "hawks" of my life, and spiral into a frenzied dance of evasion, darting here and there while God desperately tries to corral my flailing spirit? *I am here. You are safe.*

Next time life sends a hawk my way, I pray that I will pause to remember that I am safe in my net with the best zookeeper on earth looking out for me.

Lord, keep the hawks of my life at bay, and when they circle, remind me that You are there to help me along the way. —Ashley Kappel

Digging Deeper: Colossians 3:15;
2 Thessalonians 3:16

JOURNEY THROUGH GRIEF: Well-Lived
"Well done, good and faithful servant!"
—Matthew 25:23 (NIV)

Days before my father's funeral, I went through hundreds of photographs to display his life on giant foam boards. I created a video montage, wrote his eulogy, and typed up his favorite hymn in English and Spanish.

In my sorrow, I found comfort in presenting his life to those who would come to say goodbye. They all knew and loved him, but did they know the whole story? Did they know the impoverished little boy, the pastor who graduated seminary at the age of 54, the loving husband of more than half a century, or the golfer who made a hole-in-one as a senior citizen after just a few years of learning?

Every picture, every word, gave testimony to a life well lived—not by wealth or worldly achievements but through perseverance, compassion, faith, and love. What more could you ask for in the life of a man?

Toward the end of the service, one of my cousins unexpectedly stepped up to speak. "As many of you may know, I'm an atheist," my cousin said. "I have never questioned my assertion that God does not exist . . . until right now."

He went on to say that if such a great man could put his faith in the Lord, who was he to think that God is not real?

The day I laid my father to rest was not dominated by sorrow as I had expected. What I felt, above all, was gratitude for the purposeful life he lived. A purpose still very much alive.

Lord, may I live a life so filled with purpose that it ripples through the lives of others, well after I come home to be with You. —Karen Valentin

Digging Deeper: Philippians 1:6; 2 Timothy 4:7

Wednesday, June 10

So be truly glad. There is wonderful joy ahead, even though you must endure many trials for a little while. —1 Peter 1:6 (NLT)

The moment my husband and I saw the words Crazy Woman Canyon on the map, we designated it our adventure for the day.

Located west of Buffalo, Wyoming, an uneven dirt road meanders along Crazy Woman Creek through soaring rock cliffs and towering trees. Boulders the size of a school bus had broken off and rolled toward the creek over the years, creating multiple driving obstacles and a rough ride. But our four-wheel-drive vehicle conquered the difficulties like a professional bull rider. After miles of rugged wilderness, the terrain leveled out, the forest thinned away to an open meadow, and we stopped in awe of the beauty before us—a 180-degree vista stretching for hundreds of miles over Wyoming's spacious hills and valleys.

Later we heard there are two stories about how this canyon got its name. Both of them revolve around women who suffered tragic losses and went insane as a result. Reflecting on the contrast between the area's natural splendor and the heartbreaking stories surrounding it, I thought about the sudden turns our own life can take.

One second everything is grand, and the next one brings hardship. Sometimes the trouble results from our actions. Other times we're impacted by the behavior of family or strangers. Many times the trials come from an act of nature or the effects of illness. Regardless of the problem, God always rewards endurance and provides relief.

In the same way that our bumpy ride through Crazy Woman Canyon ended with a magnificent view, the Lord promises the end of our personal trials will give us a greater reward: peace and joy.

Heavenly Father, bless us with strength to endure life's trials, faith to trust Your promise they will end, and abundant joy when we complete the journey. Thank You for traveling with us along the way. —Jenny Lynn Keller

Digging Deeper: Isaiah 55:12; 2 Thessalonians 1:3–5; James 1:2–4, 12

Thursday, June 11

You anoint my head with oil; my cup overflows. —Psalm 23:5 (NIV)

Worries over church finances knotted up my mind as the horseshoer, Jim Bob, set Jack's hoof down and picked up his tools. I'd recently become church treasurer, although I lacked any accounting background. Wrestling with payroll and nonprofit corporation taxes had nearly defeated me.

The horseshoer lifted Jack's knotted tail and asked if my tail comb had broken in the past two months. I hung my head. Last time I let Jack's tail get knotted, conditioners didn't help. Jack hated my tugging so much that I ended up cutting it off.

"Use olive oil," Jim Bob said. "Pour it on heavy and run him in sagebrush. It'll comb out on its own."

It wouldn't hurt to try the oil, but I could do better than sagebrush for a comb. Every day after that, I combed Jack's tail while he ate grain. I untangled the bottom 2 inches in 10 minutes. Then I freed two more the day after that. Bit by bit, inch by inch, Jack's tail unraveled. The impossible task became possible. Jack tolerated small doses. Combing was rhythmic and calming for Jack and for me. Before long, the knot was gone.

Just as the simplest advice from an expert helped me free the hopeless knot in Jack's tail, I needed to ask for guidance with the church's finances. After one hour with a tax professional, the solution was just as simple.

Lord, thanks for smoothing my path and for reminding me that asking for help doesn't mean that I've failed. —Erika Bentsen

---

Friday, June 12

**The seed falling on good soil refers to someone who hears the word and understands it. This is the one who produces a crop, yielding a hundred, sixty or thirty times what was sown.
—Matthew 13:23 (NIV)**

I was still stewing over something that had come to mind in my morning prayer time, an unpleasant memory—a moment when I hadn't behaved at my best. *Why do these things come up when I'm sitting here in prayer, Lord, offering myself up to You?* I wondered. No answer. At least not then.

A good while later, after I'd eaten my breakfast, done some work, and finished my lunch, I was putting stuff in the compost bucket we keep in the kitchen—an apple core, a lemon rind, the toast that I'd burned. I was disgruntled to note that the bucket was full. Now I'd have to take it down the block to the compost bin in our neighborhood. What a bother. It would have been so much easier to dump it in the trash.

And at once I made the connection. Dump it in the trash? Wasn't this whole compost effort a great spiritual reminder of the nutrients that could be found in our griefs and regrets, our painful times of mourning, when we put them into the Lord's hands? What seemed to be only useless loss could be transformed by God's power into rich soil.

As I dumped the bucket into the bin, I could almost smell that process happening. This trash could become just like the fertile soil Jesus spoke of. Transformative.

Lord, help me dig deep and grow in Your fertile soil, seeing how the pains and sorrows of life are healed and changed. —Rick Hamlin

Digging Deeper: Ecclesiastes 3:1; Romans 12:1–2; 2 Corinthians 5:17

Saturday, June 13

THE BIRDS OF MY NEIGHBORHOOD: Messages of Hope and Healing

Then the word of the Lord came to Elijah: "Leave here, turn eastward . . . I have directed the ravens to supply you with food there." . . . The ravens brought him bread and meat in the morning and bread and meat in the evening. —1 Kings 17:2–4, 6 (NIV)

The farmers around me have been blessed with abundant harvests the past few years. And along with them we've been blessed by an abundance of crows. Crows in the corn have been a theme in poems, songs, and popular culture for millennia. Usually it's not a positive image. After all, a flock of them is called a murder. Crows are often seen as robbers or harbingers of disaster of some sort. But being the contrarian I am, I don't find them so. I have some support in the Bible. In Scripture, ravens—a relative of crows that share much of the same symbolism—can also convey messages of hope and healing. In today's Bible passage, they feed the prophet Elijah.

I find these big black birds fascinating. They caw to each other, loudly. They swoop and soar. They are an avian breed of Walt Whitman's singing a song of their selfhood. I sometimes, to my chagrin, do that too.

Crows are fascinated by shiny things. At least that's a long-held folk belief. Like the crows, I often am too. Sometimes I'm too loud. Oftentimes too easily distracted. Even in the silence of Quaker worship, if I spy an interesting car zipping by outside the meeting room windows, I'm captivated. Or I offer a message that comes more from myself than God's Spirit.

I want to be like the ravens in the Elijah story, providing spiritual sustenance but not getting too distracted or full of myself. If I do, I must step back and recenter.

**You who are never distracted, teach me
to focus my life in and on You. Call to me
with the voice of love and correction. Amen.**
—J. Brent Bill

Digging Deeper: Luke 10:38–42

Sunday, June 14

The one who was dying blessed me.
—Job 29:13 (NIV)

A friend I had worked with, Wally, was diagnosed with cancer. Months later tests showed the cancer wasn't slowing. He decided to stop the chemotherapy. I wanted to see him. I was uncomfortable with what I would say and wondered if he would even want visitors in his final days. I shared my concern with a mutual friend who said, "Call him anyway."

I asked God to guide me in the call with Wally and to find a comfortable way to spend time with him. Early the next morning, before I even called, another friend called asking if I would join him in spending an afternoon watching a baseball game with Wally. Wally loved baseball. His team was in the playoffs. While he couldn't go to the game, he invited us to come to his home and watch it on TV.

After we arrived, Wally shared the latest on his situation and then quickly moved us into baseball. It was a joyful afternoon. Three friends hanging out together—watching a game, exchanging stories, talking baseball, and enjoying pizza. It was the last time I saw Wally.

I will always remember that once I asked for God's help, everything fell into place in a way that exceeded anything I could have planned. Nothing about our time with him was uncomfortable—except saying goodbye. My friend and I were blessed with a lasting memory of being with Wally doing something he loved.

Dear God, lead us to become comfortable spending time with others in their most difficult days. Help us remember that it is not about our words but about Your presence and words through us that bring comfort in their time of need.
—John Dilworth

Digging Deeper: Psalm 23:3–4; Proverbs 3:5; John 3:16

Monday, June 15

All of you who were baptized into Christ have clothed yourselves with Christ. —Galatians 3:27 (NIV)

I was sorting some old files recently when I came across my baptismal certificate, dated June 15, 1951. I was nine then, and attending a Christian camp, where my minister-father was the camp dean.

I remember that during a chapel message I learned that I needed to be baptized, but I was afraid to "go forward" in front of all those campers. I have since learned that many people are afraid of baptism, for different reasons. My wife was one of those people; baptism scared her because of her fear of drowning.

On the last day of camp, the chapel speaker presented the Crucifixion of Christ with such drama that I was overwhelmed with love for the Lord, who had suffered so much for me. Tears rolled down my tender young cheeks, and I knew I had to find a way through my fears.

So I went to my father and said, "Daddy, I want to be baptized, but I'm afraid to go forward." He hugged me and said, "That's great, Danny! I am baptizing some campers right after lunch, and you can just join them." I was so relieved.

The sky was cloudy when I waded out into the shallow, rocky creek to be immersed by my own beloved father. I was wearing blue jeans and a white T-shirt when he lowered me into the water, but when I came up, I was clothed in the righteousness of Christ. It was the happiest day of my life and a fresh start for the future.

Love is what got me past my fears that day, and I still find that love is stronger than fear.

Thank You, Lord, for offering us a new chance at life. —Daniel Schantz

Digging Deeper: Ephesians 4:23–24; Colossians 3:9–10

Tuesday, June 16

THE LONELY AMONG US: Becoming a Contact Initiator

Do not seek revenge or bear a grudge against anyone among your people, but love your neighbor as yourself. I am the Lord.
—Leviticus 19:18 (NIV)

Throughout my twenties, I lived alone and moved frequently. I was predictably lonely in each new place but loneliest upon returning to my hometown, where my friends were busy with lives that excluded me. I longed to hang out as we had before but balked, as many lonely people do, at initiating contact, certain it was the wrong time, they were busy with something more important, and maybe they didn't even like me anymore.

Eventually I married, had kids, and settled into my own busy life, unconsciously becoming like my old friends: oblivious to the lonely ones surrounding me.

When I later became a believer, it struck me that the command to love my "neighbors"— etymologically "near ones" in Greek as in English— didn't mean far-off strangers but people I was close to but didn't really love. Friends who'd abandoned me. Disgruntled coworkers. Siblings who'd become physically and ideologically distant.

Remembering my lonely years, I decided to initiate contact in these relationships. It was hard initially, especially without some business or holiday to prompt the exchange. Who calls just to chat? What would we talk about? What if we got on an irritating topic?

Our resulting interactions simultaneously confirmed and dispelled my fears. People *don't* call to chat, making such calls pleasant surprises. People *are* preoccupied with more important things, the discussion of which helped us know each other better. Sometimes they irritated me, and I them, but our burgeoning habits of listening grew us. My discovery that each one shared my desire for closeness—*and* my reluctance to initiate it—rendered God's love mandate an effortless delight.

> **Father-God, help me hug close those You've put near me.** —Patty Kirk

> **Digging Deeper:** Mark 11:12–25; 1 Corinthians 13

Wednesday, June 17

You undid my sackcloth and girded me with joy. —Psalm 30:12 (JPS)

All my life, I'd been compulsive about saving money. My husband, Keith, sometimes called me Yulianoff the Saver, a name taken from a long-ago ad for a bank. His philosophy had always been, "When I have money in my pocket, I spend it." We compromised on a reasonable amount of spending: I paid the down payment on the house, and he paid the monthly mortgage, until, by banking two-thirds of my corporate salary for a year, I had saved enough to pay the 30-year mortgage off in 14 years.

After he died, saving became impossible for me, because I kept refusing to take anything more than a pittance from my retirement account (into which his had been absorbed). Without Keith's Social Security income, all the expenses we had been sharing landed on me, and of course, the cost of everything went up much faster than any cost of living allowance. I shared my growing dissatisfaction with the administrator of my accounts, and Dana said calmly, "Well, if you don't want to spend it, your heirs will have a good time spending it for you."

That took a while to sink in. I had always been taught that when God greets you after you die, you will be scolded for every bit of joy you had denied yourself in life. I wanted to be careful enough so that I would not run out of money before I ran out of a pulse, but I discovered soon that part of joy for me was the joy of giving to organizations that helped others. And I was pretty certain I could justify that if God asked me about it later.

It took a great deal of willpower for me to start spending any of the money I worked so hard to save, O Lord, but I am delighted when I can use it to help people. I know You'll approve when I get there. —Rhoda Blecker

Digging Deeper: Ecclesiastes 5:19; Proverbs 11:4

Thursday, June 18

Every time I think of you, I give thanks to my God. —Philippians 1:3 (NLT)

Lou, a former member of the church in Armonk, New York, where I served as the founding pastor, sent a text with several pictures of a building. Underneath he wrote, "What a strange feeling . . . like it never existed." I didn't recognize the building or location but kept looking until it came back to me. This was where the La Quinta Hotel had been located, the place where our church had gathered for worship. Now on that site was a warehouse.

At first I felt like Lou—with the hotel gone, it was as if the people we had known then and the times we had shared had never existed. Then the memories came rushing back of the moments, conversation, services, and gatherings we had as a church. It reminded me that the building is not the church—the people are the church.

When my son was seriously injured in a car accident, it was the people of the church who prayed, visited him at the hospital, and cooked dinners for us. In our most difficult season, the community of faith surrounded us with love, care, and support.

There's a saying that goes, "People come into your life for a reason, a season, or a lifetime." Although it has been more than 15 years since I served that congregation, I was blessed by the people God put in my path and our times together.

Lou summed it up well at the end of his text: "What we had during our time was very special in so many ways." Even if it was for a season.

Lord, thank You for the people who come across our path or into our life for a reason, season, or lifetime. —Pablo Diaz

---

Juneteenth, Friday, June 19

Let us not become weary in doing good, for at the proper time we will reap a harvest if we do not give up. —Galatians 6:9 (NIV)

My community's Juneteenth celebration this year was the largest my town had seen. The Juneteenth Sneaker Ball, replete with a live R & B band, dancing, a delicious soul-food meal, and an ever-popular 360-degree photo booth, was a spectacular event. The most fun of all was enjoying the dancing, eating, and socializing while guests sported their favorite high-top Nikes, Vans, and Jordans.

During the program, we enjoyed our meal of fried chicken, macaroni and cheese, and candied sweet potatoes while listening to the vision of the justice and equity organization that sponsored this annual event. The organization honored various people and organizations that were leading our community in diversity and equity efforts. A high-light was cheering on my husband, Anthony, and our good friend Brad as they received accolades and a commemorative award for the community organization they had cofounded 3 years before. I couldn't have been prouder to witness the honor they received for their commitment to providing free monthly community gatherings that promote antiracism through education.

Another standout of the evening was the racial, economic, and cultural diversity of people on the stage and in the audience. The people working toward equity, justice, and unity were representative of the people who live in my community—Black, White, Indigenous, Asian, Hispanic, and every other color and creed. On that night, we celebrated the freedom from enslavement that the original Juneteenth represents, while envisioning an even greater freedom and flourishing for people of all races, cultures, and socioeconomic groups in our county, our country, and our world.

Lord, help us not grow weary as we continue to work for liberty and justice for all.
—Carla Hendricks

Digging Deeper: Philippians 2:1–8; 1 John 3:16, 4:16–21

Saturday, June 20

Beware of practicing your righteousness before other people in order to be seen by them, for then you will have no reward from your Father who is in heaven. —Matthew 6:1 (ESV)

"Do you think I'll ever be famous again?" the older man asked me. We were outside at a community event, and he was a stranger. "I'm 80," he said. "This is when you say, 'You don't look 80.'" He smiled. "I once was a famous artist. If I tell you who I am, you would recognize my name. But now, no one knows me."

I leaned in. He was talking to me, but there was no context. I suppose it was because I was standing near him. Or perhaps the thought had just come to him, and he had to ask someone.

"Do you want to be famous?" I asked.

"Maybe," he said. "What about you? Do you want to be famous?"

"What's it like being famous?"

"I don't really know. I was famous until I wasn't." Then he smiled. "I heard the potato salad is good. Nice talking to you."

He walked away. I still have no idea who he was or is, or if it matters—but since then I've thought about our conversation and what it means to be famous, especially today when so many are famous simply for being famous.

I settled on the sentiment of the verse Matthew 6:1: find your passion and pursue it; do it with the intention of love and not to be seen.

Lord, thank You for the lesson from a stranger's heart that was guided by Your Word.
—Sabra Ciancanelli

Digging Deeper: Proverbs 22:1; Ecclesiastes 4:4; Luke 14:11; James 4:6

Father's Day, Sunday, June 21

Father of the fatherless and protector of widows is God in his holy habitation.
—Psalm 68:5 (ESV)

I stepped into the little cafe deep in the Honduran interior. I was excited. As a touring musician representing Compassion International, I was being given the rare opportunity to meet Henry, my family's sponsored child. I spotted him at a table, his back to me, holding a picture of my family in trembling hands. I couldn't fault his trepidation. I was a little nervous myself.

"*Hola*, Henry," I said.

He turned and stood. Eight, but small for his age. Hair slicked. Pressed white shirt and blue slacks. His eyes an equal blend of tension and innocence.

Up to now I'd only heard Henry's story through letters. His mother battled cancer. He'd never known his father. But there, looking down at this little man trying so hard to put on a brave face, my already cracked heart broke completely. I knelt, pulled him into a hug, and silently vowed that this boy who'd already endured so much would be fatherless no more.

It strikes me that I'm much like Henry. Here I sit in the shadowland clinging to a picture. Waiting by faith, not by sight. But my Advocate is on the way. Soon I will see Him face to face. I'll feel His arms around me. I will look upon my Father, and I will forever be His son.

How time flies! Henry has grown into a fine young man. Through the years, letters and the internet have done much to diminish the distance. He's coming for a visit this spring. My son. I can't wait to hug him and welcome him home.

Dear God in heaven, thank You that we are orphans no longer but adopted as Your children. Happy Father's Day. —Buck Storm

Digging Deeper: Isaiah 64:7; 2 Corinthians 6:16–18; 1 John 3:1

Monday, June 22

THE FIVE LOVE LANGUAGES: Starting the Journey
What a person desires is unfailing love.
—Proverbs 19:22 (NIV)

What was missing? When my husband, Chuck, and I got married, life seemed perfect. I had found my soulmate, someone who understood me and wanted to be with me. For the first time in my life, I felt wanted and loved perfectly. Our first year was proverbial bliss, with no disagreements or misunderstandings. Or so I thought.

But I began to be afraid something was missing from our relationship. I was certain God had put us together, so why was I concerned? The courtship over, we'd returned to our normal worlds of work and other commitments. However, I wondered why Chuck wasn't showing me his love the way I expected. Why didn't he bring me flowers or gifts like other husbands did?

It's not that he neglected me. On the contrary, he checked in during the day, and if I asked him to do something, he always obliged. But I wanted more, like telling me I was beautiful (if just to make me believe it), or smart. I wanted him to give me praise and recognition.

One day I stopped by the office of the minister who married us. When he asked me how things were going, I told him I was worried. He asked why, so I gave him examples. He pulled a book from his shelf and handed it to me. "Here, you and Chuck need to read this." I took home the book, *The Five Love Languages* by Gary Chapman, and asked Chuck to read it too. As a result, our eyes were opened to understanding and appreciating the different ways that we show and receive love. Over the next few devotions in this series, I'll show you what I learned about the five love languages—acts of service, words of affirmation, physical touch, gifts, quality time— and how we use them to express our love to others.

Lord, thank You that You first loved us. Help me see how others show love and how I can show love in return. —Marilyn Turk

Digging Deeper: Proverbs 3:3; Ephesians 5:33; 1 John 4:18

Tuesday, June 23

My eyes are awake before the watches of the night, that I may meditate on your promise. —Psalm 119:148 (ESV)

When my six-year-old, Beau, was little, he got in the habit of sneaking downstairs and into our bed, a practice I loved until his tiny elbows found the curve of my spine. Nevertheless, we welcomed him in, encouraging him to find us if he needed us.

As he grew, I noticed that he no longer crawled into that safe space. I assumed he was sleeping more deeply until one night when I heard the tip-tap of his feet. He made his way to our door, paused, then turned around.

"It's OK, Beau," I said. "You can come in." I scooched over to make room for him.

"No, that's OK, Mom," he said. "I was just checking."

For the next few nights, I noticed him doing the same thing—waking up, walking down, peeking at us, then going back to his own bed.

In the light of day, we had a little chat. It turns out, Beau didn't need our snuggles or words. When he woke at night, he just needed to be in our presence for a minute before returning to the comfort of his warm bed.

It almost felt like a prayer to me—how often do I wake and need to be in God's presence before I can fall back asleep? The days are so busy that the middle of the nights feel almost holy. "Bless my neighbor." "Be with our cousins." "Help me be wise about work."

As Beau grows, we'll talk to him about saving his steps and instead turning to Jesus to find that safety while safe in his sheets. Until then, I'm glad to know that he can find peace within—with the help of a glimpse of Mom and Dad's bed.

Lord, let Your presence be my calm.
—Ashley Kappel

Digging Deeper: Matthew 6:6; John 16:33

Wednesday, June 24

I thank Christ Jesus . . . because He considered me faithful, putting me into service.
—1 Timothy 1:12 (NASB)

Several years ago my cardiologist installed a pacemaker—or peacemaker, as I call it. I had just had my annual pacemaker interrogation, which showed it was working nearly three-fourths of the time to keep my heart rate at a steady pace. I became interested in who invented this wondrous device—not expecting what I found.

Born in 1919 in Buffalo, New York, Wilson Greatbatch was fascinated by wireless radio in the 1920s. "Something was happening that you couldn't see or feel," he said. He was a radioman in World War II, then received an electrical engineering degree from Cornell University under the GI Bill.

While working for a doctor at the Chronic Disease Institute in Buffalo in 1956, he experimented with a circuit to record fast heart sounds. He accidentally plugged the wrong resistor into his circuit—and in amazement found the circuit pulsed to the beat of the human heart.

Greatbatch—a follower of Jesus—later stated, "It was no accident. The Lord was working through me." His implantable cardiac pacemaker has since saved millions of lives.

I was four years old when he made his astonishing discovery. Now, seven decades later, I am one of the millions it has saved. I am filled with gratitude, especially when I read Romans 12:5: "So we, who are many, are one body in Christ, and individually parts of one another" (NASB).

God's hand, gifting and guiding His child long before my heart knew it would need his great invention, speaks of His faithfulness to me—also His child. I hear His clear call to use the gifts He has given me to match the beat of His heart for humankind.

Father—the needs are great. But working through Your children, so are You. —Carol Knapp

Digging Deeper: Psalm 40:5; Ephesians 2:10, 4:4

Thursday, June 25

Thanks be to God, who gives us the victory through our Lord Jesus Christ. —1 Corinthians 15:57 (ESV)

In an out-of-the-way corner of a used bookstore, I found a shelf of titles labeled "Lists." Perhaps I was in a critical mood, but somehow each list seemed—I don't know. Incomplete.

Take, for instance, the book on the seven cardinal sins. Actually, there should be eight. The last one is ingratitude. I'm not talking about mere sloth or apathy—I'm talking about genuine lack of thankfulness for the profound gifts we've been given. I should know. I'm guilty of this deadly sin, and it is, in fact, deadly: dead to the blessings of this life.

Speaking of deadly: same with the five stages of grief—denial, bargaining, depression, anger, acceptance. This list misses the last, toughest stage: *Now what? Acceptance* sounds as if everything's going to be OK. It is not. Grief alters everything, and even when you've come to accept your loss, that uncertain future is still staring at you, waiting, asking, *Now what?*

Finally, there are the five love languages—words of affirmation, acts of service, gifts, quality time, physical touch. They missed one: acts of foolishness. This love language is for those of us who flail about in our relationships, desperate to communicate to our spouses, our siblings, our kids, our friends.

Luckily St. Paul saw this one coming. We can be fools for Christ, he said. Standing there in the dusty used bookstore, I realized I had found a complete list of everything we need to know—the Bible. It's only one item, but somehow it's the only list we need.

Lord, let me always remember that Jesus is the Rock of our salvation, a sure and eternal refuge, the foundation on which rests the hope of heaven.
—Mark Collins

Digging Deeper: Job 28; Hebrews 13:15

Friday, June 26

Think of the kindness you wish others would show you; do the same for them.
—Luke 6:31 (VOICE)

I was draped across my lounge chair like a human towel. It wasn't only the Phoenix heat that had sapped my energy; it was spending a week with my granddaughter Shea. Our time together in Arizona was a much-anticipated one-on-one adventure. But Shea had been adopted out of foster care, and she had a lot of baggage. And, apparently, Shea had packed all of it to bring along on our vacation.

However, for the last hour, my often-sullen granddaughter had been giggling, singing, and chatting animatedly with my friend Pam. Shea was more visibly joyful than I'd seen her in a long time. Why? Because Shea had Pam's undivided attention. As they played together in Pam's pool, Pam encouraged, challenged, and praised Shea's efforts to swim under a pool noodle, over and over again. If the sun hadn't gone down, I think Shea could have continued indefinitely.

Watching this interaction between Pam and Shea was like attending a master class on learning to love well. What Shea wanted most was to be seen, heard, and wholeheartedly accepted for the one-of-a-kind individual God created her to be. Pam brought out the best in Shea because Pam was focused on the best in Shea. She treated my granddaughter the way we all want to be treated—with love.

I can't spend every minute focused totally on Shea. When we're together, I often have to prepare meals, clean up messes, or drive carpools. It's the eternal Mary vs. Martha dilemma, evident in Luke 10. But as Jesus directed, it's best to lean toward love, erring more on the side of Mary, or my intuitive friend, Pam.

Lord, please help me focus more on loving others than finishing my to-do list.
—Vicki Kuyper

Digging Deeper: Proverbs 3:27; Luke 10:38–42; 1 Corinthians 16:14; Philippians 2:3

Saturday, June 27

For who has despised the day of small things?
—Zechariah 4:10 (NKJV)

Last week, sorting through a box of fabric scraps, I found a variegated velour remnant, too small for another pillow project, too big to trash. I set it aside, not sure why, until this afternoon, when I saw baby dolls scattered on the townhouse sidewalk, a second-grade neighbor girl hovering nearby.

"Would you like a doll blanket?"

Her eager eyes prompted me to retrieve the purple remnant. As she reached for the fabric, a second girl wistfully stepped up. Hmm.

"It's a little big for one doll," I ventured. "I think I need to cut it and make two blankets."

So far, so good. I'd just doubled the pleasure. But, what? I'd hardly stepped back to my screen door before five, then six more children appeared, dolls in hands. *Me too. Me too.* From scraps of discarded linen and wool skirts, I quickly cut out swaths—unhemmed, jagged-edged—and handed out paltry pieces all around.

You would have thought I'd given them wow-worthy ruby slippers. *Thank you. Thank you*, they chorused. As others ran down the steps, one girl lingered. I tucked her remnant around her doll, as if wrapping it in peace.

I'm sure that in a few days several of those "blankets" will be kicked under beds, abandoned. No matter. Such a small effort. Such a joyous encounter. It made their day—and mine.

Lord God of every day, open my eyes to see— and appreciate—the value of seemingly insignificant goodwill. —Evelyn Bence

Digging Deeper: 2 Corinthians 9:7–15

Sunday, June 28

SACRED THREADS: Welcoming Jesus

Here I am! I stand at the door and knock. If anyone hears my voice and opens the door, I will come in and eat with that person, and they with me. —Revelation 3:20 (NIV)

Behold, I Stand At the Door And Knock, the sampler just inside my cabin door says. The scene portrayed is straight from my childhood Sunday school classroom. I'd noticed right off that something was missing. Jesus stood at the door, but the outside knob was missing. "How will He get in?" I'd asked.

"Ahh! There's only a knob on the inside. He has to be welcomed. Your heart has a knob, too, Roberta."

Then I grew up. Life was hard. Got harder. Often the folks who showed up to help were the ones I least expected. But they acted the most like Jesus as they loved helpless, hopeless, hapless me. I welcomed them into my heart and life, and my life got easier. Richer. Fuller. Deeper.

That lesson was never more precious to me than when I fell this past year. A broken hip, femur, and pelvis took me to the end of my own resources. Jesus showed up at my cabin door in scrubs; another Jesus wielded a wrench to fix my water pipes. A lady I barely knew with a handicap-accessible van offered to drive me around to see the Christmas lights. Jesus was a recovering addict who tenderly cared for me, an immigrant who brought me the freshest vegetables from his daily restaurant deliveries.

One morning, I looked out my window to see a complete stranger mowing my grass. Jesus in jeans. The Jesus in my Victorian sampler isn't clothed in a regal robe but in the ordinary. The Son of Man who came not to be served but to serve.

> **Keep surprising me, Lord, in the ways You show up.** —Roberta Messner

> **Digging Deeper:** Matthew 20:28; Mark 10:45; John 13:16

THE FIVE LOVE LANGUAGES: Acts of Service
Dear children, let us not love with words or speech but with actions and in truth. —1 John 3:18 (NIV)

Have you ever thought someone close to you didn't love you because they didn't show love the way you expected?

According to the book *The Five Love Languages*, people give love five different ways: by acts of service, words of affirmation, gifts, touch, and quality time. The way a person gives love is the way they expect to receive it as well. Unless we identify our own love language and look for ways others show love, we may feel unloved or disappointed.

I host a book club at our house one night a month, so I spend the day preparing for it. The day of our first meeting, I began to dust and started sneezing, being allergic to dust. My husband, Chuck, took the dust rag from me and said, "I'll do the dusting and vacuuming. You just do what else you need to do." Now he cleans the house every time we have book club.

Chuck shows me his love with acts of service. He does other things for me, like going grocery shopping or taking our dog, Dolly, for a walk when I don't have time because of a writing deadline. When I recognized his love language, I quit focusing on what he *didn't* do and became thankful for what he *did* do.

The adage "Actions speak louder than words" may be a paraphrase of 1 John 3:18 in the Bible. Jesus set the example for us when He was on earth by showing His love with acts of service. He helped and healed people, then committed the extreme act of service by dying for our sins.

Lord, thank You for loving us and showing us how to love others. —Marilyn Turk

Digging Deeper: John 3:16; Romans 5:8, 12:10

Tuesday, June 30

Further, my brothers and sisters, rejoice in the Lord! It is no trouble for me to write the same things to you again, and it is a safeguard for you. —Philippians 3:1 (NIV)

Recently I came across one of my old trumpet lesson notebooks, filled cover to cover with assignments from years prior. Curious, I opened it to a random page—and couldn't believe my eyes. The topics and exercises listed were nearly the same as the ones my teacher and I had just discussed in my lesson the previous day. *What a coincidence,* I thought with a laugh. But my laugh faltered as discouragement set in. Could it be that I'd just been going around in circles for all this time?

But when I told this to my teacher the following week, he replied with a simile: "Sometimes our learning journeys are like a spring," he said. "They might go in circles, but when they do, they're never flat ones."

An image of a giant metal bedspring filled my mind as I pondered what it might be like to walk a path following its coiled shape. I'd be going in circles for sure—but, just like my teacher had said, not one of them would cover the exact same ground, because each round would delve deeper into the material than the last.

I thought then about how well the imagery also applies to the repetitive themes within the Bible. In addition to functioning as reminders, I realized now how each repetition also serves as an invitation, made by God Himself, as He circles around for us again and again, encouraging us to follow Him ever deeper, into the limitless depths of His riches, wisdom, and knowledge.

Thank You, God, for fun similes and for inviting me, again and again, into an ever-deeper relationship with You. —Erin Janoso

Digging Deeper: Psalm 32:8; Isaiah 2:3

LIVING A NEW LIFE

1 _____

2 _____

3 _____

4 _____

5 _____

6 _____

7 _____

8 _____

9 _____

10 _____

11 _____

12 _____

13 _____

14 _____

15 _____

16 _____

17 _____

18 _____

19 _____

20 _____

21 _____

22 _____

23 _____

24 _____

25 _____

26 _____

27 _____

28 _____

29 _____

30 _____

July

See, I am doing a new thing!
Now it springs up;
do you not perceive it?

—Isaiah 43:19 (NIV)

Now, in my old age, don't set me aside. Don't forsake me now when my strength is failing. —Psalm 71:9 (TLB)

When I was 77 years old, my daughter Jeanne and I took a 5-day mother-daughter car trip through the Redwoods National Park in Northern California.

Jeanne anticipated my every need. She brought a camp stool for me in case there were no seats when we wanted to stop for a long look at nature's beauty. She made sure I had plenty of water to drink, healthy snacks to eat, and the proper shoes for hiking. She even had bedding so we could crawl into the back of her car for a short afternoon nap after a long hike. Through her, I saw myself as an old person.

One day we hiked the mile-long trail in the Lady Bird Johnson Grove of giant redwoods. I was gobsmacked at the enormity and uniqueness of every giant tree. The brochure said you could walk that trail in 30 minutes. It took us over 2 hours because I wanted to gaze at, touch, walk around, photograph, and drool over every tree.

The majesty of those giant 600- to 800-year-old redwoods that stand so tall, straight, and beautiful helped me accept my own aging that day. Even though the trees are protected and helped along by park rangers and environmental groups, they grow tall, strong, and resilient on their own thanks to God's plan. Instead of focusing on the limitations of aging, the redwoods taught me to work harder at being healthy—to take more hikes, eat nourishing foods, get out in the fresh air more, stretch my limbs, and reach for the heavens.

Lord, if the mighty redwoods can survive disease, drought, fires, and earthquakes, remind me that I, too, can age with grit, gusto, and grace.
—Patricia Lorenz

Digging Deeper: Joshua 24:15; Deuteronomy 34:7

Thursday, July 2

Whoso keepeth his mouth and his tongue keepeth his soul from troubles. —Proverbs 21:23 (KJV)

I stared at the handwritten sign at the entrance to the microfiche room. CLOSED. The head librarian told me the room had closed early because of a lack of staff. It was the summer of 2020, the height of the Covid-19 pandemic.

I had driven 3 hours to this southeast Ohio county library to research the murder of my maternal great-grandfather. He was killed in 1909 at the age of 27, when my grandfather was an infant. I figured journalists back then might have covered it. I was desperate to access the microfiche room's archived newspapers to find out.

"Can't you make an exception?" I pleaded. "I've come so far!"

The librarian and I locked eyes over our respective blue surgical masks.

"I'm sorry," she said. "It will reopen Monday."

I felt my frustration rise. *I hate this pandemic. I hate these new rules. She's being unreasonable.*

I was about to tell the librarian all this when, unbidden, a deep understanding washed over me. *She's just doing her job.* I paused, took a deep breath, and, instead of dressing her down, I asked her where I could find books on local history.

Later, as I was turning to leave with two borrowed books under my arm, the librarian stopped me. "What's your great-grandfather's name and date of death?" she said. "I'll see what I can do."

On Monday I received an email from her with two articles that offered vivid details of what happened to my great-grandfather. My new knowledge drew me closer to him, to the librarian who helped me, and to God. Because of the grace of that pause, I won an ally in my quest instead of making an enemy.

God, help me pause when agitated, so I may hear You clearly. —Amy Eddings

Digging Deeper: Psalm 31:23–25; Matthew 12:37

Friday, July 3

Speaking the truth in love, let us grow in every way into him who is the head—Christ. —Ephesians 4:15 (CSB)

I dip my paddle into the water and pull back. The canoe continues toward the center of the lake. My friend Matt is in the front seat.

Matt is one of the few people with whom I can be completely vulnerable. Our friendship is too deep and long-lived for false assurances and half-truths. While canoeing, I've been sharing about a conflict I recently had with another friend. That individual had sent me a strongly worded text message, rife with accusations.

"It's the words he used that bother me the most," I tell Matt. "Selfish. Unloving."

The lake is quiet—the only sound is the dip and swish of our paddles.

"Matt, is he right? Am I those things?"

Matt stops paddling. He sets the paddle across his legs. I hold my breath. And Matt begins to laugh—heavy and deeply. The noise rolls across the lake.

I am at a loss. I had steeled myself for a number of possible responses. This one is unanticipated.

Finally, when Matt's laughter quiets, he turns to face me.

"We've been friends for a long time," he said. "I know your flaws, and I've seen you make mistakes. But I have never known you to be selfish or unloving. If that guy believes you are either, then he doesn't know you."

With the paddling ceased, the water is still. And, for the first time in days, my heart is still as well.

I am grateful for Matt's words of truth, which have struck down doubt and falsity. And I am grateful for a friendship through which I am truly known.

Lord, thank You for friends who speak truth into my life. —Logan Eliasen

Digging Deeper: 1 Thessalonians 5:11

Independence Day, Saturday, July 4

Live as people who are free. —1 Peter 2:16 (ESV)

Several decades ago my parents moved into a new home, one with a stone fireplace lacking a mantel. Mother hired a man to put one up so she could display some of her favorite things, including a beautiful piece of cut glass from my grandmother and a delicate piece of china from the 1860s, a treasure gifted from her beloved great-aunt.

After the man left, Mother carefully placed her prized possessions on her new mantel, only to find that the installation had been faulty: within moments, the mantel fell, shattering her irreplaceable items against the stone underneath.

A sentimental soul myself, I hurt for Mother's loss, but it made me think of some wise words from Benjamin Franklin: "He does not possess wealth that allows it to possess him."

Sometimes we get so caught up in protecting our treasures that they bring us more anxiety than joy. Although Mother mourned the loss of those lovely, tangible connections to her past, she had to choose between being devasted and moving on. "They were just things," she concluded. Such a simple yet profound epiphany came at an emotional cost: her wise perspective on the things she loved came at the price of losing them.

Today I'm thinking of how freedom always comes at great cost—it's something Franklin and the other founding fathers understood deeply as they risked their very lives to bestow upon us the beautiful promise of America. More important, it's something God taught us when He gave us true and eternal freedom at the cost of His Son on the Cross.

Father, let me never forget that my freedom from sin and death comes at the cost of Jesus's precious blood. —Ginger Rue

Digging Deeper: Proverbs 11:4; Matthew 6:21

Sunday, July 5

Be very careful, then, how you live—not as unwise but as wise, making the most of every opportunity. —Ephesians 5:15–16 (NIV)

It was late Friday afternoon, and I was wrapping up a busy work week. Logging off my laptop, I surveyed my desk. Stacks of papers, unopened mail, pens, Post-it notes with Bible verses, a couple of coffee mugs that belonged in the dishwasher. I snapped off the light and closed the door. I'd straighten up over the weekend.

It was gorgeous weather. On Saturday I met friends at an outdoor restaurant for brunch. I took my golden, Gracie, to the dog park, then treated her to a new toy at the puppy store. I stopped outside my building to chat with a neighbor and say hello to his dog. I watched a baseball game, took a nap, then streamed a show I needed to catch up on and ordered Chinese delivery (extra pork dumplings for Gracie).

By Sunday afternoon I was feeling increasingly guilty about the desk behind the door. It was as if a monster was living in there. The guilt only fed my procrastination. I knew Monday would be a nightmare if I didn't address the disorder. Anxious, I decided the thing to do was to google Bible verses on procrastination—a worthy way, you know, to procrastinate. The word *sluggard* came up often, each time making me wince. Then I found this, 1 Corinthians 14:40 (NIV): "Everything should be done in a fitting and orderly way."

I still find myself amazed at the way a simple verse can clear my cluttered mind. I wasn't hurting anyone but myself by putting things off. I would add this verse to my office Post-it notes—as soon as I organized my workspace.

Lord, Your Word brings order to my sometimes-messy life. Help me to do today what I shouldn't put off until tomorrow. —Edward Grinnan

Digging Deeper: Proverbs 27:1; Hebrews 12:11

Monday, July 6

THE FIVE LOVE LANGUAGES: Words of Affirmation

I have loved you with an everlasting love.
—Jeremiah 31:3 (NIV)

I handed my report card to my father, eagerly awaiting his words of praise. Scanning the card, he nodded. "That's fine." That's all I got. No "Good job" or "I'm so proud of you for making such good grades." My spirit sagged, and I hoped that maybe the next report card would bring the words I wanted to hear.

My parents didn't tell me they loved me, but I knew they did. Nor did they shower me with gifts, give me frequent hugs, spend time with me, or say words of affirmation. But they took care of me and provided for me. When I learned about love languages, I realized my parents showed love with acts of service.

People can have more than one love language, and I've learned one of mine is words of affirmation. As a child, I longed for verbal approval or praise.

Studies show that our self-esteem is greatly affected by whether or not we receive approval. Children who never receive words of approval or affirmation tend to have lower self-esteem, often becoming "people-pleasers" to meet their need. This was true for me; I became an overachiever to receive recognition and reward. Once I learned about my own desire for words of affirmation, I began to speak those words to others, especially to Chuck and my children. Most people like a verbal pat on the back like "Good job" or "Great idea."

I'm so grateful for the affirmations from the Bible: God's Word affirms His love for us over three hundred times. God will always love us. Like the words of the song I learned as a child, "Jesus loves me, this I know, for the Bible tells me so."

Thank You, Lord, for loving me and telling me through Your Word. —Marilyn Turk

Digging Deeper: Psalms 36:7, 57:10; Romans 8:38–39

Tuesday, July 7

**Call unto me, and I will answer thee.
—Jeremiah 33:3 (KJV)**

As I prepared for my graduation from the University of Tennessee, the world, as Shakespeare said, was my oyster. My dream job was waiting. I had always been drawn to investing. I'd started in grammar school, when I would buy candy and then sell it for a profit.

My father was a Presbyterian minister, and when I realized that I could help good people like him realize their financial goals through wise investments, I was motivated like never before.

And then, suddenly, my job offer evaporated. The US economy had hit a rough spot, and hiring freezes enveloped the country. The world was my oyster no more. I came home and hit the pavement.

Day after day, I visited Nashville's financial institutions, but no one needed an inexperienced investment advisor. Determined, I kept going.

A job offer from a phone company put my dream at stake. Should I give up on my dream career and accept this job? Recognizing my stress, Dad suggested that I take a break for a day of fly fishing.

Out on the water, alone with God, I realized that I had neglected to include the One who mattered most in my job search.

"OK, Father," I prayed out loud, "I give this to You. If I should accept the unwanted job offer, that's what I'll do." Finally, I was at peace.

Later I was searching through my desk for the phone rep's card when Mom handed me the kitchen phone. First American Bank was calling to offer my dream job.

Suddenly the world was my oyster again, but in a far different way. The pearl was the gift that I found out on the stream. That's where I learned that when I finally give something to God, He finds a way to answer.

Father, when we need answers, help us remember to call You first. —Brock Kidd

Digging Deeper: Psalm 86:7; Matthew 6:6

Wednesday, July 8

The Lord is my shepherd; I have all that I need. —Psalm 23:1 (NLT)

My wife's love of exercise hasn't wavered through 35 years of marriage. I have my suspicions she might actually be a clandestine superhero.

"How about a walk?" she said one day.

Now, *walk* could mean anything from a quick mile around the neighborhood to summiting Everest. As it turned out, it was somewhere in between—a steep, up-and-back climb on a local mountain trail. But it was a nice day and I felt good. Maybe even good enough to keep up with Wonder Woman. Two miles in, I questioned that logic.

She waited for me by the side of the trail as I struggled to catch up. "You OK?"

"Awesome," I lied. "Are you even breathing hard?"

"Don't have a heart attack on me."

"I'll do my best."

Two more miles, and I'm thinking the heart attack might actually be on the table. At least we'd reached the turnaround point. My wife, of course, was waiting again, jogging in place, cape billowing in the breeze.

The sweat in my eyes made me squint. "Can you feel your legs? I can't feel my legs."

"Yeah, but you made it."

A lot like life. It's so easy to focus on others and compare. To get discouraged. But looking down through the trees at the lake below, I realized it's not the difficulty of the climb that counts, it's who you climb with. In my case, a superhero wife and the gracious God who gave her to me and Who loves us both every step.

"You're right," I said. "I made it."
She smiled. "I'll race you down."

Heavenly Father, help me to keep my eyes on You and never compare. You are not only my guide but my destination. —Buck Storm

Digging Deeper: Galatians 6:4; Philippians 3:14; Colossians 2:6–7

Thursday, July 9

"But I say to you, Love your enemies and pray for those who persecute you."
—Matthew 5:44 (NRSVCE)

I used to scoff at the dramatic announcement preceding a popular television show: *"Ripped from the headlines!"*—until our own life crashed into that category.

It started with a call to the computer store for help with our printer and ended in a nightmare when scammers intercepted the call. While pretending to instruct us, they infiltrated our system and financial accounts and stole information. Finally, they revealed themselves, demanding a ransom. When we refused, they laughed, locked down our computer, and threatened to release all our information and photos to dark web sites nationwide.

Charlie and I struggled with horror, spending the next month closing accounts, filing police reports, and constantly monitoring every aspect of our life.

Since I don't believe there are coincidences in God, I had to admit there was a reason I'd been reading *The Book of Forgiving* when this happened. The book tells of people who forgave wrongs far more horrifying than ours and offers a forgiveness process. One step asks the wronged person to consider the concept of "shared humanity" and think about why the person who'd committed the wrong had done so.

No way, I thought, remembering that chilling laughter. I felt too angry, violated. Eventually, though, I let myself wonder why anyone would be so bitter and cruel. What had made him lose his empathy? How had he been hurt? What poverty—financial or spiritual—had pushed him into such a terrible place?

As I considered these questions, his power over me faded, making room for the seed of understanding and, I hope, eventually forgiveness.

**Lord, empty me of the poison of hatred
and recrimination, and make me merciful.**
—Marci Alborghetti

Digging Deeper: Genesis 44, 45:1–8; Job 42:1–9

Friday, July 10

Those the Lord has rescued will return. They will enter Zion with singing; everlasting joy will crown their heads. Gladness and joy will overtake them, and sorrow and sighing will flee away. —Isaiah 51:11 (NIV)

Nursing home visits to see my father are frequently difficult. There are times when my dad is happy to see me and other times when he just has a litany of unfounded complaints. I never know what I'll be faced with, and sometimes I'm weary before I even board the elevator to head to his room, even when my husband comes along with me for moral support.

There are days when I feel like I'm dragging and question whether my visits are even welcomed. One thing that makes the visits easier are the comforting words that the receptionist offers when signing in: "Have a nice visit," she offers with a positive lilt in her voice. It may seem rote to some, but I draw such strength from those four words, which she delivers with a smile and a genuine wish of encouragement.

So imagine my surprise and gratitude when the same receptionist told my husband and me that *we* bring positivity to *her* day when we show up! She told us that the smiles we offer to her and the giggles that we share (all due to my husband's ability to lift my spirits at most any time) help to bring a spot of sunshine to *her* day. I would imagine that in her role, the receptionist sees a lot of sadness, impatience, and woe. But to think that when I believe I'm feeling down I'm somehow enabled to bring a smile to someone else—well, that's nothing but God.

Heavenly Father, I thank You for the positive people You place in my path. And I am grateful for the ability to share Your love, even when I'm unaware that I'm doing it. —Gayle T. Williams

---

Saturday, July 11

**All God's gifts are right in front of you
as you wait expectantly for our Master
Jesus to arrive on the scene for the Finale.
—1 Corinthians 1:7 (MSG)**

I pulled into the lake's swimming area parking
lot. Willow, my German shepherd, whined with
excitement. This week was our church's youth camp
swimming and boating day. I brought my dog to our
church events because the kids loved petting Willow,
and having her there opened up chances to have real
conversations with them. Except, as I pulled into the
parking area, there was a huge sign that read "No
Pets Allowed." *No! I can't stay, but at least I'll be able to
deliver the fresh peas I picked out of the garden.*

I rolled down the windows so Willow would be
comfortable in the car while I hopped out to find my
friend. The church's busload of kids swarmed the
picnic area and the beach. For more than 10 minutes
I walked in circles, searching faces and asking if
anyone had seen her.

Then I glanced at my car, behind me, to check
on Willow. My friend's daughter stood next to her
car, chatting with her. She was right there—but
I hadn't seen her because I wasn't looking for her in
a car. I was looking for her on foot.

After delivering the peas, I drove away. About 15 minutes down the road I wondered, *How many other things am I missing out on?* While waiting, instead of relaxing and getting to know the kids, I'd been so focused on my quest that I lost my focus. I may have missed an opportunity at the beach, but on the way home Willow and I stopped at a farm supply store where we were able to make new friends with some teens.

Lord, help me to remember that the people You put in front of me are gifts from You. Amen.
—Rebecca Ondov

Digging Deeper: John 4:35; Colossians 3:2

Sunday, July 12

Give thanks to GOD—he is good and his love never quits. —1 Chronicles 16:34 (MSG)

I stayed over in Holland, Michigan, for an extra day after our annual denominational chaplains' conference to visit with some dear friends.

We met at a local restaurant on Chicago Drive, near Hope College. The satisfying Saturday afternoon meal was enhanced by the windmill-themed décor. A Bible verse from 1 Chronicles, inscribed in Dutch-style lettering some 9 inches high, bordered the ceiling.

In a bit of creative flurry some weeks later, I thought the 1 Chronicles verse would make a good connecting illustration for an upcoming sermon. But I could not recall the reference.

I sent an email to the address listed on the restaurant's website. Receiving no reply, I planned to use a different illustration.

Then, on the Wednesday morning before the Sunday I was to preach, I received a voicemail from Dan, one of the restaurant's associates. With Midwestern twang, Dan recorded, "Yes, indeed, the verse on the wall was 1 Chronicles 16:34."

Dan invited me back to the eatery, and then concluded with words adapted from 1 Chronicles: "Give thanks to the Lord, for He is good, for His mercy endureth forever . . . and ever . . . and ever . . . my man. Hey, have a great day. Bye-bye."

The illustration fit the sermon, even more so because of Dan's gracious intervention. And when I'm in need of an uplifting message, I'll scroll back through my old voicemails to July 12 and relisten to God's encouraging words of life and hope.

Loving God, we give thanks for Your tenderhearted grace and the nonstop constancy of Your presence with us. May we live as Your delight-filled children this day. Amen. —Ken Sampson

Digging Deeper: 2 Corinthians 9:13, 15; Psalm 107:8; Ephesians 5:19–20

Monday, July 13

THE FIVE LOVE LANGUAGES: Physical Touch

Jesus came and touched them. —Matthew 17:7 (NIV)

I tell people I married my husband because he massaged my feet. While that's not the whole reason, it certainly ranked him high on my list. When we started dating, I had plantar fasciitis, so walking was painful. Chuck surprised me by making me sit and take off my shoes. Then he proceeded to massage my feet. I'll never forget the tenderness in his touch, conveying his care for me, and I'm convinced my feet healed because of it.

Physical touch is another love language, and one that has far-reaching benefits. Some people recoil from touch because it invades their "space." But others express love by touching, whether in a hug, a pat on the shoulder, or holding hands.

Touch can convey a range of emotions—reassurance, empathy, comfort, love, and compassion. It's a sense that makes us feel connected physically and emotionally, and it can benefit our overall health because touch stimulates a hormone that skin receptors send to the brain. Touch can affect everyone from newborns to the elderly. One study showed that frequent hugs between spouses can lower blood pressure and heart rates, improving relationships.

Jesus clearly demonstrated the power of touch. He touched the eyes of blind men, the ears and tongues of the deaf, and a sick woman to heal them; He blessed children by putting His hands on them. He even went a step further and touched those society deemed "unclean" when He touched and healed lepers. Although He could heal without touching, He touched people anyway, shocking religious leaders of the time, demonstrating His love for people by connecting with them physically.

Lord, I'm so thankful for Your example of using touch to show love and create connection. Show me who needs my loving touch today.
—Marilyn Turk

Digging Deeper: Matthew 9:12–23, 9:27–31; Mark 1:4–42, 7:31–35; Luke 7:1–8

Tuesday, July 14

He must increase, but I must decrease.
—John 3:30 (KJV)

My parents doted on me, not because I was beautiful or smart, but because I was the unexpected child of their middle age. I relished the spot, but when I went off to college, an irreversible life change hit all three of us. I had reached adulthood, and they had reached the proverbial empty nest.

Or so they thought.

One of life's emergencies would catapult Mama and Daddy into parenting again. Ostensibly a temporary arrangement, they took in one of my older siblings' babies and fell hopelessly in love with a cutie named Constance, offering perpetual excuses to keep her just a while longer. Unlike the biblical John who knew his purpose was to "decrease," I never thought I'd see someone else become the cherished "baby of the family." But I did, and I was comforted to see my parents with purpose again—to watch the beauty of it all from an adult perspective.

Talking to Constance last evening, who now has grandchildren of her own, I was reminded of the excitement she brought to my parents' latter years—filling a space in their hearts that I will always believe extended their lives.

The perfect maestro, God orchestrates life's journeys, and when He spoke through Isaiah of one coming to prepare the way of the Lord, He knew that John the Baptizer would joyfully promote the King of kings. Bold and dedicated, John served as the preparer for Jesus until the signal to decrease halted his work. Like John, I am honored to have been a witness to God's plan for Constance, recognizing that while it may pull on the heartstrings sometimes, it always produces the music of love.

Jesus, I thank You for often allowing me a glimpse into Your unfathomable plan for my life.
—Jacqueline F. Wheelock

Digging Deeper: 1 Samuel 2:7–8; Acts 20:24; 1 Corinthians 10:24

Wednesday, July 15
JOURNEY THROUGH GRIEF: Hope Arrives
There is surely a future hope for you, and your hope will not be cut off. —Proverbs 23:18 (NIV)

"Hope arrives." I read aloud the words I'd just written on my calendar. I loved the sound of those two words, as if hopefulness itself would ring my doorbell and come to stay.

Instead, a 20-year-old aspiring actress named Hope would be staying with me a few days as she visited New York City for the first time. We'd never met— she was the daughter of a friend's friend—but within hours of welcoming her in, Hope felt like family.

"Oh, your apartment is so lovely," she said. Everything was just so lovely—her green tea from the corner deli, the tree under which she'd journaled in Central Park, the group of young people she'd met at a Bible study. Her outlook on life was wonderful to watch and a mirror to my own. I wanted to share her optimism and joy, but lately, it just wasn't there.

Hope and I rode the subway to Times Square, and I delighted in her reaction to seeing this iconic and vibrant place for the first time.

Our different responses made complete sense for that moment in our lives. Maybe it was OK if my optimism and joy for life didn't match up to hers either. I was still in the early stages of so much grief after my sister's death and then my dad's. My time and place for optimism and joy would come when I was ready, but for now, I was simply happy to recognize its brilliance in someone else.

Lord, thank You for the seasons of our life, as painful as some may be. Because even in seasons of despair, I can recognize and give thanks for the

blessings of my past, while looking forward to new ones yet to come. —Karen Valentin

Digging Deeper: Ecclesiastes 3:4; Romans 12:12

Thursday, July 16

"For I know the plans I have for you," declares the LORD, "plans to prosper you and not to harm you, plans to give you hope and a future." —Jeremiah 29:11 (NIV)

It was a hot day in July when my 13-year-old son told me there was something strange happening to his vision. Everywhere he looked, he saw static, like an old television set.

Eventually we were sent to a neuropathologist at the University of Minnesota and given the official and very rare diagnosis of Visual Snow Syndrome. No known cure, lifelong, constant, but it won't get worse. In the light, my son doesn't notice the visual disturbance as much, but in the darkness, even when he closes his eyes, his vision is filled with moving static. The doctor reassured my son and said that he also had the syndrome, and that it hadn't stopped him from living his life. He said this was my son's new normal.

I was devastated and asked God why He had allowed this to happen. It was all I could think about for weeks. But whenever I brought it up to my son, he would kind of frown and say he had forgotten about it until I reminded him. Finally, one day, my son simply said, "This is my new normal, Mom." And in that one sentence, his perspective shifted mine.

He had come to terms with the diagnosis and had found peace, accepting God's plan for his life. That was the day I decided I would accept it too. Just like the doctor, my son can use this rare diagnosis to do something rare and wonderful with his life. This is his new normal, and God has a plan to use it for my son's good and His glory.

> **Lord, help me to trust Your perfect plan for my life and the life of my loved ones.**
> —Gabrielle Meyer

> **Digging Deeper:** Joshua 1:9; Psalm 112:7; Romans 8:28

Friday, July 17

THE LONELY AMONG US: To Be Lonely Is to Be Human
My command is this: Love each other as I have loved you. —John 15:12 (NIV)

Experts say loneliness is not only a universal human experience but also essential to human well-being. Like hunger, thirst, and pain—without which we wouldn't eat, drink, or seek healing when injured—loneliness makes us value and pursue the many benefits of community God planned for us.

Upon creating Adam, God says it's "not good" for him to be alone and immediately provides a companion. Being alone is, to emphasize God's words, bad for us: physically, psychologically, and spiritually. Loneliness prompts us to perform the healthy and good work of befriending—that is, loving—others.

Throughout Jesus's life on Earth, He repeatedly models the spiritual importance of companionship. As a boy, He engages His teachers at church. In His first public acts of ministry, He attends a wedding with His mom, makes wine for the guests, and gathers Andrew, John, Peter, and the rest of his twelve apostles. He befriends Mary and Martha, dines with tax collectors and prostitutes, and touches the sick and outcast. In calling His various companions "apostles" or "disciples," we perhaps overlook them as His friends.

Jesus Himself, fully human, surely suffered loneliness. He commented, "Foxes have dens and birds have nests, but the Son of Man has no place to lay his head" (Luke 9:58, NIV). As He nears His death, close friends betray and reject him and fall asleep while He suffers in Gethsemane. Still, He keeps seeking their company. After all, it's not good to be alone.

When we're lonely, we long for others to befriend us. Jesus shows us a corrective to loneliness: intentionally, relentlessly, even in our loneliest moments befriending others.

> **Jesus, my brother and friend, help me love others even when I feel betrayed, abandoned, and ignored.** —Patty Kirk

Digging Deeper: Ecclesiastes 4:7–12

ANGEL WHISPERS: Acting in Uncertainty
Whosoever shall smite thee on thy right cheek, turn to him the other also.
—Matthew 5:39 (KJV)

Writing my check in the grocery store line, I carelessly laid it down on the revolving counter, only to see it devoured. I stood perplexed as the cashier rather loudly pointed out my stupidity.

Feeling humiliated, I headed for the door clutching my groceries . . . when the angel whisper said: *Buy her a rose.*

Absolutely not. Do you think I'm crazy? I silently responded. Almost out the door, I stopped. *Buy her a rose.*

Back at the flower display, I obeyed the whisper. As I approached the checkout clerk, she looked harried, then almost frightened.

"You've obviously had a hard day and I've certainly made it more difficult . . . I'm sorry."

I handed her the rose and left.

What happened next? I went home, cooked dinner, and enjoyed my family. I never saw the woman again. The next Sunday, teaching a senior-high class, I shared the story, and that was pretty much it.

Let me offer a disclaimer here. I in no way believe that I've been chosen to receive these angel whispers. The suggestions to do something good are available to us all. It's simply a matter of listening and acting on the opportunities as they come. And they don't all turn out well. I once felt I was supposed to buy a sandwich for a seemingly homeless man. He threw the sandwich back at me.

Still, it's a chance worth taking. The rose? Only God knows.

But, funny thing, I recently ran into a young man from that long-ago Sunday school class. "Hey, Pam, would you tell me that rose story again?" he asked.

**Father, even in my uncertainty, let me listen.
Let me hear. Let me act.** —Pam Kidd

Digging Deeper: Proverbs 23; Matthew 5:44

Sunday, July 19

**Behold, I am doing a new thing; now it springs forth, do you not perceive it? I will make a way in the wilderness and rivers in the desert.
—Isaiah 43:19 (ESV)**

About a week ago my son Henry played *Live Video for Cats* on our big-screen television, and larger-than-life pet mice scampered across the screen. Not a minute in, four of our five cats lined up to watch. Kirby, our 15-year-old grumpy white cat who has never noticed the television, awakened to its magic. A world had opened for him, and whatever was on the screen—a movie, the news, anything that moved—became his prey.

Last night he jumped straight into the air during a ketchup commercial. I'm not sure what to make of his newfound energy and how he has suddenly become aware of what seems like a window to another world.

"It's brought new life into him," Henry said.

As I watched Kirby transform from a grumpy old cat into a kitten again, I thought about the importance of play and experiencing new things. The last time I was in the attic, I saw a gigantic cobra kite we had gotten as a family gift but never tried to master. It's time to take it down, dust it off, and get it up in the sky to see what windows may open in my own life as I chase the wind.

Heavenly Father, help me take the time and effort to experience new things and embrace the gift of being alive. —Sabra Ciancanelli

Digging Deeper: Proverbs 1:5; 2 Corinthians 5:17; Revelation 21:5

Monday, July 20

THE FIVE LOVE LANGUAGES: The Language of Gifts
Every good and perfect gift is from above.
—James 1:17 (NIV)

"What beautiful flowers!" I said, admiring my friend's arrangement. "What's the special occasion?"

She said, "Oh, those are from Tom. He keeps me stocked in flowers, stopping at the grocery store to get a fresh bouquet on his way home. For special occasions, he gives me a dozen red roses."

I smiled, hoping my skin hadn't turned green. Flowers are not my husband's love language. A frugal man, he thinks they're a waste of money because they don't last.

Gifts are nice to receive, especially when they're a surprise and given from the heart. My shelves display odd pottery and artwork my children and grandchildren gave me. My heart warms whenever I look at them, because they represent love to me.

I like to give gifts too. Buying for my sons was fun, but now that I have daughters-in-law and a stepdaughter, I have even more fun buying girly gifts. It's such a joy to see their smiles when I give them something they like. Of course, buying gifts for grandchildren is even more fun.

God gives us many types of gifts, not because of who we are but because of who He is. He can give us whatever we ask or need. He provides food for us, as Jesus did when feeding the five thousand (Matthew 15). He gives us peace (John 14:27). He gives us His Word and wisdom (Luke 21:15). He gives us healing through physicians, medicine, and miracles. But best of all, He gives us salvation and eternal life by giving His life, a gift of ultimate love.

Lord, You are the giver of gifts. Thank You for being so generous to us. Show me what I can give to others. —Marilyn Turk

Digging Deeper: Matthew 7:11, 11:28; John 10:25; 1 Corinthians 12:1–11

Tuesday, July 21

As for God, his way is perfect: The Lord's word is flawless; he shields all who take refuge in him. —Psalm 18:30 (NIV)

How many times have I looked at my calendar and thought, *Whew, when things settle down, life is going to get easier*? It happens to me at least once a month, often at the start of a new sports schedule, the end of a trial stretch for my lawyer husband, or when I see the wide-open expanse of summer days.

But life isn't like that, is it? When a void opens, something else pops right in to fill it up. I've joked that afterschool activities are like a gas—they fill the space they are given!

This year I caught myself saying it again, this time around a bad stretch of family sicknesses. We were passing colds and coughs back and forth and I thought, *Man, life will be better when we get past all this.*

At that moment it dawned on me: I kept thinking of all these hiccups as detours taking me off my perfect road, but these weren't detours— this was the road!

Once I realized that all of this life wasn't getting in the way of my grand road map, I was a lot happier. I still get stressed about calls from the school nurse and other intrusions into my carefully organized days, but now I know to take a breath and remember that this is all part of God's plan. What better navigator could I ask for on this epic road trip of life?

Lord, help me remember that life isn't designed to be squeaky clean and perfect. Grant me the patience to navigate the curves as we travel the road of life together. —Ashley Kappel

Digging Deeper: Philippians 4:6–7; 1 Peter 4:12

Wednesday, July 22

Oh, call your brothers "My People," and your sisters, "Lovingly Accepted." —Hosea 2:3 (JPS)

My friend Don gave me one of the pots he'd thrown on the wheel in his garage. I loved Don's work. He would combine rough surfaces with smooth ones, creating harmony with colors I had not thought would go together. He had the eye of every good visual artist, and as a verbal artist, I envied his perception. So when he presented me with the pot—which I still admire when I see it in my kitchen—I was delighted.

I thanked him and told him how beautiful I thought it was, and he surprised me by saying, "Let me show you the flaw."

"What flaw?" I asked.

He took the pot and turned it in my hands so that I could see a place near the base where the glaze on a shiny part was deeply scratched. "That's not a mistake," he said. "I built it in."

Naturally, I asked why. He said, "I studied in Japan. My teacher taught me never to do a perfect job." I asked why not, and he just shrugged.

Of course I thought about that every time I looked at the pot. I loved that pot, and slowly, over time, I began to realize that if I could deeply love something despite its flaw, how much more important it had to be to love some*one*, even if I saw a flaw in that person.

Thank You for teaching me, Greatest of Teachers, that all of Your creation is good, even if there are flaws to be found. —Rhoda Blecker

Digging Deeper: Genesis 1:31; Leviticus 19:18

Thursday, July 23

. . . that I may know how to sustain the weary one with a word. —Isaiah 50:4 (NASB)

I treasure words—speaking them, hearing them, reading them, writing them. A letter from my mother to her mother when I was a year old says, "I think Carol Anne will talk before she walks." It happened.

I have a note by Psalm 29 that exclaims, "This is the Voice!" The psalm describes the voice of the

Lord as "majestic" and "powerful." It "shakes the wilderness" and "makes the deer to calve."

The book of Genesis records God speaking the world into being. Colossians 1:16 (NASB) says of Jesus, "For by Him all things were created."

What wonderful divine words Jesus brought to this earth. He spoke and people were healed; wind and waves calmed; demonic spirits fled; the dead were raised. He wrote in the dust and hateful accusers walked away.

The thought came one day, *Jesus must have had to be so careful with His words because of their power.* He could not utter anything idly or thoughtlessly.

I felt the weight of my own careless words— thrown in judgment, in impatience, in accusation. I also felt the lightness that came from knowing my written and spoken words have encouraged. *What a contradiction I am,* I confessed to Jesus. *Teach me the sustaining power of good words.*

In stepped my six-year-old granddaughter. During a visit, I remarked to one of the adults I was chatting with that I wasn't good at most things— except words. I didn't know that my granddaughter, coloring in a book nearby, was listening. She came over to me saying, "Grandma, you're good at being a grandma." The beauty of a word that builds up.

Jesus, You built this world with Your words. May I add to its beauty with mine. —Carol Knapp

Digging Deeper: Genesis 1; Isaiah 55:10–11; 2 Thessalonians 2:16–17

The Lord had said to Abram, "Go from your country, your people and your father's household to the land I will show you."
—Genesis 12:1 (NIV)

I've been spending ages in airports lately, and as those hours have accumulated, I've noticed the strange way I think about my time there—almost like it's in suspended motion, set aside from the normal forward momentum of life, caught in the transitory space between where I'd been before and where I'm heading next.

"Liminal spaces," I've heard places like that called. From the Latin word *limen*, meaning threshold, they're not fully one thing or the other, existing only in the in-between. And they can be disconcerting. My brain likes to know where to look for its predictable certainties. When I'm instead faced with something that defies classification, that forces me to glimpse my vulnerability and lack of control, it can feel unmooring. Sometimes it can even be downright scary, when I recall the tortuous waiting that had come after a loved one's recent health diagnosis.

But it's also often been precisely these times in my own life that I'd classify as the most profound. Would the perception of control and certainty be worth wishing those away? It occurs to me that would be like allowing my anxiety to force dusk and dawn to give up their in-between-ness, to pick a side already. "Are you night or are you day?"

But clearly, they cannot be one or the other. Because they're both. And they're neither. And it's exactly this in-between that gives them their beauty.

Thank You, God, for the liminal spaces in my life that disrupt my status quo. I know it's necessary if I'm to continue to grow in my walk with You. Please help me recognize the uncertainty they bring as a gift and grant me the courage to make the leaps of faith they require. —Erin Janoso

Digging Deeper: Psalm 27:14; Matthew 12:40

Saturday, July 25

Some trust in chariots and some in horses, but we trust in the name of the LORD our God. —Psalm 20:7 (NIV)

On our final morning in San Diego, my husband, Kevin, our daughter, Katelyn, and I meandered our way along the boardwalk to Seaport Village. The past 3 days had been filled with delicious food, good conversation, and strolls along the ocean. An ideal vacation.

But in the back of my mind, a conversation with a magazine editor had spun around and around. He wanted me to tackle a new project, something out of my comfort zone. I preferred to stick with what I knew, to play it safe.

At the carousel at Seaport Village, we stopped to peer through the gate at the fifty-four animals that had been hand-carved in 1895. Besides traditional horses, there were giraffes, camels, and even a blue dragon.

"I want to ride the carousel," I declared.

Katelyn stared at me, shocked. To be honest, I was surprised as well.

Due to unsettling motion sickness, I usually experienced carnival rides from the sidelines, holding everyone's jackets and snapping photos. Did I really want to risk an incapacitating bout of nausea?

The animals and carnival music drew me in. I paid my money and climbed on, determined to join the fun, no matter the outcome. I was tired of playing it safe. With that, I also had the answer to my work dilemma. I would face my fear and step into the unknown.

Round and round, up and down, I rode with my family without one queasy qualm.

I rode the blue dragon.

Jesus, in the unknown ups and downs of this day, thank You that You ride with me as I face my dragons. —Lynne Hartke

Digging Deeper: Psalm 34:4; Isaiah 41:10

Sunday, July 26

Praise the Lord! How good it is to sing praises to our God, for he is gracious, and a song of praise is fitting. —Psalm 147:1 (NRSVUE)

It was a summer Sunday, and I was visiting my sister, Gioia, in the Southern California suburb where we grew up. She still lives there and happens to go to the same church where we worshipped and got baptized more years ago than I dared to count.

"Do you want to sing in choir?" she asked.

"Sure. But wait, how can I join the choir if I haven't been to rehearsal on Thursday? Aren't those choir rehearsals always on Thursday nights?"

"In the summer it's just whoever shows up on Sunday mornings," she said. "We'd go to the church at eight o'clock, rehearse, and then sing at the nine o'clock service."

"Count me in," I said.

I might have been a little groggy when I woke up—jet lag—but I was all ears and eyes in the sanctuary. I wanted to point to the steps and exclaim, "That's where I sang my first solo," or gesture to a choir stall, "That's where we tenors always stood in high school choir," where we sang "Pass It On" and "Tell It Like It Is," and where we burst into "O Holy Night" at midnight on Christmas Eve.

Hallowed ground. Churches are like that, not because of the buildings but because of what goes on in them, what prayers have been heard, what scriptures read, what sermons preached, and what lives changed. On a summer Sunday, I could feel that past, present, and future tremble in the very stones as we gathered together singing God's praise.

How glorious it is, Lord, to sing in Your house.
—Rick Hamlin

Digging Deeper: Isaiah 12:5;
Acts 16:25; James 5:13

Monday, July 27

THE FIVE LOVE LANGUAGES: Quality Time
Surely I am with you always, to the very end of the age. —Matthew 28:20 (NIV)

Growing up as the youngest and only girl in my home, I was accustomed to spending time alone. In my career, I worked outside my office traveling, so I wasn't in an atmosphere with coworkers around me. I was so used to being on my own that it was a surprise to learn my husband wanted me to spend my nonworking time with him.

Chuck wanted to do everything together, whether eating, fishing, or working in the yard. I'd never had so much togetherness with one person. What I learned was that one of my husband's love languages is quality time. And quality means more than being in the same room. It means paying attention to the other person when having a conversation and interacting, which sometimes takes effort. It means putting down the cell phone and engaging with the person you're with. If you observe couples in public, very few seem to be spending quality time together, even if they're sitting at the same table.

Jesus showed us how to give quality time to others. He spent almost every day with His disciples, talking and eating with them, traveling with them, and sharing experiences. He even went out of His way to spend time with a Samaritan woman. When He wasn't with His disciples, He spent time with His Father in prayer. His Word tells us He wants to be with us, too, so much so that He'll never leave us alone.

Most of us remember people who spent quality time with us with feelings of love and acceptance. With Jesus as our guide, shouldn't we commit to spending more time with those we love?

Dear Lord, You are our constant companion, sharing our ups and downs. Thank You for Your constant love and for being with us always. —Marilyn Turk

Digging Deeper: Matthew 17:9; Mark 9:30–31

Tuesday, July 28

In the morning, LORD, you hear my voice; in the morning I lay my requests before you and wait expectantly. —Psalm 5:3 (NIV)

I recently discovered Adelynrood, a summer retreat house north of Boston. Opened more than 100 years ago, this oasis of calm offers personal retreat space as well as spiritually themed conferences and workshops.

One of the charming traditions there lingers with me long after I have returned to everyday life: Greeting the Sun by responsively reciting the "Canticle of the Sun," composed by St. Francis of Assisi in the thirteenth century. Each morning at seven o'clock sharp, retreatants and staff position themselves on the first-floor screened porch and second-floor porch directly above it. One group begins the Canticle, the next recites the second verse, and so on. All else is still, save the birdsong and breeze soughing in the pine boughs.

I savor this morning meditation on so many levels. Praising God for creation reminds us that God is near to us in His creation, right now. It's the perfect way to begin a new day.

How I cherish the presence of my fellow retreatants! Praying aloud with my faith friends enriches the closeness I feel, both to them and to God. Best of all, this feeling of fellowship stays with me when I return home, where I live alone and offer the morning meditation in the company of my cat—yet another creature to bless my morning.

Lord of creation, thank You for the joys of the morning: sunrise, companionship, and prayers that endure. —Gail Thorell Schilling

Digging Deeper: Isaiah 50:4; Lamentations 3:22–23; Matthew 18:20

Wednesday, July 29

One who has unreliable friends soon comes to ruin, but there is a friend who sticks closer than a brother. —Proverbs 18:24 (NIV)

A few weeks after a friend retired, we got together for lunch. He lamented a change he was experiencing from several work friends in their response to him. Replies to his voicemails and texts were slow in coming, if even answered at all. "You learn quickly after you leave who are your situational friends," he said. I started thinking about situational friends.

Not long after, I went to the funeral of a friend, Bob. His grandson, Adam, shared a powerful tribute to him. Adam's mom and dad (Bob's son) were divorced. Adam told us how much it meant to him that despite the divorce, his grandpa kept his relationship with Adam's mom strong. "Grandpa always remembered Mom at Christmas, her birthday, and other special occasions. He brought her gifts, stopped for visits, and called her. And when she experienced tough challenges, Grandpa was there to help. With Grandpa, Mom's change in status didn't change his friendship with her," Adam said. Bob was a forever friend.

I have more situational friends than forever friends. All my friends are valuable to me. At one time, some may have been more present in my life, but for various reasons, like work changes and relocations, I don't see them as often. This includes both my situational and forever friends. What

I took away from these two experiences is that I need to become more intentional and timely in my replies to all friends who reach out.

Dear Lord, You put many people into our lives— some for a lifetime, others for a while, and some only for a moment. Help us to respond to each of them in ways that say they are valued!
—John Dilworth

Digging Deeper: 1 Samuel 20:42; John 15:13; 3 John 1:13–14

Thursday, July 30

SACRED THREADS: The Well That Will Never Run Dry

Jesus answered, "Everyone who drinks this water will be thirsty again, but whoever drinks the water I give them will never thirst."
—John 4:13–14 (NIV)

My sister, Rebekkah, rounded up the samplers she thought best told my story. The sweet, folksy mottos I understood. But *The Old Oaken Bucket*? What did a well and a bucket have to do with me?

"It's one of your best chapters," Rebekkah insisted. My eyes took in the mustard, sage green, and red palette that had called my name in a back-in-time antiques shop. Before I developed a problem with prescription opioids and felt like an outcast. "You're the woman at the well, Roberta," Rebekkah said. "You searched for everything, but it all let you down." Her eyes held the pain of living the desperation with me.

But Jesus had sought me out. He knew everything about me yet loved me more than anyone. He hadn't just delivered me from a prison of pain and addiction. He'd restored my body, my mind, my spirit. Given me a brand-new start. A brand-new life.

I often marvel at the yellowed paper on the back of that sampler. Words written in 1862 by an invalid who stitched threads salvaged from discards. What compelled her to create such beauty in her own difficult life, her sewing akin to planting a tree whose apples she would never see? I imagine her hunched over the perforated paper, the work of her hands far more than mere needle and thread. She was nudged by the Jesus at the well that will never run dry. Stitching a promise for an unknown someone who would live two centuries later. For me. My cup runneth over.

Your promises are hidden everywhere, Lord, even in dusty antiques shops. —Roberta Messner

Digging Deeper: John 4:14, 7:38

Friday, July 31

He hath made every thing beautiful in his time. —Ecclesiastes 3:11 (KJV)

Spending summer days at the cabin my grandfather built on a rural Alabama lake was one of the great pleasures of my childhood, and today, the pleasure remains. My wife, Corinne, and I have come here from our home in Nashville to relax and find time together.

The sun is setting on our first day. Almost leisurely, it inches behind the mountain that lies on the other side of the lake. Slowly it paints the sky in bright orange and sets the lake afire with ripples of color.

It is the golden hour.

I call out to Corinne, "Let's sit outside and enjoy the sunset."

"It's a shame that we have to come down here to see it," she says wistfully.

We sit contented, just being together, at peace with the twilight of day.

One star pops out of the darkening sky, and then another.

"You know," I say, "my grandfather carefully chose this spot for the cabin for its view of perfect sunsets."

Corinne smiles, having heard this story more than once. She is a patient woman.

"I think he was on to something," I say finally. "There's just something about a sunset. No two are ever alike. The colors vary. They spread across the sky like contemporary paintings, a constant surprise. And even on the darkest day, we know for sure the sun is setting back beyond the clouds. I think there's meaning here—a gift."

Corinne smiles. "Maybe it's God's way of reminding us of the beauty He has created. It's always there, even when we forget to see it. Even when we are too busy to look."

Father, Your beauty is waiting for us. Help us remember to take time to see. —Brock Kidd

Digging Deeper: Matthew 6:28–29; Philippians 4:8

LIVING A NEW LIFE

1 _____

2 _____

3 _____

4 _____

5 _____

6 _____

7 _____

8 _____

9 _____

10 _____

11 _____

12 _____

13 _____

14 _____

15 _____

16 _____

17 _____

18 _____

19 _____

20 _____

21 _____

22 _____

23 _____

24 _____

25 _____

26 _____

27 _____

28 _____

29 _____

30 _____

31 _____

August

Therefore,
if anyone
is in Christ, he is
a new creation.
The old has
passed away;
behold,
the new has come.

—2 Corinthians 5:17 (ESV)

Saturday, August 1

Those who know your name trust in you, for you, LORD, have never forsaken those who seek you. —Psalm 9:10 (NIV)

"The federal laboratory has invited me back to do research," our third son, Samuel, says. "I've decided to take a gap year before medical school. This experience will be good for my applications, and I'm passionate about the work."

My husband, Lonny, and I listen. We're not sold on gap years, but Samuel is a grown adult. He spent a summer working in this lab a year ago. It's in North Carolina. We're in Iowa. Should Samuel need us, it's more than an "I'll be right there" distance away. These are his first big steps toward independence—and away from our protection.

As Samuel shares about his research, I see joy in his eyes. I taught Sam to read. To write. We flipped flash cards for math facts. He loves to learn, and digging deep adds fuel to the fire of his curiosity and passion. The Lord made him this way. As I listen, my mind drifts to Samuel's birth.

Lonny and I struggled with infertility after our first two boys. We lost a babe and then prayed for years. Our family and friends prayed with us. Our whole church prayed for this child we'd already named Samuel because, like Hannah in the Bible, we'd asked the Lord for him.

And the Lord answered our prayer.

Suddenly it seems shameful to hold Samuel too tightly now.

I feel Lonny's hand wrap around mine, and when he squeezes gently, I know we're of the same mind. We know the Lord's name. We know it in the Word. We know it by prayer, petition, and praise. His faithfulness is scripted on our lives like our names are scripted in the Book of Life.

We know that soon Samuel will ask for our blessing. And we'll trust in the Lord.

Lord, I trust You with my children because I know Your faithfulness. Amen. —Shawnelle Eliasen

Digging Deeper: Psalms 28:7, 37:3; Isaiah 26:3; Jeremiah 17:7–8

Sunday, August 2

Your word is a lamp for my feet, a light on my path. —Psalm 119:105 (NIV)

My Bible has a lot of circles adorning its pages. It started when our pastor mentioned in a sermon that when we come across the word *therefore* while reading Scripture, we need to pause, go back, and check out *what it is there for*. Here's an example:

Romans 8:1 (NIV): "Therefore, there is now no condemnation for those who are in Christ Jesus."

In other words, because Christ died in our place by taking the penalty for our sins upon Himself, we are free of judgment.

Those were the first words that I started circling.

Then a short while later, a Bible teacher pointed out that when studying God's Word, it is important to look for *if* and *then* when listed. Often God's Word has a list of blessings He is longing to give His children.

For example, 2 Chronicles 7:14 (NIV) says: "*If* my people, who are called by my name, will humble themselves and pray and seek my face and turn from their wicked ways, *then* I will hear from heaven, and I will forgive their sin and will heal their land" (emphasis added).

More circles covered my Bible's pages.

The next circles came from a devotional on Zechariah and Elizabeth. How often I'd read the story leading up to the birth of John the Baptist. What the devotional pointed out was one lone word in Luke 1:7 (NIV): "*But* they were childless because Elizabeth was not able to conceive, and they were both very old" (emphasis added).

The *but* spoke of years of longing, disappointment, regret, and grief.

What I find profound as I read through my Bible is that every *but*, *if*, *then*, and *therefore* always circles right back to Jesus.

Lord, I write circles in my Bible while You write circles on my heart as I study and meditate on Your Word. —Debbie Macomber

Digging Deeper: Matthew 4:4; Hebrews 4:12

Monday, August 3

Let your ear be attentive and your eyes open to hear the prayer your servant is praying before you day and night. —Nehemiah 1:6 (NIV)

I was eight years old when my mother was diagnosed with cancer. It was a confusing and depressing time for me. I wanted my mother to get better, but I also didn't want anyone in the family to know I was scared that she wouldn't get better, so I kept my fears to myself.

However, one day I was so desperate for reassurance that I went out the back door and sat on the porch. I wanted to pray for my mother, but I didn't want anyone to see me.

When I knew no one was nearby, I looked up in the sky, where I believed God lived, and asked God to help my mother get better. That was it. It was a simple prayer. I was happy because it was the first time I had really prayed. Fortified by this prayer, I went inside incredibly happy.

Although my mother died soon after this prayer, praying for my mom prepared me for the time when, a few years later, I had a brain tumor and had to navigate another scary time. Praying for Mom gave me the courage to ask God for help, and it taught me that prayer was something I could turn to when life became difficult. Praying for Mom planted the seeds that continue to sustain me to this day.

O Lord, thank You for always being close to us. Amen. —Adam Ruiz

---

Tuesday, August 4

My times are in your hands. —**Psalm 31:15** (NIV)

When our grandchildren came to visit last summer, my husband, Kevin, and I took them to the indoor aquarium to escape the 110-degree Arizona heat. I had hoped to spend our time outside—at playgrounds and swimming pools—but the record temperatures thwarted that desire. The same thing had happened in previous years, making the aquarium our fallback plan for entertainment.

As a former country girl, I worried my grandkids would not have the childhood memories I had of tree climbing and bike riding all over the neighborhood. My siblings and I had played kickball, baseball, and hide-and-seek until the sun set on late midwestern evenings; our time was measured by how tall the corn grew in neighboring fields.

In comparison, here we were surrounded by air-conditioned safety, concrete walkways, and glass-enclosed exhibits.

But the grandchildren loved the aquarium.

"Can we touch the stingrays, Grandma?"

"The rescued turtle has no back flippers."

"Look at the beautiful jellyfish."

As we packed up our gear to head home, my grand-daughter Madelyn reminded me to take a photo next to the penguin wall, something we did each time we visited. The children ran to compare their heights to a mural painted with different penguins, from the 24-inch African penguin to the 48-inch Emperor penguin. As they smiled and lined up for the photo, I knew my grandchildren's childhood might not be the same as mine—measured by corn growing in agricultural fields—but that didn't reduce its validity.

My grandchildren's memories are measured in penguins. But it's more than that. Their memories are measured in time spent with us.

Jesus, may I measure time not by what I do but whom I love. —Lynne Hartke

Digging Deeper: Psalms 39:4, 90:12

Wednesday, August 5

Forget about deciding what's right for each other. Here's what you need to be concerned about: that you don't get in the way of someone else . . . —Romans 14:13–14 (MSG)

Gracie, my golden, is a cheerful dog who strikes up friendships with new dogs easily, bounding up to them, assuming the play posture, and bursting into zoomies, even at age nine. Admittedly, she's a bit of a show-off.

Hiking today we ran into a couple with a chunky white Lab named Hector. Our dogs stopped, sniffed, stood stock-still. In the blink of an eye they were fighting, growling and snarling and snapping their jaws, kicking up the dirt.

We managed to pull our dogs away from each other and apologized before going our separate ways.

"What got into you?" I hissed. "You know better!"

But Gracie was back to her tranquil self, as if she hadn't done anything wrong. Dogs. It's a good thing people don't act like that. But do I? Sometimes?

I consider myself an affable guy. I like meeting people. Yet there are those occasions when something about the other person triggers me. Maybe I don't like their handshake, their body language, or they mumble. Then I'm off to the races, judging, rejecting, jumping to conclusions—taking the person's inventory, as we say in the Twelve-Step Program. Romans 14:13 (NIV) says, "Let us stop passing judgment on one another."

Gracie's got an excuse: she's a dog, and she has her reasons. I have none.

Lord, help me embrace everyone You bring in my path today as a brother or sister. —Edward Grinnan

Digging Deeper: Matthew 7:1–5; James 2:13

Thursday, August 6

LIFE LESSONS FROM GAMES: Take the Hint
The LORD will guide you always; he . . . will strengthen your frame. —Isaiah 58:11 (NIV)

I love working in my garden, but my back used to hurt for the rest of the day. The anti-inflammatory gel I applied only relieved it until I gardened again.

One day I rested after gardening while the gel soaked in. I find it relaxing to play games on my cell phone. Depending on my energy level or mood, I might choose a card, word, number, or sorting game. Sometimes the game even gives me clues to my life puzzles.

This time I chose Solitaire. I like that Solitaire gives me hints when I get stuck. The small price I pay for a hint is to wait through a short ad.

That day, the ad for Bend caught my attention. It's a free app that guides you in daily stretches. I'd read that you should stretch before activities like gardening, but I'd never had a plan. Maybe doing 5 minutes of stretching every morning would head off my back pain?

I downloaded the app and chose the Wake Up routine. Every morning at eight o'clock I get a phone reminder from Bend. The app shows me the stretches and counts the time for each one. After 5 minutes it tells me how many days in a row I've stretched.

A few days later, I skipped applying the gel to my back after gardening. Since then, I haven't used it once. My back is tired if I garden too long, but there's no pain. And I can touch my toes for the first time ever! I'm glad I took that hint.

Dear Lord, in what other areas of my life do I need to take Your hints? —Leanne Jackson

---

Friday, August 7

Therefore, as God's chosen people, holy and dearly loved, clothe yourselves with . . . kindness. —Colossians 3:12 (NIV)

I was eight years old. My family was visiting my grandparents, who lived on the opposite side of the country. We all went out to lunch, and my grandparents brought along two of their good friends. I still remember their names—George and Dorothy Patterson.

After lunch we all moseyed through the gift shop attached to the restaurant, and my eight-year-old eyes landed on a small ceramic pitcher and bowl set. The bowl was 1½ inches high and 3 inches wide; the pitcher 3 inches tall and 2½ inches wide. They were made in Italy, each with a blue base and a decorative band of fruit around its top. Why at that age I was attracted to those items I have no idea, but I admired them out loud.

We left the shop, and as we were at our cars saying goodbye to the Pattersons, Mr. Patterson handed me a box. In it were "my" little bowl and pitcher set. I was speechless. Why would a man who hardly knew me bestow upon me such a wonderful gift?

Though this was many years ago—and no doubt Mr. Patterson is no longer on this earth—I will never forget him, nor the kindness he showed me. That pitcher set sits on a shelf in my study still. I see it every day. It reminds me that even a small act of kindness can mean a huge amount and reverberate through the years.

Lord, thank You for this daily reminder that even a little bit of kindness goes a very long way. —Kim Taylor Henry

Digging Deeper: 1 Corinthians 13:4; Galatians 5:22

Saturday, August 8

Blessed are they that mourn: for they shall be comforted. —Matthew 5:4 (KJV)

Fifty years ago, I had been Katie's maid of honor. Now she was gone. This afternoon I would join a small family gathering to distribute her ashes at her family homestead.

I had emailed Sherry, another bridesmaid now living in County Waterford, Ireland. Yes, she would join us in spirit. At the time of the scattering, 8:30 p.m. Greenwich Mean Time (3:30 p.m. in the eastern part of the US), she would light a candle. Both family members and I appreciated her comforting gesture from 3,000 miles away.

Later, home alone and reflecting on Katie's passing, I found another email from Sherry. She had forgotten that she had tickets for a concert that night at Lafcadio Hearn Japanese Gardens. "No matter. I'll bring Katie's candle."

Her story continued, "A woman just said to me, 'I think you're carrying a special soul with you.'" Sherry told me that she had replied, "That's exactly what it is," and explained her mission. The woman on staff gave her a small lantern to shield the candle from the wind. "Now we are surrounded by love and music and thoughts of Katie," Sherry concluded and attached a photo of the glowing lantern beside a bed of bright-pink coneflowers.

Sherry's candle and a stranger's kindness toward a "special soul," however unknown, lessened my lonely grieving. We shall, indeed, be comforted—sometimes by unlikely sources.

Holy Comforter, who knows our sorrows, we trust Your loving care. —Gail Thorell Schilling

Digging Deeper: Isaiah 61:2–3; Jeremiah 31:13; 2 Corinthians 1:4

Sunday, August 9

I will instruct you and teach you in the way you should go; I will counsel you with my loving eye on you. —Psalm 32:8 (NIV)

My husband and I were home alone. It seemed in a blink of an eye we went, as parents, from carpools and spring break vacations to teenagers with driver's licenses taking college road trips with their friends. Despite the paths they venture off on, we always want our children to find their way home.

Watching our children explore their new independence made me think of my first beach trip with my siblings. Our dad had surprised us with a weekend at Carolina Beach, where we walked the Atlantic shoreline, collected seashells, and soaked up the Southern sun.

On the ride home, I'd claimed the front seat. It was no surprise when my dad handed me the same map he'd used for the trip down. I spread the map across my lap and noted our starting and ending points.

My dad calmly advised me that I was in charge of charting the path home. He would—he emphasized—only go where I told him to go. I'd never been completely responsible for the road map before. Although I didn't realize it at the time, my dad was showing his confidence in me. Not only that I could get myself home, but that I could also lead others as well. We arrived home safely and with only a couple of short detours.

I've shared that experience with my children several times. Even with life's detours, God is confident that we will find the way back home to Him. His grace, His way, and His Word will lead us home.

Father, thank You for Your Word that keeps me on the straight and narrow path. When I deviate from Your plans for my life, it's Your Word that lights my path. —Tia McCollors

---

Monday, August 10

**When Jesus heard this, he said to them, "Those
who are well have no need of a physician, but
those who are sick; I have come to call not the
righteous but sinners." —Mark 2:17 (NRSVCE)**

One of my favorite prayers is about gratitude. It
reminds me to praise God, not just petition Him.
But I always hesitate at a part that thanks God for
suffering as part of His plan. Can anyone be truly
grateful for suffering?

Those lines troubled me most when in the midst of
my own deep suffering. Shaken by physical, emotional,
and spiritual pain, I could barely accept that this was
part of God's plan, never mind feel grateful.

Not long after that illness receded, I met with a
sick friend. I intended a short visit, because he was
in the same hospital where my suffering had begun,
and the thought of being there brought back anxiety-
producing memories. I found him very ill, weakened,
and confused by intense pain and medication.

I told him what I'd learned of sickness and God's
plan. "We can never truly understand our suffering
until we are with Him. And maybe then, we won't
need to understand."

"I feel afraid of dying, being judged," he said
bleakly.

"It's OK to be afraid," I answered, and then leaned forward so that he could look into my eyes. "But I do not feel afraid *for* you; God knows you and we trust in His mercy."

Peering into my face, he began to slowly nod. When I left, much later than I'd planned, he looked comforted and more peaceful.

Walking out of the hospital I'd promised myself to never enter again, I understood how suffering had enabled me to help my friend. And I did thank God, wondering where it might lead me in the future.

Generous Lord, thank You for Your great gifts that sometimes come in forms I don't recognize.
—Marci Alborghetti

Digging Deeper: Job 40:3–5; Psalm 73:13–16, 21–26

Tuesday, August 11

Jesus Christ is the same yesterday and today and forever. —Hebrews 13:8 (NIV)

I took my wristwatch to the jeweler for a new leather band, and she suggested a new watch. Based on my timepiece's age and make, the lady declared it not worth the cost of her services and showed me several of the current popular models. By remembering the manners my mother taught me, I managed a polite "no, thank you" and left the store. While the jeweler's professional assessment was correct, she didn't know the priceless sentimental value I placed on my mother's old watch.

When I found someone willing to replace the watchband, I told him about the jeweler's comment. He smiled, charged me much less than anticipated, and said, "Ain't no need to change something that works."

On the way home I drove my 44-year-old car through heavy traffic and recalled the man's wise words. Thanks to my husband's care, our antique vehicle runs great. The same phrase applies to my father's 55-year-old riding lawnmower, which we use every summer, and the 42-year-old Bible I read every day. Yes, I know everything in this world eventually dies or wears out, but not God. He was here in the beginning and will remain forever, meaning He was, He is, and He is to come.

Best of all, the Lord keeps promises He made long ago and never tires of renewing our spirit despite our age or condition.

God, thank You for being the one constant in this ever-changing world and never changing Your mind about loving us. —Jenny Lynn Keller

Digging Deeper: 1 Samuel 15:29; James 1:16–17; Revelation 1:8, 22:13

Wednesday, August 12

I have calmed and quieted my soul, like a weaned child with its mother; my soul is like the weaned child that is with me. —Psalm 131:2 (NRSVUE)

Growing up in Oakland, California, I remember our car trips to visit my father's family in Detroit, Michigan. We generally crossed Nevada at night both ways to avoid as much heat as possible in our non–air-conditioned cars. Supper and breakfast alternated between Reno and Salt Lake City, depending on whether we were coming or going. Before seat belts, my dad rigged up a foldaway bed so my sister and I could sleep in the back seat with our feet barely touching. Stopping at brightly lit gas stations, we woke to groggy trips to the bathroom and my parents commenting on how hot it still was at 3 a.m.

While on the road, I found the murmur of my parents' quiet conversation and the monotonous highway hum securely soothing.

In the early 1970s I began a rhythm of praying through the Psalms every month, which I still continue more than 50 years later. On life's journey, my wife, Candy, and I have had three sons and four grandchildren. We have lived in five states, experienced unemployment and career changes, weathered health challenges—including my wife's Alzheimer's diagnosis in 2016—released all of our parents into God's eternal care, and grieved national and global tragedies. Along the way Psalm 131 has grown increasingly rich as I imagine myself as a child curling up on God's lap.

Those soothing night drives across Nevada were a precursor to the feeling of resting securely in God's loving care when I am drawn into angst at events in my life and world over which I have no control. No words—just God's comforting embrace.

O God of the safe, soft lap, we relinquish our anxieties to You. —Norm Stolpe

Digging Deeper: Psalms 11, 121; Matthew 6:25–34

Thursday, August 13

In quietness and confidence shall be your strength. —Isaiah 30:15 (NKJV)

My grandfather messaged me today. Even though he passed away decades ago, he spoke to me through three words on a wooden sign he carved long before I was born: "Living for Jesus." My grandmother had placed the sign above the doorframe in her rustic summer cabin, which sits nestled in the Maine woods beside a pond.

Sitting in the cabin amid peaceful silence, I pondered my grandfather's message. "Living for Jesus." *What did that mean for you, Grandpa? How did you live for Jesus?* I barely remember my grandfather, who died suddenly at age 59, but I knew he was a zealous evangelizer. In fact, it was a ministry to lumberjacks that first took my grandparents to Maine. But how did "Living for Jesus" play out in Grandpa's daily life? Perhaps it would surprise him that here, decades later, his carved sign is still speaking. I am thinking about those words and how they apply to my own life. How am I living for

Jesus? What in my existence reflects a life lived for the Lord?

My thoughts turned to my grandmother, who lived 28 years beyond her husband and who now also has passed on. What was it like for her when her husband unexpectedly died? I then noticed hanging on the wall a framed piece of burlap imprinted with the words of Isaiah 30:15, "In quietness and confidence shall be your strength." As these words sunk in, I realized that Grandma had also just messaged me, reminding me to be still and trust in God amid life's hardships.

Lord, thank You for loved ones who followed You and left evidence of their faith. May we do the same for future generations. —Lisa Livezey

Digging Deeper: Exodus 14:14; Psalm 107:29; Isaiah 26:3–4; Mark 4:39

Friday, August 14

If anyone serves, they should do so with the strength God provides. —1 Peter 4:11 (NIV)

For two decades I've organized a senior lunch at my church. Six times a year some twenty people gather for a potluck and a program. I've drawn on a large pool of acquaintances, asking if they'd present their interest or expertise, pro bono.

But my network is shrinking. Or maybe I'm getting discouraged and tired. Last month, having run out of ideas, I pulled out a card game I'd squirreled away.

I wrote a short description: "We'll explore the origins of common sayings/idioms. What's the meaning behind 'crocodile tears'? Or 'chip off the old block'? Together we'll guess, learn—and laugh." Or so I hoped.

That morning, I spontaneously bought a dozen roses, thinking that it would add cheer to the space. Finding no vases, I laid the buds willy-nilly on the tables. The gathering was small but engaged. Delving into idioms prompted personal stories. Lalitha, from Asia, said "crocodile tears" in her language would be "tears as large as eggs." Hearing the phrase "hair of the dog that bit you," Daisy shared the childhood memory of a neighbor's fierce dog.

A special grace settled over the event. Afterward, a participant named Mary said, "For an afternoon it made me forget my worries." And another named Sandra: "I had a song in my heart as I walked home."

Hmm, when I was about ready to throw in the towel, my heart heard God whisper, *No, it's not yet time.*

Lord, show me if and when it's time to stay on, veer from, or quit the course. —Evelyn Bence

Digging Deeper: 2 Peter 1:1–8

Saturday, August 15

THE LONELY AMONG US: I Bet There's a Facebook Group for That!
Again I say to you, if two of you agree on earth about anything they ask, it will be done for them by my Father in heaven. —Matthew 18:19 (ESV)

During the years when I taught fiction-writing courses, my students' stories often featured characters who didn't fit in. Outsiders. Loners. Such stories had no characters beyond the lonesome protagonist and, importantly, no interaction.

"People won't read books without dialogue," I taught. "*You* don't want to read books like that."

My friend Susan and I were recently discussing struggles that make us feel helplessly alone. Hers included dealing with her ailing mom and young daughter's school problems. Mine was dealing with my daughter's attention deficit disorder and how it affects our relationship.

"I bet there's a Facebook group for that!" Susan said. That's where she goes whenever she's struggling with something. She explained how discovering others with the same problem made her feel better, less alone, heard.

Her experience reminded me of the relief of connectedness I feel when, making nervous small talk in a crowd of strangers, I encounter among the attendees a fellow believer, a spiritual sibling I didn't even know I had. Whoosh, my social anxiety evaporates.

Sharing similar experiences, whether positive or negative, connects us and can illuminate the pathway out of loneliness.

Father, help me share my experiences with others, for their sake and my own. —Patty Kirk

Digging Deeper: Deuteronomy 6:4–9; Luke 8:16–18

THE BIRDS OF MY NEIGHBORHOOD:
God's Fierce, Tender Love

But I trust in you, Lord; I say, "You are my God."
My times are in your hands. —Psalm 31:14–15 (NIV)

I was out walking in the woods the other day, checking the eager beavers' work. They've been cutting down my trees for the building of their new dam. So far, they've downed thirteen small trees. As I stood there, I heard a cooing I recognized.

I scanned the treetops and finally spotted a pair of bald eagles. We've been blessed with eagle couples since shortly after we built our house here in 2004. Extinct in Indiana until repopulation began in 1989, there have been a number of eagle couples who've nested along our creek and raised young ones in the past 20 years. I've come to know their call. It's a tender sound, not at all like the scary screeching sounds assigned to eagles in movies.

I find it amazing that such a huge bird as a bald eagle has such a gentle sound. They are majestic, fearsome-looking birds. One I would not really like to see swooping down at me as if I were prey. It's enough to see them take flight toward me when I really ruffle their feathers by getting a bit too close to the huge nest.

As I stood there thinking about this fearsome bird and its gentle calling, I thought about the fierce, tender love God has for each of us. I often think of those things as opposites—fierce and tender. But

I realized that they're really not so far apart when I thought about how I love my family and friends: my instinct is to defend them, the same way God fiercely loves us and watches over us.

O Glorious Guardian and Gentle Carer, teach me the way to love fiercely but gently, ever following Your example. Amen. —J. Brent Bill

Digging Deeper: Romans 8:31–39

Monday, August 17

So in Christ we, though many, form one body, and each member belongs to all the others. We have different gifts, according to the grace given to each of us. —Romans 12:5–6 (NIV)

As a first responder on the local ambulance crew, I work not only with EMTs and paramedics but with firefighters, police, and sometimes funeral home staff. On a recent motor vehicle accident, the firefighters cut the patient out of the car, police officers apprehended the impaired driver who had caused the wreck, and we attended to the injuries of the patients and transported them to the hospital.

Perhaps the most striking similarity between firefighters, medics, and police where I work is their nearly universal and passionate assertion that nobody wants the other person's job. Many firefighters wouldn't touch medical if their lives depended on it; many medics don't want to fight fire; and many police seem satisfied to clear a scene from potential threats so medics can focus on patient care. But all of them are most vehement when they say they don't want to trade with the funeral home.

A friend's husband discovered his calling as a funeral director the hard way. He had trained to work the ambulance as an EMT, but he quickly realized he had no stomach for working with people in pain. He would freeze up when he knew his actions would cause additional discomfort, even if it was ultimately helping the patient. That prompted him to discover his gift in burial services—a vital role that caused no pain.

We all need one another. Our differences are what give us strength as a team. All of this made me wonder: do I need to rely more on other people's differences in my everyday life?

Precious Lord, You designed us so our differences are what can unite us. Please help us to value and celebrate one another's unique and wholly individual strengths.
—Erika Bentsen

Digging Deeper: Galatians 3:26; Ephesians 2:11–22, 4:7, 4:16

Tuesday, August 18

Hope deferred makes the heart sick, but a longing fulfilled is a tree of life. —Proverbs 13:12 (NIV)

There have been times this year when less-than-happy news swirled about me. So when a drop of good news falls my way, I welcome and savor it, and I look for the lesson God may be providing.

At one point, a work colleague faced a serious health challenge, and another dear colleague moved to a new job, leaving a huge void. I felt so sad about my whole work world, and I was anxious as I realized that my own workload was about to triple. I prepared myself for a few months of rough going. And I kept reading the Word and praying that the Lord would grant me peace in this situation.

But just as I settled in for the storm, some sunshine began to appear: After a lengthy and tedious search, my sweet mentee finally landed a full-time job that enabled her to start afresh in a new state. Later, we received news that helped settle my father's long-term legal case, a dilemma that had weighed heavily on my whole family for several years. As gospel singer Tye Tribbett once said in a song that has become my mantra, "He turned it!"

There was a time in my life when I would have easily settled into the sadness that was lingering in my life. But God. As a believer, I praise the Lord for the ability to worship Him in all circumstances—both easy and difficult. I now settle in the knowing that He will cover us at all times, in ways that I can't even begin to fathom.

Father God, You are here for all those who have hope in You. And I am grateful for Your omnipresence that surrounds and protects me always and in all ways. —Gayle T. Williams

Digging Deeper: Psalm 9; Matthew 28:20; Romans 8:31

Wednesday, August 19

JOURNEY THROUGH GRIEF: Mami's Grief
You keep track of all my sorrows. You have collected all my tears in your bottle. You have recorded each one in your book. —Psalm 56:8 (NLT)

"That was fun, right?" I said to my mother after getting back from Connecticut.

We'd just spent 4 days at my cousin's house. My father had passed a few months ago, and my mother was now spending more time with me.

"Yes, we had a wonderful time with the family," she agreed.

I watched her smile begin to scrunch, before sobbing into her open hands.

"How dare I?" she cried. "How can I enjoy myself when he's not here to enjoy it with me?"

For 54 years, my father enjoyed many experiences with his beautiful bride. They'd dance in the kitchen with no music at all, hold hands everywhere they went, and join in harmony whenever the other would spontaneously sing out loud. They worked together as equal partners in our home, cooking together, washing dishes, and folding sheets into small, neat squares. Their love didn't fade in their many years together. Even in the depths of dementia, my father never forgot his great love for my mother.

Now that he was gone, she struggled with her grief. Good days were met with the guilt at the thought she might be forgetting him, while bad days were met with guilt because she felt she was being ungrateful for their many years together.

That day, I encouraged my mother to grieve without judgment and recognize it as something beautiful in all of its forms. Grief is hard, but it's the only expression of love we have left to give.

Lord, You know my heart even more than I do, especially in the fog of despair. When I'm struggling to be kind to myself as I process painful emotions, remind me there is no ingratitude or lack of love in my heart when I grieve—there is only love. —Karen Valentin

Digging Deeper: Psalm 31:9; John 16:22

Thursday, August 20

A joyful heart is good medicine, but a crushed spirit dries up the bones. —Proverbs 17:22 (ESV)

I looked at my computer's desktop, cluttered with icons and documents, and began deleting and sorting. I found pictures of my dog from years ago, when he could see. My son Solomon's high school graduation photos. Then I went down a rabbit hole of settings and saw the options for screensavers and, on a whim, chose bubbles.

Now, instead of my computer going to sleep when I pause from typing or scrolling, colorful bubbles fill my screen and nudge one another into different patterns.

I don't know what caused the demise of these fun animated things our computers used to do when we were resting. I guess technology made them obsolete, but this new setting, these floating bubbles, has changed my day. Who knew this little adjustment would bring back a familiar feeling from decades ago, when these colorful animations that came to life during work pauses were the rage?

I suppose part of the fun is that piece of me—the one that was in awe of the magic of a screensaver—comes to the surface, and with it the realization that all those memories, all of the inventions and experiences, live within me and are a catalyst for all of the memories of this rich and beautiful life.

I read somewhere about a study that showed people who bounce back from life's challenges often use nostalgia to feel upbeat and happy—and now, as these bubbles bump against one another in a calm and mesmerizing pattern, I completely agree.

Dear Lord, guide me to find life's little gems, small changes that I can make that bring me joy.
—Sabra Ciancanelli

Digging Deeper: Psalm 32:11; Galatians 5:22–23

Friday, August 21

Cast your burden on the Lord, and he will sustain you; he will never permit the righteous to be moved. —Psalm 55:22 (ESV)

I am not a plumber.

My kids don't quite understand this truth.

Which is how I found myself staring at the open walls of my son and daughter-in-law's new spa shower second-guessing my work. Triple shower heads and faucets—not a simple operation. But after a half hour of checking and rechecking every connection, I was fairly certain everything was solid. Nothing left but to turn on the water main and look for leaks.

Dry as a bone.

Until it wasn't.

I noticed a drop, then another. I groaned and dug for a wrench.

I'm a fixer by nature. My first instinct is to attack life's problems myself. Even more so when they affect my family. I need to *handle* it. Which is why I so often find myself back in Give It to God 101. Yes, I should know better. After all, I'm not a kid. You'd think I'd have graduated this particular class by now. But invariably I find myself tightening here, refitting there. I check and recheck. Still, the leaks come. And, once again, I'm sitting in a front-row school desk taking down notes. The most important lesson? *The water will drip until you take off the tool belt and hand it to the One who not only fixes but makes things beautiful and new.*

Back in my kid's shower, I finally get the leak to stop. And another starts. Uh-huh, time to call a professional.

No, ladies and gentlemen, I am not a plumber. Thank You, God, I don't need to be.

Lord, sometimes these trust lessons hurt. Thank You for Your patience with me. I give it all to You.
—Buck Storm

Digging Deeper: Proverbs 3:5–6; Isaiah 41:13; Matthew 11:28

Saturday, August 22

Don't be anxious about tomorrow. God will take care of your tomorrow too. Live one day at a time.
—Matthew 6:34 (TLB)

The older I get, the more I dream about something big, new, or exciting happening in my life. Perhaps I'll receive a writing opportunity, or a publisher will become interested in some of my unpublished books, or maybe I'll find someone to go with me on an adventure to Europe, Africa, or Iceland. Could it be possible that I would meet a man and actually have a date? It's been years since Jack died, and I'm ready.

Any of those things would have given me something to hope for and something to do, two of the main ingredients for happiness. But the days kept on passing—ordinary days with nothing too exciting about any of them.

Finally, I decided to organize monthly lunches in area restaurants for a dozen or more women in my neighborhood. Choosing restaurants with foods from lots of different countries, sending out text-message invitations, making reservations, arranging to pick up my favorite octogenarians in what is now known as my BOLT (Blue Old Lady Taxi), and then enjoying the meal and afternoon with a group of gabbing, highly entertaining lady friends brought a great deal of happiness into my life.

I loved the meals and the comments afterward about how much fun we'd had. Planning them gave me a sense of purpose. I was using my excess time wisely. I learned that I didn't need a big job or a gentleman caller or an exciting trip to get rid of the blues. I just needed a purpose and the grace to gather people together.

Lord, thank You for giving me the courage to step out and get things going around me. Keep our lunches grace-filled. —Patricia Lorenz

Digging Deeper: Galatians 6:9; Philippians 3:13–14

Sunday, August 23

How abundant are the good things that you have stored up for those who fear you, that you bestow in the sight of all, on those who take refuge in you. —Psalm 31:19 (NIV)

I wound my arm back and chucked a tennis ball into the yard. My parents' Labrador puppy, Hazel, bounded after it.

It felt odd to sit on the porch with just my mom. I'd grown up with four younger brothers—a full house. The youngest two still lived with my parents. But I hadn't seen them all weekend.

"What are the boys up to?" I asked. I watched Hazel hunt for the ball, her nose pressed to the ground.

"Sports and work," my mom said. "They've been busy this summer."

I remembered past summers when the boys had spent full afternoons in the backyard pool. A lot had changed in the last few years. The boys had grown more independent. My parents had sold my childhood home. Our family dog, Rugby, had passed away unexpectedly.

"Do you ever wish you could go back to the way life was?" I asked.

Hazel fished the ball out from where it had landed amid the leafy hostas and rushed back at full speed.

"I'm grateful for the good days I've had," my mom said. "But the ones in front of me are full of goodness too. And I don't want to miss future blessings by wishing for past ones."

Hazel returned and dropped the ball on the porch. I tousled her ears, and she licked my face recklessly. Hazel was so much different from her predecessor. She was wild and wiry. Rugby had been sturdy and still.

And though they were different, they were both very good. And today this puppy was showing me that I could appreciate the new without forgetting the old.

Father, thank You for the blessings You have given me and for the blessings yet to come.
—Logan Eliasen

Digging Deeper: Philippians 4:19

Monday, August 24

Each day is God's gift. . . . Whatever turns up, grab it and do it. And heartily!
—Ecclesiastes 9:8–9 (MSG)

"You make the world a better place," announced the well-placed sign. I was at the checkout counter of our West Point Post Exchange (PX for short—it's like a department store for Armed Forces members and retirees). Other uplifting quotations from Helen Keller, Ralph Waldo Emerson, and Winston Churchill surrounded the cash register.

I thanked Senior Store Associate Carmine for his heartening, tastefully presented citations. "Keeps you in the right frame of mind!" came his rousing response.

Hearing Carmine's words, I recognized the animated voice behind the PX's "blue light special" announcements: "Attention all shoppers. Welcome to your West Point Main Exchange. Check out the coolers in front of the register for today's bargain."

I inquired further. "How do you maintain, day after day, your cheer-filled demeanor, Carmine? Seems positive energy even comes across in your in-store announcements."

With a hush-hush manner, Carmine showed me his "Good Vibes Only!" spiral notebook. Pages of handwritten passages. Highlighted sayings. Tabbed indexes for themes of "teamwork," "discover your potential," "don't quit," "stay positive," "lift up people during the day."

"My old supervisor encouraged me to write things down. I did. Now I love it."

As I gathered my purchases to leave, Carmine's satisfying "Have a great day! Nice talking with you!" gave inspiration to take with me and pass on. My frame of mind was buoyed up. And I was grateful.

Glorious God, keep us alert and watchful for sightings of Your grace this day. Enable us to make Your world a better place, through the kindness and encouragement we offer others. Amen.
—Ken Sampson

Digging Deeper: Joshua 1:6; Psalm 84:5, 7

Tuesday, August 25

Your word is a lamp to my feet and a light to my path. —Psalm 119:105 (ESV)

The pitter-patter of eight puppy feet rouses me each morning, followed by playful barks. Our two dogs, Bella and Coco, have an internal timer that lets them know when to wake us up so they can be let outside. One Monday morning my husband observed, "I'm surprised Bella hasn't fallen down the stairs yet." Our much-older dog, Bella, had gone blind. Despite her condition, Bella's quality of life remained consistent. I agreed with my husband. It really was quite remarkable that she came down from my daughter's room each morning as usual with no hindrance.

Not long after my husband's observation, I came down with a dreadful cold, and not wanting to spread it, I found myself sleeping on the sofa with Coco. Morning came, and hearing Coco's pattering feet, I knew it was time to wake up and go out. Instead of running to the door, Coco ran upstairs. Curious, I peered up the stairs and watched as Coco guided Bella down the steps. Coco would take two steps down, and Bella would follow him. When they got to the bottom of the stairs, their morning patters and barks proceeded normally.

My heart leapt at the discovery of this little secret between friends. Like Bella, I am blessed to have a friend who journeys life's path with me— my God. The Great Comforter remains steadfast at my side as I navigate my way down the stairs, and my grateful soul rejoices!

Father God, let Your Word light the path of my life while remaining close to You. Amen.
—Jolynda Strandberg

Digging Deeper: Proverbs 4:26–27; Isaiah 41:8–10; John 10:22–30

Create in me a clean heart, God, and renew a steadfast spirit within me. —Psalm 51:10 (NASB)

A prestigious position had opened up at the radio station where I worked, and I wanted it. I thought it was a great fit for me. I had the skills, the drive, and the smarts for it. I knew a lot of talented people would be applying, but I was pretty confident I'd outshine them all.

You probably know where this is heading. I did not get the job.

I was angry and hurt. I was jealous of the winning candidate, then ashamed that I was jealous. I was grateful for the great job I still had as a newscaster but afraid that I had hit a ceiling and would advance no further.

I got these tangled emotions down on paper. I talked about them with my closest confidants. I petitioned God over and over for the grace to accept this outcome. And I finally did.

Weeks went by. I felt depleted. I hated Mondays. I made a lot of mistakes on the air. I bumbled through my newscasts and missed my cues.

A friend asked if I was harboring any resentment toward my employer.

"I'm mad that I didn't get that job!" I thundered. "They don't value me!"

I was surprised. I thought I had dealt with this. But, like a dandelion, my pain had a long taproot. I had cut the obvious flower, my disappointment over not getting what I wanted. But it took my friend's insightful question to show me that my insecurities had turned a job offer into a referendum on my worth. Once I brought this crooked thought to the surface, it withered and died.

God, resentment wears many masks, like indifference, irritation, listlessness, and boredom. Keep me steadfast in my resolve to root it out when it comes. —Amy Eddings

Digging Deeper: Hebrews 12:15

Thursday, August 27

I am not worthy of all the unfailing love and faithfulness you have shown to me.
—Genesis 32:10 (NLT)

This morning I had to throw away an old pair of shoes, and I almost wept. I felt like I should at least perform some kind of goodbye ritual, like a shoe funeral.

Good shoes are indispensable to me because I have bad feet and because I do a lot of hard, physical work: lifting heavy bags of sand, pushing a wheelbarrow, slogging through thick mud, crunching along over gravel, and shoveling hard clay soil.

I have to buy expensive shoes, but even they wear out fast. For months I have been patching up these shoes with "miracle" glues. I hate to throw away old shoes because they are the most comfortable ones. Just when they are perfect, they begin to fall apart.

The way I feel about shoes is the way I feel about old friends. I get very attached to them. We have been through good times and hard times together. My old friends are not much to look at these days. They are a bit grumpy and forgetful, but they are still good-hearted. I dread losing even one of these godly companions, but age is causing us to drift apart because of our limitations. It's harder for us to see, to walk, to hear. We don't eat out together anymore, because we can't hear in noisy restaurants.

Recently, when I heard that one of my good friends was dying, I expected that I would be weighed down with grief. Instead, my mind was flooded with rich and happy memories. This nudge from God made me realize that as long as I have those memories, my friend is not gone. And the hope of renewing our friendship in heaven gives me perfect peace.

O Lord, make me worthy of my friends.
—Daniel Schantz

Digging Deeper: 1 Samuel 18:1; John 15:15

Friday, August 28

As we have opportunity, let us do good to everyone, and especially to those who are of the household of faith. —Galatians 6:10 (ESV)

Mark was one of our "adopted" children through our church's college student ministry, and one who would teach our family an important lesson about doing good when we have the opportunity.

The first time we asked him to our home for a meal, I asked what kind of desserts he liked. "Anything but chocolate," he said.

I gave Mark a hard time about this every chance I got. "How can anyone not like chocolate?" I'd tease. Or I'd tell our young guests, "For dessert, we have brownies—or strawberry shortcake, for those strange folks who don't like chocolate." Mark would always grin and thank me for "putting up with" his preferences.

With his birthday coming up, I asked Mark what his very favorite dessert was. "Carrot cake," he told me. I spent an entire day making him one from scratch, lining my pans with parchment, grating carrots, toasting nuts, and mixing cream cheese frosting. It was exhausting!

Naturally, I couldn't miss the opportunity to rib Mark a little more. "I hope you realize how much you are loved," I said. "And I hope you enjoy this carrot cake, because it's the last one I will ever make!" Sweet Mark laughed. Then he thanked me and made sure to tell me how delicious my cake was.

My husband and I were heartbroken when, a few years after graduation, Mark died in a car accident. Driving to and from the funeral, all I could think about was how glad I was I'd made Mark that carrot cake, and how badly I wished I could make him another one.

Father, let me love and serve those You put in my life for as long as I can. —Ginger Rue

Digging Deeper: Romans 12:11; Philippians 2:3–8

Saturday, August 29

May your fountain be blessed, and may you rejoice in the wife of your youth. —Proverbs 5:18 (NIV)

It was a Saturday date night, and my husband and I decided on sushi at one of our favorite Asian restaurants. After ordering we chatted and caught up, eagerly waiting for the sushi and chicken fried rice we had ordered. From my seat, I had a perfect view of two other couples. An older couple sat in the booth to the right. In the adjacent booth sat a very young couple—they couldn't have been more than 20. I quietly observed both couples, watching their interactions, and pondered their stories and what had brought them together.

The younger couple wore cheeky grins and sat chest-forward, as if an invisible magnet pulled them closer to each other despite the table separating them. The older couple wore relaxed smiles that you'd expect old friends to flash at each other and sat back against their seat cushions. I sensed chemistry and wonder between the young'uns—the excitement of a budding relationship. I sensed comfort and camaraderie between the goldens—the satisfaction of having built a life together.

As Anthony and I sat across the restaurant from them, I pondered what others would see in us. Perhaps they could detect the ever-present fatigue of full-time work and supporting young adult sons and teen girls. Maybe they saw that we were at a stage in our marriage when we had to work at romance but felt comfortable in our friendship. Hopefully, they saw that we were moving toward the depth of relationship I could see in the older couple. That one day we'd sit back with the satisfaction of having built a life together.

Lord, help me to always cherish the gift of marriage and family, remembering they are a gift from You. —Carla Hendricks

Digging Deeper: Proverbs 5:18, 18:22; Ecclesiastes 9:9

Sunday, August 30

As they rode along, they came to some water, and the eunuch said, "Look! There's some water! Why can't I be baptized?" He ordered the carriage to stop, and they went down into the water, and Philip baptized him. —Acts 8:36–38 (NLT)

Baptism, by default, is a communal event, not a private one. It's a public witness of faith in Jesus that welcomes the individual into the community of believers. When Donnie, a member of our congregation who is in his late forties, requested to be baptized privately due to his discomfort in front of crowds, the elders and I honored his request.

The Sunday of the baptism, we waited for everyone to exit the sanctuary after worship before heading to the baptismal font in the front of the chancel. I was joined by two elders, Donnie, and his girlfriend, Lois. We were the only people in this sacred space. But it felt like the entire congregation was present.

After a few words about baptism and its meaning in the life of a believer, I asked Donnie, "Putting your whole trust in the grace and love of Jesus Christ, do you desire to be baptized?" He replied, "I do." I dipped my fingers into the font filled with water and did the sign of the cross on his forehead, saying, "Donnie, I baptize you in the name of the Father, the Son, and the Holy Spirit."

After the prayer, the elders and I welcomed him into the church. Donnie was grinning from ear to ear. Tears of joy rolled down Lois's face. I imagined God smiling at us and a great celebration in the heavenly realm. I was proud of our elders, who, knowing how important the religious traditions and rituals are in our church, didn't let them get in the way of love and compassion.

God, may Your love and compassion guide our decisions and actions as people of faith.
—Pablo Diaz

Monday, August 31

You shall anoint for Me the one I point out to you. —1 Samuel 16:3 (JPS)

The LA Archdiocesan Spiritual Direction Program was a 3-year commitment. I had signed up for it when a Christian man I knew from the office demanded that I become his spiritual director, and I figured I'd better find out how to do that.

Before graduation, we were required to conduct a one-on-one weekend retreat. We gathered on the campus of Mt. St. Mary's (it was an Archdiocesan program, in which I was the only Jewish participant). Each of us prospective directors was assigned a directee to work with.

I was unsure about my own ability, and it was a lot harder going into the first session, but I muddled through it.

When we all—directors and retreatants—gathered at the end of the retreat for a final session, I felt a great relief that it was over, knowing I'd done well. But then the instructor held up a small pot of holy oil and said we were each to anoint our directee. Something about the act of anointing hit me like being stomped on by an elephant. All my confidence drained away again. I watched the other directors as one by one they dipped a finger in the pot and made the sign of the cross on the foreheads of their retreatants.

When it was my turn, I cradled the pot in one hand, dipped my forefinger into the oil, and tried not to freeze at the thought that I was a person who was standing in for God, since it would have been false for me to do a cross. As I hesitated, inspiration came, and I drew a heart on her forehead to bless her with God's love.

I trust in You, Lord of Holiness. It always astounds me when You seem to be trusting in me.
—Rhoda Blecker

Digging Deeper: Exodus 29:7; 1 Samuel 15:1

LIVING A NEW LIFE

1 _____

2 _____

3 _____

4 _____

5 _____

6 _____

7 _____

8 _____

9 _____

10 _____

11 _____

12 _____

13 _____

14 _____

15 _____

16 _____

17 _____

18 _____

19 _____

20 _____

21 _____

22 _____

23 _____

24 _____

25 _____

26 _____

27 _____

28 _____

29 _____

30 _____

31 _____

September

And this is the confidence
that we have toward him,
that if we ask anything
according to his will
he hears us.

—1 John 5:14 (ESV)

Tuesday, September 1

ANGEL WHISPERS: God's Messengers
A good word maketh [the heart] glad.
—Proverbs 12:25 (KJV)

Here's an amazing truth: you can be God's messenger, His angel whisper.

I'm checking my emails when a note pops up from a *Walking in Grace* reader named Phyllis.

"So many times, we neglect to do this, but I wanted to take time to thank you. I wanted to let you know that your work with the children in Zimbabwe is precious. God sees your efforts."

Another day, I open a letter and a beautiful fluffy feather falls out. "An angel feather for you," my friend Julie writes.

Ah! I believe, with all my heart, that an angel whisper floated into my friends' heads, straight from God. *Pam needs a bit of a boost.* They listened. They heard. They acted.

I wish I could show you the profound impact their acts have had so far.

And now, it's my turn and yours. The whispers are there, hanging near, waiting for us to bring God's messages to others. Recognize God's opportunities. Develop the angel whisper habit.

Call Mr. Smith. Make cookies for a neighbor's children. Send a thank-you to your high-school teacher. Ask the friend who recently lost a loved one to lunch. Stop and praise the work of a laborer who might not otherwise be appreciated. Buy that grumpy cashier a rose!

Who says we can't change the world? Bring comfort? Spread joy? Send surprises, like feathers that float from envelopes?

I'm in. Are you?

Father, keep sending Your messages, Your angel whispers, Your opportunities for us to make life better for others. I'm in. I'm ready. —Pam Kidd

Digging Deeper: Isaiah 40:11; Romans 12:15

Wednesday, September 2

We were gentle among you, like a nursing mother taking care of her own children.
—1 Thessalonians 2:7 (ESV)

We took our fourth son to college. As I held Gabriel, I wanted to squeeze him until he turned back into a little boy. White-blond hair. Eyes green and warm as summer. I wanted to pull him onto my lap and read *Mike Mulligan and His Steam Shovel*. But I opened my arms and let him go.

A week later I got an email from the director of women's ministries at my church inviting me to serve as a table leader for Bible study. I was honored to have been asked. My husband, Lonny, and I were new to this body, and it was much bigger than we were used to. I'd even asked the Lord to let me serve in this way.

But not now. Life lately had been an ongoing process of letting go. Raising and releasing boy after boy. Leaving behind our home-teaching lifestyle and taking on other jobs. How could I give when I felt gutted?

Yet, when a second email arrived, I committed.

Our ministry director spoke with exuberant joy at our leader training session. "I am so very excited for you to care for the women at your tables," she said. "The verse the Lord has brought to my heart over and over is from 1 Thessalonians." And as Sylvia read Paul's words, my spirit swelled with purpose in the Lord's provision.

I could lead these women with gentleness! I could love and nurture and nourish women with the same fierce tenderness with which I'd held my babies to my breast.

Suddenly the compassionate care of the Father overwhelmed me. In His grace, He would allow me to continue to love others. In His goodness, He would bring fresh life and resurrect my heart.

Lord, thank You for allowing me to love others for Your glory. Amen. —Shawnelle Eliasen

Digging Deeper: Ephesians 2:10; 1 Thessalonians 5:11; Hebrews 10:24–25

Thursday, September 3

LIFE LESSONS FROM GAMES: Take Breaks
Remember the Sabbath day by keeping it holy.
—Exodus 20:8 (NIV)

It's early Thursday morning and my enormous to-do list is taunting me. It includes everything I'd planned to get done today, plus the things that had poured over from Monday, Tuesday, and Wednesday. I have no idea where to start.

I decide to start by playing Wordscapes, a game on my cell phone. It doesn't count as procrastination if it relaxes me, right?

Immediately I ask myself, *Relax??? What am I thinking? I can't do this! There's no way I can make one word out of these six weird letters, let alone twelve words. It's hopeless.*

Blank spaces for twelve words are set up like a crossword puzzle. I've done it before. *Maybe I can make one short word, just three letters. I did it!* I study the two blank words that cross it, easier now with one letter filled in. *Got one!*

I'm stuck. I put it away. After breakfast I go back to the puzzle, hoping my subconscious has been working. *It has!* Quickly I see one word, then another. I keep going, and before long I've made all twelve words. The game congratulates me, "Victory!"

Lord, I know it's just a game. And I know my to-do list is long, but can I win there too? I quickly pick the easiest item on my list and do it. I cross that off. I complete a second task. Before the third, I take a break. I return refreshed.

I know I won't finish it all today, but by dinner-time I'll declare, "Victory!"

Friday, September 4

As iron sharpens iron, so one person sharpens another. —Proverbs 27:17 (NIV)

Just a few more minutes, I tell myself, adding 2 minutes to my alarm before snuggling back into the blankets. It's four in the morning, and I don't want to get up yet. Soon my alarm is going off again, though. I have to get up now.

Technically, I could sleep for another hour or two and still have time to get to work. My older sister, Katie, doesn't have that time, though. She leaves for work before six, so if we want to go for a walk together, we have to start around four.

Groggily, I get up. I've been wanting to get up earlier to exercise before work, but if I'm on my own I'm usually more motivated to sleep than wake up. I like walking with Katie, though, because we help hold each other accountable. We both have to get up early, and we can't make fake excuses for sleeping in. That is helpful for me, because I'm really good at fake excuses—telling myself that I should wait until next week to start a new habit, that I have time to do something later; the list goes on and on.

"All right, I'm ready," I say. "You got the key?"

"Yep, let's go," Katie answers, opening the door and letting me slip past.

Though we never discuss it, Katie helps hold me accountable for many things, like going to church, Sunday school, or Bible study. It's sometimes tempting to sleep in, to leave right after the service instead of staying through Sunday school, or to skip Bible study. But having someone else there who notices this and mentions it helps me to not give in to those temptations.

Lord, thank You for opportunities to be held accountable, so that I can't just take the easy way out. —Rachel Thompson

Digging Deeper: Galatians 6:2; 1 Thessalonians 5:11

Saturday, September 5

Give, and it will be given to you. Good measure, pressed down, shaken together, running over, will be put into your lap. For with the measure you use it will be measured back to you. —Luke 6:38 (ESV)

To paraphrase a Pope—the English poet Alexander Pope, that is—to give is divine. Today I saw a wonderful example of that and a reminder that I can do more.

Several times a week my golden, Gracie, and I haul our trash and recyclables to the transfer station known affectionately hereabouts as The

Dump. It's as good a place to catch up on town gossip as it is to get rid of stuff that's cluttering up the basement. Billy, Chuck, and Bob, The Dump Meisters, are always willing to lend a hand. And a treat for Gracie. They have a box of them for all the ride-along dogs.

This morning I watched a young mother lugging a bulky laundry bag of clothing to the big metal used-clothing bin, run by a county agency that redistributes the items to families in need. A little girl was running to catch up, shouting, "Mommy, let me help! Let me!"

Mom seemed slightly exasperated. After all, it was Saturday, and there were probably errands to do. But she let the little girl pull out an armful of sweaters and shirts from the bag and lifted her up so she could reach the slot at the top of the bin and put them in. They repeated this until the bag was empty. It must have been a bit of a workout for Mom. Then the girl ran back to their van skipping and clapping her hands.

This, I felt reminded, was what Christ asks of us. Not just to give, but to give joyously.

What a good mother I saw today, Lord, teaching the lesson of giving as You taught us. And a reminder, too, that it is time to clean out my own closet. —Edward Grinnan

Digging Deeper: Proverbs 11:24–25; Matthew 6:21; 2 Corinthians 9:7

To every thing there is a season, and a time to every purpose under the heaven.
—Ecclesiastes 3:1 (KJV)

It was almost fall when I found a long-lost treasure: an acorn cup. It sat solitary on our back patio, as if just waiting for me to find it, a key to open a beautiful memory.

When my older daughter was in preschool, I told her stories about fairies using the empty tops of acorns to shield themselves from danger or rain, a lovely idea I'd picked up from Shakespeare's *A Midsummer Night's Dream*. Oh, how she marveled at the thought, her big blue eyes sparkling! The two of us would go outside and search for acorn caps, and later, I'd often find several tucked inside her little purses. Perhaps she was saving them as gifts for the day she would finally meet some fairies, for surely they were as real as you and I in her magical, childhood world of make-believe.

As I picked up the little acorn cap, the memory flooded my soul with the taste of bittersweet. That little girl with the sparkling blue eyes had long since become a woman. The daily realities of adulthood had swallowed up her childhood sense of wonder. Her little purses had been traded for her college backpack. The days of collecting fairy treasures had passed away.

A few days later I saw her from a distance at the preschool where she worked. The little children clung to her, arguing over who would get to hold her hand. I saw my now-grown daughter comforting a little girl on the playground, holding her on her lap and consoling her.

And, perhaps, whispering in her ear the secrets of the fairies.

Father, thank You for childhood wonder and the passing on of love to our little ones. —Ginger Rue

Digging Deeper: Psalm 127:3–5; 1 Corinthians 16:14

Labor Day, Monday, September 7

The Lord God, even my God, will be with thee; he will not fail thee, nor forsake thee, until thou hast finished all the work for the service of the house of the Lord. —1 Chronicles 28:20 (KJV)

On Labor Day last year, rather than hosting the usual backyard BBQ, I found myself an ocean away in Scotland. There, I witnessed a special type of labor—childbirth.

The birth took place in a community hospital that bordered a busy harbor on the North Sea. The mother—my daughter—brought forth a son, and I reveled in the miracle of this beautiful new life, recognizing that a different type of labor was now beginning: that of raising a child.

Once my daughter was settled in her hospital room, I headed out to a coffee shop overlooking the ocean. I watched the fishing vessels busy at work and chatted with the woman sitting solo at the next table, learning that her husband had the beginnings of dementia. Whenever he got in his car, she was unsure of where he might end up. It was a stark reminder that yet another type of labor—caregiving—may be required of us in life's later years.

The ways we labor throughout our lives will extend beyond the wage-earning workplace to spheres like the family homestead, parenting, and end-of-life care. On this day, let us rally under the words of an old hymn: "Come, labor on. Cast off all gloomy doubt and faithless fear! No arm so weak but may do service here. Though feeble agents, may we all fulfill God's righteous will."

Lord, give us Your courage and strength this day as we work at the varied tasks You have set before us. Help us to do Your will in all things. —Lisa Livezey

Digging Deeper: 1 Chronicles 28:20; Psalm 104:23–24; 1 Thessalonians 1:3

Tuesday, September 8

The LORD bless you and keep you; the LORD make his face shine on you and be gracious to you; the LORD turn his face toward you and give you peace. —Numbers 6:24–26 (NIV)

For 19 years I had been praying a nightly blessing over my children from Numbers 6:24–26.

The night before our oldest daughter left for college, I watched her finish packing and I wondered how in the world I was going to let her go. I had been dreading this day for years. So many fears and uncertainties ran through my head as the clock ticked by, and even though she was eager to start this new journey, I knew she was nervous too.

The night before she left, I prayed the blessing over her with tears in my eyes.

We drove the 100 miles away from home, moved her into her dorm, and met her lovely roommates. When it was time to say goodbye, all the families were invited into the performance hall. As the ceremony was coming to an end, the school president invited the choir to circle the room and they began to sing "The Blessing," from Kari Jobe and Elevation Worship, inspired by the prayer from Numbers 6:24–26.

As we listened to the familiar words, my daughter and I began to weep, and in that moment I felt God whisper reassurance into my heart. For 19 years I had blessed my daughter; now I was handing her over to a community that would continue to bless her. No matter what, God's blessing would follow her all the days of her life.

Lord, when I'm worried about my loved ones, remind me that You are always with them, and I have nothing to fear. —Gabrielle Meyer

Digging Deeper: Isaiah 41:10; Philippians 4:19; 3 John 1:2

Pray without ceasing.
—1 Thessalonians 5:17 (NASB)

"Anna in the temple" is one of my favorite Bible people. Not much is said of her, except she was a prophetess of the tribe of Asher, was married just 7 years, and had lived as a widow to the age of 84. The other thing is she never left the temple.

What she was doing all those years in one spot is hard to picture with my life's zigzags. Luke writes of her that she was "serving night and day with fasts and prayers" (Luke 2:37, NASB). Anna was one of two people in the temple to whom the Holy Spirit revealed the newborn Jesus was the Messiah the nation of Israel awaited.

I think, *Isn't serving God taking action? How can sitting around praying be serving?* But then I find in the last chapter of Colossians phrases such as "devote yourselves to prayer, keeping alert in it" (4:2, NASB)—and Epaphras is "always striving earnestly for you in his prayers" (4:12, NASB).

OK—this is beginning to sound like real effort. I read in James 5:17 that Elijah also "prayed earnestly"—some translations say "fervently."

My middle name is Anne, named after an Anna. Could I possibly begin to pray in a way that serves God like she did? I will have to quit saying to others I'll pray for them, and then only do so once. No more running down a prayer list quickly—or popping off rote repetitions. I recognize I even forget or stop praying when nothing seems to be happening.

Chagrined, I study those words—devote, alert, laboring, earnestly—and know prayer is a deep commitment. And God, who is a deep listener, hears.

Jesus—teach me to pray as You did—fervently, with rejoicing and groaning and tears.
—Carol Knapp

Digging Deeper: Jeremiah 29:12; Luke 1:36–38; Romans 12:12; Hebrews 5:7

Thursday, September 10

Be patient like those farmers and don't give up. —James 5:8 (CEV)

The June sun beat down on me as I stood at the garden nursery gazing at the apple trees. *Should I buy one?* This past spring, when I had checked on my baby apple trees, I was crushed to discover that rodents had eaten the bark nearly all the way around the base of one, even though I had a plastic collar on it. Worse yet, they had chewed through the cambium layer, which carries the water and nutrients throughout the tree. *Should I just give up on it, pull it, and plant a new one?*

In my mind's eye, I could see my baby tree when I saw what the animals had done. I had called my brother. He'd had the same thing happen to him. Several of his had bloomed and seemed to thrive but died midsummer. There was only a slight chance my tree would live. As is, it wouldn't have enough nourishment to support its structure. He coached me to literally butcher the tree, leaving only a few scaffolds and pruning them to just a couple feet long. After doing that and painting the wounded bark, only a skeleton remained. I prayed over what was left and asked God to bless it.

A light breeze rustled the tags on the rows of apple trees. They looked so perfect compared to my little tree that was struggling to survive. I sighed. *But I'm not ready to give up on mine, nor on my prayer.*

I'm glad that I didn't—because in September I harvested a dozen apples from its homely, but healthy, branches.

Lord, when I've done all I can do and things look bleak, please remind me to not give up but instead to rely on You. Amen. —Rebecca Ondov

Digging Deeper: Psalm 71:14; 2 Corinthians 4:7–12

Friday, September 11

Peace I leave with you; my peace I give you. I do not give to you as the world gives. Do not let your hearts be troubled and do not be afraid. —John 14:27 (NIV)

When I think about the attacks on America that took place on September 11, 2001, my mind turns to the thousands of lives lost. These were just ordinary people, doing their everyday tasks, and then suddenly and so very tragically, their lives were lost.

I suppose that's why whenever I visit the Kensico Dam Plaza in Valhalla, New York, near my home, I am drawn to The Rising, a memorial structure created by architect Frederic Schwartz that is dedicated to the 110 people connected to Westchester County who lost their lives in the 9/11 attacks. It's a beautiful sculpture of stainless steel that offers a perfect spot for remembrance, prayer, and reflection. The name of each Westchester victim is etched onto the memorial, and it's rare that I visit the plaza without spending some time perusing the names.

As an editorial writer for a local newspaper at that time, it was my job to read pieces about the victims, but it was a privilege more than an obli GPBK1535_Walking in Grace_LP-QCcrx.pdf gation to learn so much about them: what they did for a living, how they achieved in school, what their hobbies were, and how much they were loved.

It's been a quarter of a century since that dreadful day, but my frequent visits to The Rising give me hope that the Lord will provide better days for us all, even as I solemnly focus upon their lives lost.

Father God, may Your peace surround those survivors who have suffered such great losses in the 9/11 attacks. May their lives and the love they showed to others never be forgotten by those who knew them, and those who didn't. —Gayle T. Williams

Digging Deeper: Psalm 23:4; Isaiah 49:13

To get wisdom is to love oneself; to keep understanding is to prosper. —Proverbs 19:8 (NRSVUE)

"I did it!" my two-year-old grandson, Silas, announced proudly from his car seat. "I did it."

What did he do? It was more a matter of what he *didn't* do. He got from one place to another on a short drive without getting carsick. On longer journeys he's old enough to get some Dramamine, usually mixed in with yogurt and maple syrup so he won't spit it out. But this was just a 4-minute drive from their home to the place where we'd get a pizza dinner.

It runs in the family. "Ricky's funny tummy," my mom used to call it. Did I not do it? Yes, indeed. I remember staggering off the merry-go-round at a Pasadena playground beneath some eucalyptus trees and getting sick. Ugh. For years afterward the smell of eucalyptus—usually so soothing and fragrant—made me nauseous.

And then Silas's father, Tim . . . well, as a boy, I remember driving us home from church on Sunday and having to pull over so he could step out and get some fresh air, just in the nick of time. Dare I admit that we'd send him off to school on the school bus with a plastic baggie that he could use, should he need it?

Jesus's great commandment, to love your neighbor as yourself, has two parts, and often it's that second part that is hardest to put into practice—to love yourself. I think Silas has just the right answer. When you've achieved some spiritual victory, no matter how small, let yourself celebrate. After all, God knows. You did it.

Lord, let me feel Your love and power, reminding me how to love myself as I love others.
—Rick Hamlin

Digging Deeper: Deuteronomy 16:15; Mark 12:31; Ephesians 5:29

Sunday, September 13

The sheep hear his voice. He calls his own sheep by name and leads them out. —John 10:3 (NRSVUE)

I enjoy sitting on our porch greeting people who walk by. I regularly greeted a man who lived at the group home for older men on our block. I often saw him as he strolled the neighborhood.

Before long, he greeted me first. "Hey, guy!" Once he picked up an old chair one of our neighbors had put out for trash. He was struggling to carry it while using the cane he needed for his limp. I went and offered to carry it for him. He handed it to me with a happy "Thank you."

I said to him, "My name is Norm. I see you almost every day, but I don't know your name."

"My name is Jim." He smiled. "Hey, Norm, I'm glad I don't have to keep calling you 'Hey, guy.'

I don't have a chair in my room, and this will be better than sitting on my bed. Just leave the chair by the steps. I'll get it later." He was obviously embarrassed to invite me into his room.

From then on he called, "Hey, Norm!" and I often went down to the sidewalk just to chat with Jim. He has since moved from that group home, but I am convinced calling each other by name connected us with a bond of human dignity.

Scripture tells us that God calls us by name and invites us to call on Him by name. God's own image connects us.

Our Father in heaven, thank You that You not only know us by name, but You also welcome us to personally call on You in the name of Jesus.
—Norm Stolpe

Digging Deeper: Exodus 33:12, 17–19; Psalm 9:10; Isaiah 40:26, 43:1

Monday, September 14

DOORS OF OUR LIFE: Closet Door

The LORD says, "Forget what happened before, and do not think about the past. Look at the new thing I am going to do. It is already happening. Don't you see it? I will make a road in the desert and rivers in the dry land." —Isaiah 43:18–19 (NCV)

At the beginning of our relocation project, my husband and I agreed to reduce our living space and possessions, believing less square footage meant fewer stored items. Years later, we're still working on the junk reduction and have run out of time. Our closets posted No Vacancy signs and demanded we deal with their overcrowded conditions.

OK, not really. But every time I open a closet door, the abundance of junk reminds me something must be done. Why have I kept items I haven't seen or needed in years, like high school prom dresses and college textbooks? Out of sight, out of mind? I wish. The truth is I always know they are there and detest my procrastination. Another truth revealed itself when I opened a box, found my parents' divorce papers, and recalled those sad times. Similar to the physical items I stowed away, I also stored painful memories and refused to deal with them.

Wow, talk about a sobering moment. Elimination of the physical junk suddenly became easier. Removal of the negative emotions required heavenly help, knowing only God possesses the power to forgive a wrong, wash away its stain, and forget it ever existed. Through trusting in Him, we can forget the past, live in the present, and travel in the new direction He provides for us—a future free of useless clutter and filled with abundant hope.

God, thank You for revealing the junk in our lives and removing it. Remind us lighter travel makes the journey easier and more joyful.
—Jenny Lynn Keller

Tuesday, September 15

. . . and with your feet fitted with the readiness that comes from the gospel of peace.
—Ephesians 6:15 (NIV)

Movies depicting cowboys at full gallop whooping it up around cattle always make me cringe.

My coworkers and I loaded three cattle trucks in under 2 hours and nobody had to raise their voice. I admit it; I love sorting cattle. When done calmly in a well-designed corral, it's almost like a choreographed dance. One step can make all the difference. Cattle don't like to be singled out but will move toward an "escape" or toward a group. They need just a moment to think and an opening to move toward. Positioning myself one step at a time is often all that is needed to change the direction of an animal's travel, or that of an entire herd.

My walk in faith is much the same. My will to follow God's direction doesn't need to be flamboyantly loud, with wild shouting and waving arms. I simply need to take one step, calmly, in the right direction at the right time.

Understanding cattle body language, so that you know which step to take and when to take it, is an art form. Some people possess the natural ability to read a cow. Others, like me, are slower to learn it.

Mending broken fences or re-sorting the herd from a misstep can be motivating instructors. Textbooks can teach theory, but in order to learn the dance, you've got to get out there and move.

Faith, I'm learning, is the same. If I don't practice it, do I have it? All it takes is one step.

Dear Lord, may I dance with You? You can lead.
—Erika Bentsen

Digging Deeper: Habakkuk 3:19;
2 Corinthians 5:7; Hebrews 4:16

Wednesday, September 16

THE LONELY AMONG US: Listening to the Lonely

Understand this, my dear brothers and sisters: You must all be quick to listen, slow to speak, and slow to get angry. —James 1:19 (NLT)

My daughter Charlotte got a job in Seattle, where several old dormmates of hers lived, and was instantly social. Knitting group one night, book club the next, meeting at the climbing wall on the weekend. Her husband, Reuben, had no ready-made Seattle friends and, since he worked remotely, no easy ways to make new ones. Lonely for the first time in his life, he organized social activities his own college buddies had liked—soccer games, ski trips, board games—for Charlotte's expanding group of friends and spouses. Their response was lukewarm. Worse, getting together with them only made him feel more alone.

I was honored when Reuben confided in me. I remembered my own loneliness when I lived alone in then-divided Berlin. My friends' activities—like getting together with other West German transplants to watch their hometown soccer team on TV—only intensified my loneliness. My recent research into loneliness ratified my experience: joining existing communities often exacerbates loneliness.

How to advise Reuben? I pray-worried. *Say that I survived the experience, and he will too?* (Negative advice for a present sufferer.) *Say having kids made me view those lonely days with nostalgia?* (Seemed like pressuring him about grandchildren.)

I couldn't solve Reuben's problem, of course, but our ensuing conversations and his own eventual solution—befriending working-from-home neighbors—taught me an important truth about both helping the lonely and giving advice: paying attention is the simplest and best way to love others.

Help me, Father, to listen to those around me and love them as You do. —Patty Kirk

Digging Deeper: Job 13:1–17

Thursday, September 17

A word fitly spoken is like apples of gold in pictures of silver. —Proverbs 25:11 (KJV)

Over the years, friends and family in New York State have encouraged me to move "back home" in retirement. One person even emailed me ten benefits of my choosing a particular town. I read the list and soon returned a cordial and noncommittal reply, in effect saying, "Thank you for your concern. I continue to downsize as I consider various options..."

I received another email in response: "I wish you well in making your future plans but am also aware of the wisdom of Proverbs 6:9." The vague reference piqued my attention. I opened my Bible. In short, the verse read, "Wake up, you sluggard."

Considering my temperament, the accusatory noun is way off base. A painful emotional sting turned to resentment that I was tempted to nurse. But a friend nudged me to reply truthfully, if vaguely. A day later I wrote, "I admit that I don't find the proverb very helpful, though I appreciate your concern."

My kind but terse email sent the Scripture quoter back to Proverbs. "I'm mortified," she soon responded; she'd meant to commend Proverbs 16:9 (NIV): "In their hearts humans plan their course, but the LORD establishes their steps." Quite a different message!

Decades ago yet another proverb—*a word fitly spoken*—had rooted in my spirit. I thank God that here and now, the Spirit used its wisdom to mend a breached relationship.

Lord, as I communicate with friends, family, and strangers, give me words that promote peace, understanding, and goodwill. —Evelyn Bence

Digging Deeper: Proverbs 16:13–24

Friday, September 18

Now faith is confidence in what we hope for and assurance about what we do not see. —Hebrews 11:1 (NIV)

My daughter, Olivia, got super lucky this year. As a fifth grader in her last year of elementary school, she was tapped to be the school mascot when events called for someone to dress up as the larger-than-life owl. We kept her identity under wraps to keep the mystery alive; she didn't even tell her little brothers!

Her career as an owl began at kindergarten Meet the Teacher night, where her little brother Beau was getting his start. It was only after the day was over that she whispered to him that she had been the one he high-fived inside the owl costume.

A few months later, Olivia sported the owl costume again, this time for their winter festival. That night, she again told Beau it had been her inside the costume. "I know, sissy," he said with cool, quiet confidence. "It's always been you."

For Beau, there was never a question that his sister would be the one inside the slightly creepy enormous owl costume. Of course it would be her!

I feel at times like I am surprised to find God where He has always been. I enter my lows, and He is there. I reach the mountaintop and am shocked to see Him there beside me. I need to remember what it is like to have the faith of a child, to simply know that my Savior will always be who He says He is.

Lord, remind me that I am never alone, and that You are always good and faithful. —Ashley Kappel

Digging Deeper: Matthew 18:1–5; James 1:17

Saturday, September 19

For where your treasure is, there your heart will be also. —Matthew 6:21 (ESV)

When I was growing up, Jane Goodall was my hero. I remember sitting on the bus with an article I had torn out of a magazine and being in awe of her life, which seemed magical and powerfully filled with purpose. I had only been working at *Guideposts* magazine for a year or so when they did a cover story on her, and I read a beautiful piece about how she kept small objects in a trinket bag as reminders of hope—a leaf, a feather, and a stone. The feather she kept was from a peregrine falcon that—despite the odds—made a comeback from potential extinction.

It reminded me of the way my grandmother always kept a horse chestnut in her pocket that she rubbed when she worried, and now my mom does the same. Every autumn, I ride my bike down to

Clermont State Park and find just the right one for her to hold on to for the year.

I don't keep things in my pocket, but I do slip important things in my phone case. Feathers I find that seem like signs, a photograph of my nephew and sister—both in heaven now—and a Post-it note my husband put on the coffee maker one morning that says, "I love you," with a heart.

My dad always kept a baby picture of my oldest sister in his toolbox. I remember seeing it when I was asked to get a screwdriver and thinking the small black-and-white photo with yellowed tape on the edges was a peek inside his heart.

I am fascinated by the things people keep and what they hold dear—the scraps of life that are precious because of love and sentiment—and what that reveals about our hearts.

Heavenly Father, thank You for the amazing power of love. That is the one and only treasure here on earth. —Sabra Ciancanelli

Digging Deeper: Matthew 19:21; Luke 12:34; 1 Timothy 6:10

Sunday, September 20

"Blessed are the merciful, for they will receive mercy." —Matthew 5:7 (NRSVCE)

"He can't afford to stay here," Charlie said of a friend searching for a three-bedroom apartment in New London. Our Connecticut city had become more expensive lately, and even retirees like us were disturbed about housing costs. Our friend was particularly burdened because he wanted an apartment large enough for his adult son and granddaughter to continue living with him.

"He could find a nice one-bedroom if he'd tell his son to get himself together," I said. Charlie and I had often discussed how manipulative the son was, often leaving our friend to care for his granddaughter while he disappeared on what he called "important business." We'd hoped our friend would come to his senses.

Later I received a text from a colleague, who'd finally broken down and gotten her kids a pet. "It's amazing what we do for our kids!" she texted.

I stared at the words, suddenly filled with self-dismay. How easily I had, with no children of my own, decided our friend should give up on his son! What made me so sure I knew the right course for him?

But bigger questions were more disturbing. What if every time I didn't measure up, God turned away from me? How often had I ignored God's grace because of my "important business"? What if my Father treated me the way I expected our friend to treat his son and granddaughter?

Father, I feel humbled by how often You could justifiably turn away from me, and grateful that You don't. —Marci Alborghetti

Digging Deeper: Luke 15:11–32; John 4:46–54

Monday, September 21

THE BIRDS OF MY NEIGHBORHOOD:
Traveling Together

I rejoiced with those who said to me, "Let us go to the house of the Lord." —Psalm 122:1 (NIV)

Autumn is here, and so my bird feeders are back up. It didn't take long for the birds of my neighborhood to find them. And deplete them. As I went out to fill them, a distant sound fell on my ears from high above. It was a muted, rattling bugle cry.

I looked around, trying to spot what I knew were sandhill cranes high in the sky. I love that sound. It can carry over 2 miles. It grew louder as they drew closer. I finally spied them, specks at about 2,000 feet, calling to each other on their pilgrimage to warmer climes. To me it was a sound of encouragement. "Come on!" "You can do it!" "We're in this together!"

Then I thought of the little flock of Friends (as Quakers are known) that I am part of and the pilgrimage to the face of a loving God that we're on. I wondered what sort of encouraging calls we offered one another. We share our joys and concerns as we gather every Sunday. Some of us are there in person. Others, from Florida, Kentucky, Iowa, and more, are on Zoom.

Every week, since we share leadership, someone offers a message, often out of their own spiritual journey. These are almost always pastoral and supportive. We travel together, like the sandhill cranes, no matter where we're geographically located.

Just as sandhill cranes who journey together, so, too, are we people of faith social creatures. Meant to travel the way of the spirit together. There are times we may be alone, but hopefully we are never so alone that we can't hear the call of our fellow travelers.

Loving Encourager who calls us to You, help us to be encouragers to one another on our pilgrim way.
—J. Brent Bill

Digging Deeper: Psalms 122:1–4, 132:1–18

Tuesday, September 22

For who is God save the LORD? or who is a rock save our God? —Psalm 18:31 (KJV)

I have an English degree, but I teach in a geology department. It's been quite a learning curve for me. I used to refer to metamorphic rock as *metaphoric* rock until someone corrected me. Turns out metamorphic rock is the result of temperature and pressure. The original material actually changes into something new.

Huh. Who knew?

Jesus was a teacher too—*rabbi*, they called Him. His disciples also encountered a steep learning curve—mostly unlearning what they had learned over a lifetime of different experiences. He taught them to doubt their own senses—*you have eyes but you cannot see, ears but you cannot hear.* Instead, He said, *Rely on faith, that thing that isn't seen, that faith in something bigger than ourselves, and that faith that will save us from . . . us.*

He chose to build His church on a place that seemed empty and barren—a rock.

It wasn't barren for long. And I bet it was metamorphic rock—rock that had been transformed forever into something new.

Or maybe it was metaphoric rock. That would work too.

May the words of my mouth and the meditations of my heart be always with You, my rock and my salvation. —Mark Collins

Digging Deeper: Isaiah 28:16; 1 Peter 2:6

Wednesday, September 23

Dearly loved friends, don't always believe everything you hear just because someone says it is a message from God: test it first to see if it really is. —1 John 4:1 (TLB)

It was a new church, at least new to me. So I decided to try an evening Bible study group. With more than seventy women in attendance, we broke up into groups of ten to get better acquainted. To start us off, our group leader asked, "What scripture do you turn to when you're really struggling with life?"

Not being one who fears going first, I shared how I turned straight to the Psalms when I felt overwhelmed. I talked about how the psalmists' authentic emotional depth bonded me to them like dear friends and helped me be more emotionally authentic with God in return.

One by one, the rest of the group shared their most helpful "scriptures." Kinda. Each woman shared the name of a devotional or Christian book they turned to for encouragement. Not the Bible. That's when I started to get nervous. I knew who wrote the words that they were describing: emotional, opinionated, imperfect human authors like me. Our words may be inspired by the Bible, but they aren't God's words. They're ours.

I didn't end up becoming a part of this church, but it taught me a valuable lesson—how important it is for me to make certain what I write lines up with Scripture. It also taught me to encourage my readers to be like the Bereans in Acts 17:11. They checked everything Paul said against the words God had already provided. Please, dear readers, do the same for me.

God, may what I write accurately reflect Your message and nature. Let it always lead others straight back to You. —Vicki Kuyper

Digging Deeper: Psalm 19:7–11; Acts 17:11; Romans 15:4; 2 Timothy 3:16–17

Thursday, September 24

I urge, then, first of all, that petitions, prayers, intercession and thanksgiving be made for all people. —1 Timothy 2:1 (NIV)

I was wrapping up things at work to leave on an overseas trip. I got a message to see my manager, Patrick, before leaving. I stopped by his office expecting a question about something coming up while I was away. As I walked in, he said, "I need you to do something for me while you're in Jerusalem. Will you go to the Wailing Wall and pray for me and my family?"

"Sure. What would you like me to pray?" I asked.

"Pray general prayers, whatever you choose," he said.

I had worked with Patrick for years. We had never really talked about our faith. On the flight over, I thought about what I would pray for him and his family. I wrote out the prayer and folded it into a small square. At the wall, I stood silently praying for him and his family. After praying, like multitudes before me, I pushed the folded prayer into a crack in the wall. I felt especially close to Patrick and his family thousands of miles away. I was surprised he had asked me to pray and blessed that he did.

The significance of praying in Jerusalem at a location where people of different faiths have been praying for thousands of years warmed my soul.

I took special care with this prayer, for I felt I was standing on holy ground.

Dear Lord, thank You for the blessing of interceding for others. Help us treasure the sacred trust that comes with each request. Guide us to take special care with every prayer whenever we are asked to pray. —John Dilworth

Digging Deeper: 1 Kings 8:28; Ephesians 6:18; Colossians 1:9

Friday, September 25

Just as a body, though one, has many parts, but all its many parts form one body, so it is with Christ. —1 Corinthians 12:12 (NIV)

It was a perfect autumn day when my nine-year-old grandson and I went to East Park to shoot hoops. The trees presented a kaleidoscope of vibrant colors. I pointed out my favorites to Sev: orange, red, brown, and yellow. Then my grandson surprised me. He pointed to a tree saying, "Those leaves aren't really red. They are magenta. And the tree next to it is like burnt sienna." On and on he went, identifying the colors of the trees with names like cerise and sepia. Where I'd seen only brown, he'd seen bronze. The leaves I'd identified as orange, he insisted were mandarin orange.

In that moment, the many Bible verses about different parts of the body and the different gifts given by the Holy Spirit came to mind. Some, like me, see basic colors. Others, like Sev, view the world with a wider palette. I thought of people in my church family, all of us singing praises together during the worship service, but Mary's and Dennis's voices rise above the rest. My hands frequently serve in the kitchen washing dishes after a church potluck, but there are others with hands that can skillfully paint a wall mural or decorate a beautiful wedding cake.

The Bible is very clear: whatever we do, we should do for God's glory. I hope Sev will grow up to use his discerning eye to serve the Lord. Whether you see brown and gold leaves this fall or bronze and amber ones, praise God for the beauty of autumn.

Dear Lord, I want to glorify You, please You, and thank You with my unique gifts. In Jesus's name.
—Shirley Raye Redmond

Digging Deeper: 1 Corinthians 12:21–27; Ephesians 1:22–23; Colossians 3:17

Saturday, September 26

My God will meet all your needs according to the riches of his glory in Christ Jesus.
—Philippians 4:19 (NIV)

Our daughter, Christine, couldn't contain her excitement on the phone. She and her husband,

Taun, had gotten a puppy. I couldn't believe it. How in the world did she get a dog? It's not that I don't like dogs. Christine, like me, is allergic to dogs, cats, and so many other things. She and her husband had no plans to get a dog. As she revealed when I asked, it just happened in God's mysterious way.

Christine and Taun had reservations at a restaurant. In the same plaza, the local pet store had several puppies out in an area for people to pet them. My daughter and husband had a good time playing with one puppy before going to dinner.

While at dinner, it dawned on Taun that Christine had no allergic reaction to the dog. She wasn't sneezing and had no watery eyes, hives, or nasal congestion. Taun said to her, "I think we found the right dog for you." After dinner they decided to go back to the pet store and spend more time with the same puppy. Once again, Christine was fine. On the spot they decided to purchase the Bernedoodle puppy with black, curly poodle fur and a white face and paws. Christine named the dog Frida, after her favorite Mexican artist, Frida Kahlo.

Frida fills their quiet home with lots of love, joy, and energy. It's the perfect gift for a wonderful, loving couple. And my wife, Elba, and I now have a wonderful grand fur in our lives.

This got me thinking how God knows all our needs. The perfect gift for our daughter and son-in-law, Frida is more than a dog—she's family.

Thank You for the gift of our dogs, cats, and other pets. They, too, are answered prayers that fill our hearts with love. —Pablo Diaz

Digging Deeper: Matthew 6:7–8; 2 Corinthians 9:8

Sunday, September 27

JOURNEY THROUGH GRIEF: Brandon's Wisdom

Consider it pure joy, my brothers and sisters, whenever you face trials of many kinds, because you know that the testing of your faith produces perseverance. —James 1:2–3 (NIV)

"Brandon broke his collarbone this evening," my son's teacher said over the phone. My 15-year-old son had landed in Cuba just a day earlier for a weeklong marine biology expedition. A day later, his trip ended. He would require surgery, and school leaders were booking tickets to bring him home immediately.

After the shock wore off, I went into self-pity mode, a familiar space the past few months. This opportunity for Brandon was supposed to be the beacon of better things to come and a respite from grief.

"Yes, it's going to be a life-changing adventure," I'd say proudly when speaking to others about his upcoming trip. Now I pitied my son for being robbed of this experience, regretted the money spent to send him there, and sympathized with what I imagined would be a long and painful recovery.

At the airport, I spotted my poor little broken boy descending the escalators. He waved with his good arm, and he was smiling the whole ride down. I embraced him gently and asked how he was doing.

"Good," he said, as if I'd just asked how his school day went.

He wasn't in pain, didn't seem sad, and was excited to tell me about his short trip to Cuba. I reassured him that he had every right to be upset.

"Oh, Mami," he said, petting my head like a puppy dog. "What good is that going to do?"

In that moment, as my son refused to take on the weight of self-pity, I could feel my own lift from my body.

Father, thank You for creating me with emotions. Help me to accept how I feel for a season, without wallowing and becoming stagnant.
—Karen Valentin

Digging Deeper: Romans 8:28; 1 Thessalonians 5:18

Monday, September 28

Our citizenship is in heaven, and from it we await a Savior, the Lord Jesus Christ, who will transform our lowly body to be like his glorious body. —Philippians 3:20–21 (ESV)

"Hey Buck, I hate to tell you, but the guitar you loaned me has a crack in the side. It's totally separated."

I knew what my friend was talking about. An old repair. It must have come loose in transit. Nothing major. It wasn't like it was one of my more expensive instruments. It was older—vintage might be a kinder term—and had seen a whole lot of life. I imagined it living through a war or two. After all, not every war is fought on a battlefield. More struggles than we probably like to admit are fought right here on the home front. In bedrooms, kitchens, living rooms—you get the picture. I'm sure that guitar could tell stories.

I guess I'm a little vintage too. I've definitely had my share of repairs. Like my old guitar, every so often I feel one or two of them might be coming apart. Unlike my old guitar, I'm not all that sure I sound better with age.

But even as I grumble, I remember God's promise—that one day this fleshly tent of mine, weak and battle-scarred as it is, will be transformed into something perfect and new. He is here. His love surrounds me and hope lifts, fills, and thrills me. And even though there are some buzzes in these braces and scratches in the body, in the hands of the Master Luthier I find myself in tune again.

And He reminds me there are songs left in me yet.

Heavenly Father, I am nothing—wood and strings—unless You are the musician.
—Buck Storm

Digging Deeper: 2 Corinthians 5:1–6; 1 John 3:2

Tuesday, September 29

Woe to the world because of the things that cause people to stumble! Such things must come, but woe to the person through whom they come! —Matthew 18:7 (NIV)

I may have to give up Wordle, an online game. Not because I'm not good at it. My win ratio is 98 percent, and I most often guess the word of the day in three or four tries. It's because of my friend Leslie. Well, not exactly *because* of her, but because of what happens when I see her Wordle score on Facebook each day.

Wordle is a popular web-based word game in which players have six attempts to guess the five-letter word of the day. A game of skill and chance, success is often determined by the word chosen to start the game, which will give you a hint about what letters the word of the day has and what position they're in. Think of it like hangman or Scrabble, only played alone, word by word.

Leslie routinely shares how many tries she took to get the correct Wordle answer. When I see her social media posts, I've often done better. I smile with satisfaction and deem myself superior. *What kind of friend does that?*

Can you guess what my problem is? I'll give you the answer in five letters: PRIDE.

Maybe I don't actually need to give up Wordle altogether. Perhaps changing my start word could prompt me to be less GREEN. ABIDE would remind me to stay close to God. PIETY might help me be nice and not JUDGE others. TRUST and FAITH are strong contenders, as I'm no ANGEL. I think the very best answer is for me to extend GRACE and REMIT. After all, judging my friend makes me an ENEMY, and that's a win for the DEVIL.

Lord, change my HEART and make me more like JESUS. —Stephanie Thompson

Digging Deeper: Matthew 7:1; Luke 6:31; Colossians 3:12–14

Wednesday, September 30

For if either of them falls, the one will lift up his companion. —Ecclesiastes 4:10 (NASB)

"September 30, 4:16 a.m.: Lord, I'm asking that You send me someone to help stack wood," I wrote in my journal.

Over the past year I'd gone through several regenerative medical procedures where a doctor had taken my own stem cells, combined them with my own platelets, then injected them into my body's sites of injury, injuries that had occurred in 1983 when a drunk driver had hit me head-on.

Miraculously, my body was healing itself. During this interim time my doctor had put restrictions on my physical activity until the cells regenerated. But right now I wasn't healed enough to stack the wood that I'd purchased for my wood stove. I had several friends who had said they'd help with anything I needed, and they had, but I hated to ask—again.

When the sun poked its head over the mountains, I donned my down vest and strolled down to feed horses. A *V* of geese honked overhead, and the nip in the air foretold of the coming winter. *God, I need help with the wood. Soon.*

At 5:47 p.m. my cell phone rang. It was Jeanne, who lived in Oklahoma—1,652 miles away. Over 30 years ago, when she and her husband had lived in Montana, we'd become best friends. Together, through our faith and prayers, we'd faced the tragedies and triumphs that life brings. Her excited voice exclaimed that she and Doug had decided— that morning—to make a trip to Montana to visit their kids and me. She asked, "Is there anything we can do for you?"

Lord, I'm so humbled and awed to have amazing friends. Most of all—that You're my very best One. Amen. —Rebecca Ondov

Digging Deeper: Proverbs 17:17, 18:24

LIVING A NEW LIFE

1 _____

2 _____

3 _____

4 _____

5 _____

6 _____

7 _____

8 _____

9 _____

10 _____

11 _____

12 _____

13 _____

14 _____

15 _____

16 _____

17 _____

18 _____

19 _____

20 _____

21 _____

22 _____

23 _____

24 _____

25 _____

26 _____

27 _____

28 _____

29 _____

30 _____

October

So then faith comes by hearing,
and hearing by the word of God.

—Romans 10:17 (NKJV)

Thursday, October 1

Your paths drip with fatness.
—Psalm 65:11 (NASB)

I often say my greatest adventure is a blank page. What thoughts will I have, what stories and conversations, what creativity, what intimate moments with the Holy Spirit? Each day begins with that thin page. When evening arrives, I am always surprised by how fat it is.

A friend bemoaned the fact that she had nothing interesting to journal. Not true, I told her. The most ordinary things hold meaning. I gave her my traffic light soliloquy.

I live on a mountain looking down a river valley. In the valley is our small town with its single traffic light—a light I can see from my mountain window. At 9 p.m. it falls into its REM—rapid eye movement—slumber, as I call its flashing yellow. If I catch it just right—at 6 a.m.—I see it wake for the day. First solid yellow—then red—then a green that proclaims, "Let's get going."

It's our secret, beginning our day together across the valley—each with meaningful work to do. That lone light encourages me. We are friends greeting each other. I turn from the window, satisfied I have marked a significant moment on my daily page.

Psalm 139:16 (NASB) says, "In Your book were all written the days that were ordained for me." Each sunrise is an opportunity to fill a new page—to make it fat with life.

My pages are my story. They matter to God. I won't live them all well. I won't live them all with joy and victory. He gives them to me anyway. It is His story that is perfect, not mine.

Every morning He is the light greeting me from my unwritten page.

My Savior, from the rising of the sun You fill my story. I cannot write it without You. —Carol Knapp

Digging Deeper: Psalm 139:1–6; Zechariah 4:10; John 1:1

Friday, October 2

LIFE LESSONS FROM GAMES:
Take the First Step
The LORD makes firm the steps of the one who delights in him. —Psalm 37:23 (NIV)

I was playing Ball Sort, a color puzzle game, when my cousin Michal called. Our aunt had moved from Chicago, near me, to Washington State, near Michal, a few years before. I was still her power of attorney.

"You need to come. Aunt Carol's memory is worse. She can't manage on her own." Yes, I would fly out. But what would I do then?

Worried about Aunt Carol, I looked at my unfinished puzzle. Absentmindedly, I made the next move. Then the next. I was startled when I won the game.

That reminded me of my favorite quote from Rev. Dr. Martin Luther King Jr.: "Faith is taking the first step even when you don't see the whole staircase." If I could faithfully trust God on this trip, what would be my first step? Text my friends to pray.

Aunt Carol embraced me at her door. Behind her, stacked boxes filled the room; they were still labeled Chicago. First step? Remove piles of unpaid bills from my bed in the guest room.

The next morning Aunt Carol poured herself a bowl of cereal and moldy blueberries. When she added milk, dead bugs floated to the top. She shrugged her shoulders. "Extra protein."

First step? "Aunt Carol, would you like to visit your sister Jo?" She nodded eagerly. On our 5-hour drive to Oregon, she forgot she lived in Washington.

We toured Aunt Jo's assisted living facility. I helped Aunt Carol move into a room near Aunt Jo, then I drove back to Washington. I spent hours putting notes on boxes in her apartment: "Carol," "Leanne," "Give away." Michal would distribute it. I paid her final month's rent. I flew home. One step at a time, the puzzle had been solved.

Steadfast Lord, I put my trust in You, every step of every day. —Leanne Jackson

Digging Deeper: Proverbs 16:9; Hebrews 12:1

Hold on to what is good.
—1 Thessalonians 5:21 (NIV)

It had been a perfect day. Our youngest daughter, home for a visit, went with us to watch her sister's daughters play soccer. The sun was shining. The air held autumn crispness. My husband and I watched our two daughters, son-in-law, and three granddaughters joyfully play a pick-up soccer game after the "real" games. The eight of us observed an afternoon eclipse through filtered glasses, then lunched outside among golden-leafed trees. We talked, walked, played, and relaxed together. A fun dinner at a local restaurant was followed by drippy, delicious ice cream and smear-faced grinning granddaughters. As dusk arrived, a spectacular sunset of orange and magenta filled the sky. We walked to a playground and, as the sun dipped low, played on the swings, ropes, and slides. It was just us on the playground, and our laughter rang clear.

As night fell, I stood still, watching and absorbing, immersed in the moment, filled with gratitude to our gracious God. *Hold on to this. Hold on.* The words kept coming to my mind. I didn't want this day of togetherness, delight, and joy to end. *Hold on.*

As we drove home that night, I thought about the many times I've tried to urge myself to "let go"—to let go of worries, concerns, irritations, and more. But just as important—perhaps even more, I realized—I need to remember to hold on: to memories, beauty, purity, loveliness, joy, laughter, love, and the blessings of this life. Hold on. Don't ever forget or take any of it for granted. *Hold on.*

Precious Lord, thank You! Thank You for every precious moment of beauty, joy, and delight with which You've blessed me. Help me to remember to hold on. —Kim Taylor Henry

Digging Deeper: 1 Chronicles 16:12; Psalm 103:1–2; James 1:17

Sunday, October 4

I will give them an undivided heart and put a new spirit in them. —Ezekiel 11:19 (NIV)

I once took our dog, Max, to a blessing of the animals service at a local Episcopal church. After the service was over, as we returned with our animals to our cars, I met a woman who had brought her hedgehog.

Yes, hedgehog.

"I've seen dogs and cats, even parrots and bunnies, at these things over the years," I said, "but this is a new one to me."

"I know. I've never seen another like Sam, either, in church. But this was good for him," she said. "He's had a really tough year."

Even hedgehogs, apparently, have difficult years and need a new start.

Don't be sheepish today about your own need to reboot, recharge, or start again. We all need to be reminded of God's blessing on us. Wouldn't it be wonderful if, once a year, we had a ritual where sanctified oil (which is used to anoint the heads of kings and queens, and which we often use at baptisms and when someone is near death) was rubbed into the palms of our hands, reminding us that they are the hands of God?

With this new spirit, Lord, I will tend Your garden with these simple hands of mine.
—Jon M. Sweeney

Digging Deeper: 2 Corinthians 5:17

Monday, October 5

Trust in the LORD with all your heart and lean not on your own understanding.
—Proverbs 3:5 (NIV)

I was talking to a colleague regarding my research for a book I was writing about Alzheimer's disease and my family called *A Journey of Faith*.

"The more I read, the more I find out that almost everything can increase your chances of developing dementia," I said. "The risks are everywhere!"

I wasn't exaggerating. Diabetes, hypertension, heart disease, obesity, high cholesterol, kidney disease, hearing loss, you name it. Doctors say these common conditions can all increase the risk of developing Alzheimer's. And there's more. Stress, diet, air pollution, depression, anxiety, addiction, head injuries, autoimmune disorders, genes, even eye disease are other possible culprits. So are poverty, race, gender, and lack of education. I hate to report this, but a peer-reviewed study from Great Britain found evidence that excessive nose picking could lead to Alzheimer's. And of course, simple aging is the greatest risk factor of all.

"There's no escaping it!" I cried. "I mean, how do we not age?"

My friend let me calm down and then said, "We carry on."

Some help that was. Of course we carry on.

Yet the more I thought about it, the more I found comfort in that simple remark. We carry on through all the perils of life. Through the setbacks and disappointments. Through even the joys and victories. We carry on because our faith goes before us, meeting us in all our days, God's love the one thing we can be sure of.

My research also yielded evidence that a strong spiritual life is a protective factor against many health problems, including Alzheimer's.

Yes, we carry on.

Lord, I follow the light of heaven to carry me through life. —Edward Grinnan

Digging Deeper: Romans 8:35–39

Tuesday, October 6

He has made everything beautiful in its time. He has also set eternity in the human heart.
—Ecclesiastes 3:11 (NIV)

"If only I had a little more time."

That was my mantra throughout grade school, as the test administrator observed her watch to see if it was time for that awful "Stop!" at the end of the reading comprehension test booklet. My dread was not so much whether I possessed the skill to comprehend. The anxiety-maker was that tyrant called *time*—would I have enough of it to complete the task?

Exam apprehension notwithstanding, through reading books I learned to recognize the everlasting gifts of love and hope—universal truths, they're often called in literature. And in the ultimate Book, Ecclesiastes 3:11 makes it clear that while beauty (and other earthly treasures like test scores) falls into the parameters of time, it is eternity that God chooses to put into the human heart.

Although time is important when taking academic classes, learning eternal truths is far more crucial. God places within the believer's heart the understanding that heaven and earth—and timed tests—will pass away, but His love lasts forever.

As a fifth grader, I had not begun to understand the potential tyranny of time in our lives. It would take the never-ending string of life's joys and sadnesses to grasp the glory of eternity residing in my heart. Had I understood this earlier, the dreaded *stop* might have been less frightening. Time ceases to hold sway when measured against eternity spent with the Savior!

Lord, please help me remember that everything on earth has a time, but eternity is forever.
—Jacqueline F. Wheelock

Digging Deeper: Psalm 31:15; Matthew 24:35; 2 Peter 3:8

Wednesday, October 7

I lie down and sleep, and all night long the LORD protects me. I am not afraid of the thousands of enemies who surround me on every side.
—Psalm 3:5–6 (GNT)

I came across an interesting story about a steep and treacherous mountain road in northern Scotland that had been engineered by General George Wade in 1753, during the Jacobite rebellion. When the soldiers reached the top of the mountain and the terrain leveled off, the general commanded his workers to "Rest and be thankful." Later someone built a large sitting bench there with the general's words on it, and now it's a popular tourist rest stop, overlooking a beautiful valley.

Inspired by this story, I built several wooden sitting benches and put them in shady spots around our yard. I put one bench by our back door, and on it I painted the words, "Rest and be thankful," adding a picture of a dove.

I see these words every evening when I come in from working outdoors all day. Dragging myself along, my muscles and bones aching and my tired mind troubled about many things, I see the words "Rest and be thankful," and they are like a fine ointment to my weary head.

Since I made that bench, I have found that rest and gratitude are like miracle drugs to me, yet they cost nothing and have no ill side effects. Counting my blessings at bedtime is not always easy, but it mellows me out and helps me to sleep. Then slumber restores my perspective on life. No matter how tired I may feel at bedtime, by morning my "thousands of enemies" have been reduced to a few toy soldiers by God's grace.

When the road of life is steep, Lord, give us rest and make us grateful. —Daniel Schantz

Digging Deeper: Psalm 127:2; Matthew 11:28–30

Thursday, October 8

The nations will see your vindication, and all kings your glory; you will be called by a new name that the mouth of the Lord will bestow. —Isaiah 62:2 (NIV)

"Hey bae" is the casual way my 21-year-old daughter, Micah, texts me to say hello. If you don't know, *bae* is a slang term of endearment primarily used among iGen people my daughter's age. I don't mind her calling me bae, as it's a friendly moniker reserved for people she likes.

After two decades of motherhood, I've been called by many mother names. I was first dubbed Ma Ma when Micah was seven months old. By the time she was three, I was Mommy. Once the preteen years hit, she settled on Mom. During her teen years, I was often addressed as bruh, a shortened word for brother, but Micah most often used it to express disbelief or disagreement with what I was saying. When she was annoyed with me in high school, she'd disrespectfully drag out the syllables of my first name in a loud tone (which I didn't like).

As my relationship with my child changed, so did the names she called me by. But no matter what name she uses, I'll always be her mother.

God changed the names of people, too, but it was to reflect their character or who they were to become. Abram to Abraham (Genesis 17:5); Sarai to Sarah (Genesis 17:15); Jacob to Israel (Genesis 32:28); Simon to Peter (Matthew 16:18); and Saul to Paul (Acts 13:9).

He promises to give me a new name in eternity, but I doubt it will be bae or one of my motherhood nomenclatures. No matter what name God bestows on me, I'm most glad I'll always be His.

Lord, grow my character to be more like You while I look forward to my new name.
—Stephanie Thompson

Digging Deeper: Isaiah 43:1; Revelation 3:12

Friday, October 9

You will be my witnesses. —Acts 1:8 (ESV)

"Miss Evelyn, are you *praying*?" The neighbor teen riding in my backseat was distressed. She had lost her valued earbuds, maybe at a school dance, maybe in the family car parked 5 miles away, maybe in a school friend's car.

This was not the first such inquiry. Over several years, several times a week I had said to her, "Can we pray for the day?" Then my "Dear Jesus..." salutation introduced petitions for strength and safety, for resolution of troubles and stresses. I added thanksgivings, though not often enough. I've been modeling. She's been listening, and prayer is gaining ground among her coping mechanisms.

On that dark Friday evening, her mom was busy. She called to ask if I could take her around town— to retrace her steps. After recruiting someone to ride along, I drove to the school, now locked tight. We searched sidewalks. She asked the urgent question once and then again as we neared another unfamiliar destination. "Are you praying?!" Yes, I assured her— pleading silently that the lost would be found.

I prayed, knowing God is not a genie granting abracadabra wishes. And yet we're told to look to Him and ask for help.

On Friday evening we didn't locate the lost earbuds. But on Saturday morning the teen called. "Found them."

My immediate response? "Dear Jesus, thank You!" God—and the teen—heard my grateful words.

Lord, as people of prayer, may we be seen as witnesses to Your presence in the world.
—Evelyn Bence

Digging Deeper: Philippians 4:7; Colossians 1:3–14

Saturday, October 10

Do everything in love. —1 Corinthians 16:14 (NIV)

My eight-year-old son came over thoughtfully, balancing a carefully prepared selection of breakfast items he'd chosen for me. He thought of everything, including waffles with syrup, Hershey's kisses for dessert, a very full cup of milk, and a bowl of strawberries that he washed himself. It warmed my heart, and at first glance, it all looked amazing.

Closer look at the details revealed the paper plates were layered about five plates thick, the strawberries were floating in the water that had rinsed them, and the chocolates were stuck to the plate in the puddles of syrup that had leaked over the waffle edges.

However, these imperfections made his gift even more special. His only intention was giving his best for my joy. And there really was no blemish that could make his gift less valuable to me. He is on the autism spectrum, and the fact that he was able to go through all the steps needed to prepare my meal was amazing. He gave all that he knew how to give.

How often I have given what is easy to give from excess. I have church donations withdrawn on auto renew, yet it has been almost a year since I have checked in personally with the ministry itself. I pray at someone's request but don't stop and talk when I see them passing by.

This breakfast was a sweet reminder that the most joyful gifts come from a truly pure and selfless heart.

Lord, remind me daily, and moment by moment, to have sincere motives to give all that I can for Your Kingdom, and not only what is easy.
—Nicole Garcia

Digging Deeper: 2 Corinthians 9:7; Philippians 2:3; Colossians 3:14; 1 John 4:7

Sunday, October 11

The purpose in a man's heart is like deep water, but a man of understanding will draw it out.
—**Proverbs 20:5** (ESV)

Our busy nine-year-old son, Jacques, had a hard time sitting through any church service. We tried engaging him with fidget toys, holding his hand, and sitting up front. Nothing seemed to work. In a final effort, we decided to try attending a later service time. A later service time allowed for Jacques to expend his zoomies before service, and the lower attendance lessened the distractions he encountered.

My family walked through the back door of the chapel that first Sunday at a new time anxiously, not knowing what to expect. Immediately we were greeted with huge hugs from Ms. Deny, a long-time volunteer.

As we listened to the readings during service, Jacques, however, still squirmed and grew restless. I gave him "the look," which made no difference. Ms. Deny, noticing our situation, very quietly came to Jacques and asked him to help her.

Ms. Deny had Jacques help her collect the offering and count attendees. He came back to me and sat quietly for a while, then he went back to Ms. Deny at the end of service to help pass out bulletins. As we left the chapel, Ms. Deny gave Jacques a hug and said, "I love you. I will see you next week." And we have seen her every week since.

It turned out the time of service and number of people made no difference for Jacques, but Ms. Deny, well, she *was* the difference. She gave purpose to a little boy who needed it. And she encouraged him with warm hugs and special "I love yous." My family is blessed to call this place home!

God of all things holy, may I continue to seek and refine Your purpose for my sacred life.
—Jolynda Strandberg

Digging Deeper: Romans 8:26–30; Ephesians 2:8–10

Monday, October 12

I have learned, in whatever state I am, to be content. —Philippians 4:11 (RSV)

In mid-October one of my friends echoed a sentiment I hear often this time of year. "Well, summer's gone. It's getting colder and darker, and we still have two and a half months until Christmas."

Here in Wisconsin, peak leaf color maps are updated daily. The changes come quickly, evoking regrets. "Oh no! We're already too late for the prime brightness of Door County." Unlike spring's return to life and the promise of summer, autumn is a transition into dimness and dormancy. To be sure, every season is someone's favorite, but for those who don't enjoy autumn, lamenting for the season just past and feeling impatient for the one approaching empties joy from the present.

I remember a conversation that the same friend and I had a while back, when she commented that she especially celebrates warm, sunny days that aren't too hot or cold.

I'd grinned. "Not complaining about the weather is a spiritual discipline. It teaches us to adapt to what we cannot change and savor what life brings. Singing in the rain is ecstasy."

She chuckled and said, "If I'm watching through a window by a cozy fireplace."

"I understand," I acknowledge. "But I just get grumpy by bemoaning the days that don't measure up."

She nods and smiles.

The great spiritual teachers of many generations and traditions agree that peace and wholeness are found by living in the present moment. Regret comes from living in the past, anxiety from trying to live in the future. Delighting in whatever the current season brings and savoring each day's weather empowers wonder in each present moment.

God of every moment, alert us to Your closeness through whatever comes in the present.
—Norm Stolpe

Digging Deeper: 2 Corinthians 12:10; 1 Timothy 6:6–8; Hebrews 13:5

Tuesday, October 13
THE BIRDS OF MY NEIGHBORHOOD:
All God's Children
The Spirit himself testifies with our spirit that we are God's children. —Romans 8:16 (NIV)

When early autumn arrived, I started gathering our various bird feeders to clean and hang them. Most go up on tree limbs in a little patch of flowers and decorative grasses where our old farm hand pump is. We can see those feeders clearly from our kitchen and breakfast nook windows.

It doesn't take long after filling them with black oil sunflower seeds for the birds to find them. It's a delight to watch, from the varieties of birds that make their way to the feeders. Cardinals. Black-capped chickadees. House sparrows. Tufted titmouses. Flickers. House finches. White-breasted nuthatches. And more. Some take up residence in the bushes lining the side deck. Others perch in the mulberry tree close by. Some wait their turn while others swoop down, hoping to cut in line. Their flight plans vary—some come in straight while others go up and down, perhaps to avoid the watchful eyes of the red-tailed hawk that sometimes sits on a limb at the edge of the woods.

As I watch the various birds, with their different colors and flying patterns, it would be easy to see them as different. But they share one thing—their birdness. It reminds me of all the various types of humans there are. So many differences. And yet we all share our humanness. And we are all beloved children of God.

That's something I need to be reminded of. Especially in a time when I am noticing, with annoyance, our differences. Thank you, cardinals, black-capped chickadees, house sparrows, et al.—and God—for that reminder.

Thou who made us all, help me to see the beauty and Your image in each person I encounter today. Amen. —J. Brent Bill

Digging Deeper: Genesis 1:26–31

Wednesday, October 14

She watches over the affairs of her household and does not eat the bread of idleness.
—Proverbs 31:27 (NIV)

My mother, who passed away nearly a decade ago, was the best housekeeper I've ever known. Managing an orderly, clean home was one of her greatest virtues, and she kept a beautiful home to prove it. Over the years I can almost hear her voice in my ear, repeating the words I've heard her say countless times during my childhood and adult years.

From spiritual advice: "Daughter, you know cleanliness is next to godliness."

To the esoteric: "Always keep plants in your home. You want to have life growing in your house, along with the humans."

To instructional: "Put extra energy into detail cleaning, like those baseboards and corners."

My mother, a lifelong educator and a college dean when she retired, once confided in me that if she'd had the vision at a younger age, she would have started her own cleaning business. With her passion for clean homes and her gift of leadership,

I know she would have flourished at such a venture.

Even though I'll never become the meticulous housekeeper Mom was, her voice still speaks through mine, as I train my own children. On Saturdays, during a cleaning spree, I marvel at all the things I learned from my mother. And how much I feel her presence—reminding me that she's gone but not forgotten.

Lord, may my parents' voices continue to live on in my heart and through my own words as I encourage my family and others. —Carla Hendricks

Digging Deeper: Proverbs 31:10–31; Titus 2:3–5

Thursday, October 15

THE LONELY AMONG US: All These Things

Seek ye first the kingdom of God, and his righteousness; and all these things shall be added unto you. —Matthew 6:33 (KJV)

My brother Larry has many friends. He organizes block parties, has been in a men's group for decades, bikes with buddies, and interacts extensively online. He's the poster child for those who believe that friends in abundance ensure a long and happy life.

I have friends, too, but fewer, and spending as much time with them as Larry does seems— like getting the requisite 8 hours of blessed sleep daily—unattainable. The day just isn't long enough to provide health and happiness. Where does Larry find time to grocery shop, keep a clean house, buy garden seeds, write in a café, and watch the Oklahoma City Thunder trounce the Celtics?

Recent wellness scholarship touts the even greater value of lesser relationships—so-called weak ties, acquaintances you interact with throughout the day. I have lots of these. Baristas debating a grammar question while brewing my dark, smoky lapsang-souchong tea. Fellow customers who catch me examining the shrink-wrapped ham or olive oils and solicit my opinion. Pickup drivers who pass gray-haired me running and want to discuss it. The thought comforts me briefly, till another wellness mandate captures my worries.

Sometimes, in seeking friends and other well-being essentials, I forget all about the inventor of well-being: God Himself, who offers us everything we need if we just seek Him first.

Help me remember, Father, to seek You first in my social pursuits and everything else. —Patty Kirk

Digging Deeper: Matthew 6:19–34; Luke 10:38–42

Friday, October 16

Do not let your hearts be troubled and do not be afraid. —John 14:27 (NIV)

I was 18 and on a trip to London with my high school English class. We had no cell phones or GPS, just good old-fashioned maps to get around the city. Since we were given free time to explore, my boyfriend (now my husband) and I went off on our own.

That evening we were supposed to meet the group, but we ended up stopping at the wrong metro station and became lost. We thought it would be faster to go by foot, but we were soon off the main drag and in the middle of a dark neighborhood.

Panic began to overwhelm me, and I could no longer make rational decisions. My boyfriend was a strong guy, and he tried to reassure me, but I couldn't see beyond my fear. In the span of a few minutes, I became convinced that something horrible was about to happen.

As we walked around a bend, I could hear someone coming toward us and my panic increased. So when a middle-aged nun walking a sweet little dog appeared, I was speechless. It was the opposite of what I'd expected. After she kindly gave us directions, we discovered we were very close to our destination.

I realized something profound that evening. Fear clouds our perspective and makes us expect the worst-case scenario. Faith clears the way and tells us to look for the best outcome. Whenever fear starts to paint a dark picture in my thoughts,

I remind myself that things aren't always as they appear. Something good is just around the corner.

Lord, when fear overwhelms me with lies and negative thoughts, remind me that faith is there to point me toward safety. —Gabrielle Meyer

Digging Deeper: Joshua 1:9; Psalm 23:4; 2 Timothy 1:7

Saturday, October 17

Moses was one hundred twenty years old when he died; his sight was unimpaired, and his vigor had not abated. —Deuteronomy 34:7 (NRSVUE)

In my late 70s, I am aware that my vision is diminishing and my vigor declining. A year ago I curtailed driving in the dark, snow, and ice. After my wife, Candy, was diagnosed with Alzheimer's in 2017, we moved from Texas to Wisconsin to share a duplex with our son David and his family. Our son Erik joined us in 2022, so with grown grandson Sam, I have four other drivers to chauffeur me.

I am writing this right before Daylight Saving Time ends, and I'm considering the increasing darkness and aware of the approach of the Wisconsin winter. Having lived in Minnesota, Illinois, New Jersey, and Wisconsin before living in Texas, I actually welcome winter. In our three-generation household, I am exempt from outdoor chores, including snow shoveling. I am thankful to have relinquished lifting anything heavy and most stair climbing. The family picks up more and more without bemoaning my decline. Instead I hear, "Dad, we can start taking care of that now."

I have been inspired by the example of Mechthild of Magdeburg (1207–1282). She had an active life of spirituality, service, and teaching. When she went blind and lost the physical ability to feed or dress herself, she moved into a Cistercian convent, where the nuns cared for her. She left us this prayer in her collection of meditations: *The Flowing Light of the Godhead*:

Lord, I thank You that since You have taken my sight from me, You serve me through the eyes of others. Lord, I thank You that since You have taken from me the strength of my hands and the strength of my heart, You now serve me with the hands and hearts of others. —Norm Stolpe

Digging Deeper: Psalm 71:9, 17–18; Psalm 90:10, 16–17; Luke 2:25–38

Sunday, October 18

**May your blessing be on your people.
—Psalm 3:8 (NIV)**

Many years ago, before I worked as a hospital chaplain, members of a gang moved into the neighborhood where my family lived. A month later they brutally ended the lives of four children.

Although what transpired happened to a family unknown to me, I was severely traumatized. *Oh God,* I wondered, *how could You have allowed this to happen?*

A week later, desperate for solace, I attended a prayer meeting at my parish. At the end of the meeting, the pastor of the church, Father Thomas, walked in. Someone asked if he wanted to speak a word to us. With his eyes closed, Father Thomas took a deep breath and softly said, "Evil has visited us this week and seems to be winning. But we must remember that we have goodness on our side, and we must bless the power of good so that it overcomes this darkness."

Father Thomas's words transformed me. From a traumatized person whose faith in God and humanity had been shaken to the core, his words not only brought me peace but also gave me a sense of calling.

Soon after, I began working in a church, and eventually even worked with gangs in our city before moving on to hospital chaplaincy. Interestingly, even as a chaplain, I still encounter young men who are involved with gangs. However, thanks to the powerful words of Father Thomas, I continue to bless the power of good anywhere and everywhere I am sent.

O Lord, blessed are we who call upon Your name. Amen. —Adam Ruiz

Digging Deeper: Psalm 21:6; Isaiah 44:3; Ephesians 1:3

A gentle answer turns away wrath, but harsh words cause quarrels. —Proverbs 15:1 (TLB)

I'm not sure if it's getting older or living alone that makes me cranky, but there are things that really bug me. For example, every fall when the snowbirds from Ohio move into their condo directly below mine for the winter months, they put a big, gray, oversized cement rabbit in the beautiful common garden area out back behind our two condos.

I dislike that rabbit so much that the minute it appears in mid-October, I start thinking about tossing it deep into the bushes so it will never be seen again. I feel justified because our association rules state that owners are not allowed to put anything on the common grounds.

Normally I am kind and soft-spoken and always get along with my neighbors. But when that tacky rabbit appears in my beautiful backyard area amid all the flowering bushes, plants, and palm trees, my blood pressure rises.

One year during the week that ugly rabbit appeared I came across a verse in Matthew. "One day's burden is enough for one day." That hit me smack in the face. Why did I let that cement rabbit irritate me day after day after day? Instead of staying angry for 6 months, maybe all I was entitled to was one day of it being a burden for me. One day. Then I should forget it.

So now I don't dream about tossing it in the bushes. I let it be, knowing that for 6 months a year I won't have to look at it.

Now when I'm upset about anything, I try very hard to only let it fester for one day. Then I take a deep breath, smile, and get on with my life.

Father, help me be a good neighbor 12 months a year. —Patricia Lorenz

Digging Deeper: Proverbs 22:24–25; Isaiah 63:3–9; Ephesians 4:31

Tuesday, October 20

This is the genealogy of Jesus the Messiah the son of David, the son of Abraham. —Matthew 1:1 (NIV)

A notice from a genealogy website arrived saying that there was new information on a relative, my great-grandfather's sister. When I logged in, I discovered someone had uploaded a photo of her, and for the first time, I saw my great-great-aunt, who bore an amazing resemblance to my grandmother.

Later I showed my mom the photo on my phone. "Look at that!" she said, leaning in as her eyes widened. "I've never seen her before. She looks so much like my mother!"

Years ago, when my father was ill and living halfway across the world, I found comfort in diving deep into the records of the past. Discovering my lineage made me feel connected; somehow, facts, dates, and records made me trust that things made sense. Even now, when I am worried or my life seems out of control, I find myself drawn to get back to my genealogy.

Looking at my family tree, I'm struck by all those lives and stories, all those faces—and the amazing mystery that a stranger can upload a photo to a website and bring such delight to my mother's face.

There's something beautiful about resemblance and belonging—the way that my oldest son looks like my husband's brother who died years ago, and how my brother has the mannerisms of my father. Family trees can make you feel like you fit into the order of things, just as the Bible's intricate web of genealogies affirms a sense of belonging and the enduring promises that are passed down from one generation to the next.

Heavenly Father, thank You for the connections that keep me grounded in faith. —Sabra Ciancanelli

Digging Deeper: Genesis 5:1–32; Leviticus 26:45

Wednesday, October 21

When I am afraid, I put my trust in You.
—Psalm 56:3 (NIV)

I was driving home from a friend's house with my dog in her carrying case next to me. She was becoming increasingly overwhelmed by the sound of a loud car motor nearby. She glanced up at me from behind the see-through mesh window on her bag, whimpering, concerned. Her eyes went to my face, seeking reassurance. I noticed that as long as she could see me and hear my voice, she settled down.

I tend to focus on the things I fear or feel I am failing at, and I become filled with certainty that the outcome will be bad. Lately I have been particularly overwhelmed by motherhood. My oldest son, who just became a teenager, has had some struggles at home and at school. So often I find myself examining everything I must have done wrong as a parent. I use my own strength to find him counseling, have conversations with teachers, and communicate with my ex-husband and try to parent with him.

I exhaust myself in fear and in trying. But when I look at God, I have an opportunity to receive His peace. When I fix my eyes on the Lord, the worry and fear dissipate. The situation might not change, but knowing the Lord is my guide through the difficulties provides me with the ability to exchange the fears about my son's well-being and future for reassurance that we have a Protector helping us through.

Lord, please help me to seek Your face consciously and continually and to hear Your voice over the voices of fear and worry. —Nicole Garcia

---

Thursday, October 22

The eyes of the Lord are on the righteous, and his ears are attentive to their cry. —Psalm 34:15 (NIV)

It's small-group night at our house. My husband, Lonny, and I joined this ministry at church a year and a half ago. We prayed for others to join the two of us for fellowship, accountability, and prayer. The Lord provided. Lonny and I remove a table and push the furniture to the perimeter of the room to accommodate sixteen soul-siblings who have become our family in Christ.

The front door opens again and again. Soon our home is filled with the extravagant joy of believers. It's only when we sit to study that I notice that my friend Laura is quiet. Later, when the last couple leaves, I text my friend.

"R u okay?" I ask.

Her reply comes fast. "I'm downhearted. Please pray." Then she adds, "Thank you for seeing."

Of course I see my friend. Her feelings matter to me. When she's downcast, there's a shadow on my own soul. The beauty of this intimacy overwhelms me. Especially when I compare it to being known by the Lord.

Our heavenly Father knows the very hairs on our heads. He knows our thoughts. Our beginning. And our end. He knows our hearts. Our worries.

Our actions. Our sin. He knows our weaknesses and strengths. And in the book of Zephaniah, we're told that even in knowing us, the Lord rejoices over us still.

Oh, to be this known and this loved!

I will surely pray for Laura. She's one of my closest friends. But what a blessing it is to understand that she's in the care of the One who sees us to the center. And in grace and mercy, our Father loves us still.

Lord, thank You for knowing, loving, hearing, and seeing us. Amen. —Shawnelle Eliasen

Digging Deeper: Psalm 139:13–14; Zephaniah 3:17; Luke 12:7; Romans 5:8

Friday, October 23

Behold, I am with you always, to the end of the age. —Matthew 28:20 (ESV)

Tubes glow. The turntable starts to spin, and I lower the needle gently. The speakers crackle. I love that sound. A piano starts, then the vocal, and in an instant I feel both happy and sad. *Nostalgic* would be the right word. There is a scratch on the record, and it will skip right after the first chorus, but I'll be ready to advance it just enough to keep the song going. Then I'll turn the lights low, sit back, and listen to the rest of the album. As always, the music will take me places. Some good, some painful, but all of them a part of the soundtrack of my life.

Sometimes it's good to revisit the old, well-worn paths of the past. To embrace both the joy and the melancholy. To remember where we came from and the things that shaped us. I smile as I listen, my mind filled with old apartments and old friends. Some are gone now. An image surfaces—the first time I saw my wife. Then the first time we kissed. I remember a young man's dreams and goals. Some realized, some reshaped, some simply lost.

But most of all, I remember that I was never alone. Even when I wandered places I had no business being. This is the true benefit of hindsight—I can see my Friend clearly. The record plays on. And in every verse, every chorus, His voice is there.

Life hasn't always been easy, but life has been good. Because He has been good.

So I will remember.

God, You alone have been the true constant. You are Father and Friend. You are my past and, more importantly, my future. —Buck Storm

Digging Deeper: Psalm 77:11–12; Isaiah 46:9

Saturday, October 24

Moses' arms soon became so tired he could no longer hold them up. So Aaron and Hur found a stone for him to sit on. Then they stood on each side of Moses, holding up his hands. So his hands held steady until sunset. —Exodus 17:12 (NLT)

I slid the keycard into the hotel-room door. The light blinked green as the lock clicked.

I held the door for my grandparents, who were in the hallway behind me. My grandpa paused before entering the room. "Do you want help getting the luggage from the car?" he asked.

I hesitated. From where I stood, I could see our suitcases on the hotel dresser—exactly where we'd left them that morning. My grandpa had been struggling with his memory lately, and he was tired from our day at the museum.

"Dad," my mom said, "our luggage is already inside. This is the same room we stayed in last night."

My grandpa's face creased with confusion. Then embarrassment. Then frustration.

"My memory isn't what it used to be," he said.

The silence was heavy. Alzheimer's ran in my grandpa's family. His mother's memory had slipped away years before. At the end, she hadn't even recognized him.

I wanted to assure my grandpa that everything would be OK. But I couldn't guarantee that. And I wouldn't break the silence with untruth.

My mom placed a palm to the side of my grandpa's face. "When you forget, we will help you remember."

Her words were striking. Not denial or false assurances, but a promise born of love. A guarantee that, even if his memory failed him, his daughter would not.

Jesus, help me to stand steadfast for others in times of uncertainty. —Logan Eliasen

Digging Deeper: 1 Corinthians 15:58; Galatians 6:2

Sunday, October 25

**The soothing tongue is a tree of life.
—Proverbs 15:4 (NIV)**

When a group of young adults from an international ministry came to speak to our congregation, I found myself conflicted as they shared of their experiences from their home countries of Switzerland, South Africa, Mexico, France, and other places around the world. Their love for God was energizing and palpable.

While thrilled for them, I also found myself sucked into the comparison game. As they were out traveling the world—seeing new people and going to exciting places—I was stuck in Arizona. I had lived in the same house, in the same city, and had attended the same church for 38 years. My discontent grew as they continued to share beautiful, vibrant stories about God's love around the world. In the color scheme of life, my life was beige. Beige and boring.

At the end of the service, I went to talk to a young woman from Switzerland. Joy permeated her countenance as she asked for details of my life.

My life? She wants to hear about my life?

I reluctantly admitted all the sameness of the past 38 years of my existence.

Rather than yawning, she listened intently before sincerely gushing, "Oh how wonderful! One day I want to be able to say that I have grown deep roots and loved people for 38 years."

As she turned to talk to another person, her gracious words washed over me, causing a shift in my perspective. Where I saw sameness, she saw deep roots. Where I saw beige, she saw beauty. What a gift of words to me!

Jesus, may my words—internal and external—be words of life. —Lynne Hartke

Digging Deeper: Proverbs 4:23; Ephesians 4:29

Monday, October 26

Be strong and of a good courage.
—Deuteronomy 31:6 (KJV)

The memories come back in a flood as I watch my nephew, Charlie, step out onto the field. I sense a familiar courage in his determination to be a football player.

I'm back now, on the Hillsboro High School football field. The smell of cut grass and the sounds of the cheerleaders and the people in the stands are muffled by Coach Anderson's yells and the thick breathing of my teammates. We are fired up and determined, a tight team of young warriors suited up and ready to face the obstacles on the other side of the line. I wear my jersey with great pride. Number 66.

Today, as I suit up in a coat, a tie, a starched shirt, and shoes that shine, the past is a reminder. Always ahead are obstacles of one form or another. On the other side of the line are competitors and questions about the best game plan as I manage the portfolios of those I serve.

As an investment advisor, I lead a team, chosen carefully for their ethical standards as well as their broad financial expertise. You might call me the coach. If they succeed, we all win.

In high school, number 66 represented something far greater than myself. It stood for a team, a school, and a greater entity that pulled it all together and made possible the opportunity to play, to learn, and, yes, to find courage.

And aren't we all members of a greater team? One where our loving Coach, our Father, God, gives us life with the obstacles that teach us to be strong? One who allows us to choose His game plan and to follow it through with the courage it takes to win.

Father, I wear Your number proudly. Give me the courage to win this game called life for You.
—Brock Kidd

Digging Deeper: 2 Kings 6:16;
Psalm 31:24

Tuesday, October 27

Truly I tell you, whatever you did for one of the least of these brothers and sisters of mine, you did for me. —Matthew 25:40 (NIV)

"Erin," my friend said. "Hey Erin, what is it?" I blinked, the hallway lights bright in my eyes. I was still upset, but my friend's sincere tone was registering.

My friend and I were part of a committee that'd been charged with working through a difficult problem. Decent progress had been made until a major wrinkle had been discovered. Many of the others wanted to just let it slide. I, however, felt certain that would end up costing us dearly.

The committee had reached an impasse that had made me think more than once of Bartimaeus, the blind man in Scripture who had been brushed aside by the crowds of his day. Like him, "Just be quiet already" was the unspoken message I kept hearing, loud and clear. It's incredibly hurtful to be made aware that others don't find your voice worth listening to.

But now, faced with my friend in the hallway outside another painful meeting, I recalled a different part of Bartimaeus's story. Because while the crowds had brushed him aside, Jesus hadn't. Jesus had not only heard Bartimaeus's calls, He'd allowed Himself to be stopped by them. And then He'd centered on the very voice the crowds wanted to silence. "What do you want me to do for you?" Jesus asked (Mark 10:51, NIV).

"Hey Erin, what is it you need?" my friend was asking me.

I could feel the similar question's impact. Which is when I realized it probably wasn't just the restoration of his sight that changed Bartimaeus's life that day. Being noticed—and truly heard—are powerfully healing and transformative as well.

Thank You, God, for helping me understand the profound difference the simple acts of noticing and listening can make in a life. —Erin Janoso

Digging Deeper: Mark 10:46–52; Luke 13:12

Wednesday, October 28

Let him have all your worries and cares, for he is always thinking about you and watching everything that concerns you. —1 Peter 5:7 (TLB)

In Florida we don't have the gorgeous fall leaves or snow that the northern states enjoy. But we do have weather changes, sometimes all in the same day.

One crisp October day it felt like all four seasons packed into one. When I got out of bed at 6 a.m. it felt like winter to this tropical climate dweller at a temperature of 57 degrees. By 10 a.m. spring arrived—68 degrees. Summer began around 3 p.m. when my air conditioner kicked on at 82 degrees. And by 7 p.m. it felt like a crisp fall day with temperatures around 73.

On days like that I spend a lot of time in my clothes closet. Long pants and sweater in the morning. Midday, short sleeves and shorter pants. Lightweight jacket in the evening. Layering is a way of life here in Florida.

I noticed that layering also seemed to be the way everyday stress and anxiety happened in the years after my husband, Jack, died. Living alone, worrying about anything that might go wrong with my condo or car, plus worrying about two of my children who were experiencing health problems, plus worrying about the skyrocketing costs of everything in my life felt like heavy, scratchy wool coats on my bare skin.

Those were the days when I stayed longer in the swimming pool to pray longer, more serious prayers. Then other days, when all seemed right with the world, I took off the layer of proverbial wool and felt free as a bird.

I suppose that's what grace is. Knowing that God, prayer, and faith are the perfect wraps to get us through whatever is bothering us.

Lord, thank You for giving me the grace to know when to layer on more prayers, more faith, and more confidence in Your healing.
—Patricia Lorenz

Digging Deeper: Psalm 37:4–5;
Matthew 6:25–34; Luke 8:14, 21:34–35

JOURNEY THROUGH GRIEF: A Place to Heal

My God will meet all your needs according to the riches of his glory in Christ Jesus.
—Philippians 4:19 (NIV)

I put together the large artist's easel and placed it next to the tall dresser filled with tubes and bottles of paint. Markers, colored pencils, and paintbrushes sat in clear containers on my work desk. Everything I needed to create art was at my reach. I sat in the small sitting area by the Murphy bed that would only come down for visitors and marveled that my little art studio was finally complete.

The art studio was once an open dining room in my New York City one-bedroom apartment. I'd slept on the couch after having kids so they could have their own space. Craving solitude, I'd eventually commissioned walls to go up and make a bedroom to call my own. When my parents had moved in so I could help care for my father, I added a bed in my living room and slept there again, for over a year. While I'd missed having a place of refuge, my father's care was more important.

Now I take out my paints and pour colors onto my next creation. Art has always been my therapy. My little room continues to transform—it has been a place to break bread, a place to retreat, and a place to give love and care to my father. It's been 1 year since my father has passed, and my mother no longer lives with me, but I still sleep in the living room. Having a place of solitude is no longer a priority. My room has transformed again, to a place where I can heal.

Lord, thank You for the provisions You give as the seasons of life change. Circumstances change, but my spirit always find sustenance in You.
—Karen Valentin

Digging Deeper: Proverbs 17:22; 3 John 1:2

Friday, October 30

You can't hide behind a religious mask forever; sooner or later the mask will slip and your true face will be known. —Luke 12:2 (MSG)

When I picked my granddaughter up after school, I couldn't help but roll my eyes. Thankfully I had sunglasses on, so nine-year-old Shea was none the wiser. She was wearing a head-to-toe costume of her favorite video game character, complete with a stuffed tail sticking out the back.

No, it wasn't Halloween. On that day, Shea would sport her dragon costume. Today was just another day for Shea. Last month, she'd worn a superhero costume almost everywhere we went. Last weekend, when we attended a Hispanic heritage festival, she'd sported a large wolf-head hat. And when Shea wasn't wearing a costume, she was usually cloaked in a sweatshirt with the hood up, hiding her sweet little smile in the shadows.

When I asked Shea why she liked wearing costumes so much, she said they made her look cool. But I think a more accurate answer would be that Shea doesn't feel "cool" on her own. Calling attention away from the "real" Shea feels safer for her. By wearing a costume, Shea's actually trying to blend in.

How often do I do the very same thing? I paste on a smile when my heart is breaking. When Christian friends discuss theological issues I disagree with, I keep my lips sealed. When invited to pray in a group, I comply outwardly by bowing my head, while inwardly God and I wrestle over whether this truly is intercession or just gossip masked as prayer requests. Yes, my granddaughter and I have much more in common than I care to admit.

Father, You always see the true me. Help me be that woman both inside and out, transparent about my flaws, questions, weaknesses, and all.
—Vicki Kuyper

Digging Deeper: 1 Samuel 16:7; Proverbs 11:3; 1 Peter 3:3–4

Saturday, October 31

The Lord is close to the brokenhearted and saves those who are crushed in spirit. —Psalm 34:18 (NIV)

Early on the morning of Halloween I got a call from our son Ted. His voice was a low whisper when he spoke.

"Howie died last night."

Howie was our two youngest grandsons' dog. He'd been perfectly fine a few days earlier. His death had been sudden, happening overnight. My heart immediately went out to Mason and Oliver, as they loved Howie.

"I'm bringing Howie to your house."

"You're what?"

"Mom, please, the boys aren't ready for this. I want to wait to tell them until after Halloween."

Groaning inwardly, I agreed. Ted could bring Howie to the house. As I contemplated what he had said, I realized how unready I was for many of the losses in my own life. I certainly wasn't ready to lose my parents, or to bury a son. Nor was I ready to say goodbye to one of my best friends, who had died from cancer.

Really, are any of us ever ready to face such devastating losses? I don't know how anyone can get through times like these without faith. It's the comfort we received from the Lord that enables us to look to the future, when we will be with those we've lost. Knowing that is what makes us ready.

Lord, we all face losses in life, some more devastating than others. How grateful I am for the comfort You offer and the promise of eternal life in You. —Debbie Macomber

Digging Deeper: Psalms 73:26, 147:3

LIVING A NEW LIFE

1 _____

2 _____

3 _____

4 _____

5 _____

6 _____

7 _____

8 _____

9 _____

10 _____

11 _____

12 _____

13 _____

14 _____

15 _____

16 _____

17 _____

18 _____

19 _____

20 _____

21 _____

22 _____

23 _____

24 _____

25 _____

26 _____

27 _____

28 _____

29 _____

30 _____

31 _____

November

But if we walk in the light,
as he is in the light,
we have fellowship with one another,
and the blood of Jesus his Son
cleanses us from all sin.

—1 John 1:7 (ESV)

Sunday, November 1

I have called you by name; you are mine.
—Isaiah 43:1 (RSV)

Parishioners in my church wear nametags to underscore our mission: "A place to belong, whoever you are, just as you are." In fact, once newcomers have been greeted, they are offered a nametag. The little card allows us to know one another and immediately envelops newcomers in our spirit of hospitality.

You see, for 9 years after moving to New Hampshire, I had struggled to find a church family, a spiritual home. The first church I attended burned down the year I arrived. That congregation combined with another miles away. The long drive often kept me home during snowy weather. Finally I moved an hour closer to work and severed my tenuous connection.

But my big-city church didn't feel welcoming. Everyone seemed to know everyone else and to ignore me. I felt invisible. I drifted away and eventually stopped going altogether. Instead, on Sundays I guided tours at the Canterbury Shaker Village, a place that offered a spiritual lift but left me craving church community. Then a newspaper ad promising "A place to belong" drew me to St. Paul's Episcopal, where the welcome was palpable—especially my new nametag. People spoke my name! I existed!

That was 17 years ago. I continue to worship and serve in ministries at St. Paul's, thoroughly embraced by my beloved community there. I've learned the importance of names. In fact, if you drop by, I hope I'll be the first to say, "Welcome! My name is Gail. What's yours?"

God of many names, may we be quick to acknowledge the individuality of Your people.
—Gail Thorell Schilling

Digging Deeper: Nehemiah 9:10; Isaiah 49:1, 56:5

Monday, November 2

The LORD is near to the brokenhearted and saves those who are crushed in spirit.
—Psalm 34:18 (NASB)

It was not a beautiful day in the neighborhood. My husband discovered me already on the couch when he got up. Randy moved gingerly around me, so my face must have said it all. Bleary-eyed, I groped for my coffee and spilled it. It was all I could do to not fan the embers of annoyance.

Last night I'd gone to bed early, but the wind had howled all night. BlueDog had to go out at 11:30. Then both dogs started barking at something around 1 a.m., although I found nothing. Then Randy woke me at 3 a.m. to ask me what the dogs had been barking at. Then RooDog conjured up a gastrointestinal display at 4 a.m., the result of some unidentifiable treasure she'd found and eaten in the pasture. I know this because I *almost* got her outside in time. I finally fell asleep about the time I needed to get up.

Over what was left of my coffee, Randy read aloud some dismal news from an online article having to do with environmental issues I'd been covering. What I'd feared most was now happening. Hopelessness, exhaustion, and anger dwarfed me. This whole day, although it was barely dawn, was doomed.

But then Randy put down his phone and opened his Bible. He read Romans 12 to me. The words washed over me like a soothing balm to my troubled soul. I clung to the hope, the healing, and the promise. It's a beautiful day after all.

No matter what goes on around me, Lord, Your Good News can restore my soul. —Erika Bentsen

Digging Deeper: Proverbs 25:25; Romans 12

Tuesday, November 3

Still I cling to your laws and obey them.
—Psalm 119:83 (TLB)

I inherited a small book from my grandpa Porter Knapp titled *Never*. Published 139 years ago in 1887, it lists all the things one should never do when choosing a spouse, taking care of your house, interacting with family, dressing, eating, speaking, traveling, or forming beliefs and habits, seeking happiness, etc.

Never marry a woman who talks too much; you always will be tired and never will have any family secrets.

Never wear clothes so tight they pinch you—give your body room to move freely.

Never forget that persons who know everything, know almost nothing.

Never forget that a single man earning $10 a week can save four of it and live better than he does and be happier.

Never expectorate while at the table—such persons should be kicked out as hogs.

The book has 123 pages of advice, much of which doesn't apply to our current lives. However, there is one that does: "Never forget that it is not necessary to be rich to be happy. It is not necessary to be great. It is not necessary to be dandled in the lap of luxury."

The day I read that quote I received the tax bills for both my condo and my deceased husband's condo. I certainly didn't feel rich that day. But I loved the book's advice that happiness does not revolve around riches, greatness, or luxury. I paid the bills, then thanked God that I had a whole year to save for next year's bills.

I also appreciated even more the real rules we Christians have to live by: the Ten Commandments.

Jesus, You gave us a whole new set of rules for living that worked 2,000 years ago and still work today. Never let me forget them. —Patricia Lorenz

---

Wednesday, November 4

My dear brothers and sisters, take note of this: Everyone should be quick to listen, slow to speak and slow to become angry, because human anger does not produce the righteousness that God desires.
—James 1:19–20 (NIV)

This morning a little abandoned kitten who recently found her way into my life leaped onto my lap. She soon took a playful swat at my fingers as they moved on my computer keyboard. Her little claws drew blood. I grimaced in pain and am still not happy! But I sensed that God had somehow spoken to me.

All of us will sometimes "scratch the hand" of those who love us most. Jesus and His disciples certainly found this to be true. But somehow a life that is spent in sharing intimacy and friendship also creates what Native Americans call "blood brothers and sisters."

I am learning that there is no lasting intimacy without a trace of wound or conflict. And the richest friendships and marriages have scars to show from wounds gained in the quest for depth and maturity. Jesus found this to be true too. His closest friends betrayed Him. His mother misunderstood Him. His father disappeared from the gospel story. And Jesus likely hurt the feelings of His disciples when He grew angry and rebuked them.

There is no mature love without conflict. No intimacy without pain. And no maturity without immaturity. We will all be scratched and bleed many times by the sharp little claws of a kitten— or person—who is seeking above all to love and be accepted.

Father, help me to love those who have hurt me in attempting to love me. And may they forgive me too. Amen. —Scott Walker

Digging Deeper: Proverbs 15:1; Matthew 5:9, 18:15–17

Thursday, November 5

Likewise the Spirit helps us in our weakness. For we do not know what to pray for as we ought, but the Spirit himself intercedes for us with groanings too deep for words. —Romans 8:26 (ESV)

In my years as a magazine editor, I've received my share of reader mail—most of it positive, I'm happy to say. I try to read every letter, even the ones with nearly indecipherable handwriting.

I can't possibly answer every one, and for the most part the writers tell me they don't expect me to. I pray for those who ask for prayers, and even for some that don't. I am humbled by the generosity with which my correspondents share their lives. I learn things about people that amaze and inspire and sometimes amuse me. I love a letter that makes me laugh.

The one kind of letter I hesitate over is a letter from an incarcerated person. It's not that I lack compassion for them. On the contrary, I can think of nothing more unendurable than to be deprived of freedom, whatever the reason. Often they ask me to do things for them I can't possibly do.

But there was a letter today from an inmate named Jon. He wrote, "I won't tell you what I'm in for, or for how long. One way or the other, I deserve to be here. What I need most is the strength to face my past, the courage to change, and all the prayers I can get. Mostly that."

Jon's letter has stayed with me. His ask was so honest and simple. He needs all the prayers he can get. Mostly that. I thought you might help me answer his call.

Lord, there are many kinds of prisons and prisoners. Hear our prayers for all who need to break free of the shackles that keep them from You. —Edward Grinnan

Digging Deeper: Colossians 4:2; James 5:16

Friday, November 6

Whoever abides in me and I in him, he it is that bears much fruit. —John 15:5 (ESV)

Last summer I planted a tomato vine in my backyard. I'm not much of a gardener, so I didn't expect much, but I must've picked a wonderful plant at the nursery because it grew and grew and produced many beautiful red tomatoes. Whenever I sliced one, I marveled at how much redder it was than those from the grocery store.

Even into the fall, the tomatoes kept coming. September, October . . . well past its supposed expiration date, my plant kept producing more and more perfect fruit, and the vine stayed green and tall. By November, though, the main tendrils had become brown and dry. Reluctantly I decided it was probably past time to pull up my plant.

I went outside to clear the bed near my window. Imagine my surprise to find that, on its "deathbed," my tomato plant still had two lovely little yellow blooms on it! How in the world did the vine manage to keep trying to produce when it was clearly on its last gasp?

Besides giving me a summer's worth of tomatoes, my plant seemed to be giving me a bit of a spiritual message: Just because I'm getting older doesn't mean I should just give up. My energy and endurance will fade more and more as the years pass, but Jesus told His followers to "bear much fruit." I pray that when my earthly body sees its final winter, I will end my time here still striving to grow and give with all I have, having little blossoms of promise in my soul.

Lord, may I bear much fruit for You as long as I live! —Ginger Rue

Digging Deeper: Matthew 7:17–20;
John 15:16; Colossians 1:10

Saturday, November 7

**So I say to you: Ask and it will be given to you; seek and you will find; knock and the door will be opened to you. For everyone who asks receives; the one who seeks finds; and to the one who knocks, the door will be opened.
—Luke 11:9–10 (NIV)**

Ours was not a musical family. Dad had a guitar he never played. We kids plucked at the strings, but none of us thought to learn to play it ourselves. As part of a music program in school, I took up the recorder. The hope was to graduate to clarinet and join the band. I liked the recorder and practiced regularly. But my family could not afford a clarinet, and I stopped.

The algorithms of my social media accounts must have sensed this forgotten pleasure. A video ad for guitar classes popped up frequently. "Many adults wish they knew how to play an instrument," the teacher said.

Yes, that's me. But I can't do that, not now. If I was meant to play music, God would have kept me on the path toward that clarinet.

I remembered my dad and that lonely guitar in his closet. His dream of playing it died with him.

Perhaps he, like me, told himself he wasn't musical. Maybe he, like me, found validation for that self-imposed limitation by saying, "It must not be what God wants for me."

So many of my cages are of my own making. But it's easier for me to blame God or my childhood than it is to confront that truth. I forget that God is the Great Encourager, here to help me see past my limitations.

And God has. I've been playing the ukulele now for 2 years. Yes, I am musical.

God, forgive me for using You to explain the shackles I place on myself. —Amy Eddings

Digging Deeper: James 1:5

Sunday, November 8

"If you love those who love you, what credit is that to you?" —Luke 6:32 (NRSVCE)

Most pastors prepare for sermons. They pray, research, make notes, and sometimes even write out their sermons. That was the case when a local pastor started a sermon about how to understand the conflict and violence in our world. He began to outline the religious history of a certain conflict, explaining who was in the right and why.

Then abruptly, he stopped, as if he'd just recalled some long-lost and important memory. After a lengthy pause, he put aside his notes, looked directly at us, and exclaimed, "It doesn't matter! What we are supposed to do is love each other. That is all that Jesus asked, and that is everything. No excuses." And he ended there.

I don't know about others, but as my initial shock passed, his words hit me hard. How often do I make excuses for my meanness, selfishness, *unlovingness*? I tell myself it's OK to dislike the apartment manager who is sullen and unhelpful. Surely I'm justified in complaining to the supervisor of the sales clerk who scoffed at my ignorance about computers. The neighbor who lets his dog bark incessantly deserves my contempt.

Yet if I truly want to follow Jesus, there is no reason, no justification, no excuse for not loving the other, or at least not trying. It really is that simple—and that difficult.

Jesus, Lord, help me to release all that keeps me from loving. —Marci Alborghetti

Digging Deeper: Romans 8:31–39;
2 Thessalonians 1:1–4

Monday, November 9

I have fought the good fight, I have finished the race, I have kept the faith. —2 Timothy 4:7 (NIV)

Are you feeling unnoticed? Ignored? I have a foolproof solution: wait till you turn 64½, and all of a sudden you're Mr. or Mrs. Popular.

My mailbox is groaning under the weight of large envelopes chock-full of supplemental insurance plans. (My mail carrier is groaning too.) Each brochure promises the best deal on Medicare Part B or Part C or Part D or parts unknown. I hope one of these plans offers a free pair of glasses to read all the fine print.

Ironically, none of these long-term health plans can give me what I most need: long-term health. I'm fortunate enough to be in mostly good shape, but there's no doubt that the aches are getting achier, the creaks are getting creakier. Age is gnawing away at my brain cells, too, leaving tiny holes where my memory once was. (There's a name for this process, but I can't remember it.)

I can feel my own mortality creeping up from behind and closing in. As every driver can tell you, the objects in the mirror are closer than they appear.

There's more than some comfort, then, in knowing that the end won't be the end, that something awaits us at the exit ramp, redemption for our many wayward journeys. Still, I wish my healthcare coverage was more generous—I think I pulled a muscle carrying large envelopes from the mailbox.

Lord, in peace I pray to You, in humility I pursue You. You are the way, the truth, and the life.
—Mark Collins

Digging Deeper: Ecclesiastes 9; John 14:3

Tuesday, November 10

LIFE LESSONS FROM GAMES: Keep Your Goal in Mind
Jesus said, "Feed my sheep." —John 21:17 (NIV)

Thanksgiving would be sadly different for my family. For over 30 years, we had helped serve a free meal at a downtown church. I referred to the coordinator, Barb, plus the regular volunteers and guests as our Thanksgiving Family. Since Covid, the church decided that an Indianapolis agency would prepare and deliver Thanksgiving meals to area homes.

What about the unhoused people who relied on our meals? One regular guest ate two meals as he told me about the family and job he used to have, before he lived under the nearby bridge. Four meals in his sack were for his next few days.

My husband washed pots, as he had in college. Barb and I met each summer to plan the volunteer schedules. Our young daughters loved dishing up meals alongside adults and later supervising the serving line. I enjoyed sitting down, after our guests were served, to a meal I hadn't had to cook.

Still mulling it over, I opened Words with Friends on my phone. It was my turn. My daughter Katie and I always keep our goal in mind—to have fun! We play cool words instead of bland ones that might be worth more points. We conspire to tie our scores at the end. All those ties baffle the game, whose goal is counting wins.

What if we kept our family goals but found new Thanksgiving traditions?

Now we buy carryout meals the day before Thanksgiving. We text with Barb on Thanksgiving, and I meet her for lunch every summer. We support programs that feed our unhoused neighbors throughout the year.

Precious Lord, I will never change my goals to love You, love my neighbors, and feed the hungry. —Leanne Jackson

Digging Deeper: Matthew 22:37–39; John 15:13

Veterans Day, Wednesday, November 11

GOD makes his people strong. GOD gives his people peace. —Psalm 29:11 (MSG)

Staff Sergeant Loic St. Gal de Pons was my chaplain's assistant when we deployed to Afghanistan. Always at the ready, he had my back in the most difficult and uplifting of combat settings. He remains my battle buddy.

Now both of us are retired. I recently coordinated to honor "Sergeant St. G" with an Emerson Foundation Medallion from the Military Chaplains Association. Funds from this foundation provide seminary tuition scholarships for chaplains in training.

As Loic now serves in security with a West Coast aerospace firm, I communicated with his supervisors, Sean, Carlos, and Josh, about the possibility of a formal recognition ceremony for the presentation. Their response was an enthusiastic "Yes!"

The Thursday afternoon before Veterans Day weekend was the day. I joined the celebration on an online video call. Loic's mom and sister attended. Members of the security team added snacks and gifts.

As Sean read the words of the Emerson Foundation citation, concluding with "Thank you, dear servant-leader and friend," my heart seemed to overflow. Soldierly excellence, infantry skills, professional competence—all were embodied in the one we recognized. We applauded God's guiding hand on a life and calling of service.

A couple of days later I received an email with the subject heading, "Thank you, Battle Buddy!" Loic wrote: "The best Veterans Day I've had since retiring from active duty."

This day, may our gratitude extend to all veterans who have likewise willingly gone into harm's way on our behalf.

Almighty God, be near all military who now wear the cloth of our nation, in isolated and danger-filled postings around the globe. Amen.

—Ken Sampson

Digging Deeper: Psalm 85:1; Mark 8:34; Romans 12:1

Thursday, November 12

Choose you this day whom ye will serve.
—**Joshua 24:15 (KJV)**

The pressure is on. I have to make a choice.

Here I am, sitting in my office, 2 weeks before Thanksgiving, wedging in a few minutes between appointments and wondering how I'm going to fit everything I need to do into this busy day. And then it comes: a text from my mother.

Brock, she writes, *you are last on the list. I am copying it here. You must make your choice for Thanksgiving dinner.* Every member of the family gets to choose one item on the menu.

When a missive comes from Mom, it's time to put everything else aside. The list is long and names every family member, sixteen in all. It begins with what Mom calls "givens." These are established facts in her annual ritual.

Turkey. Bebe's cornbread dressing. Giblet gravy. Abby's cranberry sauce. Pumpkin pie.

Following givens, I scan the list of names: *Harrison, country ham. Charles, fried chicken. Kristi, mac and cheese.*

Hmmm, pretty heavy on protein, I think, reading on.

Corinne, turnip greens. Keri, mashed potatoes. Ella Grace, deviled eggs. Abby, green peas. Little David, sweet potatoes with marshmallows.

I smile, thinking of the people as I read what they picked. But the process makes me consider the harder choices I make daily: Reaching out to a person who lives on the street. Listening patiently to a worried client. And striving to choose God's directive throughout the day.

Back to the list, I type out my answer, and this one is easy. *Mom, I cannot wait for my favorite meal of the year. My choice is fixed: caramel pie!*

Father, how good You are. Amid life's busyness, You toss me a choice of pure pleasure. Thank You.
—Brock Kidd

Digging Deeper: Job 34:4; Proverbs 16:9

Friday, November 13

THE ENDS OF THE EARTH: The Joy of Creation
Then God surveyed everything He had made, savoring its beauty and appreciating its goodness. —Genesis 1:31 (VOICE)

The sun had set after 10 p.m. and risen shortly after 3 a.m. I awoke at five o'clock, afraid to miss out on the beauty of a morning in the Antarctic's Weddell Sea. I wasn't disappointed. When I opened the drapes of my cruise ship cabin, an art gallery of icebergs stretched as far as I could see. The air was frigid but still, turning the surface of the water into a mirror, offering a perfect reflection of the clouds and frozen landscape above.

As the sun eased higher in the sky, the light continually changed, turning walls of ice into shining silver, and rounded blue bergs into floating gems. Emperor and Adélie penguins dotted distant ice floes like poppy seeds. The frozen, pastel-colored world was silent, except for the sound of my camera's shutter, which hadn't stopped clicking since I opened my balcony door. Shivering, I grabbed my parka and put it on over my pajamas. I couldn't take time to put on warmer clothes. I didn't want to miss a moment.

I thought of how this incomparable beauty would have gone unseen if our ship hadn't anchored here. Yet every day around the world, untold beauty goes unappreciated by the human eye. God created it because it gave Him pleasure, whether others saw it or not. I felt a kinship to my heavenly Father in that moment and also an intense gratitude for the joy I receive from creating something beautiful, whether in words, in watercolor, in sugar-filled frosting, or via photo. Whether it's recognized by others as a masterpiece or not, the joy of creation is its own reward.

Father, thank You for this wild, wonderful world You've created. Exploring it is a privilege I never take lightly. —Vicki Kuyper

Digging Deeper: Psalm 24:1–2; Isaiah 40:12; Romans 1:20; Revelation 4:11

Saturday, November 14

THE ENDS OF THE EARTH: Becoming a Truth Teller

Fix your thoughts on what is true and good and right. —Philippians 4:8 (TLB)

It looked like something out of a dark fairy tale. The black, twisting tower rose almost 100 feet above the ocean waves. I'd been photographing random icebergs of all shapes and sizes for almost 2 weeks as our ship explored Antarctic waters, but there was no way this was just a weird, skinny pinnacle of dirty ice. Located about 7 miles from Deception Island (a flooded volcanic caldera in the South Shetland Islands), I figured this enigma had to be some bizarre outcropping of volcanic rock. Nonetheless, because it was so isolated—and downright creepy-looking—its image remained in my mind long after I returned home. As soon as time allowed, I headed straight to the internet for answers.

What I found made me laugh. Apparently in 2016, some folks were studying images on Google Earth and came to believe this bizarre anomaly was evidence of a kraken, a huge sea monster–sized squid. Funny thing, though, it always stayed in the same place. It's amazing what we normally rational human beings can convince ourselves is true.

If I want to be a truth teller in every area of my life, I need to make certain the truth I'm telling is based on fact, not fiction. That means doing my research. Having been a freelance writer for over 40 years, I study a wide variety of sources, including God's Word, before sharing something I've seen on the internet or TV, or even heard from a trusted friend. If I want to be honest and truthful with God and others, first I need to know what's actually true.

Father, guide me into truth in every area of my life, both big and small. —Vicki Kuyper

Digging Deeper: Proverbs 4:18, 12:17; Colossians 2:8

Sunday, November 15

THE ENDS OF THE EARTH: Following God's Will

You need endurance so that after you have done what God wants you to do, you can receive what he has promised. —Hebrews 10:36 (GW)

Who says penguins can't fly? A violent gust of wind lifted the little gentoo right off his feet and deposited him on his back in the drifting snow. The penguin popped back up. Immediately another gust sent him airborne, then dropped him in the snow again. He got up again. I watched that persistent penguin continue waddling against the wind up the steep slope of Deception Island's volcanic caldera. I sighed. We shared the same path.

I was trying to keep my own feet on the ground. My legs may be longer than a gentoo's, but I'm still a vertically challenged grandmother in her late 60s who was attempting to hike the frozen slope of a still-steaming Antarctic volcano. The trail wasn't long, under a mile each way. But it was slick, alternating between boot-swallowing drifts of snow and patches of ice where skates may have been more appropriate footwear. But I was curious to see what was at the top of the ridge. So I decided to take a lesson from the penguin and just keep moving.

The penguin made it to the ridgeline, and so did I. But while my penguin companion continued ascending, presumably headed home, I headed back down to a cozy cruise ship. Proud of my accomplishment, I thought, *I may be getting older, but I can still do hard things.* Like helping care for my grandkids, continuing to love my ex-husband and his partner, and doing what I believe God wants me to do. One small step at a time.

Lord, teach me how to be patient with myself when I face challenges, never giving up on what You want me to do. —Vicki Kuyper

Digging Deeper: Isaiah 58:11; Romans 5:3–4; James 1:12

Monday, November 16

For there is nothing hidden that will not be disclosed, and nothing concealed that will not be known or brought out into the open. —Luke 8:17 (NIV)

When our daughter, Micah, was young, our favorite family vacations were spent at Disneyland and Walt Disney World. Micah loved the magical experiences of walking through the theme parks, going on the rides, meeting various costumed characters, and hunting for Hidden Mickeys.

A Hidden Mickey is a deliberately placed representation of a Mickey Mouse head—one circle (head) with two smaller circles (mouse ears) on the top. We most easily saw the image in the geometric patterns of carpeting or wallpaper when we stayed at resort hotels. Often Micah would spot a Hidden Mickey pressed into the concrete floors or on wall murals when we stood in line for rides. Once, the unmistakable tri-circled design even exploded in the sky during a fireworks display at the Magic Kingdom. Truly an *aha* moment, it felt like we were part of a subtle reminder that only true Disney enthusiasts could share.

When I was younger, I expected to find God at my church, and I did. But as I've matured, I find enjoyment looking for other representations of Him. Noticing the changing seasons, I see His hand in all of creation. When I'm lonely and my husband spontaneously calls during his workday, I feel God near. As I smile at a harried office clerk, I catch a glimpse of Him. When I'm bored, waiting in line, and a child giggles, I know He's there.

These *aha* moments in God's Kingdom fill my soul with wonder. I can't help but think they are intentionally placed in my life as a subtle reminder of His presence.

Dear God, thank You for not being hidden from me and for surprising me with Your presence.
—Stephanie Thompson

Digging Deeper: Deuteronomy 4:29;
Isaiah 55:6; Romans 1:20

Tuesday, November 17

Be kind and compassionate to one another, forgiving each other, just as in Christ God forgave you. —Ephesians 4:32 (NIV)

I have always loved quotes. Growing up, I once debated with the librarian in my hometown of Tivoli, New York, that eight was old enough to read an adult encyclopedia of famous sayings. So it brings me joy that for the past two decades, part of my job has been creating newsletters that feature the famous words of others.

Although my mind isn't great at remembering most of the quotes in their entirety, their sentiments live in my heart and sometimes rise exactly at the right moment.

This morning a favorite piece of a saying came to mind when the cashier at the bank was rude. As my nerves rattled, "Err on the side of kindness" came to mind, and I smiled instead. She looked down at her keyboard, and then she smiled back. "It's been a hard day," she said, explaining that the network and online banking had been down all day and that most customers had not taken this inconvenience well.

As I went back to my car, I sent her positive thoughts and prayers, and the words of Plato came to mind: "Be kind, for everyone is fighting a hard battle."

Heavenly Father, may I always be compassionate and err on the side of kindness.
—Sabra Ciancanelli

Digging Deeper: Psalm 141:5; Matthew 5:7; Luke 6:35

Wednesday, November 18

When hard pressed, I cried to the LORD; he brought me into a spacious place.
—Psalm 118:5 (NIV)

Like many these days, I struggle with stress, triggered not just by too much work but any disruption to my normal routine: appointments, visitors, deadlines, my accountant husband's tax season—you know, life in general. I'm also a perfectionist, as incapable of abandoning a stressful endeavor as of doing just an OK job. I have to do it flawlessly. My students aren't all progressing? I'm a bad teacher. My daughters struggle? I'm a bad mom.

The pandemic snarled my routine, made teaching impossible to do perfectly, and constricted my time for writing and other revitalizing ventures like birding and gardening, stressing me to beyond bearing and forcing me to retire a decade earlier than planned.

Retirement offered an immediate, near-total release from these stresses. No more appointments, deadlines, paper grading, or strategizing about how to teach better. Time to run, cook healthier meals, notice birds again. I spent my first utterly free summer in my garden, producing so many tomatoes I ran out of freezer space; I gave tomatoes away by the bagful and canned homemade tomato paste just to free up the kitchen. When the garden produce dwindled, I took up abandoned writing projects and soon sat hunched all day, daily, at my computer.

To my surprise, my stress problem persisted. Fellow retirees tell similar stories: "I thought I'd have all this free time, but I'm busier than ever and still never manage to get things done!"

What is this frantic spirit that ensnares us? Scripture offered vexing answers—wrong prioritization and sin—but also this comforting promise: that God invites us into His spaciousness and rest.

Help me choose the roomy relaxation You offer, Lord. —Patty Kirk

Digging Deeper: Matthew 11:20–30; Luke 10:38–42, 12:16–21

Thursday, November 19

Whatever you do, work at it with all your heart, as working for the Lord, not for human masters, since you know that you will receive an inheritance from the Lord as a reward. It is the Lord Christ you are serving.
—Colossians 3:23–24 (NIV)

I scanned the crowd for my friend Sam. I hadn't seen him since we graduated college. Sam now worked for a ministry in South America, but he was on furlough visiting churches stateside. When I learned that one of his stops was near my home, I was excited to reconnect.

"Logan?" a familiar voice said. Sam broke through the crowd and embraced me. Though he was a decade older, he had the same joy I remembered.

We took turns exchanging questions and catching up. Sam told me about his job. He worked primarily with youth—many of whom were victims of domestic violence. His ministry was focused on breaking cycles of violence and spreading the love of Christ.

I enjoyed hearing about Sam's work. But when he asked about mine, I felt uncomfortable. Sam was working for the Kingdom. His story made me feel mine was deficient. I shared about my career practicing law, internally questioning the value of my profession.

When our conversation wound down, Sam and I said goodbye. But his final words surprised me.

"It has been so uplifting to see a friend today," he said. "I know you have a busy life. Thank you for using your time to bless me."

Sam's words eased the discomfort that had been growing in me. They reminded me that my ability to serve Christ was not inhibited by my job or where I lived. Both provided unique opportunities for me to love others. And I was now encouraged to seek out those opportunities.

Jesus, help me to do everything through You and for Your glory. —Logan Eliasen

Digging Deeper: Romans 12:4–8; Ephesians 4:11–13

Friday, November 20

THE BIRDS OF MY NEIGHBORHOOD:
Practicing Perseverance
You need to persevere so that when you have done the will of God, you will receive what he has promised. —Hebrews 10:36 (NIV)

Our woods, unsurprisingly, are filled with woodpeckers. Red-bellied woodpeckers. Downy woodpeckers. Northern flickers. And more. But my favorite is the pileated woodpecker.

They are large birds. Almost as big as a crow and with a wingspan that can be almost 30 inches. I like to watch them because they are so methodical. They are busy but don't seem to be in a hurry. Instead, they set about a task and stick with it. The holes they make are not messy or random, like some other woodpeckers. Instead, they make large, rectangular marks in the trees, as they search for carpenter ants, other ants, woodboring beetle larvae, and termites.

There was once a pileated that used our chimney flue cap as a way to amplify his mating drumming sounds. It worked out well for him, because it allowed him to produce a louder sound than he could in a tree. Nothing I could do could discourage him. He stuck to his task.

Though his drumming annoyed me, I admired his persistence in this task as well as his others. While I am methodical, sometimes, if the task feels too big or difficult—whether physical or spiritual (like loving my enemies or those who annoy me)—I am tempted to give up and move to something else. Yet Scripture praises us when we press on. Perseverance. A gift from God.

Thou who perseveres in Your love and care of me, regardless of my inattention or spiritual laziness, guide me in the way of steadfastness. Especially in this world that calls me with shiny, attention-grabbing things of little worth. Amen.
—J. Brent Bill

Digging Deeper: Hebrews 12:1–3

Saturday, November 21

But now, this is what the Lord says ... "Do not fear, for I have redeemed you; I have summoned you by name; you are mine." —Isaiah 43:1 (NIV)

At a family gathering, my adult great-nephew was holding forth in my living room. His personality was such that when he spoke, he prevailed. No one heard me—foremost and including him—when I called him by his given name.

"Shannon," I called through the noise. Needing only a few words with him, I tried to be patient, but after a few unheard tries, I called him by his childhood nickname. "Poochie!"

His head jerked toward me. "Ma'am?" The room erupted in laughter, but I was struck by the deeper implication of the name rooted in his heart.

In Isaiah 43, God reminds the Israelites of their roots—that they are and always will be called by His name. Though they knew they were set apart unto God, all too often they did not behave as such, neglecting to respond to His call.

God reminds Israel—and, by extrapolation, us—that as believers we are loved, protected, strengthened, redeemed—and, above all, never nameless. But sometimes it takes a reminder, like the affectionate monikers we are often assigned as children, to pull us back into the safety of His name.

In the moments when the waters of life cover our chins, He says, "I have redeemed you ... you are mine" (NIV). Israel is God's child, called by His name—even as we, through the sacrificial Lamb, are adopted into the family of Christ and rescued by His name.

What a breathtaking privilege to serve a God who showers personal, loving reminders upon us of who we are in Him.

Father, when I think of the times You have spoken ownership over me and my trials, I simply want to worship. —Jacqueline F. Wheelock

Digging Deeper: Isaiah 9:6; Acts 4:12; 1 Corinthians 6:11

Sunday, November 22

Command those who are rich in this present world not to be arrogant nor to put their hope in wealth. —1 Timothy 6:17 (NIV)

Over the years I've managed to save a little nest egg that will probably cover me for about a year in assisted living, should the time come that I can't manage the steps up to my second-floor condo. But meanwhile I enjoy a comfortable life thanks to a decent monthly Social Security check plus a dividend check every now and then.

As a child of parents who grew up during the Great Depression, frugality has been a way of life for me. I love nothing better than finding a real bargain at a thrift store. I enjoy restaurants where the prices are reasonable, and yes, sometimes I succumb to inexpensive "early bird" dinners.

So when it comes to being a charitable giver, I admit I'm not that generous. When I slip a ten-dollar bill into my church envelope, I tell myself that it's the equivalent of my rich friends and relatives giving $300.

In the little book I found titled *Never*, published in 1887, it lists rules for general living. One of them is, "Never forget that there can be no charity without a sacrifice, and that gifts made by millionaires cannot be classed as charity."

That line made me rethink my giving habits. If a sacrifice needs to be part of giving, then I was falling short. That day I decided to sacrifice one restaurant meal a month, or some expensive convenience food, and start contributing food and money to the meals-for-the-hungry program at church.

Somehow giving feels better when it requires more of an effort and a slice of my own comfort.

Gentle Jesus, thank You for providing for me. Now help me to be as generous as You were when You walked this earth. —Patricia Lorenz

Digging Deeper: Malachi 3:10; Matthew 6:1–4; Luke 21:1–4; 2 Corinthians 9:7–9

Monday, November 23

Bear with me a little longer and I will show you that there is more to be said in God's behalf. —Job 36:2 (NIV)

When I was in seminary, morning prayer always ended with the prayer leader asking the community, "And for what else shall we pray?"

My friend Martín would often pray that we get good grades on our exams. Really, Martín? Good grades? We knew better: we should be praying for the poor or for the victims of violence, not praying that we get good grades. Sadly, that seemed a bit selfish to me.

One day, at lunch with Martín, I asked him why he prayed for good grades. Smiling, he replied, "I've always been told that whatever is important to us is also important to God. Jesus said the very hairs of our head are all numbered. I figured if that little detail was important enough to include in the Gospels, then even something as ordinary as grades is important too."

Wow! Martín's response had given me a bigger view of God and a bigger view of my life too. Believing that even the little details in my life are important to God was a good first step in believing that all of reality has infinite value.

Being faithful in the little things, being grateful for the little things: that's what Martín taught me. I had a spiritual conversion that day, a conversion that still carries to this day.

O Lord, give us eyes to see Your glory in all of creation. Amen. —Adam Ruiz

Digging Deeper: Leviticus 23:40; Psalm 13:5; Luke 1:47

Tuesday, November 24

He says to the snow, "Fall on the earth."
—Job 37:6 (NIV)

"Good grief," I said to my mom as I clicked off the car radio. "It's almost like they think they're reporting from a war zone or something!" Snow was predicted, and the weather update that'd just played had mentioned, in tones of breathless gravity, a polar vortex, a bomb cyclone, and a coming "snowmageddon."

The language was so extreme—these kinds of storms just happen sometimes during this particular season. Most of the time they're nothing out of the ordinary.

Winter's always felt more like a friend than a foe to me. I've sometimes even found myself looking forward to it. Probably, I thought, because of how bad I am at prioritizing my own rest. When I'm chronically tired, there's just something about the long, dark nights and frozen weather that seem to grant me permission to do what I struggle with otherwise: to pause and be still. To breathe. To replenish.

It's a type of permission the world at large struggles with too, I know, as I think about the exhausting *do, do, and do more* energy that permeates just about everything. Winter weather, with its capacity to bring things to a standstill, sure does get in the way of that kind of striving. No wonder the language describing it is often so resistance-heavy.

We think we don't want to stop, that we can't. Yet the snow falls anyway.

God created us to need rest. And then, as if He knew we'd struggle with that, He also created a season whose weather occasionally blesses us with no other choice. What a gift.

Thank You, God, for winter. I pray for Your help accepting rather than resisting the opportunities and invitations it brings to slow my pace, refocus my attention, and find my rest in You.
—Erin Janoso

Digging Deeper: Psalm 4:8; Matthew 11:28–29

Wednesday, November 25

Be transformed by the renewing of your mind.
—Romans 12:2 (NKJV)

"Could you please . . . just . . . get out of my way!" said the woman at the grocery store the other day, trying to make her way to the self-checkout on the day before Thanksgiving.

The store was crowded. The atmosphere was tense, with too many people with too little free time in too small a space, and too few employees to help out.

There was very little by way of Christian charity in the store that day. I wasn't feeling it or showing it either, to be honest.

Loading bags into the trunk of my car 20 minutes later, I saw the angry woman again. Her car was beside mine. She, too, was unloading her stuff. We both sighed. She must have remembered me, standing behind her inside several minutes before. She smiled a meek smile and said, "I do better when there isn't so much going on around me."

"I get it," I said. "Me too."

And I do get it. "God is found in the soul not so much by addition, but by subtraction," said the Christian preacher and mystic Meister Eckhart in one of his many sermons 700 years ago in Germany, at a time when it was uncommon to hear messages from the pulpit of a practical nature.

In other words, it's really hard to be who you are—a person who belongs to God—when everything around you feels like chaos.

Lord, give me clarity today, and quiet, and at least a few moments alone with You. I will listen.
—Jon M. Sweeney

Digging Deeper: Proverbs 4:25; Matthew 6:6

Thanksgiving, Thursday, November 26

For I am sure that neither death nor life, nor angels nor rulers, nor things present nor things to come, nor powers, nor height nor depth, nor anything else in all creation, will be able to separate us from the love of God in Christ Jesus our Lord. —Romans 8:38–39 (ESV)

It's Thanksgiving Day, though it doesn't feel like it. Normally, my full family gathers to celebrate. We share a meal that spills across the dining room table. And we take turns sharing what we are thankful for.

This year is different. One of my younger brothers was delayed while traveling home, so we have postponed our traditional dinner until tomorrow. Since my mom spent all day in the kitchen preparing for tomorrow's meal, we ordered a pizza this evening. My brothers stopped by the table to pick up slices, then headed in different directions.

I expect tomorrow will feel odd as well. The day after Thanksgiving marks the beginning of Christmastime. But my family will be a season behind.

As I sit at a quiet table, I consider what I am thankful for this year. Ordinarily, the focus of American Thanksgiving is food and family. These are blessings that I intend to appreciate tomorrow. But tonight is lean on both. So I reflect on something that is never in short supply.

Tonight I am thankful for the love of Christ. Here, at the crossroad of holidays, I am grateful that God came to earth in the form of a child. And I am in awe that, because of Christ's birth, I received the gift of salvation.

An unexpected event has prevented my family from gathering on Thanksgiving. But nothing in this life or the next can separate me from Christ's love.

And for that, I give thanks to my Lord and my Savior.

Jesus, thank You for the infinite depth and persistence of Your love. —Logan Eliasen

Digging Deeper: Romans 5:8;
1 Thessalonians 5:18

Friday, November 27

**So speak encouraging words to one another. Build up hope so you'll all be together in this, no one left out, no one left behind. I know you're already doing this; just keep on doing it.
—1 Thessalonians 5:11 (MSG)**

A county program is encouraging citizens to see themselves as "askable adults." The phrase refers to people in the community whom teens can talk to, a way of bridging a great generational divide.

I haven't signed up for the seminar, though on some level I've been in this category for more than a decade, serving as an "extra grandma" to a neighbor girl with special needs. Most days she calls at least once and often jumps right in with a request. I've recently identified categories: (1) "Miss Evelyn, I have a question," maybe a vocabulary definition or a what-if scenario. (2) "Miss Evelyn, I have a problem," maybe a lost key or a homework deadline. (3) "Miss Evelyn, I was wondering if you could—" maybe provide transportation or a missing ingredient for dinner. There's also an ongoing barrage of curious *whys*, often about God, whom she values as her heavenly Father.

I can't always come through for her—and maybe shouldn't. On a practical level, as she gets older, she needs to rely on her family, engage her own ingenuity, practice self-advocacy, and pray faithfully.

Yet when I see her name on my caller ID, I pick up, ready to listen. In recent weeks, I've noted an unexpected opening line: "Miss Evelyn, how was your day?" I smile and give a quick report. The new question gives a deeper, personal meaning to being an askable adult.

Lord, help me to remain faithful to this deeply rooted intergenerational relationship.
—Evelyn Bence

Digging Deeper: Romans 15:1–13

Saturday, November 28

"For I know the plans I have for you," declares the Lord, "plans to prosper you and not to harm you, plans to give you hope and a future.
—Jeremiah 29:11 (NIV)

My mother-in-law, Kim, was shocked. My in-laws had gifted a Thanksgiving trip to Key West to their kiddos and grandkids. We spent our days sightseeing and our nights, well... "Puzzles?" she asked. "Are you really doing puzzles again?"

The year leading up to the trip had been tiring. We had friends who were hurting and job decisions to make. Puzzling proved a way to make something make sense. At last, everything could fit perfectly. "If I had known puzzles would keep you all around the table for hours, I would've been buying them for years," Kim said.

If you haven't done large puzzles before, there's something calming about slowly working toward a large, attainable goal. Everyone helping has a role— Will is our shapes master, organizing pieces by ins and outs, and Maddie is all over borders. And while you work, conversation flows easily even about difficult topics. There's no eye contact; all eyes are on the puzzle.

Long after the vacation ended, we kept puzzling in our little family of five. Many nights I can snag at least one of my children to come help me with whatever the current scene is, and while they build with their fingers, their worries, joys, and updates tend to spill from their mouths.

Building puzzles may seem silly to some, but for us it has become a way to make sense of the greater world, one piece at a time. I'll forever be grateful to my in-laws for kicking off what has become a prayerful practice for both me and my children.

Lord, I know I can't see the whole picture right now, but help me find the pieces to build my life in a way that glorifies You. —Ashley Kappel

Digging Deeper: Isaiah 40:8;
Philippians 4:13

First Sunday of Advent, November 29

CHRISTMAS BLESSINGS: A Light Shines in the Darkness

When Jesus spoke again to the people, he said, "I am the light of the world. Whoever follows me will never walk in darkness but will have the light of life." —John 8:12 (NIV)

For the December meeting, members of our church women's group were asked to bring a favorite nativity to display in the sanctuary. We could also explain why we'd chosen that particular one. I liked the idea but didn't plan to participate: I live in the country and had already been to town for after-school Joy Club. Besides, it was cold and windy.

At the last minute, I changed my mind. Although I love all of my nativities, I took the mahogany, hand-carved figures my oldest grandson, Ryan, brought from a mission trip to Rwanda. When it was my turn to share, I used Ryan's words: "The people we worked with were very poor but didn't want charity," he'd said, "so I bought nativities to provide extra income for some of the families."

The Rwandan figures joined Beth's fifty-piece Willow Tree set; it had been her mother's. Joan's glass figurines were a family favorite. Sharon's cross with lighted silhouettes inside was new, but there were stories behind almost all the others. We even found a set that originally graced a children's classroom but had been in storage for decades.

Amazingly, when we plugged in the cord to the stable, the light still shined on The Holy Family.

The light also illuminated a dark spot in my heart. It was well worth the time and extra drive to town to begin the Christmas season focused on Jesus, not myself.

Lord Jesus, thank You for lighting my heart and life, not only at Christmas but every day of the year. —Penney Schwab

Digging Deeper: Matthew 4:12–16; 2 Corinthians 4:6; Revelation 21:22–26

Monday, November 30

**Taste and see that the LORD is good; blessed is the one who takes refuge in him.
—Psalm 34:8 (NIV)**

Because both my parents came from large farming families, I grew up with a plethora of cousins, many of us born in the baby boom years following World War II. We lived in the same neighborhood and attended the same church. We shared family vacations and most holidays—often around the kitchen table. After my parents, aunts, and uncles passed, my cousins and I kept in close contact, although many of us had moved to larger cities, seeking employment opportunities. We would ask one another about our family recipes, especially those tied to our German heritage. Thanksgiving was my mother's bread stuffing and her borscht soup, Aunt Gerty's Jell-O salad, or Aunt Betty's coconut pie. Memories all rolled into the very best of what it was to grow up as Adlers.

Family, food, traditions. It was the same in Christ's day. The Passover meal. The wedding feast in Cana. The feeding of the five thousand. How often food is mentioned in the Bible, bringing community together.

After several years of scribbling down recipes over the phone, my cousins and I decided to create a family cookbook. It was a labor of love, including photos of our parents and a few from our childhood. The recipes were far more than a list of ingredients. They were compiled with happy memories of growing up in small-town America, where food was more than a delicious meal—it was tradition.

My children were the ones who titled the cookbook. When we loaded them into the car to visit my parents, they'd be excited and cry out, "Oh goody, we get Adler food."

Adler Food and so much more.

I treasure my family, Lord, and the traditions passed from one generation to the next. How blessed I am. —Debbie Macomber

Digging Deeper: 1 Corinthians 10:31; Hebrews 10:24–25

LIVING A NEW LIFE

1 _____

2 _____

3 _____

4 _____

5 _____

6 _____

7 _____

8 _____

9 _____

10 _____

11 _____

12 _____

13 _____

14 _____

15 _____

16 _____

17 _____

18 _____

19 _____

20 _____

21 _____

22 _____

23 _____

24 _____

25 _____

26 _____

27 _____

28 _____

29 _____

30 _____

December

And without faith it is impossible
to please God, because anyone who
comes to him must believe that
he exists and that he rewards
those who earnestly seek him.

—Hebrews 11:6 (NIV)

Behold, all things have become new.
—2 Corinthians 5:17 (NKJV)

While decorating for the holidays this year, I decided to assemble my own outdoor greenery arrangements. I had been feeling outdated and inadequate while attempting to learn a new computer platform, and thought perhaps a hands-on project would bring some joy. Following a set of instructions for the amateur gardener, I donned boots and jacket before heading outside to gather materials from the yard and surrounding woods.

The first thing listed was not something native to Pennsylvania woods—3-inch-diameter birchwood logs. Maybe if I found branches of similar size, they could be painted white. Perusing my property's perimeter, I noticed some long bamboo pieces. These might work! I cut away brambles and pulled them out from beneath leaves and dirt. Dragging them home, I used a rusty vintage saw to cut the bamboo to three varying lengths. I spread out an old sheet on the garage floor and found a half-used can of white spray paint. Perhaps it was the garage temperature or maybe it was the paint can's age, but when pressing the nozzle, only a couple drips of white paint emerged. I pressed again, causing another dribble—and suddenly, voilà! The paint drops were creating a snowy effect on the bamboo. From there,

I added evergreen cuttings, sprigs of holly berries, and—wow!

Friends and family are complimenting my outdoor arrangements, saying they look professional. I chuckle because they resulted from buried bamboo pieces, a broken paint can, and fringe greens cut from dormant bushes.

Lord, sometimes we feel outdated, broken, and on the fringes. Please take these things about us and transform them into something remarkable.
—Lisa Livezey

Digging Deeper: Isaiah 43:19; Ezekiel 36:26; Romans 6:4; Titus 3:5

Wednesday, December 2

Never will I leave you; never will I forsake you. —Hebrews 13:5 (NIV)

Our daughter, Natalie, is the culinary czar of the family, specializing in breads. Her French bread is a buttery mouthful of paradise. When I pressed her for the secret of great bread, she just shrugged and said, "Bread isn't that hard to make. You just have to be there for it."

"Just be there." It sounds so simple, but it can be miserably hard to do. My mother, Virginia, successfully reared us six children on a preacher's salary alone. She was there for us, night and day. A hundred times a week I would go to her with questions. "Mom, what does the word *exacerbate* mean?" She would smile. "That's when you make things harder for me by tracking in mud on my clean floors."

My mother was wise, creative, and selfless. She could have had a great career, and she did, as the full-time mother of Danny, Tommy, Mark, Bob, Gloria, and Linda. And without her constant presence, my father, Edward, would surely have faltered in the ministry.

I try to "be there" for my wife. She talks a lot, which means that I do a lot of listening. However, I'm a little hard of hearing, and my brain is often "out to lunch." When she tells me the complicated plot of her latest mystery novel, my eyeballs turn to stone, and she glares at me.

"You are not listening to me!"

"Uh, well, I was thinking . . . about how much I love you."

Her face softens to a smile. "Nice save," she says.

That doesn't always work, however, so I have ordered a hearing aid.

Thank You, Father, just for being there, whenever we need to talk. —Daniel Schantz

Digging Deeper: Galatians 6:10; Philippians 2:4

Thursday, December 3

They who wait for the LORD shall renew their strength; they shall mount up with wings like eagles; they shall run and not be weary; they shall walk and not faint. —Isaiah 40:31 (ESV)

One day many years ago, when my daughter was eight, she was wearing a winter ski mask on a cold December morning. I said to her: "Hey, honey, you look like a ninja. You could rob a bank."

I think we had just seen a Disney movie with bank robbers in it, and I knew that she and her friends talked about ninjas a lot.

She responded in her usual matter-of-fact way, "No, I couldn't. My legs are still too short. I wouldn't be able to outrun the cops."

Where do kids learn these things?

Where do we adults unlearn them?

We are sometimes told that God criticizes the human imagination in the Bible. This is true. When you read "the imagination of the heart" it is code for "your ungodly leanings," as if imagination is bad because it is in opposition to faith. You'll find a lot of this, for instance, in the prophet Jeremiah.

But there is another kind of imagination—the kind we love to see in our children, and that we often lose as we grow older. I'm talking about the creativity and vision that come when someone is open to possibilities. Then, we are able to imagine ourselves in the metaphors of eagles' wings, and running long races, and waiting on the Lord—all creative, imaginative metaphors from Scripture.

God, illumine my life today with Your creativity and imagination. Help me to see and hear the unexpected! —Jon M. Sweeney

---

Friday, December 4

LIFE LESSONS FROM GAMES: Celebrate Successes

**LORD, save us! LORD, grant us success!
—Psalm 118:25 (NIV)**

My husband, Dave, was practicing the violin when he suddenly doubled over with abdominal pain. He lunged for his pain pills and water, then slumped on the couch.

It was Dave's second pain attack that day. The previous month he'd had days in a row without a single pain attack, and never one this severe. I worried, *Is his tumor growing? What will his next scan show?*

His tumor randomly squeezes a large blood vessel and nerve in Dave's abdomen, causing severe pain. As a nurse, I tend to look for another cause of the pain, some variable we can control. Diet? Exercise?

Dave doesn't like me to hover during a pain attack. I went to the next room to pray for him. I resisted the urge to ask God, "Why?" Then I opened Number Match on my phone.

I quickly remembered why I like playing it. Those fun emojis! One celebrates my move with "Well spotted!" Another winks, "Line cleared!" When I win, I get a gold star and "Congratulations!"

God whispered, *Are there successes to celebrate hidden in Dave's cancer journey?*

I started a list.

1. Dave's tumors are neuroendocrine, not the more common and fatal adenocarcinomas.
2. December 4 marks 10 years since his diagnosis!
3. His oncologist is caring and highly experienced.
4. Between his pain attacks and doctor appointments, Dave gets to enjoy his hobbies: violin, golf, biking, and woodworking.

Gracious Lord, I celebrate Your many blessings, especially those hidden in our sufferings.
—Leanne Jackson

Digging Deeper: Psalm 145:7; 2 Corinthians 4:7

Saturday, December 5

Keep your life free from love of money, and be content with what you have, for he has said, "I will never leave you nor forsake you."
—Hebrews 13:5 (ESV)

Money woes. If the prayer requests we get at Guideposts.org are any indication, money worries rival health issues as the number-one concern.

I remember when my late wife, Julee, and I were newlyweds, living in a one-bedroom sublet. I was a lowly assistant editor, basically entry level, and paid accordingly. Julee was waiting tables at night and going from audition to audition during the day. We pinched every penny till Lincoln cried uncle. Still, the first of the month always threatened doom. How many times did we count the change in our pockets to see if we would make it?

"I got a callback for an audition," Julee said one night, sounding hopeful as we scribbled numbers on a legal pad. "You said you might get a raise this year, maybe even a promotion."

Sure, I thought. *As if we can count on any of that.*

"Don't worry, Edward. Someday we'll be on easy street." Julee loved to say that.

Later that night I prayed: *Lord, we don't need to be on easy street. Just help us get to* easier *street.*

As the years passed, we found our feet financially. Things worked out. Not everything, but enough. Eventually we got a mortgage and put a down payment on a house.

"See?" Julee said. "Easy street."

I smiled. Not exactly. A mortgage is another money thing to worry about. But my wife had a point. We were on easier street, just as I had prayed for.

Father, we all have money worries at some point in life. Yet how often have I allowed those worries to obscure Your grace? Remind me that the one thing I can count on is You. —Edward Grinnan

Digging Deeper: Proverbs 10:22;
1 Timothy 6:10

Second Sunday of Advent, December 6

CHRISTMAS BLESSINGS: It Is Well with My Soul

Mary treasured up all these things and pondered them in her heart. —Luke 2:19 (NIV)

The deep grief I felt when my husband, Don, died has receded, and I've adjusted to living alone. But holidays, especially Christmas, are still tinged with sorrow. That's why I accepted an invitation to attend a "Blue Christmas service" in a nearby town.

The church was packed with people. A slide show recognized each person who had died during the year. There were some familiar faces. A friend of mine had died in a car accident, and a person close to my daughter had taken his own life.

After songs and prayers, the pastor gave a meditation on the life of Horatio G. Spafford. Mr. Spafford knew a lot about grief. His son died of scarlet fever in 1871. On November 22, 1873, his four daughters died in a shipwreck tragedy while sailing to England with their mother, Anna, who was rescued. Upon reaching England, Anna telegraphed her husband the tragic news: "Saved alone." Mr. Spafford boarded a ship to England. After the ship passed over the place where the tragedy occurred, he was inspired to write the lyrics to the hymn "It Is Well with My Soul."

Following the meditation, candles were lit, prayers said, and tears flowed freely. We grieved lost loved ones, then sang together Mr. Spafford's words of faith: "Whatever my lot, Thou hast taught me to know, it is well, it is well, with my soul."

This same song was sung at Don's funeral. My heart was comforted and my spirits lifted. I was ready to celebrate the coming of Jesus into the world.

Lord, like Mary, may I treasure up memories in my heart, assured that in You, all is well with my soul.
—Penney Schwab

Digging Deeper: Psalm 103:1–5; Isaiah 51:11–12; John 16:20–24

Monday, December 7

Then God said, "Let the waters abound with an abundance of living creatures, and let birds fly above the earth across the face of the firmament of the heavens." —Genesis 1:20 (NKJV)

It is a chilly winter day, and I am in my quiet study carrel on the top floor of the Mercer University library. As I sat down at my desk to write this *Walking in Grace* devotion, I suddenly heard a sharp peck on the window glass nearby. Startled, I looked to see a beautiful female cardinal sitting on the windowsill and gazing straight into my eyes. It was a moment of delight, and for a brief second, the gift of a return to Eden.

I did not know this young bird, nor did she know me. And she is instinctively "wired" to be wary of human beings. Yet for a few seconds, we had a "conversation" without words. Sitting very still, I tried my best to convey a message with my delighted smile: *Thanks for dropping by! Thanks for this wonderful surprise!* In response, she pecked on the ledge, perhaps for a breakfast treat, and peered at me as if smiling. However, such a gift is momentary, and suddenly, as if coming to her senses, she flittered and flew off into an eternity of time in which I hope we will meet again.

I do believe that the greatest quest and hope of all "God-breathed life" is for the experience of unity—of not being alone or frightened or separated by a pane of glass or instinctive fear. For a brief moment today, I did catch a glimpse of Eden. I did savor the scent of God's sweet nature.

Dear God, bring into my awareness today the beauty of Your creation. May I soon be surprised by Your joy and Your presence! Amen.
—Scott Walker

Digging Deeper: Psalms 25:14–18, 51:11–12; Romans 8:38–39

Tuesday, December 8

For great is his love toward us, and the faithfulness of the LORD endures forever. Praise the LORD. —Psalm 117:2 (NIV)

My husband, Lonny, and I followed the nurse down the hall, but I lagged. It was the day of my foot reconstruction. Mobility was an issue, and each step brought jagged-edge pain.

But that was nothing next to my nerves. There would be lots of hardware. Months of recovery.

"I'm scared," I whispered.

"I know," Lonny replied.

In a matter of minutes, it would be too late to run. Too late to hide. A window showed dawn on the horizon. On a normal day, I'd be heading to work in the outpatient lab downstairs.

"Here we are," the nurse said, stopping outside an open door. My heart pulsed in my ears.

Then I heard my friend's voice.

"Shawney, wait! Please wait!" I turned to see my dear friend Jenny. It was time for her to open the lab, but there she was. Breathless to catch us.

"This is a good thing," she said. "You're going to be better. You're going to be fine." Her wide green eyes spoke confidence and truth.

Jenny was always helping me. Teaching me phlebotomy when teaching was tough. Standing outside my draw room when patients or veins were difficult. Bringing lunch when I didn't have time to brown-bag it. But this kind of help stirred me to the center. And when Jenny's arms went around me, I felt the sacred sureness of God's love.

A half hour later, I lay in bed in a gown. Tethered to an IV pole. Surgeon's initials on my leg like a tattoo.

But my soul was settled. The Lord had shown His faithfulness and love.

Lord, thank You for reminding me of Your care. Amen. —Shawnelle Eliasen

Digging Deeper: Lamentations 3:23; Psalm 86:15; James 1:17

Wednesday, December 9

I praise you because I am fearfully and wonderfully made. —Psalm 139:14 (NIV)

While shopping in my favorite home-goods store, I came across the most adorable Christmas kitchen towel set. They displayed scenes of Santa Claus walking various breeds of dogs wearing red or green bows, scarves, and sweaters. In lieu of a doggie leash, Santa guided the cute canines with a string of red and green Christmas lights.

I loved the whimsical towels, but not just for the bright colors and fun doggies. I'd found my favorite Christmas décor motif ever—Black Santa. These towels, featuring a brown-skinned Santa, reminded me of my introduction to Black Santa, and that transported me back to my childhood.

It was my fifth birthday, and my parents had invited my closest cousins and best friends to my birthday party. Since people tend to be focused on Christmas by the time my December 9 birthday arrives, my parents hosted a Christmas-themed party. I couldn't be more excited to enjoy the candy canes, hot chocolate, and fun holiday decorations. Little did I know, my parents had a big surprise in store for me. Midway through the party, in walked none other than Santa Claus. He had a big belly, long white beard, a huge sack slung over his shoulder, and brown skin like me!

Several decades later, I chuckle at my naivete back then. At the time I couldn't understand why, underneath the beard, Santa resembled my dad, or why my father had missed Santa's appearance. But I knew one thing: I loved this Black Santa guy. He reminded me that I was seen and valuable, the same thing God reminds me often. That in His eyes, I am valuable and seen—exactly for who I am.

Father, thank You for seeing me and reminding me how valuable I am in Your eyes. —Carla Hendricks

Digging Deeper: Psalm 139:13–16; Matthew 10:29–31

Thursday, December 10

As we have therefore opportunity, let us do good. —Galatians 6:10 (KJV)

All my life, our family had "gone about doing good." I've tried to carry on this great tradition, and now my wife, Corinne, and I were looking for ways to include our children.

"Your mom's group is doing their annual toy drive," Corinne reminds me.

I load up our kids and head for the store.

"Remember," I instruct as we drive along, "we are shopping for kids that might not get anything at all for Christmas."

"Why won't they get anything for Christmas?" asks little David from the back seat.

"Well, some children live in shelters because they don't have homes." The car grows quiet; the girls have stopped their chatter. "Some children only have grandparents, and others have families who are very poor because their parents have lost their jobs. All are good people going through hard times. God wants us to help."

A shopping marathon follows. Ella Grace concentrates on things girls might like. Mary Katherine is studying games that families can play together. David centers on "boy things." We fill one buggy, then another and another.

Later, when it's time to deliver the toys to our friend Darlene at Spruce Street Baptist, where the toys will be distributed, David and I are on our own. We carry armloads of toys and set them on tables. David insists on organizing them into categories.

We leave, but outside David hesitates. Tears fill his eyes. "Dad, I brought the money from my bank. I wanted to give it to the children." As we leave a second time, Darlene says goodbye with a big smile.

I am perfectly sure that God is smiling too.

Father, lead us toward Your good, and we will follow. —Brock Kidd

Digging Deeper: Proverbs 3:27; Hebrews 13:6

Friday, December 11

For whosoever shall call upon the name of the Lord shall be saved. —Romans 10:13 (KJV)

As snowflakes started to fall, I was grateful I'd ordered my groceries online. All I had to do was drive to the store, pop my trunk, and all the provisions I needed for the week would be loaded in. Simple, right?

"Any coupons?" the young man asked before finishing up my order.

I sighed. My $5 off coupon was sitting on my kitchen counter at home. There was nothing I could do about it now. As I drove home, feeling $5 poorer, I mentally chastised myself. My absentmindedness had cost me money. Again.

It was so frustrating. It felt like every transaction I made had a special trick to master. If I clipped or clicked a coupon, downloaded an app, typed in a promo code, or made a purchase at a certain time of day or day of the week, I'd "win" and save money. Paying the regular price made me feel not only like I was throwing my money away, but also that I wasn't smart enough to play the consumer game.

But before I made it to my driveway, which was only a 5-minute drive from the store, God stopped my negative thoughts by grounding me in gratitude. He assured me He never played games. Jesus didn't provide me with a discount coupon or BOGO offer. There were no hidden costs, expiration dates, or exclusion clauses behind His gift of life and love. Jesus paid for everything, once and for all. No strings attached. Buoyed by grace, I unloaded my trunk with a smile on my face and gratitude in my heart.

Jesus, help me to let go of the little things that trip me up during the day and focus more on the big things, like Your gifts of love and grace.
—Vicki Kuyper

Digging Deeper: John 3:16; Ephesians 2:8–9; Titus 3:5

Saturday, December 12

Thanks be to God for his inexpressible gift! —2 Corinthians 9:15 (ESV)

"Mom, I need fifteen more 8 x 10 canvases," my nine-year-old son, Jacques, belted from his room.

Fifteen! I just bought eight of them, I thought to myself. Puzzled, I walked into his room to investigate the situation. Upon inspection, I found he *did* use all the canvases previously purchased. When I asked him why he needed fifteen more, he explained for Christmas he was making a personalized painting for each classmate in his third-grade class.

Astonished by Jacques's heartfelt gifts, I peered closely at his paintings and found he incorporated each person's name along with their favorite colors, hobbies, books, animals, and games. "How do you know each person's likes and favorites?" I asked. Jacques then pulled out a stack of papers each student had filled out detailing their preferences.

Astounded by the thoughtfulness, organization, and planning Jacques embraced for these class Christmas gifts, I immediately planned to get him more canvases. Jacques's thoughtful gifts humbled my heart.

My own gift-giving this year looked much less personal and was more convenient. In an effort to love others better, like Jacques, I decided to replace all of the gift cards on my list with more thoughtful expressions of love—a picture ornament of the grandchildren for my mom, an engraved picture frame for a fellow horse mom, and prayer journal for a dear friend. Thanks to Jacques, I expressed a truer meaning of Christmas by how I loved those close to me this year.

Heavenly Father, may our love for each other be a true testament of Your love for us, in Your holy name. Amen. —Jolynda Strandberg

Digging Deeper: Matthew 1:18–25, 22:36–40; John 1:19–23

Third Sunday of Advent, December 13

CHRISTMAS BLESSINGS: Treasures and Traditions

So then, brothers and sisters, stand firm and hold fast to the teachings we passed on to you, whether by word of mouth or by letter.
—2 Thessalonians 2:15 (NIV)

I decided not to decorate for Christmas. I felt a bit guilty, because my husband, Don, had loved every display and every ornament. But getting them out alone would take several hours and multiple trips to the basement.

However, a couple of weeks before Christmas I hung a quilted wall hanging, made by my dear friend Martha, over the fireplace. The panels portrayed the birth of Christ in vivid shades of blue, green, and gold. It looked out of place all alone, so I put a needlepoint picture of the Holy Family in the dining room.

One thing led to another, and by day's end the house was decorated. Four nativity sets were displayed in the dining room. The pewter one with exquisite, tiny figures was a gift from Don. Another was handmade from corn husks; 40 years earlier I spent my Christmas money to buy it from a mission agency. The small, vividly painted tin figures were from Mexico. A stable with rough-cut wooden figures was a favorite with my children. A bowl of pinecones adorned the living room coffee table. I even set out the basket of coasters that were handmade from old Christmas cards. They're a bit tacky, but I like them.

When I lit the candles on the Advent wreath and saw the angel collection reflected in the light, I was thankful I'd kept alive the tradition Don loved. Every decoration brought precious memories and helped me move toward Christmas Day with joy.

Thank You, Jesus, for treasures and traditions that draw me closer to You. —Penney Schwab

Digging Deeper: Joshua 4:4–7; Psalm 29:1–2; Isaiah 60:13

Monday, December 14

DOORS OF OUR LIFE: Bedroom Door
I wait quietly before God, for my victory comes from him. —Psalm 62:1 (NLT)

If you ever regretted following through on one of your spur-of-the-moment brilliant ideas, I sympathize with you. My dimly lit lightbulb notion originated with our need for a second office, and our bedroom immediately popped into my mind. The concept of a dual purpose made sense to me, considering we used the space for 8 hours or fewer each day. Why waste large windows with gorgeous views on closed eyelids?

The next day I moved my desk into the bedroom's dormer nook and closed the door during work hours—until winter rolled around and daylight time decreased. All I wanted to do by sunset was sleep. Good night, home office; hello, bedtime. Like so many times in the past, I had marched full steam ahead with my hasty idea and achieved mixed results. *Help me with this office issue,* I prayed. Would I ever learn God knows what I need and will provide it?

As Christmas approached, I spent extra time decorating and baking in our great room/kitchen. While preparing to celebrate the birth of God's son, I focused more on Him and less on me—and that led me to the solution to my office problem. With the large island as my desk, snacks in the refrigerator, and roaring fire in the fireplace, the great room made a much better working space. And I learned a valuable lesson about being in a space where I can listen to His wisdom.

Nowadays I constantly remind myself no issue is too large, small, simple, or complex for the Creator of the universe. As the first and everlasting multitasker, He is more than able to give me what I need now and forever through His Son Jesus Christ.

God, thank You for opening the doors of our life if we close them to You. Help us remember to seek You first for all of our daily needs.
—Jenny Lynn Keller

Digging Deeper: Psalm 121; Isaiah 58:11; Luke 18:27; Philippians 4:19

**I will repay you for the years the locusts have
eaten—the great locust and the young locust,
the other locusts and the locust swarm—
my great army that I sent among you.**
—Joel 2:25 (NIV)

"Are you comfortable?" my husband, Lonny, asks.
He tucks a knit blanket around me as I stretch on
the sofa. "Is there anything that you need?"

There is not.

I've had reconstructive foot surgery. Lots of
hardware. Lots of recovery. Lots of time.

But I am good, because I'm home.

I sit and pat the sofa seat. Lonny sits beside
me and cradles me in his arms. The fire crackles.
Our Labrador breathes a rhythm of rest. And
contentment in my soul overflows so mightily that
it's surely in the air around us.

For years, I'd been in a place of letting go. The
home where we'd raised our boys. A lifestyle of
home teaching. An identity of being a five-boy
mama. But life moved forward, and that practice
of opening my hand to let go left an emptiness of
heart.

But as the Lord restored what the locusts had
gnawed from Israel, He has restored the goodness to
my life too. There's delight in seeing my sons stretch
their roots and wings. Our smaller home is a haven
for others—furniture often pushed to the perimeter

so saints can study His Word. Caring for my husband brings a depth of satisfaction I've never known. And even this new pup beside us is a reminder of new life.

"Did you hear me, Shawnelle?" Lonny asks. "Can I get you anything?"

But I'm drifting off to sleep in this comfort, knowing the Lord has graciously given all I need.

O Father, You lavish blessing after blessing when we don't deserve a thing. Amen.
—Shawnelle Eliasen

Digging Deeper: Psalms 23:1, 34:10; Matthew 6:33; Philippians 4:19

Wednesday, December 16

Surely I am with you always, to the very end of the age. —Matthew 28:20 (NIV)

I pick through hangers, looking for a sweater for my grandma. Every year, I buy her one for Christmas. She likes simple, neutral colors. And, because she's active, she prefers lightweight clothing.

I come across a cream-colored cardigan. I pull it off the rack to inspect the loose weave. The sweater is dainty—just like her. Perfect. I drape the sweater over my arm and head to the front of the department store. Halfway there, my phone rings. I answer.

"Hey, Mom," I say. "Just finishing Christmas shopping. Can I call you in a bit?"

"Logan," Mom says. Her voice is shaky. "I'm at the hospital. Your grandma had a stroke."

The world spins.

Mom explains that, because my grandma received treatment quickly, the likelihood of permanent damage is reduced. They are running tests now, but we won't get results for some time. While Mom speaks, I grip the sweater tightly, my fingers pressing through the woven pattern.

My mom promises to call me when the test results come in. Then she hangs up.

I feel unmoored. My grandma is hurting, but there is nothing I can do to help. And, because I live hours away, I can't even sit with my family in the waiting room.

I feel alone. Awash with fear and doubt.

But, as I cling to the sweater, I choose to also cling to a promise. My Lord will never leave me or forsake me.

Though I cannot help my grandma in this dark hour, I know that she is not alone.

Lord, even in times of uncertainty, You are steadfast. —Logan Eliasen

Digging Deeper: Joshua 1:9; Psalm 94:14

Thursday, December 17

Do not remember the former things, nor consider the things of old. Behold, I will do a new thing, now it shall spring forth. —Isaiah 43:18–19 (NKJV)

In every move I've ever made, something gets broken or goes missing. When my then-husband and I moved from a three-story house to an apartment, I lost Christmas.

Our stately Victorian house in rural Ohio invited a yuletide extravagance of trees, wreaths, candles, and strings of lights that would not fit a small apartment in Cleveland. We boxed up the decorations and called a local charity to pick them up.

One box was coming with us. It was robin's-egg blue, tied with a white ribbon. It held my favorite, most meaningful ornaments. Each one reminded me of a trip, a person, or a special time in my life.

The blue box with the white ribbon was not supposed to go to the local charity. But somehow, it did. We called the charity immediately when we realized the error, but the box and its contents had already found a new home. I was heartsick.

"Why don't you start another collection?" a friend said.

I recoiled. *I can't do that! Those ornaments were irreplaceable!*

Then came the thought that freed me: they became valued through the alchemy of my intention, attention, and time.

Behold, I could do a new thing.

About a month after our move, I bought a collection of glass ornaments of Santa Clauses from around the world. They're charming little fellas. I look forward to getting to know and cherish them, one Christmas at a time.

God, give me the strength to begin again.
—Amy Eddings

Digging Deeper: Revelation 21:1, 4

Friday, December 18

If any household is too small for a whole lamb, they must share one with their nearest neighbor. —Exodus 12:4 (NIV)

Colorful wrapping paper flies through the air, as memory yields an image of a toddler tearing open her gifts.

Was it her birthday? Christmas? I simply cannot recall.

Truthfully, the specific occasion didn't seem to matter as the chubby little one gasped her way from gift to gift. An only child, she had become used to mountains of presents, and it appeared her interest had moved from the fun of seeing the actual toys to the studied pursuit of how deeply the family audience could be impressed. I ask myself, *Was the excitement of the toys the draw that day, or was it a matter of coaxing the family toward the next round of thunderous applause?* The latter, I'm afraid.

Granted, attention-seeking is a trademark of two- and three-year-olds—pointing toward a tendency that follows throughout life if unchecked. But reminded of God's decree to the Israelites during the night of the first Passover, insisting they share the lamb where needed, I wonder: When do we grow up enough to ask, "Is this too much? With whom can I share my blessing?" rather than "How impressed are you with my latest stash that I have no intention of sharing?"

Instead of quickly becoming numb to God's gifts—flinging them into a cloud of forgetfulness as soon as they have caught everyone's eye—perhaps we could straightaway touch the heart of God by offering gratitude for each blessing, shucking the selfishness of toddlers while embracing their enthusiasm, and looking to share with our neighbors.

Jesus, help me accept my blessings as occasions not for self-importance and accumulation but for gratitude, shaping me into the person You want me to be as I continue to grow up in You.
—Jacqueline F. Wheelock

Digging Deeper: Romans 12:3;
Philippians 2:3–4

Saturday, December 19

An intelligent heart acquires knowledge, and the ear of the wise seeks knowledge.
—**Proverbs 18:15** (ESV)

I was getting dressed and ready for a party we were hosting, going over the appetizers and last-minute things to do, when the roar of the vacuum came up through the floorboards—music to my ears.

I remember a time when the sound of the vacuum cleaner was an annoyance that I ran from. As a child, it was a catalyst for me to hide in my room with a book or go outside before I was roped into doing the carpeted stairs.

When my nephew was born, the noise of the vacuum was the only sound that lulled him to sleep, and because they lived next door, I would hear the white noise most early evenings—a sound that I learned to tune out.

That night, the vacuum's motor continued to ebb and flow downstairs, and I was filled with gratitude for whoever it was—one of my sons or my husband—who had taken it upon himself to plug it in and do a quick once-over before our guests arrived.

As I looked in the mirror, I thought about change, the transformative power of life's experience that can fundamentally alter my reaction to a sound, bringing me away from annoyance and toward love and gratitude.

Heavenly Father, thank You for this life and its layered experiences that fill me with awe.
—Sabra Ciancanelli

Digging Deeper: Isaiah 43:19; Romans 12:2; Ephesians 4:23

Fourth Sunday of Advent, December 20

CHRISTMAS BLESSINGS: Joy to the World

Taking the child in his arms, [Jesus] said to them, "Whoever welcomes one of these little children in my name welcomes me."
—Mark 9:36–37 (NIV)

We always do the traditional Christmas story for our Sunday school program. This year, though, God nudged us to acknowledge that wars and poverty would prevent any joy for millions of the world's children. But what could we do? The answer, it turned out, came in telling more of the Christmas story than usual.

We had eight participants. Props were simple. The "stable" was a grass tiki hut. Mary and Joseph were plastic and Baby Jesus a well-loved doll. There were canes for shepherd's crooks. The tiny angel had wings and tinsel in her hair. The five wise men wore gold paper crowns; two of them had also been shepherds. (The Bible mentions three gifts, not the number of wise men.)

The program began with the prophecies from Micah and Isaiah; the angel's message; and the shepherds' visit as told in Luke. The wise men presented their gifts but "returned to their country by another route" (Matthew 2:12, NIV). We followed Matthew's account of the flight of the Holy Family to Egypt to save Jesus from King Herod's wrath. Although Herod didn't kill Jesus, he ordered the killing of all baby boys under the age of two.

The program closed with this request: "Will you please remember to pray for today's children who are in danger due to poverty and war?"

Then we sang "Joy to the World." Troubles abound, but we rejoice that Christ's birth gives us precious gifts of hope, peace, joy, and love.

Jesus, the world hasn't changed much since Your birth. Thank You for coming into it for the sake of all of us. —Penney Schwab

Digging Deeper: Isaiah 11:6–9; Matthew 2:18–23; Luke 18:17

Monday, December 21

It is good for the heart to be strengthened by grace. —Hebrews 13:9 (ESV)

For decades, every year in mid-December, the mailman delivered a big carton with telltale packaging. I would joke with the out-of-town sender, "You're the shipping-tape aficionado. I can hardly wrestle the box open."

She wanted to guarantee safe delivery. She'd scoured vintage shops, then individually wrapped six or more gifts: serving dishes, maybe table linens, a piece of jewelry, or a hat. Oh, and a box of chocolates or book of poetry.

In return I usually sent two modest, lightweight finds—clothing accessories or kitchen doodads. The exchange, though lopsided, seemed to work for us. We both appreciated the sentiment and anticipated the moment of revelation, opening the gifts.

But at this stage of life, my home is small, and my shelves are full. The physical heft has become, well, burdensome. I wondered and maybe worried, *How will she react if I suggest a change?* At Thanksgiving last year, Christmas plans crept into our phone conversation. I sensed the Spirit's nudge and tentatively asked, "What would you think of cutting back on the gifts?"

"Oh, I've been thinking the same thing. Shopping isn't as easy as it used to be." Perfect timing. I felt graced, newly confident that our friendship would weather a new season.

Weeks later her box arrived, smaller, lighter. Bonbons, vintage leather gloves, two books. But some things never change. I still struggled with the tape.

Lord, thank You for relationships that remain stable even as we—and our needs—change.
—Evelyn Bence

Digging Deeper: 2 Corinthians 8:7–14

Tuesday, December 22

Meanwhile we groan, longing to be clothed instead with our heavenly dwelling.
—2 Corinthians 5:2 (NIV)

Why was that song stuck in my head? All December I had hummed it from waking up until going to sleep. "I'll Be Home for Christmas" refused to stop. It left me feeling sad.

Are you trying to tell me something, Lord? I prayed.

The first Christmas I remember noticing that song, I was with my new husband and his family instead of with my parents and siblings. I heard it on the radio and Mom did too; we cried on the phone. Thirty years later, our daughter Katie spent her first Christmas with her husband Brian's family. Katie and I didn't cry; we celebrated a week later.

This year we'd do the same. Celebrate with our daughter Emily at the Christmas Eve service and put up our tree and stockings. The five of us would exchange gifts over the New Year. So why was I singing that sad song over and over?

God's gentle voice asked, *What did you do lately that might have triggered that song?*

I'd visited Mom. She's in memory care; can't walk, can't talk, doesn't know me. Then I'd found an earlier photo of her. Smiling like herself, eyes twinkling. *That's it!*

Shortly after that photo was taken, a nurse coming to work on an icy January morning found Mom wheeling her walker toward the front door. In one of her last full sentences, Mom told the nurse, "I want to go home."

God whispered, *She wants to be with Me, Leanne. Her heavenly home.*

My sadness faded, replaced by God's peace.
I hummed, "Precious Lord, take my hand..."

Loving Lord, I pray for all those who long to go Home with You. —Leanne Jackson

Digging Deeper: Matthew 5:3; 2 Timothy 4:18

Wednesday, December 23

Therefore comfort each other and edify one another, just as you also are doing.
—1 Thessalonians 5:11 (NKJV)

Fresh pine scent filled the room and twinkle lights on the Christmas tree glowed. I snuggled in my recliner. Several years ago it'd become a tradition to tuck my handmade "quilt of comfort" around me. I traced the square Mom had cross-stitched that read, "Children are for hugging." When I did, it brought back memories of the first Christmas my family celebrated after Mom died.

It was a late, blustery evening a couple days before Christmas when my brother, sister-in-law, and I had picked up family from the airport. We'd decided to grab a bite to eat at a restaurant. Unfortunately, the heat wasn't working, so we all sat bundled in our winter coats. Our hearts were colder than the room. Nobody spoke. What was there to say? Mom, the cornerstone of all our holidays, the one who always made them fun, wasn't here anymore.

The following day we gathered with heavy hearts at my brother's home. Dad brought in a suitcase with the words "Becky and Linda sent gifts." When he opened the suitcase there was a handmade lap-quilt for each of us. After Mom had died, with Dad's permission, they'd gone into Mom's sewing room and gotten her fabric, unfinished quilting squares, and cross-stitch, then sewed a quilt for each of us. Tears welled in our eyes.

Now, all these years later, I pull the quilt under my chin, remembering how that Christmas changed me. Like many others drowning in the sorrow of a "first Christmas" without a loved one, I remember that first Christmas without Mom like it was yesterday. How grateful I am for the continued gifts of God's joy and comfort that He gives all year-round.

Thank You, Lord, for Your comfort, especially through family and friends. Amen. —Rebecca Ondov

Digging Deeper: Psalm 119:76; 2 Corinthians 1:3–4, 7:4

Christmas Eve, Thursday, December 24

CHRISTMAS BLESSINGS: Beloved Community

Therefore, since we are surrounded by such a great cloud of witnesses . . . let us run with perseverance the race marked out for us, fixing our eyes on Jesus, the pioneer and perfecter of faith. —Hebrews 12:1–2 (NIV)

Today is too busy, I thought as I hurried to teach Sunday school. I left immediately after the worship service for the 40-mile drive to a Christmas Eve luncheon hosted by my son Patrick and his wife, Patricia.

The meal was delicious and the company delightful. Dessert was a cheesecake competition. I sampled all four entries and picked my favorite. But I had to leave before the winner was decided to meet my daughter, Rebecca, for our 5 p.m. candlelight service. Afterward, she and granddaughter Olivia were joining me for a light supper.

Rebecca and I walked in just before the prelude started—a lovely duet rendition of "O Holy Night" played by a mother-son duo. We slipped into a pew behind a family with two little girls in red Christmas dresses who couldn't sit still. Elsewhere babies cried and other kids wiggled. I'd had noisy, wiggly kids, too, and was thankful for all the children at the service.

Scripture readings were interspersed with carols. A beautiful solo beckoned us to follow Jesus from His birth in Bethlehem all the way to the Cross of Calvary. We went forward for Holy Communion, then each took a small candle and made a circle completely around the church. The lights went off. The flickering light of glowing candles lit the faces of those around us as we sang an a cappella version of "Silent Night."

The day was busy, but oh, so good! Christmas was almost here.

Thank You, Lord, for family time, noisy children, shushing parents, and the great cloud of witnesses that make up this beloved community.

—Penney Schwab

Digging Deeper: Luke 2:4–20; John 1:9–14

Christmas Day, Friday, December 25

CHRISTMAS BLESSINGS: Past and Present

Praise be to the God and Father of our Lord Jesus Christ, who has blessed us in the heavenly realms with every spiritual blessing in Christ.
—Ephesians 1:3 (NIV)

I welcomed a quiet Christmas Day. There would be five of us for dinner and opening gifts, but afterward we'd connect with our scattered family through texts and calls. I finished meal preparations early, so I spent some time remembering past Christmases.

The year I was 12, Christmas was a great disappointment. Santa brought me a bicycle even though I'd begged for a poodle skirt (the latest fad in the fifties). But I enjoyed riding the bike for years, while poodle skirts were soon out of fashion.

Another Christmas, husband Don and I got stuck in heavy snow 8 miles into a 2-hour trip to celebrate with family. After a fervent prayer for help, a road grader cleared the way, and we arrived in time for dinner.

Once, amid complicated family issues, three of us went to a hotel for Christmas dinner. The room was packed, but I felt incredibly lonely. When a busy server stopped at our table to refill coffee cups, I told her I was sorry she had to work Christmas Day. "Honey," she replied, "I volunteered! I'm blessed to serve Jesus by serving His people." Her words were the one note of cheer.

Years have passed and times are mostly good. I was again reminded of that when our oldest son, Patrick, said our Christmas table grace: "Thank You, God for a year full of blessings—a wedding, a new baby, family trips, and especially for the presence of Your Son Jesus Christ in our lives."

I am blessed and grateful. Thank You, Jesus!
—Penney Schwab

Digging Deeper: Numbers 6:24–26; Psalm 103:1–2; Matthew 5:3–10

Saturday, December 26

Each of you should use whatever gift you have received to serve others, as faithful stewards of God's grace in its various forms. —1 Peter 4:10 (NIV)

On the quiet morning the day after Christmas, my aunt slipped away into eternity. Although it was sudden and unexpected for us, an indescribable peace settled over our family. We were in the season to celebrate the birth of the One who came to save us, and we could take comfort in knowing that my aunt's earthly death meant her heavenly reward.

We hadn't celebrated the Christmas holidays with my aunt, but we'd recently spent 4 days together during Thanksgiving and enjoyed her delectable delights. She was known for her baked goods, specifically her chocolate, red velvet, and pink lemonade cakes. When I'd called her on Christmas afternoon, she'd just finished baking three layers of a chocolate cake and set it out to cool, to be completed with frosting later.

Although my aunt had fought cancer during the previous months, doctors had recently told her that there were no longer signs of cancer in her body. She'd been awaiting one minor procedure but other than that was eager to testify of her healing to anyone who would listen. While enduring treatment, she faithfully served others and organized her church's community outreach efforts for the unhoused members of her community every Friday. Her heart was to serve. She did so sacrificially and with a sweet spirit. Almost as sweet as her chocolate cake.

Our family still talks about that unfinished cake. She left things behind for us to finish. Not just the frosting of her famous cake but her life's commitment to service.

God, thank You for the time You've given us to spend together with our family and friends. And for the loved ones who have gone on before us, we will honor their legacies with service.
—Tia McCollors

Sunday, December 27

Even the Son of Man did not come to be served, but to serve, and to give his life as a ransom for many. —Mark 10:45 (NIV)

One day several years ago, my little niece lightly poked a vein in the center of my mother-in-law's hand. "Why do your hands have blue worms?" she asked.

Slightly embarrassed, Helen laughed gently and explained that the veins on our hands become more visible as we grow older.

I'm of the age now where "worms" have made an appearance on my hands as well, along with brown spots and various scars. Not the most attractive to the untrained eye, but a small price to pay for the many ways my hands have served me over the years. They've held my babies, scrubbed countless surfaces, and prepared meals for my family, church potlucks, and the bereaved. I have a bit of an attachment to the scar I got slicing tomatoes at my grandmother's house when I was a teenager. If not for that slip of the knife and the resulting forever-raised tissue, I'm sure I would have long ago forgotten that moment. So in a weird way, I guess I wear my "worms" and other imperfections with . . . maybe not pride so much as gratitude.

Helen's hands have lovingly cared for three children and nine grandchildren. They have lain gently on feverish foreheads, softly brushed away tears from chubby cheeks. Her hands also happen to make the best buttermilk biscuits this side of heaven, having that "feel" for the dough that takes years to achieve.

I think my mother-in-law's hands are beautiful, especially in the eyes of the Lord. They are a servant's hands that have spent a lifetime folded in prayer.

Father, let me truly be "the hands and feet of Jesus," serving others with love. —Ginger Rue

Digging Deeper: John 13:14–15; 1 Corinthians 12:27

Monday, December 28

When I look at the night sky and see the work of your fingers—the moon and the stars you set in place—what are mere mortals that you should think about them, human beings that you should care for them? —Psalm 8:3–4 (NLT)

"I saw some shooting stars a moment ago!" I whisper to my older sister, Katie, as I step inside and away from the cold December air. It's around 5 a.m., and I hadn't been expecting to be able to see any shooting stars.

Meteor showers are one of my favorite things. Growing up I loved going out and trying to see one streaking across the sky. My parents' house was perfect for watching them too. They live outside of town, so there's not much light pollution, and they have open areas where we could watch the stars without trees or buildings blocking our view. We'd set up chairs, blankets, and sometimes air mattresses, and I'd count how many shooting stars I saw—I wanted to see if I could spot more than my siblings.

I had read that last night was supposed to be the best time to see the meteor shower, but I hadn't been able to stay up late to watch them. I'm also renting a house in town now, so I thought I'd miss them entirely because of the light pollution. Instead, I had a perfect, clear square of sky resting above me—and that's when I saw those shooting stars.

Katie and I leave a bit later. As Katie drives, I watch out the window for more shooting stars. I don't see any more, but that's OK. Even though I didn't experience shooting stars the way I was used to, I'm thrilled with what God showed me.

Lord, thank You for the stars and for Your many blessings. Please help me to remember in this coming year to be grateful for everything, big or small. —Rachel Thompson

Digging Deeper: Psalm 147:4;
Isaiah 40:26

Tuesday, December 29

Sometimes there is a phenomenon of which they say, "Look, this one is new!" —Ecclesiastes 1:10 (JPS)

The late fee and the interest charges on my credit card bill were appalling. I always pay the balance in full, and I mail the check in plenty of time, but they had posted the check to my account one day late. People were saying that the US Postal Service had slowed a great deal, but I had had no trouble sending checks before this. When I complained to friends, they were generous with stories about not having to write checks at all.

I had rejected the idea of changing the habits of a lifetime, but over time, I set up some automatic payments for the internet and my home utilities on my credit card. I got used to checking all the charges when I wrote the check to pay off the credit card every month. But the big penalties for late payment of the card on that statement made me angry enough to set up autopay for that, as well. It didn't occur to me that I couldn't pay off my credit card bill by credit card.

I would have to use the bank account, and that was a whole new level of distrust. I grilled the bank about its security against hacking, asked how many people were using the service, demanded to know their safety record, and then began interrogating my friends to find out who had given someone access to their bank account and what that experience had been like.

Finally my friend Susan threw up her hands in exasperation and asked, "Didn't it ever occur to you that technology could possibly be one of God's gifts to us?"

Go ahead, God, tell me what You want me to do, even if it takes twisting my arm or hitting me upside the head. —Rhoda Blecker

Digging Deeper: Genesis 28:16; Proverbs 3:5

Wednesday, December 30

But godliness with contentment is great gain. —1 Timothy 6:6 (ESV)

I try to avoid the grocery store the day before New Year's Eve, but I needed one last thing. I expected chaos and wasn't disappointed. Which is why I noticed the two couples sitting at a table next to the deli section. Late 80s, probably, white hair shining in the fluorescents, dressed for a day out. They chatted over ice cream, a pocket of serenity in the heart of the holiday panic. One of them noticed me watching. She smiled and waved. I returned both, suddenly happier.

Sometimes I struggle with aging. As I get older, it's easy to look back with longing on youthful days. Milestones loom and pass and, though I fight it, it bothers me. My body complains, but not as loudly as my heart and spirit.

Those couples encouraged me. They were life-survivors. They'd lived the storms of time and were stronger for it. They weren't mourning the past or stressing about the future. They were simply enjoying the *now*. A hard-earned skill that I'm slowly (sometimes painfully) realizing only comes with the blessing of years.

The seasons roll on; we can't stop them. Leaves fall and days grow short. But I'm reminded that even in this, I can rest. I can enjoy the now with the knowledge that this physical life is only the beginning. Life's earthly summer fades, but winter must and will give way to spring. The beginning is near. What peace to live in the hope of God's promise.

Lord, my mind and emotions sometimes fail. But my heart and spirit long for our face-to-face meeting. May the stars make me humble and the storms make me strong. —Buck Storm

Digging Deeper: John 16:33; James 1:12; 1 Peter 5:10

Thursday, December 31

The LORD . . . lifteth up. —1 Samuel 2:7 (KJV)

For some, New Year's Eve is about parties and all manner of celebration. In New York City the giant ball in Times Square drops at midnight and, with much revelry, ushers in a brand-new year.

Once the festivities seemed important, but now I'd rather be home with my family. There's sparkling grape juice for the kids and they're off to bed, allowing my wife, Corinne, and me a quiet time to count our blessings as the year draws to an end.

It's now, as every Southerner knows, that black-eyed peas, essential to luck and prosperity in the coming year, must be put in a big pan of water to soak for cooking on New Year's Day. Serve them with cooked greens and a big pan of crispy cornbread, and you are ready for a blessed New Year.

"Each pea that you eat brings more good luck, Brock," my grandfather used to say.

But then came the year when a trip with Corinne's family took us away from home and all our traditions. Not that I'm superstitious. Let's just say I was a little worried.

God, I know this is silly, but . . . the black-eyed peas . . .

I felt a bit sheepish even breathing the words.

Suddenly our trip was cut short, and late on New Year's Eve, we were home.

I was considering the peas, thinking how lucky my life had been so far, wondering if the grocery store was still open and if there was such a thing as canned black-eyed peas.

Passing the refrigerator, I swung the door open on a whim. It was all there. Peas, greens, cornbread. "Just in case," the note from Mom read.

God, sometimes I worry about something so trivial, and yet You are a step ahead. A new year is coming. Stay with me, God. Stay with me.
—Brock Kidd

Digging Deeper: Psalm 23:5; Proverbs 8:32

LIVING A NEW LIFE

1 _____

2 _____

3 _____

4 _____

5 _____

6 _____

7 _____

8 _____

9 _____

10 _____

11 _____

12 _____

13 _____

14 _____

15 _____

16 _____

17 _____

18 _____

19 _____

20 _____

21 _____

22 _____

23 _____

24 _____

25 _____

26 _____

27 _____

28 _____

29 _____

30 _____

31 _____

Marci Alborghetti and her husband, Charlie, have had a year of adjusting to the many changes in their lives, including a new address and continuing health challenges. "For someone who does not like change, it seems that I have much too much of it in my life these days!" Marci says. "But it does push me to understand how utterly dependent we are on God's grace, help, healing, and forgiveness. I can't say I've reached the point where I view everything with peace and equanimity—the way I should!—but I do feel the Lord drawing me closer to that."

Marci is also grateful for her and Charlie's church community and the prayer circle she participates in within that community. "Praying for others is a real comfort," she observes, "especially on days when I don't feel very productive in the ways of the world, I can feel productive in the way of prayer."

Evelyn Bence of Arlington, Virginia, writes: "In 8 years, a hydrangea in my yard has blossomed only once. But as I'm writing this in the spring, the buds portend a bush full of blossoms. I'm anticipating color, beauty, and new life. Even before I planted the hydrangea, a neighbor girl 'adopted' me as an extra grandmother. She's now a young woman, honing skills for a culinary career. I like to think her interest in food service started in my galley kitchen. It must say something about me that this year I gave up my 28-year-old sedan for a 4-year-old SUV. My friends and family applaud this upgrade, feeling I'm safer on the road. And I continue to benefit from the grace-filled fellowship of a small-church congregation, where 'everybody knows your name,' as the song goes."

 **Erika Bentsen** walks in the newness of life where every day is a treasured gift. "I wish everyone felt the joy that comes from Christ," she says. "He makes each day new." She continues to serve Him in the varied adventures that come her way as a first responder in a rural area. "I'm impressed with our ambulance crew," she says. "The professionalism is outstanding and the team is fun to work with." Some of the calls are crazier than the plot of a TV show, but she feels God beside her. "This is His work," she says. "I'm doing my best for Him."

Erika is illustrating her eighth children's book, a sequel to *The Not So Sleepy Sheepie*, a collaboration with her niece, Haley. "I'd love to illustrate one of my own stories, but it's tough to say no when there are so many delightful projects to do!"

BlueDog is still on guard no matter what Erika is doing. "He's all heart. Not bad for being 112 in dog years." Erika welcomes readers to check out her website at erikabentsen.com, although she admits she rarely has time to blog now that she has rebuilt her cow herd.

 **J. Brent Bill** is a photographer, retreat leader, and Quaker minister. He's also the author of numerous books, including *Holy Silence: The Gift of Quaker Spirituality* and *Amity: Stories from the Heartland*, a collection of short stories. He has been a local church pastor, a denominational executive, and a seminary faculty member. He lives on Ploughshares Farm, about 50 acres of former Indiana farmland being converted into tall-grass prairie and native hardwood forests.

 "The circle of the year passes almost unnoticed," says **Rhoda Blecker**, "but every day is so full that sometimes I think busy, busy, busy. There are morning chores—sometimes enough of them that I don't get around to eating breakfast until afternoon. But I never miss my morning coffee.

When we moved up to the Pacific Northwest almost 20 years ago, I didn't even know what a latte was. My husband was the coffee drinker, not me, and sometimes other denizens of the area asked why I moved up here in the first place if I didn't drink coffee. So, eventually, I started, and now the jolt of caffeine gets me through mornings when eating doesn't make it onto the to-do list. Chocolate used to be my muse, but now it seems that coffee is fighting it for pride of place, and I am happy to go along with whichever wins."

 **Sabra Ciancanelli** of Tivoli, New York, writes, "This year, my youngest graduates from high school, and my oldest graduates college. Navigating these two milestones has filled my plate with college applications, planning celebrations, and everything else under the sun. In the midst of the shuffle, I am preparing my heart for the days ahead and the bittersweet challenge of letting go. When things get to be too much, I sit on my front porch and reflect on the many blessings that have led us to this momentous time. Something about the calm breeze helps me reframe my focus and embrace the days ahead with faith and anticipation of the future yet to unfold."

"I received an invitation to my upcoming high school reunion," says **Mark Collins**. "I don't remember much of those years, except a verse from the school hymn 'Eternal God, Whose Power Upholds': 'Dispel the gloom of error's night/of ignorance and fear/until true wisdom from above/shall make life's pathway clear.' I tend to dwell in the 'ignorance and fear' part, but life's pathway is anything but clear." Lighting the way for this Pittsburgh pilgrim is his wife, Sandee, and three grown daughters. "I am eternally grateful for whatever divine guidance led me to my present coordinates," muses Mark. "Had I followed my own faulty internal GPS unit, I would be orbiting Pluto by now, listening to an endless loop of *rerouting . . . rerouting . . . rerouting . . .*"

"This past year has been a time of fun and adventure," writes **Pablo Diaz**. "My wife, Elba, and I went on a 10-day cruise to the Eastern Mediterranean. It was amazing. We traveled to Croatia, Montenegro, Greece, and Italy. Experiencing the scenery, local culture, cuisine, and people was awesome. I can't believe we are now planning for our next cruise.

"Elba, who has never been into sports, is playing pickleball with friends. On my days off I go out and play with her. We enjoy playing together outdoors in the sunshine, competing—well, I do—and exercising, yet having a good time. It has added value to our wonderful relationship.

"I also had the opportunity to travel to the Dominican Republic for continuing education. I spent several days observing and learning from leaders in a nonprofit ministry impacting children and youth by providing the message of the gospel. I returned to my ministry with energy and a deeper appreciation for God's work abroad and home."

"Great times with family and friends, enjoyable trips, and opportunities to serve filled our year," writes **John Dilworth**. "One highlight was the fulfillment of a long-held dream, in a small way. Since my youth I have wanted to hike the Appalachian Trail—never enough to do it! Last fall my wife, Pat, and I drove the entire Skyline Drive and Blue Ridge Parkway from Front Royal, Virginia, to Cherokee, North Carolina. A very special moment was coming upon a large black bear that was just standing in the road. Before disappearing into the woods, the bear teased us with a brief performance.

To remember the experience, we selected a black bear for our annual Christmas tree ornament. Taking time along the way for short hikes to be a part of the grandeur and beauty of God's magnificent creation proved sufficient to satisfy my longing to hike the Appalachian Trail!"

"My focus in the last year has been making more room for joy," writes **Amy Eddings**, who rejoins the *Walking in Grace* family after a 5-year hiatus. "I'm learning the ukulele and guitar, and I have an introduction to improv class on my calendar." Amy divorced in 2021 after 20 years of marriage. "I'm discovering and sharing my vulner-abilities," she said, "and making regular trips to the Southwest desert landscapes I love." She also swims across the Hudson River at an annual swim with friends she knows from her 28 years in New York City. Amy continues to work as a public radio broad-cast journalist and anchor of NPR's "Morning Edition" on WKSU in Cleveland, Ohio.

"The past year was one of change," says **Logan Eliasen** of Des Moines, Iowa. "I purchased my first home, which brought with it many new responsibilities. One concept the

Lord taught me through that process, and throughout the year, was balance. I often feel pulled in many different directions by my obligations. But I'm learning to identify the proper balance points in areas of my life. Balance between working and resting. Between lawyering and writing. Between remembering what is gone and embracing what is to come. And I am truly grateful that I follow a Carpenter-King who demonstrated perfect balance for us."

"I wasn't surprised to learn that the theme for *Walking in Grace* 2026 is new life in Christ," says **Shawnelle Eliasen**. "The Lord is intimate and knowing." Shawnelle and her husband, Lonny, live near the banks of the Mississippi River in LeClaire, Iowa. They have five sons, four of them now in college or beyond. "I've gone through many changes. There has been so much letting go, from home teaching to raising boys and releasing them to live independently. But there is peace and contentment in this new life. Of course, most important is our salvation and the new life Jesus gave when He released us from our sin sentence. But how kind of the Lord to make this earthly life full of fresh joy too."

"Over the last year, I have been learning about the things that I love doing and about the positive things that make me who I am," says **Nicole Garcia**. "There's been a lot of self-reflection, counseling, hard days, and painful healing. But it's all coming together for His purpose and will.

"I recently moved into a new townhome with my two boys. We love it there. My son with autism loves stairs, and it's two floors. I have also spent a lot of time making new memories and staying active on the weekends with amusement parks and trips to the beach. I have taken up new hobbies, such as gardening and birding. I have continued old habits like traveling. I also started going to a new church that I love and am blessed by. I assist in the special-needs and children's ministries there. I am grateful to have found a new home church, as I have been looking since the divorce."

"Forty years ago, on a warm fall day, I walked into the *Guideposts* offices at 747 Third Avenue in midtown Manhattan," recalls **Edward Grinnan**. "I had never heard of *Guideposts* magazine—and *Guideposts* had certainly never heard of me. But I really needed a job and I'd gotten a call from a recruiter. I imagined *Guideposts* might be a travel magazine. Substitute *journey* for *travel*, and it wouldn't be so far off. I was only prepared to commit to 1 year while I worked on my résumé and rebuilt the sobriety I'd lost—along with my previous job—in a disastrous relapse after several years in a twelve-step program. Frankly, *I* wouldn't have hired me. Yet coming to *Guideposts* proved the greatest of God's unexpected blessings. These last few years I have reduced my role as editor-in-chief in anticipation of retirement, though I hope to remain part of this inspiring family of writers and help on other projects. By the way, I never found out how an employment agency I'd never heard of got hold of my résumé and connected me with the interview that day, and I never heard from them again."

Rick Hamlin is a busy writer, singer, husband, and father, but if you asked him what role he's proudest of, it's the most recent one: he's Gramps. He and his wife, Carol, are thrilled to be the grandparents of four precious grandkids—and by the time this appears in print, there might be another one on the way. Their older son, Will, and his wife, Karen, live in San Francisco and have two kids, including little Ricky (where did they get that name?). Their younger son, Tim, and his wife, Henley, live in Connecticut with their two kids. "We've got family from coast to coast." They're always in church on Sundays, but most often at Christ Church in Greenwich, where Tim—aka Rev. Tim—is an Episcopal priest. "We're needed to help look after the children." He and Carol were thrilled to write a history of that church as it recently celebrated its 275th anniversary.

Lynne Hartke explores desert trails with her husband, Kevin, in Chandler, Arizona, where they are on staff at a church and where Kevin is also the mayor. After purchasing a canoe, she anticipates additional adventures on the lakes near their cabin in northern Arizona. A breast cancer survivor, Lynne was named a Voice of Hope with the American Cancer Society in 2018. Lynne is a speaker and author of *Under a Desert Sky: Redefining Hope, Beauty, and Faith in the Hardest Places*. The couple has four grown children and four grandchildren. Connect with her at lynnehartkeauthor.com.

"Every year I contribute to *Walking in Grace*, I'm amazed at how quickly time is flying by," says writer and child advocate **Carla Hendricks**. "Life continues to evolve, and as I age, so do my children and extended family members. I lost two dear cousins this year—an older cousin in his eighties who was a beloved mentor; the other cousin, a bestie since birth, was a mere 45 years old. And yet life goes on. . . . At this moment, I am waiting for my baby girl to return my car so I can run some errands. I marvel that she is a sophomore in high school and driving, while my oldest son is 27 years old, on his own, and enjoying his career teaching and mentoring teens in an inner-city Nashville school. My youngest son is working in downtown Nashville (with his own health insurance plan!), and my oldest daughter is working and attending community college. My husband, Anthony, and I just attended our nephew's college graduation. And now that my oldest niece is a mom, I have taken on the title of 'G-Auntie,' since 'great-aunt' makes me feel ancient!"

"I feel time passing at lightning speed, and I treasure every precious moment," says **Kim Taylor Henry**. "My husband, David, and I have resumed our travels, including Greenland, Iceland, Greece, and twelve other countries in Europe. We have been blessed with many great adventures and much breathtaking beauty. Yet my favorite thing remains our time with our family. I thank God we have all been gifted with great health. With God, health, and family, we have everything. I'd love it if you would visit me at my website, kimtaylorhenry. com and/or email me at kim@kimtaylorhenry.com. Also, please check out my books on Amazon—*Making God Smile, Living the Fruit of the Spirit One Day at a Time,* and *Do I Still Matter? The Secrets of Aging with Faith and Purpose.*"

 **Leanne Jackson** is thankful that her grown children live within easy driving distance. To visit their two daughters and son-in-law between holidays, she and her husband, Dave, drive 2 hours to meet them halfway for the day. "No one has to pack, cook, or clean; we just visit! And did I mention there's a bookstore?"

Leanne says, "Readers often tell me, 'My grandmother introduced me to *Guideposts* magazine.' I grew up reading my parents' *Guideposts,* then started my own subscription in college. I return the blessings by sharing my *Walking in Grace* devotions with you!" Leanne invites you to visit her at leannejacksonwrites.com.

 **Erin Janoso**'s mom received some difficult health news in November. Quickly, plans and priorities became reordered, and things that had seemed big-picture before gained a

different perspective. Happily, though, a stable status quo seems to have been found for her for the moment—something she and her family are thanking God for every day.

In the meantime, regular life has continued to roll forward in her home of Fairbanks, Alaska. Her daughter, Aurora, is 11 and in the fifth grade. Aurora plays the oboe in her school's band and has spent the past year getting quite tall. Her husband, Jim, reports that his microscopy business is doing well, taking him to various places within Alaska, as well as McMurdo and Palmer Stations down in Antarctica.

Erin still loves playing her trumpet, and has recently picked the violin up again as well. Her writing, substitute teaching, and volunteering on behalf of Fairbanks schools and music education remain important to her. Most of all, she is incredibly grateful for the time she gets to spend with the people she loves, doing things that bring her joy.

 **Ashley Kappel** lives in Alabama with her husband and three children. This year, Ashley was diagnosed with breast cancer, so the theme "Living a New Life" has hit close to home as so much of her life is now new—treatments, routines, and hopes. She has learned that "new" doesn't have to mean "bad," and that this "new" life she gets to

live is pretty great too. She would appreciate prayers for ongoing health and the hearts of her family. Ashley continues to work as an editor and unpaid laundress for her family of five and moonlights as the biggest fan of her children's activities and her husband's passions, as well as her own. Her goal for the next year is to laugh more than ever before.

Jenny Lynn Keller is an award-winning author who transforms her family's rowdy adventures into stories filled with hope, humor, and plenty of Southern charm. Follow their fun on her blog at jennylynnkeller.com and facebook.com/jennylynnkeller. Her beloved true animal stories appear in Callie Smith Grant's compilations *The Horse of My Dreams*, *The Dog Who Came to Christmas*, *The Cat in the Christmas Tree*, and *Second-Chance Horses*.

For **Brock Kidd**, this past year was a constant reminder of Ecclesiastes 3:1 (NLT), "for everything there is a season . . ." The Kidd family season could be summed up in one word: busy. "Life for us is good, but hectic," he says. "At work, I am fortunate to have built a great team over the years to serve our clients well. At home, I have a great wife in Corinne, who is involved in lots of good works, three kids still at home, and one out on his own. There are lots of ball games, plays, and even horse shows. On a recent walk with our dogs and youngest daughter, I was walking ahead of her, rushing through the walk so I could get to the next thing. 'Slow down, Dad!' It hit me like words from heaven. Sometimes we should all be reminded to slow down and enjoy all that God has for us."

"Ah! Living a new life! Could there be a better thought than this?" wonders **Pam Kidd**. "How well I remember our son, Brock, as a young boy, always— as I see it now and to borrow a phrase from the great John Lewis—in 'good trouble.' Every night as we tucked him in, there was the reminder: 'Today's blackboard is wiped clean . . . we all start fresh tomorrow!'

"The years roll by. We all slip up at times. Disappointments happen. But our lives are measured in moments. We see Brock loving his work, his family. We see Keri, our daughter, the best of mothers, who can't let any opportunity to do good slip by. I see my husband, David, head of our family, inquisitive, intelligent, supportive, and always leading us toward renewal. How can I not wake up each morning to new life!"

 **Patty Kirk** heartily resists "retirement"—tire herself again?!—but has found her first year of not teaching creatively productive, spiritually enlightening, and a thousand times less stressful. She has resumed working on writing projects she had to sideline while teaching and now works part-time for her husband's CPA firm.

Her daughter Lulu completed her PhD in comparative literature. Lulu also graduated from hunting with a crossbow to a gun, and immediately upon arriving home over Thanksgiving, shot a ginormous doe. After many YouTube videos, Patty single-handedly field-dressed it, hung it from their old swing set, skinned it, and butchered it.

Patty's other daughter, Charlotte, is happily homeowning in Seattle. She and her husband, Reuben, now throw Christmas parties and trade dog-sitting favors with friends. The indoor soccer league Reuben organized won its first game this past year. For Christmas, Patty got grow lights and soil-blocking equipment and fulfilled a dream of growing her own garden plants. Almost every seed from her ever-growing collection—some as old as 1998—unexpectedly germinated, producing hundreds more seedlings than she has room for in her garden.

Carol Knapp and husband Terry are celebrating new freedom with the success of Terry's fourth spine surgery. They took a 1,200-mile road trip—much of it through their home state on scenic Highway 93—and the back made it. Other travels carried them to their first Florida visit for a grandson's autumn wedding beneath a magnificent live oak in an elegant outdoor setting. Then another first—Thanksgiving with Carol's brother in the Nashville area. Before leaving, visiting family gathered for deeply meaningful prayer— thankful for new closeness. It was a tough winter. Within 3 months from idea to gone, Carol and Terry's nearby daughter and family moved to Kentucky for his employment at The Ark Encounter. While clearly the right decision, she struggled with accepting the change—and felt new comfort from God. On the horizon is Carol's first children's book, which will be released in February 2025. *Capi's Sensational Hair* tells the surprising story of a weeping willow in a city park. A second book, *Coldilocks and the Three Polar*

Bears, draws on Carol's Alaska connection. Living new life daily with Jesus is Carol's greatest peace and hope.

 "It's been a wild and wonderful year for me, as I've traveled from the tropical climes of Hawaii to the frigid shores of Antarctica," says **Vicki Kuyper**. "Although my love of adventure, photography, and writing about God's astonishing world is a core part of who God created me to be, spending time with those I love (and those God wants me to love!) is always paramount. As my grandchildren get older, and so do I, I'm spending less time babysitting and more time just hanging out with my five grandchildren and their parents. What a joy! My entire family is a blessing I never take for granted. Without my sweet sister Cindy, who's a professional wildlife and travel photographer, I'd never have traveled to the amazing places I've explored—and the ones on the calendar for the coming year, which include Zambia, Rwanda, and remote Tlingit communities of Alaska. With so much of life to live and love, writing may take a bit of a back seat in the season ahead. But I have an inkling God will continue opening doors for my words, at the right time and the right place, for as long as He gives me breath."

Lisa Livezey is a freelance writer and spiritual blogger with a journalism degree who seeks to encourage those laboring in life's daily trenches. She serves on staff at Heart of the Father Ministries—home of the book *Unbound*. Lisa lives in the Philly suburbs with her husband, David, whom she credits with giving her name alliteration. Together they are blessed with five children and six grandchildren. They can sometimes be spotted sailing the Chesapeake Bay on summer weekends. You can find more of Lisa's reflections in Guideposts' *Strength & Grace* magazine and on her website, lisalivezey.com. She publishes a weekly 1-minute photo devotion at lisalivezey.com/olivetree and enjoys hearing from her readers.

"Recovering from the death of my youngest son Andrew—who died February 20, 2024—has been the most difficult thing I have ever done in my life," writes **Patricia Lorenz**. "During the months after he died, I organized all the letters he ever wrote to me into a 2-inch-thick notebook that I kept on my dining room table so I could stop and read his words frequently. I kept ordering more reprints of photos of Andrew, mailing them out to relatives and friends all over the country. I put framed photos of my son in every room in my home. I finally figured out that I will never recover from his death. The pain is only known and felt by other parents who have lost a child. But time has also taught me that life is here. I have three other children, nine grandchildren, one great-grandson, numerous other relatives, and many friends who also need my love, energy, and time. Now I find purpose in writing, painting, working out in the pool, and swimming at least 2 hours a day, playing cards with friends, meeting new friends, volunteering at the airport, exploring parks, and traveling around the country and the world. It's what I do. I live. Gratefully."

Debbie Macomber is a #1 *New York Times* best-selling author and one of today's most popular writers, with more than two hundred million copies of her books in print worldwide. In addition to fiction, Debbie has also published three best-selling cookbooks, an adult coloring book, numerous inspirational and nonfiction works, and two acclaimed children's books. Celebrated as "the official storyteller of Christmas," Debbie's annual Christmas books are beloved, and five have been crafted into original Hallmark Channel movies. She serves on the Guideposts

National Advisory Cabinet, is a YFC National Ambassador, and is World Vision's international spokesperson for their Knit for Kids charity initiative. A devoted grandmother, Debbie and her husband, Wayne, live in Port Orchard, Washington, the town that inspired the Cedar Cove series.

"I've started making expressions and acts of gratitude a regular practice in my life," says **Tia McCollors**. "Maybe it's just me, but I look at the world a tad bit differently since I turned 50 years old. For one thing, time has moved a lot faster than I ever expected, and aging isn't as bad as it seemed at 13, when I thought everyone in this midlife age was archaic. Quite the contrary. I'm happier, freer, and clearer about my journey in life. I'm thankful for the way the tapestry of my life has been woven by God's hands. Acknowledging those things and journaling about them gives me peace."

Tia expresses her creative side through writing, speaking, and trying new recipes and DIY projects that she finds on Pinterest. You can connect with her online at TiaMcCollors.com, through her "Fans of Tia" Facebook page, or follow her on Instagram @TMcCollors.

Roberta Messner writes from her 124-year-old log cabin, at the table where Alex Haley once wrote *Roots*. It's a place saturated by the memory of her own roots in the form of vintage and antique motto samplers. Stitched by unknown—yet precious to her—artists, one sampler even hails from Pawling, New York, the birthplace of positive thinking and home of *Guideposts'* founders, Dr. Norman Vincent Peale and Ruth Stafford Peale. In her series in this year's *Walking in Grace*, "Sacred Threads," you'll learn how samplers celebrate Roberta's faith as well. "It's a faith that never grows old, yet is new every morning," Roberta says. This year found her recovering from fractures from a traumatic fall, an experience she calls the best-worst year of her life. "The challenges were endless, but I found that no matter what life throws at us, the difficult and the beautiful can live in the very same moment."

Gabrielle Meyer grew up above a carriage house on a historic estate near the banks of the Mississippi River, fueling her passion for the past. As a teenager, she discovered her interest in genealogy and traced her ancestors back to the original settlers in Jamestown, Virginia, in 1607. As a young woman, she went on to work for the Minnesota Historical Society, where she fell in love with the rich history of her state and was inspired to write fiction and nonfiction inspired by real people, places, and events.

She currently resides in central Minnesota, on the banks of the upper Mississippi River, not far from where she grew up, with her husband and four teenage children. By day, she's a busy homeschool mom and small business owner, and by night she pens fiction and nonfiction filled with hope. Her work currently includes historical and contemporary romances, cozy mysteries, and home and family articles. You can learn more about Gabrielle and her writing by visiting gabriellemeyer.com.

 "With biocellular regenerative medicine, I'm getting a new lease on life," says **Rebecca Ondov** of Hamilton, Montana. "I'm amazed at the progress scientists and doctors have made after discovering that they can use the person's own stem cells and platelets to heal." With the treatments she's received, it's the first time since she got hit by a drunk driver decades ago that she is on her way to living pain-free. "For me, to have no back pain is a miracle from God. He is my greatest healer."

The hardest part of recovery was asking friends to help with so many chores. It has truly made her appreciate the gift of friendship. The second-hardest part was slowing down her lifestyle so she could heal. She says, "It was like looking at the world through a magnifying glass. I marveled at the beauty that surrounded me, from watching the neighbor's honeybees pollinate my flowers to sitting on the porch facing the Rocky Mountains and pondering God's love. But now I'm ready to get back into the swing of things."

Rebecca loves to connect with her readers on social media. To find out how, go to her website: RebeccaOndov.com.

Shirley Raye Redmond has sold hundreds of articles to such publications as *Focus on the Family Magazine*, *Home Life*, *The Christian Standard*, *Woman's Day*, and *Chicken Soup for the Soul*. Her writing has appeared in multiple Guideposts devotionals as well as three Guideposts fiction mystery series. Her children's book *Courageous World Changers: 50 True Stories of Daring Women of God* (Harvest House) won the 2021 Christianity Today Book Award in its category. She has been married for 50 years to her college sweetheart, Bill. They are blessed with two children and five precious grandchildren. Shirley Raye lives in northern New Mexico where she enjoys green chiles in nearly everything—even brownies! She enjoys birdwatching for fun and recently added a Lewis woodpecker and a Clark's nutcracker to her life list. Shirley Raye loves hearing from readers through her Facebook page or via her website at shirleyrayeredmond.com.

Ginger Rue has been enjoying traveling with her husband, Dwight. A recent trip was to Purgatory Ski Resort in Colorado with Dwight's brother and sister and their families. "I'm the only one of us twelve who fell on the ski trip," Ginger says. "But what makes that hilarious is that I wasn't even skiing at the time. There they were, going down double black diamonds without a scratch, and I slipped on ice taking out the garbage! Probably for the best that I stay off the mountains." The trip got even more interesting when a blizzard nearly snowed them in. "It was pretty scary driving to the airport on all that ice, unable to see the road at all, especially for a bunch of Southerners," Ginger says. "But now we all joke that we 'barely made it out of Purgatory!'"

Adam Ruiz believes that the human history is a hope-filled story. In his life journey, there may have been many people and encounters that have helped to strengthen his own sense of hope. One of those blessings came early in life when copies of *Guideposts* magazine would regularly arrive at his family's home. Inspired by the stories he read as a child, Adam now uses copies of *Guideposts* to help the patients he visits as a hospital chaplain for Norton's Women's & Children's Hospital in Louisville, Kentucky.

A native Texan, Adam now calls the Bluegrass State home where he lives with his wife, Denise, and their two fur babies, Buddy and Molly. A Roman Catholic and graduate of both Oblate School of Theology and Louisville Presbyterian Seminary, Adam believes his cultural and educational diversity has helped broaden his sense of people and the world. When not working or writing, Adam loves to read books, play chess, and hang out with his family.

"Now in our eleventh year in the Hudson Highlands of New York State, some 50 miles north of New York City, my wife, Kate, and I continue to enjoy the stability of being in one home and location for an extended period," says **Ken Sampson**. "We're grateful for the perspective, balance, friendship, and enriching grace offered by our children and friends made over the years.

"This past summer, Kate remarked, 'Lean and mean, what can I say?' in response to my change of eating habits and loss of a significant amount of weight. This all came about due to a variety of heart-related tests at our local Veterans Affairs Healthcare. I still relish food—it's just that now it's different types.

"Also, I've returned to enjoying the wonders of being in the field with soldiers. I hiked a 9-mile section of the Appalachian Trail with my old Army buddy, Perry. The next weekend, I traveled to Great Sacandaga Lake for a less strenuous but equally delightful camping experience with my daughter Jenn. We've just returned from a New York City trip to meet our son Michael, son-in-law Steven, and granddaughter Chanel for her first opera, *The Magic Flute*. We remain blessed."

 A new arrival stirred up the peaceful lives of **Daniel Schantz** and his wife, Sharon, of Moberly, Missouri, this past year. A baby girl named Eve Riviere was born to their granddaughter Hannah in 2023. This is Dan and Sharon's third great-grandchild.

Dan and Sharon are adjusting to the losses of aging. Sharon's quilting has slowed down, due to seemingly intractable dermatitis on her fingers, and she walks a lot slower these days. More and more the two of them are kept busy just taking care of each other, and some days it's "the blind leading the blind."

For their anniversary, Dan bought Sharon a small piano and a large-print hymnbook. Although Sharon has not played the piano for more than 30 years, she picked it up again in a few days. Now Dan is comforted by the sounds of "Showers of Blessing" and "Heavenly Sunlight" drifting into his study from the living room.

Gail Thorell Schilling of Concord, New Hampshire, never thought she would start snorkeling in her seventies, but a cruise to the Caribbean with a dear friend provided the opportunity. Gail savors each God-given day as a gift—or surprise! She reveled in having three of her four children and their families in New Hampshire for Christmas, then visited her other grandchildren in California en route to Singapore. There she provided childcare for her grandson during a school break and celebrated familiar Holy Week traditions in a new city with new friends. "What a joy to find beloved community wherever I go!"

"I still live on the farm several miles from town," writes **Penney Schwab** of Copeland, Kansas. "I'm delighted to have three great-grandchildren, Talyn, Andrea, and Nolan. A somewhat reluctant traveler, I enjoyed several trips during the year. The first was to South Dakota with my sister and brother-in-law; later we attended the Chickasaw Elders Conference in Oklahoma. Son Patrick and family took me to Maine, where I did the 3½-mile Jordan Pond hike—thanks to help on the big rocks from grandson David. Thanksgiving was spent with son Michael and family in Ft. Collins. Although I gave up trying to maintain the flowerbeds my late husband, Don, planted and hired professional help, I still mow and water. My dog, Pepper, jumps on people and barks at coyotes, but she's a joyful walking companion. There are some difficult times, but I find comfort in Psalm 46:1, 'God is our refuge and strength, an ever-present help in trouble' (NIV). Blessings abound! Thanks be to God!"

Norm Stolpe retired from his pastoral ministry when his wife, Candy, was diagnosed with Alzheimer's in 2016. He cared for her as his life and calling until she passed from this life into the inheritance of the saints in light in 2024. He drew on their experiences as he wrote devotions for Guideposts' magazine *Strength and Grace*. He still reads *Strength and Grace* for daily encouragement on this next leg of his life journey. As he continues to discern God's call on this unfamiliar path, he is recognizing opportunities for mutual conversations, some planned but most serendipitous. Some folks just need an empathetic listener and some are looking for his perspective, but most of all Norm is enriched by chatting with people at a personal level without being identified as a pastor. He is learning how to listen in new ways.

Norm shares a duplex with his son and daughter-in-law, David and Rachel, and their grown children, Sam, Elizabeth, and Erik. He delights in their involvement and care as he embarks on what he's thinking of as his homestretch. He finds stability in Psalm 31:14–15 (NIV): "I trust in you, LORD . . . My times are in your hands."

Buck Storm didn't exactly tell the truth on the Los Angeles apartment application when he and his wife married in 1989. He listed his profession as "writer." He figured it wasn't much of a stretch—after all, he wrote songs and would get to books eventually. But life has a way of sidetracking.

Those songs would up taking him around the globe. It took 25 years and a lot of miles for Buck to become a novelist, but several books in now, he's made good on that application. Buck spends his days writing and spending time with his wife, Michelle, his grown children, and three granddaughters. His nights are often spent out playing music with the popular Northwest band The Buckley Storms, a songwriting collaboration project with his son, Ransom. God's mercies are new every morning and Buck is blessed beyond words. "Thank You, Jesus. I feel Your arm around my shoulder. You are *good*. And the best part is knowing the journey will never end!"

 **Jolynda Strandberg** has served for 27 years as a civilian working for the military, currently as a director of religious education. She and her family reside in Clarksville, Tennessee. This year she and her family welcomed Ellie, a cute little quarter horse who has stolen her family's hearts.

 **Jon M. Sweeney** is an award-winning author who has been interviewed by the *Dallas Morning News* and *The Irish Catholic*, on radio with NPR and the BBC, and on

television at *CBS Saturday Morning*. He's a rare author found in scholarly journals as well as Romper.com and *Catster Magazine*. Jon's books on Franciscan spirituality have sold about a quarter of a million copies. He is also the author of thirty other books on spirituality, biography, and memoir, including *Thomas Merton: An Introduction to His Life and Practices* and *Sit in the Sun: And Other Lessons in the Wisdom of Cats*. Jon is religion editor at Monkfish Publishing, and editor of *Living City* magazine. He speaks at literary and religious conferences, in churches and independent bookstores. He is a Catholic married to a rabbi, and their interfaith marriage has been profiled in national media. He lives on Milwaukee's East Side, and his youngest child is now very much a teenager.

 "I work as the manager of a university help desk, which is pretty much exactly what I wanted to do post-graduation!" says **Rachel Thompson**. "At work I enjoy getting to troubleshoot and problem solve while helping students, faculty, and staff with various technical issues. When I'm not at work, some of my favorite pastimes are reading, writing,

walking, playing games, and spending time with my family."

This year's *Walking in Grace* 2026 theme, "Living a New Life," is close to **Stephanie Thompson**'s heart. As empty nesters, she and her husband are focusing on their marriage more than ever before. "Michael and I had only been married 6 weeks when I found out I was pregnant," said Stephanie. That joy was shattered when her father was murdered 2 months later. "We hit the ground running in 2002 and are just now at a point where we can breathe and pour into our relationship."

One of the ways they have enriched their marriage is through travel—a vacation to a couples' resort on the Mexican Riviera and a pilgrimage to the Holy Land. "Sharing the beauty and wonder of sights around the world has brought us closer to each other and to God," she said.

While their daughter, Micah, lives away at college, the couple shares their home in an Oklahoma City suburb with Michael's 96-year-old grandmother, Linda; their 13-year-old schweenie (shih tzu/dachshund mix) named Missy; and Mr. Whiskers, a congenial tuxedo cat that appeared on the driveway one cold December day in 2013.

"I'm so thankful God made it possible for my World War II novel, *The Escape Game*, to be published," says **Marilyn Turk**. "I had planned to write this book for several years using some amazing information my husband, Chuck, stumbled across. After the book released, I intentionally took on fewer writing assignments to enjoy stress-free time with Chuck to work on our bucket list. Taking a trip to Israel was one of the things we'd wanted to do, and we were blessed to have the opportunity to discover the Bible in person. We also enjoyed an island vacation to St. Marten—except for the exciting jet-ski ride in 4- to 5-foot waves where I prayed and sang praises over the noise of the engine in order to survive! Back home, we relaxed and got our exercise taking our dog, Dolly, for walks. We are blessed and thankful for our community, our church friends, and the close proximity of most of our children and grands. One of them, Logan, started high school this year! How did that happen so quickly?"

"I knew it was coming," says **Karen Valentin**. "This season of loss came in like a distant storm. I sat in the sun, trying to absorb the last bit of light, as the dark clouds moved forward. I sang with my oldest sister and made my father laugh until my sunshine disappeared. They left this world 3 months apart from each other, and as much as I braced myself, the storm ravaged my world more than I could imagine. It takes time to heal, well after the storm rolls past. I allow myself to mourn with tears, gratitude, laughter, and despair. I process emotions in many ways, but the most healing way for me is to write. Thank you, readers, for giving me the opportunity to heal, as I share my stories of love and loss with you."

Scott Walker of Macon, Georgia, is now 3 years post-retirement from Mercer University and reports that not much has changed: he and his wife, Beth, still try to visit with friends and family as much as possible, and he continues to work on writing projects while visiting campus as often as he can. "But perhaps what I'm most grateful for is my Guideposts family—the writers and readers of *Walking in Grace* who have provided so much spiritual nourishment over the years. I pray that God will be with you always."

Jacqueline F. Wheelock is convinced that one upside to having adult children who live far away in interesting cities is the built-in opportunity for a ready vacation spot. In Jacqueline's case, her two children—Stefan, the eldest, and Alexis, the youngest—live in historical, fascinating places in Virginia and Florida, respectively.

Last fall she went on an extended vacation to Virginia, where she thoroughly enjoyed a daily view of the surrounding mountains, as well as a beautiful Saturday visit to the top of Carter Mountain. There, she sat on a bench in the sun as her children pursued some serious apple picking, and she eventually did some equally serious overeating of apple doughnuts, conveniently for sale on the mountaintop.

Occasionally, Jacqueline dreams of having her children and grandchildren nearer, but trips to places like Carter Mountain continue to show her that there are always nuggets of joy to find and history to discover, if one is willing to escape her venue and put in the time.

 **Gayle T. Williams** has been a reporter, writer, and editor for magazines and newspapers for the past 30 years, and now leads a team of public relations writers for an academic medical institution. But it is the writing that she does for Guideposts that truly feeds her soul and spirit. A native of the Bronx, New York, she grew up as a member of Harlem's historic Abyssinian Baptist

Church. These days she is a member of New York Covenant Church in New Rochelle, New York, where she is fed by a fantastic group of believers who truly feel like family. Her hobbies include word puzzles (*The New York Times'* Spelling Bee is her favorite!), listening to music—ranging from classical to classic rap—and taking long walks with her husband of 37 years, Terry. Gayle also loves baking and surprising her two adult sons, friends, and family with their favorite cakes.

SCRIPTURE REFERENCE INDEX

ACTS
1:8, 417
8:36–38, 356
13:9, 416
17:11, 392
17:27, 155

CHRONICLES 1
16:34, 286–287
22:8, 184
22:12, 82
28:20, 370
29:13, 213

CHRONICLES 2
7:14, 319
16:9, 114

COLOSSIANS
1:16, 302
3:9–10, 1, 246
3:12, 325
3:13, 169
3:23–24, 477
4:2, 148, 373
4:12, 373

CORINTHIANS 1
1:7, 285
6:12, 91
6:19, 62
8:1, 28

9:24, 209
12:12, 394
13:12, 104
14:40, 277
15:57, 259
16:14, 418

CORINTHIANS 2
1:3–4, 15
4:16, 125, 144
5:1, 58
5:2, 526
5:17, 316, 497
6:2, 69
9:11, 21
9:15, 512
13:11, 205

DEUTERONOMY
4:9, 112
7:6, 20
8:2, 151
28:5, 81
31:6, 440
32:7, 26
33:27, 109
34:7, 428

ECCLESIASTES
1:10, 537

3:1, 202, 369, 557
3:11, 54, 312, 413
4:10, 401
7:13, 159
9:8–9, 348

EPHESIANS
1:3, 531
2:8–9, 225
4:15, 273
4:16, 63
4:32, 474
5:1–2, 203
5:15, 101
5:15–16, 276
6:10–11, 221
6:15, 381

EXODUS
12:4, 521
15:13, 227
15:20, 51
17:12, 437
20:8, 364
25:2, 65

EZEKIEL
11:19, 410

EZRA
1:6, 166

GALATIANS
2:21, 77
3:27, 245
6:2, 228
6:9, 251
6:10, 37, 353,
   509
GENESIS
1:3, 2
1:20, 505
1:31, 468
12:1, 303
15:5, 173
17:5, 416
17:15, 416
22:14, 32
32:10, 352
32:28, 416

HABAKKUK
2:3, 98
HEBREWS
10:23, 109
10:24, 57
10:24–25, 199
10:35, 131
10:36, 471,
   478
11:1, 385
11:6, 496
12:1, 93–94

12:1–2, 529
13:5, 498, 502
13:8, 94, 330
13:9, 525
HOSEA
2:3, 300

ISAIAH
1:18, 18
7:4, 89
30:15, 333–334
40:31, 499
41:10, 115
43:1, 452, 480
43:18–19, 379,
   519
43:19, 270, 296
50:4, 10, 301
51:11, 283
58:11, 323
62:2, 415

JAMES
1:2–3, 397
1:17, 297
1:19, 41–42,
   382
1:19–20, 456
5:8, 374
5:16, 181
5:17, 373

JEREMIAH
17:8, 206
29:11, 292, 489
31:3, 109, 278
33:3, 279
JOB
19:2, 197
29:13, 244
36:2, 482
37:6, 484
JOEL
2:25, 517
JOHN
1:2, 6
1:5, 6
1:12, 6, 12, 33
1:48, 212
3:16, 20, 141
3:30, 289
4:13–14, 29,
   311
4:17, 121
8:12, 491
10:3, 378
10:27–28, 118
13:14, 47
14:27, 232,
   298, 375,
   426
15:5, 458
15:12, 293

15:16, 20, 195
16:20, 143
19:39–40, 140
21:6, 212
21:17, 464

JOHN 1
1:7, 451
3:18, 265–266
4:1, 391
4:10, 127
5:14, 361

JONAH
2:8, 76

JOSHUA
1:9, 117
24:15, 467

KINGS 1
1:1, 60
17:2–4, 242
17:6, 242

LEVITICUS
19:18, 246

LUKE
1:7, 319
2:19, 504
2:37, 373
5:16, 162
6:31, 261
6:32, 461

6:38, 367
8:17, 472
9:58, 294
10:33, 190
11:9, 22
11:9–10, 460
12:2, 446
12:15, 100
12:27, 165
17:13–14, 30
21:15, 298
22:19, 137

MALACHI
3:6, 108

MARK
2:17, 329
9:36–37, 524
10:45, 534
10:51, 442
11:2–3, 128
12:30–31, 21
13:7, 21
14:7, 21
15:33–34, 139

MATTHEW
1:1, 432
2:2, 8
2:12, 525
5:4, 326
5:7, 387

5:39, 295
5:44, 282
6:1, 252–253
6:21, 386
6:33, 425
6:34, 345, 431
10:8, 226
13:11, 196
13:23, 241
14:29, 34
16:18, 416
17:7, 287
18:7, 400
18:19, 335
18:20, 199
18:21–22, 189
23:5, 230
25:13, 180
25:23, 237
25:36, 78
25:40, 442
28:20, 307,
436, 518

MICAH
6:8, 21

NEHEMIAH
1:6, 320

NUMBERS
6:24–26, 371
11:4–34, 100

PETER 1
1:3, 135
1:6, 238
1:8, 44
2:16, 275
2:17, 68
2:21, 4
4:8, 55
4:10, 532
4:11, 334
5:7, 443
5:10, 72, 216

PHILIPPIANS
1:3, 249
1:6, 109,
3:1, 266
3:20–21, 398
4:6, 146
4:6–7, 90
4:8, 48, 186,
  470
4:11, 421
4:12–13, 11
4:19, 395,
  445

PROVERBS
3:5, 411
3:6, 3
5:18, 355
6:9, 384
7:3, 6

12:25, 362
12:26, 122
13:12, 339
13:20, 152
14:26, 171
15:1, 431
15:4, 439
16:3, 188
16:9, 384
16:18, 217
17:6, 220
17:22, 40, 342
18:15, 522
18:24, 200, 310
19:8, 377
19:22, 255
20:5, 419
21:23, 272
22:6, 130, 219
23:18, 290
24:10, 167
25:11, 383
27:9, 121
27:17, 366
31:27, 424

PSALMS
3:5–6, 414
3:8, 429
4:8, 235
5:3, 308
8:1, 161

8:3–4, 207,
  535
8:4–5, 103
9:10, 317
16:11, 231
18:30, 299
18:31, 390
19:1, 184
20:4, 107
20:7, 304
23:1, 184,
  280
23:1–2, 154
23:5, 239
24:1, 182
27:14, 111
29:11, 465
30:5, 193
30:12, 248
31:14–15, 337,
  573
31:15, 321
31:19, 346
32:8, 327
33:15, 214
34:8, 492
34:15, 435
34:18, 447,
  453
37:23, 407
46:1, 572

46:2, 23
46:10, 152
51:10, 351
55:22, 344
56:3, 433
56:8, 341
61:5, 25
62:1, 515
65:11, 406
68:5, 254
71:9, 271
75:1, 136
77:11, 83
78:4, 17
100:5, 170
101:6, 120
101:8, 120
102:12, 109
103:2, 174
103:11–12, 70
116:7, 176
117:2, 506
118:5, 475
118:24, 21
118:25, 501
119:11, 122
119:15, 105
119:83, 454
119:105, 318, 349
119:148, 257

122:1, 389
127:3–5, 36
131:2, 331
138:3, 158
139:7, 19
139:14, 508
139:16, 97, 406
139:17–18, 20
144:12, 147
145:9, 49
145:18, 157
147:1, 305

REVELATION
3:2, 96
3:20, 264
21:4, 52
ROMANS
4:18, 14
5:3–5, 73
6:4, III
6:5, 142
6:8, 141
8:1, 318
8:16, 422
8:18, 234
8:26, 457
8:28, 122
8:38–39, 486
10:13, 511

10:17, 185, 405
12:2, 7–8, 61, 88, 485
12:4, 163
12:5, 259
12:5–6, 338
12:12, 43
12:15, 21
14:13–14, 322–323

SAMUEL 1
2:7, 539
16:3, 358
SONG OF SOLOMON
8:7, 75

THESSALO-NIANS 1
2:7, 363
5:11, 124, 150, 192, 488, 528
5:17, 373
5:18, 179
5:21, 409
THESSALO-NIANS 2
2:15, 514
3:5, 38

TIMOTHY 1
1:12, 258
1:17, 79
2:1, 393
6:6, 538

6:17, 481
TIMOTHY 2
1:7, 46
4:7, 462
4:18, 66

TITUS
2:7, 210
ZECHARIAH
4:10, 64,
   262

AUTHORS, TITLES, AND SUBJECTS INDEX

9/11 attacks, 95, 376

Advent, 491, 504, 514–515, 524

Alborghetti, Marci, 22–23, 147–148, 282–283, 329–330, 387–388, 461–462, 543

"Angel Whispers" series, 3–4, 114–115, 196–197, 226–227, 295–296, 362–363

Apostles (Disciples), 85, 92, 129, 140, 212, 222, 294, 308, 390, 456–457; Andrew, 294; John, 289, 294; Paul, 17, 77, 92, 142, 204, 260, 364, 392, 416. *See also* Biblical figures

Ash Wednesday, 70–71, 129

Baptism, 27, 245, 356–357, 411

Bence, Evelyn, 15–16, 71–72, 103–104, 221–222, 262–263, 334–335, 384–385, 417–418, 488–489, 525–526, 543–544

Benedictine spirituality, 89

Bentsen, Erika, 6–7, 61–62, 180–181, 240, 338–339, 381–382, 453–454, 544–545

Bible, 6–7, 17, 20–21, 64, 100, 121, 180, 243, 260, 266–267, 276–277, 279, 286, 317–319, 331, 384, 394–395, 433, 454, 493, 500, 524

Bible study, 51–52, 127, 138, 219, 291, 363, 367, 391–392

Biblical figures: Adam, 174, 294; Bartimaeus, 442; Daniel, 17; David (King), 122, 184; Elizabeth, 319; Eve, 174; Hannah, 317; Herod, 524; Isaac, 32; Jacob, 416; Jonah, 77; Joseph (father of Jesus), 524; Joseph of Arimathea,

140; Magi, 9; Martha and Mary, 262, 294; Mary (mother of Jesus), 524; Nathanael, 212–213; Nicodemus, 140; Samaritan woman at the well, 308; Solomon (King), 165. *See also* Apostles. *See also* Prophets

Biblical groups: Bereans, 392; Israelites, 65–66, 100, 480, 521; Judahites, 186; Pharisees, 140, 230

Biblical sites: Bethlehem, 64, 530; Calvary, 530; Cana, 493; Eden, 505–506; Egypt, 524; Gethsemane, 294; Jerusalem, 64, 186, 393; Nazareth, 64

Bill, J. Brent, 79–80, 111–112, 154–155, 242–243, 337–338, 389–390, 423–424, 478–479, 545

"The Birds of My Neighborhood" series, 79–80, 111–112, 154–155, 242–243, 337–338, 389–390, 422–423, 478–479

Blecker, Rhoda, 65–66, 89–90, 151–152, 198–199, 248–249, 300–301, 358–359, 537–538, 545–546

Books: *Angels: God's Secret Agents*, 103; *The Book of Common Prayer*, 71; *The Book of Forgiving*, 283; *The Five Love Languages*, 256, 265; *The Flowing Light of the Godhead*, 429; *Lives of the Presidents*, 68; *Mike Mulligan and His Steam Shovel*, 363; *Never* (1887), 454, 482

Choir, 27, 79, 139, 195, 306, 372

Christ, *see* Jesus Christ

Christian mystics: Mechthild of Magdeburg, 429; Meister Eckhart, 486

Christmas, 9, 38, 68, 71, 85, 264, 310, 421, 487, 491–492, 504–505,

508–510, 512–516, 518, 520–521, 524–529; Christmas Day, 515, 531–533; Christmas Eve, 9, 306, 527, 529–530

"Christmas Blessings" series, 491–492, 504–505, 514–515, 524–525, 529–532

Ciancanelli, Sabra, 2–3, 74–75, 116–117, 167–168, 206–207, 252–253, 296–297, 342–343, 386–387, 432-433, 474–475, 522–523, 546

Collins, Mark, 33–34, 161–162, 260–261, 390–391, 462–463, 547

Communion, 16, 67, 138, 530

Compassion International, 254

Covid-19 pandemic, 22, 94, 111, 272–273, 464, 475

Crucifixion, 143, 245

Diaz, Pablo, 14–15, 99–100, 150–151, 249–250, 356–357, 395–397, 547–548

Dilworth, John, 96–97, 244–245, 310–311, 393–394, 548–549

Disciples, see Apostles

"Doors of Our Life" series, 12–14, 72–73, 117–118, 203–204, 379–381, 515–516

Easter, 27, 106, 127, 139–142, 144; Easter Monday, 143–144; Easter Sunday, 141–142

Eddings, Amy, 48–49, 162–163, 272–273, 351–352, 460–461, 520–521, 549

Eliasen, Logan, 112–114, 146–147, 188–189, 274–275, 347–348, 438–439, 477–478, 487–488, 518–519, 549–550

Eliasen, Shawnelle, 32–33, 50–51, 81–82, 107–108, 213–214, 317–318, 363–364, 435–436, 507–508, 517–518, 550

"The Ends of the Earth" series, 468–472

Epiphany, 8–9
Episcopal Church, 142,
    195, 410, 452

Father's Day, 254–255
"The Five Love
    Languages" series,
    255–256, 265–266,
    278–279, 287–289,
    297–299, 307–308
"Following Jesus" series,
    128–129, 137–144
Forgiveness, 283

Garcia, Nicole, 127–128,
    216–217, 418–419,
    433–434, 551
Good Friday, 139, 143
Gratitude, 21, 31, 84, 99,
    159, 162, 194, 238, 259,
    284, 329, 409, 415,
    466, 469, 512, 522–523,
    534
Great Depression, 481
Grinnan, Edward, 7–8,
    57–58, 94–95, 144–145,
    185–186, 231–232,
    276–277, 322–323,
    367–368, 411–412,
    457–458, 502–503,
    551–552

Halloween, 446–448
Hamlin, Rick, 17–18,
    104–105, 128–129,
    137–144, 195–196,
    241–242, 306–307,
    377–378, 552–553
Hartke, Lynne, 4–6,
    101–102, 176–177,
    220–221, 304–305,
    321–322, 439–440,
    553
Heaven, 2, 54, 59, 159,
    161–162, 353, 357, 387,
    413, 527, 532
Hendricks, Carla, 28–29,
    43–44, 193–194, 251–252,
    355–356, 424–425,
    508–509, 553–554
Henry, Kim Taylor, 10–11,
    325–326, 409–410,
    554–555
Holy Spirit, 30–31, 78,
    92, 114, 171, 187, 222,
    243, 357, 373, 384, 395,
    406, 526
Holy Week, 129
Hymns: "Come, Labor
    On," 371; "God Will
    Take Care of You," 220;
    "Immortal, Invisible,
    God Only Wise," 80;

"It Is Well with My Soul," 504; "Joy to the World," 525; "O Holy Night," 306, 530; "Pass It On," 306; "There's Something About That Name," 220; "Silent Night," 530; "St. Patrick's Breastplate," 222; "We Three Kings," 9; "What a Friend We Have in Jesus," 220. *See also* Songs

Independence Day, 275

Jackson, Leanne, 323–324. 365–366, 407–408, 464–465, 501–502, 527–528, 555

Janoso, Erin, 34–35, 40–41, 110–111, 124–125, 214–215, 230–231, 267–268, 303–304, 442–443, 484–485, 555–556

Jesus Christ, 9, 13, 24, 31, 64, 70, 85–86, 91, 94, 96, 128–131, 137–143, 153, 156, 180, 182, 184, 190, 204, 212–213, 222, 230, 233, 242, 245–246, 258–260, 262, 264–266, 288, 290, 294, 298, 302, 308, 312, 318–319, 333–334, 356–357, 368, 373, 377, 390, 417–418, 435, 442, 456–457, 459, 462, 477–478, 481, 483, 487, 492–493, 505, 512, 514, 516, 524–525, 530, 532

"Journey Through Grief" series, 52–54, 118–120, 202–203, 237–238, 290–292, 341–342, 397–398, 445–446

Juneteenth, 251–252

Kappel, Ashley, 62–63, 105–106, 131–132, 217–218, 235–236, 257–258, 299–300, 385–386, 489–490, 556–557

Keller, Jenny Lynn, 12–13, 72–73, 117–118, 203–204, 238–239, 330–331, 379–380, 515–516, 557

Kidd, Brock, 136–137, 182–183, 279–280, 312–314, 440–441,

467–468, 509–511,
539–540, 557–558

Kidd, Pam, 3–4, 114–115,
196–197, 226–227,
295–296, 362–363,
558–559

Kingdom of God, 64, 85,
473, 477

King Jr., Rev. Dr. Martin
Luther, 27, 408

Kirk, Patty, 155–157,
199–200, 247–248,
293–295, 335–336,
382–383, 425–426,
475–476, 559–560

Knapp, Carol, 37–38,
68–69, 100–101,
170–171, 212–213,
258–259, 301–302,
373–374, 406–407,
560–561

Kuyper, Vicki, 21–22,
93–94, 148–149,
261–262, 391–392,
446–449, 470–472,
511–512, 561

Lent, 106

"Life Lessons from
Games" series,
323–325, 364–366,

407–408, 464–465,
501–502

Livezey, Lisa, 60–61,
166–167, 333–334,
370–371, 497–498, 562

"The Lonely Among Us"
series, 155–157,
199–200, 246–248,
293–295, 335–336,
382–383, 425–426

Lorenz, Patricia, 24–25,
66–67, 130–131,
173–174, 271–272,
345–346, 431–432,
443–444, 454–455,
481–482, 562–563

Luther, Martin (priest),
142

Macomber, Debbie,
36–37, 90–91, 228–229,
318–319, 447–448,
492–493, 563–564

Martin Luther King Jr.
Day, 26, 28–29

Maundy Thursday,
137–139

McCollors, Tia, 26–27,
54–55, 186–187,
327–328, 532–533, 564

Messner, Roberta,

55–56, 83–84, 125–126,
165–166, 171–173,
219–220, 264–265,
311–312, 565

Meyer, Gabrielle,
122–123, 292–293,
371–372, 427–428,
565–566

Military, United States:
Navy, 17

Ministry, 78, 195, 200,
227, 294, 333, 354, 364,
419, 435, 439, 477, 499

Miracles, 2, 137, 298,
370, 415

Mother's Day, 145, 192

New Year, 527, 540, KK;
New Year's Day, 2–3,
540; New Year's Eve,
538–540

Ondov, Rebecca, 38–40,
169–170, 205–206,
285–286, 374–375,
401–402, 528–529,
566–567

Palm Sunday, 128–129
Passover, 493, 521
Patience, 18, 233

Prayer, 8–10, 15, 21,
27, 34, 39, 47, 52, 69,
89–91, 99, 106, 130–131,
138, 148–149, 158, 175,
182, 192, 195, 215, 219,
222, 241, 257, 306, 308,
317–318, 320, 329, 357,
372–376, 393–394,
402, 417, 429–430, 435,
444, 447, 457–458, 475,
483, 490, 502, 504, 513,
531, 535

Prophets: Abraham, 17,
32–33, 416; Anna, 373;
Elijah, 243, 373; Isaiah,
290, 524; Jeremiah,
500; John the Baptist,
290, 319; Micah, 524;
Moses, 17; Sarah, 416;
Zechariah, 319. See also
Biblical figures

Puritanical law, 123

Quakers, 155, 243, 389

Redmond, Shirley Raye,
51–52, 85–86, 232–233,
394–395, 567–568

Resurrection, 33, 129,
142–144, 212

Rue, Ginger, 58–59,

121–122, 153–154,
275–276, 354–355,
369–370, 459–460,
534–535, 568

Ruiz, Adam, 82–83,
158–159, 227–228, 320,
429–430, 483, 569

"Sacred Threads" series,
83–84, 125–127, 171–173,
219–220, 264–265,
311–312

Salem witch trials, 123

Salvation, 51, 298, 487

Sampson, Kenneth,
25–26, 287–286,
348–349, 465–466,
569–570

Schantz, Daniel, 11–12,
64–65, 96, 160, 210–211,
245–246, 352–353,
414–415, 498–499,
570–571

Schilling, Gail Thorell,
9, 78–79, 108–109,
163–164, 191–192,
308–309, 326–327,
452–453, 571

Schwab, Penney, 491–492,
504–505, 514–515,
524–525, 529–532, 572

Sermon on the Mount, 190

Songs: "The Blessing,"
372; "Call Me
Righteous," 92; "The
Canticle of the Sun,"
309; "Hail to the
Chief," 68; "He Turned
It," 340; "I'll Be Home
for Christmas," 527;
"Jesus Loves Me," 279;
"Tell It Like It Is," 306;
"You'll Never Walk
Alone," 196. *See also*
Hymns

St. Francis of Assisi, 309

Stolpe, Norm, 208–209,
332–333, 378–379,
421–422, 428–429,
572–573

Storm, Buck, 18–19,
157–158, 254–255,
281–282, 344–345,
398–399, 436–437,
538–539, 573–574

St. Patrick, 222

Strandberg, Jolynda,
47–48, 234–235,
349–350, 420–421,
512–513, 574

Sunday school, 26, 264,
296, 367, 524, 530

Sweeney, Jon M., 41–42, 69–70, 120–121, 189–190, 410–411, 485–486, 500, 574–575

Ten Commandments, 455
Thanksgiving Day, 68, 464–465, 467, 485–487, 489, 493, 526, 533
Thompson, Rachel, 209–210, 366–367, 535–536, 575–576
Thompson, Stephanie, 19–20, 29–30, 75–76, 174–175, 192–193, 400–401, 416–417, 473–474, 576
Tomb of the Unknown Soldier, 213
Torah, 65
Turk, Marilyn, 255–256, 265–266, 278–279, 288–289, 297–299, 307–308, 577

Ukraine, 14

Vacation Bible school, 27. *See also* Sunday school
Valentin, Karen, 52–54, 118–119, 202–203, 237–238, 290–292, 341–342, 397–398, 445–446, 577–578
Valentine's Day, 56

Wailing Wall, 393
Walker, Scott, 201, 456–457, 505–506, 578
Wheelock, Jacqueline Freeman, 31, 76–77, 91–93, 184–185, 289–290, 413–414, 480–481, 521–522, 578–579
Williams, Gayle T., 97–98, 181–182, 284, 340–341, 375–376, 579–580
Word of God, 30, 50, 62, 121–122, 138, 180, 187, 222, 279, 298, 308, 318–319, 328, 340, 471, 518
World War II, 17, 258, 492

ACKNOWLEDGMENTS

Every attempt has been made to credit the sources of copyrighted material used in this book. If any such acknowledgment has been inadvertently omitted or miscredited, receipt of such information would be appreciated.

Scripture quotations marked (CEV) are taken from *Holy Bible: Contemporary English Version*. Copyright © 1995 American Bible Society.

Scripture quotations marked (CSB) are taken from *The Christian Standard Bible*, copyright © 2017 by Holman Bible Publishers. Used by permission.

Scripture quotations marked (ESV) are taken from the *Holy Bible, English Standard Version*. Copyright © 2001 by Crossway Bibles, a division of Good News Publishers. Used by permission. All rights reserved.

Scripture quotations marked (GNT) are taken from the *Good News Translation*® (Today's English Version, Second Edition) © 1992 American Bible Society.

Scripture quotations marked (GW) are taken from *GOD'S WORD*®. Copyright © 1995, 2003, 2013, 2014, 2019, 2020 by God's Word to the Nations Mission Society. Used by permission.

Scripture quotations marked (JPS) are taken from *Tanakh: A New Translation of the Holy Scriptures according to the Traditional Hebrew Text*. Copyright © 1985 by the Jewish Publication Society. All rights reserved.

Scripture quotations marked (KJV) are taken from the *King James Version of the Bible*.

Scripture quotations marked (MSG) are taken from *The Message*. Copyright © 1993, 2002, 2018 by Eugene H. Peterson.

Scripture quotations marked (NABRE) are taken from the *New American Bible*, revised edition, © 2010, 1991, 1986, 1970 Confraternity of Christian Doctrine, Inc., Washington, DC. All rights reserved.

Scripture quotations marked (NASB) are taken from the *New American Standard Bible*®. Copyright © 1960, 1971, 1977, 1995, 2020 by The Lockman Foundation. All rights reserved.

Scripture quotations marked (NCV) are taken from *The Holy Bible, New Century Version*. Copyright © 2005 by Thomas Nelson.

Scripture quotations marked (NIV) are taken from *The Holy Bible, New International Version*®, *NIV*®. Copyright © 1973, 1978, 1984, 2011 by Biblica, Inc. Used by permission. All rights reserved worldwide.

Scripture quotations marked (NKJV) are taken from *The Holy Bible, New King James Version*. Copyright © 1982 by Thomas Nelson. Used by permission. All rights reserved.

Scripture quotations marked (NLT) are taken from the *Holy Bible, New Living Translation*. Copyright © 1996, 2004, 2007, 2015 by Tyndale House Foundation. Used by permission of Tyndale House Publishers Inc., Carol Stream, Illinois. All rights reserved.

Scripture quotations marked (NRSVCE) are taken from the *New Revised Standard Version Bible: Catholic Edition*, copyright © 1989, 1993 the Division of Christian Education of the National Council of the Churches of Christ in the United States of America. Used by permission. All rights reserved.

Scripture quotations marked (NRSVUE) are taken from the *New Revised Standard Version, Updated Edition*. Copyright © 2021 by National Council of Churches of Christ in the United States of America. Used by permission. All rights reserved worldwide.

Scripture quotations marked (RSV) are taken from the *Revised Standard Version of the Bible*. Copyright © 1946, 1952, 1971 by the Division of Christian Education of the National Council of the Churches of Christ in the United States of America. Used by permission.

Scripture quotations marked (TLB) are taken from *The Living Bible*. Copyright © 1971 by Tyndale House Publishers, Inc., Carol Stream, Illinois. All rights reserved.

Scripture quotations marked (VOICE) are taken from *The Voice Bible*, copyright © 2012 Thomas Nelson, Inc. The Voice™ translation copyright © 2012 Ecclesia Bible Society. All rights reserved.

Scripture quotations marked (WE) are taken from the *Worldwide English (New Testament)*, © 1969, 1971, 1996, 1998 by SOON Educational Publications.

A NOTE FROM THE EDITORS

We hope you enjoyed *Walking in Grace,* published by Guideposts. For over seventy-five years, Guideposts, a nonprofit organization, has been driven by a vision of a world filled with hope. We aspire to be the voice of a trusted friend, a friend who makes you feel more hopeful and connected.

By making a purchase from Guideposts, you join our community in touching millions of lives, inspiring them to believe that all things are possible through faith, hope, and prayer. Your continued support allows us to provide uplifting resources to those in need. Whether through our communities, websites, apps, or publications, we inspire our audiences, bring them together, and comfort, uplift, entertain, and guide them. Visit us at guideposts.org to learn more.

We would love to hear from you. Write us at Guideposts, P.O. Box 5815, Harlan, Iowa 51593 or call us at (800) 932-2145. Did you love *Walking in Grace*? Leave a review for this product on guideposts.org/shop. Your feedback helps others in our community find relevant products.

Find inspiration, find faith, find Guideposts.

Shop our best sellers and favorites at
guideposts.org/shop
Or scan the QR code to go directly to our Shop